Ius Gentium: Comparative Perspectives on Law and Justice

Volume 132

Ius Gentium is a book series which discusses the central questions of law and justice from a comparative perspective. The books in this series collect the contrasting and overlapping perspectives of lawyers, judges, philosophers and scholars of law from the world's many different jurisdictions for the purposes of comparison, harmonisation, and the progressive development of law and legal institutions. Each volume makes a new comparative study of an important area of law. This book series continues the work of the well-known journal of the same name and provides the basis for a better understanding of all areas of legal science.

The *Ius Gentium* series provides a valuable resource for lawyers, judges, legislators, scholars, and both graduate students and researchers in globalisation, comparative law, legal theory and legal practice. The series has a special focus on the development of international legal standards and transnational legal cooperation.

Jan Podkowik • Anna Chmielarz-Grochal
Marcin Stębelski • Jarosław Sułkowski
Editors

Gleams of Good Faith in Constitutional Law

Springer

Editors
Jan Podkowik
Faculty of Law and Administration
University of Warsaw
Warsaw, Poland

Anna Chmielarz-Grochal
Faculty of Law and Administration
University of Lodz
Lodz, Poland

Marcin Stębelski
Faculty of Law and Administration
University of Warsaw
Warsaw, Poland

Jarosław Sułkowski
Faculty of Law and Administration
University of Lodz
Lodz, Poland

ISSN 1534-6781 ISSN 2214-9902 (electronic)
Ius Gentium: Comparative Perspectives on Law and Justice
ISBN 978-3-032-06485-1 ISBN 978-3-032-06486-8 (eBook)
https://doi.org/10.1007/978-3-032-06486-8

This work was supported by Narodowe Centrum Nauki (2020/39/B/HS5/02298).

This Springer imprint is published by the registered company Springer Nature Switzerland AG
The registered company address is: Gewerbestrasse 11, 6330 Cham, Switzerland

Preface

In recent years, the phenomenon of democratic erosion has prompted scholars to seek mechanisms and ideas to protect constitutions from exploitation for short-term political goals or contentious practices by constitutional actors. Among these ideas, the concept of good faith has emerged as a response to various bad faith practices. In constitutional law, however, the notion of good faith has not been thoroughly conceptualised. It is still understood intuitively and inconsistently, with elements sometimes borrowed directly from private or international law. Moreover, it lacks a solid foundation within constitutional theory.

This volume is a contribution to the academic discourse on the role of good faith in constitutional law. By bringing together scholars from different countries who explore various aspects of the topic, the book provides a comprehensive comparative and constitutional theoretical analysis explaining the idea of good faith in constitutional law. Comparative studies covering seven different jurisdictions, as well as historical and public law perspectives, reveal eponymous "glimpses" of good faith in constitutionalism. This analysis serves as a starting point for developing a theoretical framework for good faith in constitutional law and practice, including constitutional interpretation, relations between the branches of government, and interactions between the state and the individual.

The book claims that constitutional good faith is an universal concept intended to guide the interpretation and application of constitutional standards, regardless of whether this notion is directly expressed in the constitutional provisions of a given country.

The structure, analytical approach, and narrative strategy of the book are designed to achieve the main research objective of highlighting the understanding and manifestation of good faith in constitutional law. The book consists of three main parts, preceded by an introductory chapter outlining the research problem and initial findings.

Part One: "Inspirations" examines the origins of good faith in public law and its historical sources. This section introduces the reader to the idea of good faith in jurisprudence and legal tradition and its current application in public law, which includes constitutional law. This part focuses on three key points of reference: international treaty law, where good faith governs the formation and performance of international agreements; EU law, where good faith or "loyal cooperation" shapes the relationship between Member States and EU institutions; and the Council of Europe's human rights system, in particular the European Court of Human Rights, where good faith considerations appear in assessing the compatibility of state action with fundamental rights. This section therefore provides a basic background for understanding constitutional good faith.

Part Two: "Perspectives" explores constitutional good faith in selected legal systems. The choice of jurisdictions for comparative analysis is not accidental. First, it includes countries where good faith is explicitly enshrined in constitutional provisions, and thus is a normative concept with a well-defined meaning, namely Switzerland and Romania. Second, it includes countries where good faith play a role in constitutional jurisprudence or academic debate, such as the United States, Germany, Spain, France, and Poland. These countries represent different political and legal systems with differing approaches to the concept of good faith in constitutional law, often intertwined with constitutional fidelity, mutual loyalty, or relations between central and local authorities. Each chapter in this part follows a consistent structure: examining the inspirations for good faith in each country's constitutional framework, the relevant constitutional provisions, and the role of good faith in judicial enforceability and practical application. This section enables a comparative view of the discourse surrounding constitutional good faith.

Part Three: "Manifestations" analyses good faith through the lens of constitutional theory, focusing on key areas relevant to the interpretation and application of constitutional law. It builds on the findings of Parts One and Two to propose broader conclusions about constitutional good faith in modern liberal democracies. It covers three main areas: good faith in constitutional interpretation, its role in intergovernmental interactions, and its relevance in state–private relations. The authors note that good faith constitutional interpretation requires deciphering constitutional norms to determine their objective content, regardless of the contextual goals of the interpreter. Similarly, good faith constitutional application requires upholding constitutional purposes and assumptions.

Overall, the editors' hope that this book will not only clarify the concept of constitutional good faith, but also provide a valuable analytical framework that can serve as a reference point for future scholarship and judicial decisions, especially in complex "hard cases".

***

The book is the result of research carried out at the Faculty of Law and Administration, University of Warsaw, Poland, as part of the research project "Good Faith in Constitutional Law", funded by the National Science Centre under the OPUS 20 competition (No 2020/39/B/HS5/02298).

The research team consists of Jan Podkowik, Ph.D. (Principal Investigator), Anna Chmielarz Grochal, Ph.D., Jarosław Sułkowski, Ph.D., and Marcin Stębelski, Ph.D. (Investigators), supported by research assistants: Aleksandra Kochman, LL.M., Rafał Stronk (Ph.D. student), and Jędrzej Zieliński (Ph.D. student).

Warsaw, Poland — Jan Podkowik
Lodz, Poland — Anna Chmielarz-Grochal
Warsaw, Poland — Marcin Stębelski
Lodz, Poland — Jarosław Sułkowski

Acknowledgements

Every book, regardless of its nature, is the product of the hard work and determination of its authors. The commitment of all those who share their knowledge, experience, and substantive support in good faith is also extremely important. This was certainly the case with this publication.

We would like to thank everyone who contributed to this book by sharing their inspiration, critical comments, or suggestions that forced us to reflect even more deeply. This support was crucial for the accomplishment of this project.

We are grateful that you took the time for consultations, the results of which strengthened our conviction that it is necessary to conduct this research and to continue searching for answers to the question of whether there is room for good faith in constitutional law and what good faith actually is. These conversations not only enriched the content of the book, but also allowed us to look at certain issues from a completely new perspective.

In particular, we would like to thank everyone with whom we had the opportunity – at various stages of the project – to conduct interviews that helped us understand the perspectives of different jurisdictions or to discuss our theses. In alphabetical order, we would therefore like to thank:

Leonardo Alvarez Alvarez (University of Oviedo, Spain), Maciej Berek (University of Warsaw, Poland), Piotr Chybalski (Cardinal Stefan Wyszyński University, Poland), Adam Czarnota and his team from the Centre for Legal Education and Social Theory (University of Wrocław, Poland), Monika Florczak-Wątor (Jagiellonian University, Poland), Stephen Gardbaum (UCLA School of Law, the US), Leszek Garlicki (University of Warsaw, Poland, retired judge of the Constitutional Tribunal, former judge at the European Court of Human Rights in Strasbourg), Tom Ginsburg (University of Chicago Law School, the US), Mirosław Granat (Cardinal Stefan Wyszyński University, Poland, retired judge of the Constitutional Tribunal), Marie Gren (University Paris 1 Panthéon-Sorbonne), Irv Gornstein (Georgetown University Law Center, Supreme Court Institute, the US), Mariusz Haładyj (President of the Supreme Audit Office, Poland), Christian Hillgruber (University of Bonn, Germany), Samuel Issacharoff (New York University School of Law, the US), Andrea Katz (Washington University School of

Law, the US), James P. Kelly, III (The Federalist Society, the US), Katarzyna Kubuj (Polish Academy of Sciences, Poland), Ewa Łętowska (Polish Academy of Sciences, Poland, retired judge of the Constitutional Tribunal), Małgorzata Masternak-Kubiak (University of Wrocław, Poland, judge at the Supreme Administrative Court), Anna Młynarska-Sobaczewska (Polish Academy of Sciences, Poland), David E. Pozen (Columbia University, the US), Piotr Radziewicz (Warsaw University of Technology, Poland), Aleksander Stępkowski (University of Warsaw, Poland, judge at the Supreme Court), Rosario Tur Ausina (Miguel Hernández University of Elche, Spain), Piotr Tuleja (Jagiellonian University, Poland, retired judge of the Constitutional Tribunal), Kazimierz Michał Ujazdowski (University of Lodz, Poland, senator of the Republic of Poland), Joseph H.H. Weiler (NYU School of Law, the US), and Marek Zubik (University of Warsaw, Poland, retired judge of the Constitutional Tribunal).

Your involvement in the creative process was invaluable.

An important task was the survey conducted in 2023 in the form of an anonymous electronic questionnaire in Poland, France, Spain, Germany, Switzerland, and the United States. This survey was conducted among researchers from leading academic centres in the field of legal sciences and judges of constitutional and supreme courts. The aim was to determine the current state of development of constitutional thought on the notion of good faith, the understanding of good faith as a category of constitutional law, the usefulness of this concept in legal science and practice, and its application in the activities of state bodies.

We would like to thank everyone who took the time to participate in the survey and share their thoughts.

We had originally intended to present the results of the survey in a separate chapter. However, the number of responses received is insufficient to provide a representative overview of the views of academics and practitioners from the countries surveyed on the subject of constitutional good faith. Nevertheless, the answers obtained – despite individual sceptical voices regarding the usefulness of introducing the concept of good faith into constitutional law – confirmed our initial intuitions and research hypotheses and strengthened our belief in the need for further research.

Contents

Towards Constitutional Good Faith

Jan Podkowik, Marcin Stębelski, Anna Chmielarz-Grochal, and Jarosław Sułkowski

Abstract The purpose of this chapter is to set out the theoretical and doctrinal framework for analysing the concept of good faith in constitutional law. The chapter is divided into four sections.

The first section focuses on the main features of good faith in jurisprudence, particularly in public law, as discussed in greater detail in the first part of the book. It notes that although the concept of good faith is typically associated with private law, it also has roots and foundations in the public law system. The following sections examine the existing discourse on good faith in constitutional doctrine. Section two emphasises that the concept has gained prominence in recent years in the face of the crisis of liberal democracy, as a response to instances of the instrumentalisation of the constitution and the abuse of the law to achieve undemocratic ends. Section three shows that the concept of good faith pervades constitutional law, whether it is rooted in the provisions of a particular state's constitution or emerges from case law. This concept is relevant to the interpretation and application of the constitution in both vertical and horizontal relations. The final section of the chapter undertakes a theoretical exploration of the concept of constitutional good faith, seeking to identify its main characteristics and foundations.

J. Podkowik (✉) · M. Stębelski
Faculty of Law and Administration, University of Warsaw, Warsaw, Poland
e-mail: j.podkowik@wpia.uw.edu.pl; m.stebelski@wpia.uw.edu.pl

A. Chmielarz-Grochal · J. Sułkowski
Faculty of Law and Administration, University of Lodz, Lodz, Poland
e-mail: achmielarz@wpia.uni.lodz.pl; sulkowski@wpia.uni.lodz.pl

J. Podkowik et al. (eds.), *Gleams of Good Faith in Constitutional Law*, Ius Gentium: Comparative Perspectives on Law and Justice 132,
https://doi.org/10.1007/978-3-032-06486-8_1

1 Good Faith in Public Law

Reflections on good faith (Latin: *bona fides*) usually arise when we suspect that it may be lacking. This is particularly the case when conduct, which falls within the formal legal framework appears correct at first sight, raises doubts as to its purpose or the rules of morality. We also think of good faith when there are some difficulties in judging behaviour that may be incompatible with a legal rule but is nevertheless recognised as right and morally acceptable. The introduction of the concept of good faith into legal discourse stems, to some extent, from the epistemic limitations that accompany the legal qualification of a certain event according to formal rules, but also from the need to supplement these formal rules with an axiological element.

The notion of "good faith" that permeates jurisprudence refers to two fundamental ethical categories or values that the law should embody: goodness (Greek: *agathon*, Latin: *bonum*) and faith (Greek: *pistotēs*, Latin: *fides*). Although the essence of the idea discussed here is not a simple combination of the terms "goodness" and "faith", it does draw attention to the characteristics of what we usually refer to as "bona fides" in jurisprudence. On the one hand, the concept of the "good" refers to moral values such as honesty, justice and respect for others. In Kant's view, the moral good consists in acting from a sense of duty in accordance with the categorical imperative, rather than from selfish motives and the pursuit of self-interest.[1] Fidelity, on the other hand, implies trust,[2] loyalty and a willingness to act in accordance with accepted principles or a commitment to a relationship with others. This indicates the relational nature of this conceptual category, which is particularly relevant where there are some reciprocal relationships, entitlements and obligations.

Good faith is a concept most often associated with private law, particularly in the context of contracts, the protection of property and the protection of the weaker party in a legal relationship.[3] However, its significance goes far beyond this area. In fact, the principle of good faith also has a rich tradition in public law. Some even point out that good faith was one of the foundations of public law before it entered private law. As Grzegorz Blicharz points out in the next chapter,[4] his tradition can be traced back to the thought of classical Roman law, in which honesty and adherence to the principles of loyalty to the community were an essential element of the relationship between the state and the citizens, as well as a guideline for the conduct of those who exercised power over others.

The fundamental importance of good faith is that it complements the legal order in areas where formal legal norms have certain shortcomings and where the interpretation of rules requires consideration of the ethical or social context. Good faith

---

[1] Johnson and Cureton (2024).

[2] Bishop and McKaughan (2023): "*At its most general 'faith' means much the same as 'trust'. Uses of 'faith' and 'faithfulness' closely parallel 'trust' and 'trustworthiness' and these are often used interchangeably*".

[3] See for example: Perry (2024)

[4] Blicharz (2025).

serves as an interpretive tool that allows legal norms to be read in such way that ensures the formal correctness of decisions while also guaranteeing their conformity with fundamental values.

The importance of good faith in the legal system can be considered on two levels. First, it constitutes the ethical foundation of the legal system, promoting honesty, compliance with agreements entered into and loyalty to the partners in legal relationships. In this way, it prevents situations in which actors act contrary to the spirit of the law, although formally in accordance with its letter.[5] Secondly, it plays a corrective role, allowing the strictness of the law to be mitigated where justice, the protection of the legitimate interests of the parties or the public interest so require. The concept under discussion is therefore not only a mechanism for verifying the intentions or motives of legal actors, but also a tool for strengthening the integrity of the legal system and its ethical foundations.

Jurisprudence generally distinguishes between subjective and objective good faith, which differ in how the are used to assess another person's actions. Subjective good faith refers to a person's internal belief that his or her actions are in accordance with the law and moral principles. The key question is therefore whether the person sincerely believed that he or she was doing the right thing, regardless of whether this belief was justified in the circumstances. Subjective good faith therefore requires an assessment of the person's state of mind – their intentions, motivations or beliefs. Objective good faith refers to external standards of conduct that are considered fair and reasonable in a given social or legal context. In this view, the key question is whether a person's actions were objectively reasonable and in accordance with generally accepted norms. In contrast to subjective good faith, it is not individual motives, intentions or beliefs that are relevant to the attribution of objective good faith, but rather the possibility of the behaviour in question can be regarded reasonable and fair.

2 Good Faith as a Response to the Crisis of Democracy and the Rule of Law

In recent years, references to good and bad faith have appeared in constitutional doctrine, particularly in the context of what has been described as the erosion of democracy. Of particular relevance to the problem at hand are the findings of the American constitutional law professor David Pozen, which have not only introduced the issue to academic discourse, but have also become a point of reference for other authors.[6]

[5] See for example: Whittington (2023).

[6] His work was referenced by, among others: Gardbaum (2016), Levinson (2016), Fallon Jr. (2017), McCanse Wright (2018).

In his in-depth analysis focused on his home jurisdiction, Pozen observed that the concepts of good and bad faith – found in other branches of private and public law – rarely appear in doctrine and constitutional jurisprudence. As he noted, constitutional law "has been an enclave of good faith and bad faith exceptionalism".[7] At the same time, references to these concepts, and in particular the concept of bad faith, are ubiquitous in non-legal discourse and political culture in the United States, serving as a means for participants in constitutional debates to challenge the actions of opponents accused of constitutional infidelity, dishonesty or fraud. In an attempt to explain the phenomenon of the relatively few references to these concepts in the sphere of constitutional law, especially in judicial decisions, Pozen drew attention to the peculiarities of the perception of the Constitution, which – on the one hand – is treated almost as a sacred document by a part of American legal doctrine,[8] and on the other hand remains a highly political act, regulating complex decision-making processes under conditions of opportunism or instrumentalist tendencies.[9] The political dimension of the application of the Constitution, coupled with the difficulty of proving the lack of good faith of individual actors, raises concerns about the possibility and extent of its enforcement by the courts. Consequently, it seems more justified to treat it as an unenforceable constitutional norm that exists at the intersection of law and legal culture.

While allegations of a lack of good faith or of the presence of bad faith may perpetuate existing divisions and undermine the need for cooperation and the search for compromise, thus negatively affecting the quality of public debate, the presence of these concepts in non-legal discourse helps to compensate for the insufficient enforcement of good faith in judicial practice.[10] In particular, the inclusion of the concept of bad faith in constitutional discourse may enable the identification of constitutional abuses and cases that are clearly far from the generally accepted understanding of specific constitutional standards.

The undoubted strength of Pozen's study lies not only his recognition of the presence of the idea of good and bad faith in constitutional law and his attempt to define its legal nature, but also in his attempt to create a taxonomy of constitutional bad faith around which his work focuses. Although his reflections are based on specific examples from American constitutional practice, they have a broader, universal relevance. Based on the distinction between subjective and objective bad faith, Pozen identifies eight situations that constitute constitutional bad faith. The manifestations of subjective bad faith are: (1) facially neutral government actions that are in fact based on illegitimate motives or purposes, (2) usurpation of another actor's constitutional prerogatives by deliberately violating constitutional constraints or disregarding constitutional duties, (3) inconsistent use of interpretive methodology, (4) double-heartedness or imperfect commitment to the Constitution. In turn, he

[7] Pozen (2016), p. 887.

[8] Pozen (2016), pp. 942–947.

[9] Pozen (2016), pp. 909–914.

[10] Pozen (2016), p. 953.

identifies as cases of objective bad faith: (1) unwillingness to compromise or negotiate across branch or party lines, (2) unwarranted deviations from constitutional convention, (3) evasion of the spirit of the bargain, and (4) interpretive arguments that are so unreasonable as to betray a furtive design or malicious state of mind. Additionally, referring to Sartre's definition of bad faith understood as self-deception,[11] he distinguishes two further situations of bad faith: (1) necessitarian assertion about what the law "must" mean, and (2) minimisation of inconvenient facts about the Constitution and the judicial role.

Pozen's findings have been echoed by other scholars, such as the Polish professor of constitutional law and former judge of the Polish Constitutional Court and the European Court of Human Rights, Leszek Garlicki.[12] Without explicitly defining good and bad faith in constitutional law, he identified seven situations in which any element of good faith could undoubtedly be denied. Among them he included: (1) calculated unconstitutionality, when the legislator is or should be aware of the unconstitutionality of the act, but uses sophisticated legal arguments to create the appearance of legality; (2) hypocrisy (constitutional fraud), when legal provisions have an apparently neutral form, while their real purpose is to produce completely different unconstitutional effects; (3) regulatory singularisation, which consists in adopting regulations that appear general and abstract, but whose real purpose is to resolve a specific individual issue; (4) regulatory accumulation, which consists in the adoption, at the same time or within a short period of time, of a large number of regulations which would be natural if considered separately, but which are adopted for a contentious purpose; (5) the intentional over-interpretation of the powers or scope of action of constitutional bodies or officials, especially for the purpose of dealing with a particular matter that could not be dealt with under the previous understanding of those powers or scope of action of the body; (6) the deliberate loosening of the consistency of the interpretation and rules of application of constitutional law; and (7) the deliberate creation of a stalemate or conflict in order to divert attention or play for time.

Pozen's findings have also inspired a wider integration of the concept of constitutional bad faith into scholarly discourse in the context of violations of constitutional norms, particularly in relation to so-called abusive constitutionalism. As Rosalind Dixon and David Landau point out, in liberal democratic systems, when constitutional actors, including judges, deliberately take actions designed to undermine the foundations of the democratic system, there is an element of bad faith.[13] Thus, in the doctrine, bad faith is sometimes associated with unconstitutional intentions or acting for constitutionally impermissible purposes.[14]

The Israeli scholar Yaniv Roznai also refers to the language of good faith in the context of the exercise of constitutional power and the concept of unconstitutional

[11] Pozen (2016), pp. 934–939.

[12] Garlicki (2016), pp. 17–19.

[13] Dixon and Landau (2020), p. 1326; Dixon and Landau (2021), p. 27. See also: Petrov (2024).

[14] Acar (2016); Ziółkowski (2020).

constitutional amendments.[15] He points out that constitutional amendment should be based not only on formal compliance with legal procedures, but also on adherence to constitutional values and respect for democratic principles. A good faith limitation prevents the abuse of the power to amend the constitution, particularly in the case of a constitutional amendment or an act that is "personal", which raises doubts about the abuse of a constitutional power.

Observing manifestations of bad faith in constitutional practice naturally prompts the question of what constitutional good faith entails. Paradoxically, this question has not been the subject of much analysis. As the American jurist Andrew McCanse Wright suggests in his essay, good faith is essential to the proper functioning of the entire political system.[16] It is more than simple compliance with the law. It requires "respect for constitutional values, appropriate response to cautionary signals by other constitutional actors, and pursuit of substantive partisan and policy goals tempered by mindfulness of long-term institutional health".[17] It implies, among other things, acting honestly towards other constitutional actors in the exercise of one's own competences, in particular by allowing a certain margin of discretion, and treating the constitutional system of the state as a common enterprise, as opposed to opportunism and selfish thinking.[18]

3 Glimpses of Good Faith in Constitutional Law: National Perspectives

The absence of a broader discussion of constitutional good faith, despite the recognition that certain behaviour cannot be attributed to good faith or is even a manifestation of bad faith, seems surprising for at least three reasons.

First, constitutional law is an integral part of public law, where the concept of good faith has been developed over the years in international treaty law,[19] the legal system of the European Union[20] and the legal system of the Council of Europe.[21] Perhaps the explanation for this lack of doctrinal discussion lies in the specific nature of constitutional regulation. Although both constitutional and international law regulate the activities of state institutions, international law, like private law, regulates horizontal relations between formally equal entities (private individuals in private law and between states in the law of treaties), and in their relations consent,

[15] Roznai (2023).

[16] McCanse Wright (2018).

[17] McCanse Wright (2018), p. 49.

[18] McCanse Wright (2018), pp. 47–48

[19] See: Kałduński (2025).

[20] See: Klamert (2025).

[21] See: Kochman (2025).

custom and bilateralism play a key role.[22] Horizontal relations between constitutional bodies are, in fact, rare. As the American constitutional scholar Stephen Gardbaum suggests, in areas where constitutional law regulates horizontal relations between co-equal branches of government, between constituent federal units, or where constitutional rights bind individuals, one might expect "a greater role for legal duties of good faith or their equivalents, such as 'comity' or 'full faith and credit'".[23]

Second, good faith is a normative concept. It appears in the constitutional texts of some states and thus has an autonomous meaning in these legal systems, going beyond a rhetorical label. It appears in the constitutions of some states and thus has an autonomous meaning in those legal systems. It is therefore more than a rhetorical label. For example, the concept of good faith is expressed in Article 5(3) of the Swiss Constitution, which guarantees that public authorities and private persons shall act in good faith, and in Article 9 of the Swiss Constitution, which states that everyone has the right to be treated by public authorities without arbitrariness and in good faith. In both provisions of the Swiss Constitution, good faith is an obligation of the various organs of the state towards each other and towards the citizen.[24] On the other hand, Article 57 of the Romanian Constitution explicitly imposes an obligation on Romanian citizens, foreign citizens, and stateless persons to exercise their constitutional rights and freedoms "in good faith, without any infringement of the rights and liberties of others", while Article 11 of the Constitution obliges the Romanian State to fulfil accurately and in good faith its obligations under international agreements to which it is a party.[25]

This notion also appears in other constitutions around the world, both in the context of the functioning of state authorities and public administration. For example, Article 266(2) of the Portuguese Constitution states that "Administrative organs and agents are subject to the Constitution and the law, and in the exercise of their functions must act with respect for the principles of equality, proportionality, justice, impartiality and good faith" or in Article 41(1)(h) of the South African Constitution, according to which "Authorities at every level and all state organs at every level: shall co-operate with each other in mutual trust and good faith: maintaining friendly relations; assisting and supporting each other; informing and consulting each other on matters within their common sphere of action; co-ordinating tasks and legislation; complying with agreed procedures; and avoiding legal proceedings against each other". The obligation of state organs and citizens to act in good faith, as well as the presumption of acting in good faith, is also established in Article 83 of the Colombian Constitution. Good faith is also a construction that excludes (modifies) the legal liability of public officials, including judges, for illegal acts committed in good faith. For example, according to Article 50(9) of the

[22] Gardbaum (2016), p. 159.

[23] Gardbaum (2016), p. 159.

[24] See more: Askin (2025).

[25] See more: Stănescu (2025).

Zimbabwean Constitution, "any person who has been illegally arrested or detained is entitled to compensation from the person responsible for the arrest or detention, but a law may protect from liability a judicial officer acting in a judicial capacity reasonably and in good faith as well as any other public officer acting reasonably and in good faith and without culpable ignorance or negligence".

Third, good faith appears either explicitly or implicitly in the jurisprudence of constitutional courts, sometimes as an element of other constitutional principles and sometimes as a separate, autonomous legal construct. Such jurisprudence is also found in jurisdictions where there is no constitutional provision expressing the concept of good faith. One example is the jurisprudence of the US Supreme Court, which established the so-called "good faith exception",[26] according to which evidence obtained on the basis of an invalid search warrant may be admissible at trial, as long as the officer acted in good faith.[27] In the case law of the Israeli Supreme Court, good faith is linked, inter alia, to the absence of an unlawful purpose on the part of the legislature or, more generally, to the existence of a rational justification for the action taken by the officers.[28]

The above may indicate that good faith permeates constitutional law, irrespective of the existence or specific form of its normative basis in constitutional provisions. Its concepts and scope are debated or remain unclear. This calls for a closer examination of the issue, beginning with an attempt to reconstruct the titular "reflections" of good faith as manifested in constitutional law across selected jurisdictions, culminating in the development of a theoretical framework of good faith in constitutional law and practice, encompassing constitutional interpretation, relations between branches of government, and the interaction between the state and citizens.

The reflections on constitutional good faith are conducted on complementary levels: theoretical, philosophical, dogmatic and comparative. The multiplicity of these approaches corresponds to the structure of this volume.

On the theoretical and philosophical planes, reflection on the role of constitutional good faith cannot be reduced to mere theories and methods of constitutional interpretation, but should take into account the role of the constitution in a liberal democracy. This is because it serves to limit the discretionary power of those applying the constitution and to strengthen the legitimacy of their actions. Since constitutional good faith requires normative justification, it is possible, with the help of the concept of *reflexivity*, to consider good faith as a kind of *reflexive action*. In the process of interpreting the constitution, the context conditioned by social ideas, historical experiences, and social phenomena, i.e. elements that are of interest to philosophy, history, sociology or economics, plays an important role. Hence, it is reasonably argued by Krzysztof J. Kaleta that: "the key to understanding the essence

---

[26] See eg: Tokson and Gentithes (2023).

[27] United States v. Leon, 468 U.S. 897 (1984).

[28] *United Mizrahi Bank v. Migdal Cooperative Village* (1995); in relation to the objective of constitutional amendments against the backdrop of the socially controversial judicial reform initiated by Prime Minister Benjamin Nataniah—*Movement for Quality Government in Israel v. Knesset* (HCJ 5658/23).

of good faith is a comprehensive view of constitutional interpretation. The constitution as a whole, being the product of the rational and deliberate action of the constituent power, has an identity and a function that is more than the sum of the purposes formulated in its individual provisions. Fidelity to the constitution is not only fidelity to its letter or even its spirit, but also to the broader political philosophy from which the constitution grows".[29]

In constitutional law scholarship (and thus at a dogmatic level), the key point is that the constitution operates both vertically and horizontally. Both dimensions are evident in relation to constitutional good faith. This conclusion is fully supported by an analysis of the constitutional provisions of states that explicitly normativise the concept of good faith. It is no coincidence that the constitutional laws of Romania and Switzerland, albeit with some differences, frame good faith as a duty of political actors, a requirement for public authorities to respect individual rights, and a standard of conduct for private law subjects in their dealings with the authorities and with one another.

For a long time, legal science has drawn attention to the phenomenon of the constitution – along with its principles and values – penetrating the sphere of private law relations.[30] The horizontal treatment of constitutional good faith coincides with the treatment of bona fides in civil law, so the civilian connotations of this concept are therefore not surprising. However, analysis of the effects of good faith on relations between individuals remains at the margins of the broader debate. More space is devoted to understanding good faith in state-individual relations, not least because its meaning differs in vertical relations and horizontal relations. In horizontal relations, the good faith of both parties is presumed, and overcoming this presumption requires evidence. In vertical relations, however, such a strong presumption of good faith on the part of the state is questionable. Therefore, the individual is not required to prove the lack of good faith on the part of the state (Monika Florczak-Wątor).[31]

The comparative analysis demonstrates the relevance of the findings made so far regarding the understanding of good faith in constitutional law. In Switzerland, good faith is expressed in the constitution as both a general principle of law and a subjective right of the individual. The individual's right to be treated without arbitrariness and in good faith is of an "asymmetrical" nature, as it accrues to the individual in relation to the public authority. It includes: (1) the protection of legitimate expectations, (2) the protection of acquired rights, (3) the prohibition of abuse of rights, (4) the prohibition of contradiction, (5) the protection of good faith in procedural law and (6) the interpretation of legal acts and legal relations in good faith. As Elif Askin[32] rightly notes that constitutional good faith is not only the obligation of the state to act, characterised by certainty and predictability, but also the obligation of individuals to comply with the applicable law. Viewed in this way, good faith is

[29] Kaleta (2025).

[30] Łętowska (2001), p. 125.

[31] Florczak-Wątor (2025).

[32] Askin (2025).

based on a mutual trust between the state and its citizens. It aims to balance the tension between trust and distrust, which is particularly important in times of crisis. It demonstrates that the legal system cannot be sustained by legal instruments and procedures alone. Good faith goes beyond the law by referring to the social, political and moral obligations incumbent on those applying the law.

In another country where good faith has constitutional status, namely – Romania – attention is drawn to the penetration of the civilist understanding of good faith into constitutional law. The elevation of the principle of good faith to the status of a constitutional norm is a logical consequence of the constitutionalisation of the state's legal order and the recognition of the autonomy of civil society. As Lucian-Sorin Stănescu points out,[33] public authorities are increasingly detached from their original status of irrational and abusive powers and under the rules and mechanisms of constitutional democracy, are returning to their roots as moral persons, which affects their fulfilment of their constitutionally defined tasks in terms of ensuring the primacy of the constitution and the normative priority of human rights. The jurisprudence of the Romanian Constitutional Court points to three manifestations of constitutional loyalty as a principle of law, i.e. the loyal behaviour of public authorities towards the Constitution, the loyal reciprocal behaviour of public authorities in institutional relations and the loyal behaviour of public authorities appointed to implement the will of the people.

In some countries (e.g. Germany, Spain), good faith is equated with the loyalty of constitutional actors in their interaction not only horizontally, but also vertically. In Germany, as Ann Kathrin Schnieders and Simon Strickrodt show,[34] although good faith is not explicitly expressed in the German Basic Law, loyalty or fidelity to the constitution (*Verfassungsorgantreue*) is regarded as a general principle for the implementation of the duties of the federal bodies in their mutual relations. The Federal Constitutional Court (*Bundesverfassungsgericht*), on the other hand, has developed the *Bundestreue* principle for the relationship between the federal government and the Länder, which is an expression of good faith. In effect, constitutional loyalty is regarded as a principle relating to coherent and harmonious cooperation between the organs of the various authorities and between the federation and the Länder. In both levels of the relationship, the authorities are to respect each other and not undermine each other's authority. This issue is highlighted in Spain, where tensions between Madrid and the autonomous communities are a defining feature of the country's system. As Rosario Tur Ausina points out, territorial tensions have been an important legal and political destabilising factor in recent years. They are accompanied by "an unstable coexistence between gubernaculum and jurisdictio, with significant strains on the rule of law". It is recognised that constitutional loyalty coupled with good faith can contribute to the "regeneration of the democratic system". In the complex configuration of the principle of separation of powers, horizontal and vertical, it is possible to achieve this goal by maintaining the

[33] Stănescu (2025).

[34] Schnieders and Strickrodt (2025).

desired balance and by applying "counter-power mechanics, sometimes invisible but capable of contributing to the proper functioning of the system".[35]

The logic of good faith includes, in its symbolic meaning, the oath taken before assuming public office. It imposes a moral obligation on public authorities to apply the constitution loyally, going beyond formal compliance with it. Through the oath, the collective dimension of respect for the law, including the constitution, is reinforced by the individual and moral dimension. The fiduciary nature of the duties of public office holders is emphasised in American constitutional law scholarship. Constitutional actors should act in the public interest, in good faith and not use their power for personal gain. The aim of this approach is to build trust between those in power and citizens. Ethan J. Leib points out that the US Constitution so often requires public officials to act faithfully as a basic rule of conduct that one can speak of a fiduciary conception of office permeating the law, even if it is not enforced directly as a rule of decision-making.[36] Good faith can act as an exception to protect public officials when they make a "mistake that is reasonable under the circumstances",[37] whereas ulterior motives (e.g., discriminatory) or impermissible purposes for their actions will constitute a manifestation of bad faith.[38]

Constitutions do not formalise the requirement or the means of compliance to such an extent that it can be argued that the obligatory nature of the norms derives from their constitutional formulation. Good faith does not have to follow *expressis verbis* from the content of the Basic Law for constitutional actors to be under a duty of loyalty to its provisions and each other. The presumption of good faith in relations between political actors implies an obligation on the part of state organs to cooperate in a constructive, goal-oriented manner, fostering cooperation rather than unhealthy competition. Constitutional good faith exists at the interface between law and political culture. It is this culture, rather than the constitution itself, that shapes the orientation of the constitutional actor towards its constitutional obligations. Formal compliance of an action with the provisions of the constitution is insufficient; constitutional actors should be expected to respect values and to pursue constitutional goals. Good faith can be regarded as a component of the political system and an essential element of the rule of law.[39]

The question arises about the possibility of incorporating good faith into positive constitutional law. Perhaps supplementing the formal regularity requirement of constitutional actors with a substantive requirement of good faith would help to prevent the instrumentalisation of the constitution. However, Ariane Vidal-Naquet and Xavier Magnon[40] are not fully convinced of the validity of such an addition. Establishing the objective meaning of constitutional good faith is possible, but the

---

[35] Tur Ausina (2025).

[36] Leib (2025).

[37] Pozen (2016), p. 898.

[38] Pozen (2016), pp. 902–903.

[39] McCanse Wright (2018), pp. 48, 49.

[40] Vidal-Naquet and Magnon (2025).

practical implementation of this requirement in constitutional law reveals too much uncertainty and subjectivity. It would also be necessary to establish sanctioning mechanisms to ensure compliance with good faith, which would require equipping the courts or other controlling bodies with appropriate tools to assess the actions (presumably also the intentions and motives) of constitutional actors. Ultimately, it is the voters who sanction the lack of good faith in the activities of political actors.

4 Theoretical Assumptions of Constitutional Good Faith

The conviction, already expressed earlier, that good faith is necessary for the proper functioning of a political system based on a constitution, requires elaboration at this point. This is because it is important to outline a theoretical framework for understanding good faith in constitutional law, and to provide at least an initial grasp of its basic features. Since in the studies cited above quite numerous manifestations of actions devoid of good faith have been indicated, which are thus recognised as objectionable in the constitutional perspective, it is necessary to indicate the grounds for deriving the obligation to act in good faith from the constitution, as well as to attempt to identify the defining features of constitutional good faith.

We base our findings on the assumption that acting in good faith is – in the area of constitutional law – a consequence of the constitution being endowed with the features of a specific act in the aspect of its content, form and legal force. In this way, we link the analysed category of good faith with the essence of the constitution, thereby confirming its normative character and at the same time enabling it to be treated as an obligation.

The presented approach entails a perception of the constitution that, above all, recognises its specificity of content. It is a matter of drawing attention to the fact that the regulation of issues of key importance for the functioning of the state and the determination of the status, freedoms, and the rights of the individual in the constitution is expressed through norms that vary greatly in their level of detail. Some are quite general and "from the outset" require interpretation to determine their meaning. This is because these fundamental issues, which are captured in the form of normative provisions in the text of a specific legal act – the constitution – refer to a broad context of meaning, which is both fundamental and initial for interpreting the norms. In this way, it is possible to identify a clear two-level constitutional structure extending between the text expressing the legal norms and the sphere of axiology forming the ideological foundation of the constitution. At the same time, it concerns those presuppositions which the constitution – understood in the stricter sense as a normative act – is intended to express and realise.[41]

The existence of two distinct spheres by no means implies a dismemberment of the constitutional matter that would lead to internal contradiction. On the contrary,

[41] Young (2007), pp. 467, 470.

it means that any process of interpreting the normative sphere of the constitution must take into account its more general goals and values. It therefore requires a close connection between the constitutional norms being interpreted and that sphere of assumptions not articulated in the text itself, but which give constitutional provisions their meaning.

The observation made makes it possible to formulate a further conclusion relating to the very essence of the constitution. The point is that the aforementioned two-tier structure of the constitution requires the necessary coherence of the two spheres. So that they remain complementary. In other words, the values, ideas and assumptions on which the constitution is based are not only to be taken into account in the process of interpretation, but moreover they should guide that process, constituting its content point of reference. The preservation of the coherence of the constitution must therefore involve striving for the fullest possible realisation of its premises. The injunction inscribed in the very idea of the constitution to realise the fundamental values constituting its axiological foundation determines the specific goals that one wishes to attain using this specific legal act.

The combination of the aforementioned two-tier structure of the constitution with the expectation that its presuppositions and basic ideas will determine the direction of interpretation of the norms expressed in the language of constitutional norms leads to yet another conclusion. It indicates that the constitution is – in itself – always an intentional act. This, in turn, implies that all entities interpreting and applying the constitution should take measures that – in accordance with the situation and the scope of their competence – will aim at achieving constitutionally legitimate goals. They will thus be consistent with the values and assumptions deemed to be accepted and constitutionally protected. The very recognition of the constitution as an purposeful act is therefore a consequence of its specific content and follows directly from the imperative to give effect to its provisions.[42]

The perspective outlined above allows the concept of good faith to be introduced at this point. It is understood as an attitude of those interpreting and applying the constitution, reflecting an orientation towards the realisation of constitutional aims and objectives. It constitutes, from this perspective, a consequence of a broader and more fundamental reflection on the essence of the constitution and, at the same time, places acting in good faith at the very centre of reflections on this normative act. The identification of good faith with conduct relating to the aims and objectives on which the constitutional model is based is not merely a desirable directive of action. It is not, therefore, a subjective disposition of the interpreter's will that could be regarded simply as a manifestation of a particular legal culture (or absence thereof). It is of crucial importance for maintaining the coherence of the constitution and thus preserving its meaning in that full dimension which concerns constitutional norms read in the context of the values they are intended to realise.

The necessity to act in good faith is particularly evident if we take into account the nature of constitutional norms and their frequent underdetermination, which

[42] Brzozowski (2014), p. 8.

opens space for multiple, sometimes contradictory interpretations. This circumstance makes it difficult to provide a sufficiently precise answer to the question of whether a given action does not violate the disposition of a legal norm expressed in the constitution. It is then necessary to include in the process of interpretation those elements of content that relate to the underlying assumptions and values, and then – against this background – to clarify the meaning of the norm, taking into account the constitutionally legitimate objectives. This process, as emphasised above, follows from the arrangement of the constitutional matter on two closely related levels. However, their mutual coherence cannot be preserved, and discrepancies that undermine the stability of a system based on constitutional regulation cannot be prevented, if the interpretation and application of the constitution are not based on good faith. Without this necessary orientation, which must constantly accompany the interpretation of constitutional norms, it is very easy to inadvertently instrumentalise the constitution and, in the long term, undermine its normative meaning.

At the same time, the theme outlined above indicates that the understanding of acting in good faith is closely related to another key feature of the constitution, namely its supremacy in the system of sources of law. The very principle of supremacy requires us to ask whether a given action is in compliance with the constitution and, in the case of a negative answer, to declare it inadmissible. Since conformity is always considered in two ways – whether a given norm is not contrary to the constitution and whether it serves to realise its objectives – determining this issue inevitably requires assessment in light of constitutional goals. The supremacy of the constitution, after all, does not invalidate the earlier observation about its purposive character. In effect, however, it is not possible to ensure the supremacy, i.e. to ensure that the constitution acts as supreme law, if the interpretation and application of constitutional norms are not directed towards the attainment of these goals. Otherwise, although the constitution is undoubtedly based on certain assumptions and expresses ideas and values, their realisation is not taken into account when interpreting constitutional norms. This would reduce the constitution to merely symbolic meaning, thereby significantly weakening – if not eliminating – its guarantee function. Recognising and naming good faith as an attitude oriented towards constitutional is therefore not only related to the essence of the constitution but also necessary for the preservation of its supremacy. The theoretical findings presented above make it possible not only to situate good faith within the framework of constitutional considerations, but at the same time to give good faith action a key meaning in the context of its specific content and legal force. On this basis, one may already attempt to outline the main features of such an action, and thus to introduce the further considerations undertaken by the authors of this book, particularly in its third part The identification of the perceived characteristics of acting in good faith must begin by emphasising that the reference is to its objective meaning. That is, constitutional good faith is not contingent on the subjective attitude of the subject, who may freely decide to direct his or her conduct towards constitutionally legitimate aims or to abandon this perspective in order to achieve personal aims. Nor is it dependent on the way in which one interprets the goals set out in the constitution, thereby giving them a purely subjective meaning. For this would mean that each actor could invoke his or her own understanding of certain constitutional principles and thus justify a particular action through an individual interpretation. Good faith should be understood as a formal category that signifies a commitment to the goals set out in the constitution, and thus endeavouring to give them real meaning in the process of interpreting and applying the constitution. In this way, good faith serves as safeguard against the instrumentalisation of the constitution and cannot, at the same time, be used to mask actions that run counter to its aims and objectives.

Secondly, good faith, which draws attention to the axiological context of constitutional norms and obliges one to take it into account, is not exclusively directed at a particular segment of the separated authorities. It does not concern only legislative activity, nor is its impact limited solely to the sphere of the executive or the judiciary. Since it derives from the essence of the constitution, it naturally permeates the entirety of constitutional regulation, including in its organisational and competence dimensions. As a result, a more detailed analysis of good faith is not undertaken in the remainder of the book, by dividing it according to individual authorities, but rather by examining the various types of relations that the constitution provides for. This includes both the relationship between public authorities and, separately considered, the relationship of the state towards the individual. This therefore confirms the universal character of good faith.

Thirdly, constitutional good faith, as the required attitude of those involved in the process of interpreting and applying the constitution, is founded on the mutual trust of the "parties" who, acting in loyalty to each other, orient their action towards the realisation of these common goals. The relational character of good faith understood in this way is linked to its initial characteristics derived from private law and international law. It is also confirmed at the constitutional level, which is analysed in detail mainly in the chapter on good faith in the state-individual relationship. This feature alone means, at the same time, that the normative sources of good faith on constitutional grounds may derive both from regulations addressed to public authorities and those which impose certain obligations on individuals. Therefore, also in this dimension, good faith appears as a universal category, clearly embedded in the constitution.

5 Conclusion

The above review shows that the idea of good faith is present in constitutional doctrine and practice, and even permeates the constitutional laws of different countries with different systems of government and constitutional traditions. Constitutional good faith plays an important role in the process of applying and interpreting the constitution, as well as in determining the way in which the horizontal and vertical interrelationship between state organs is maintained and serves as a kind of constitutional safeguard for the individual against arbitrariness. In these various aspects, the doctrinal assumption of the existence of constitutional good faith seems justified for several reasons. First, a purely legalistic approach may not be sufficient to prevent the instrumentalisation or circumvention of the constitution, the abuse of constitutional rights or other manifestations of abusive constitutionalism. Constitutional good faith can be seen as an essential element of the rule of law and of a political system based on the separation and interaction of powers. Second, constitutional good faith has its common denominators in the entire legal system, including constitutional law, implying honesty, loyalty and sincerity towards constitutions as supreme law (including their premises and objectives) as well as towards other constitutional actors. This substantive understanding of good faith is complemented by the requirement of honest action or conduct (the formal/procedural aspect of good faith). Third, it is seen as an obligation of public authorities and individuals, including under the horizontal operation of the constitution. Fourth, the experience of some countries allows us to conclude that constitutional courts recognise the usefulness of good faith in the interpretation of constitutional provisions, irrespective of its explicit inclusion in constitutions. This is particularly evident in vertical relations: state-individual, central authority-local authority. It is possible that federal loyalty is a kind of prototype of constitutional loyalty, which can be equated with good faith.

This chapter is by definition introductory, and its purpose is to open up the field for discussion. The studies presented in the three parts of the volume by no means claim to be exhaustive. They are, however, intended to introduce the category of good faith into the reflection on the constitution and to underline the need to closely link the process of its interpretation and application to the objectives it is intended to serve.

References

Acar A (2016) De-constitutionalism in Turkey. Verfassungsblog. Available at: https://verfassungsblog.de/de-constitutionalism-in-turkey/

Askin E (2025) Good Faith in Swiss Constitutional Law. In: Podkowik J, Chmielarz-Grochal A, Stębelski M, Sułkowski J (eds) Gleams of good faith in constitutional law, Springer Nature, Cham

Bishop J, McKaughan DJ (2023) Faith. In Zalta EN, Nodelman U (eds.) The Stanford encyclopedia of philosophy (Winter 2023 edn). Available at: https://plato.stanford.edu/archives/win2023/entries/faith/

Blicharz G (2025) Good Faith in Public Law and the European Legal Tradition. In: Podkowik J, Chmielarz-Grochal A, Stębelski M, Sułkowski J (eds) Gleams of good faith in constitutional law, Springer Nature, Cham

Brzozowski W (2014) Obejście konstytucji. Państwo i Prawo 9:3–18

Dixon R, Landau D (2020) Abusive judicial review: courts against democracy. UC Davis Law Rev 53(3):1313–1387

Dixon R, Landau D (2021) Abusive constitutional borrowing. Oxford University Press, Oxford

Fallon RH Jr (2017) Arguing in good faith about the constitution: ideology, methodology, and reflective equilibrium. Univ Chic Law Rev 84(1):123–145

Florczak-Wątor M (2025) Good Faith in Polish Constitutional Law. In: Podkowik J, Chmielarz-Grochal A, Stębelski M, Sułkowski J (eds) Gleams of good faith in constitutional law, Springer Nature, Cham

Gardbaum S (2016) Comparing constitutional bad faith. Harv Law Rev Forum 129:158–165
Garlicki L (2016) Niekonstytucyjność: formy, skutki, procedury. Państwo i Prawo 9:3–21
Johnson R, Cureton A (2024) Kant's moral philosophy. In: Zalta EN, Nodelman U (eds) The Stanford encyclopedia of philosophy. (Fall 2024 edn). Available at: https://plato.stanford.edu/archives/fall2024/entries/kant-moral/
Kałduński M (2025) Good Faith in International Law. In: Podkowik J, Chmielarz-Grochal A, Stębelski M, Sułkowski J (eds) Gleams of good faith in constitutional law, Springer Nature, Cham
Kaleta KJ (2025) Good Faith in Constitutional Interpretation. In: Podkowik J, Chmielarz-Grochal A, Stębelski M, Sułkowski J (eds) Gleams of good faith in constitutional law, Springer Nature, Cham
Klamert M (2025) Good Faith in European Union Law. In: Podkowik J, Chmielarz-Grochal A, Stębelski M, Sułkowski J (eds) Gleams of good faith in constitutional law, Springer Nature, Cham
Kochman A (2025) Good Faith in the European Convention of Human Rights. In: Podkowik J, Chmielarz-Grochal A, Stębelski M, Sułkowski J (eds) Gleams of good faith in constitutional law, Springer Nature, Cham
Leib EL (2025) Good Faith in U.S. Constitutional Law. In: Podkowik J, Chmielarz-Grochal A, Stębelski M, Sułkowski J (eds) Gleams of good faith in constitutional law, Springer Nature, Cham
Łętowska E (2001) Wpływ konstytucji na prawo cywilne. In: Wyrzykowski M (ed) Konstytucyjne podstawy systemu prawa. Instytut Spraw Publicznych, Warszawa
Levinson S (2016) Trash talk at the Supreme Court: reflections on David Pozen's constitutional bad faith. Harv Law Rev Forum 129:166–175
McCanse Wright A (2018) Constitutional good faith. NY Univ Law Rev 93:41–49
Perry C (2024) Good faith in contract law. Edward Elgar Publishing Limited, Cheltenham
Petrov J (2024) How to detect abusive constitutional practices. Eur Const Law Rev 20(2):191–221. https://doi.org/10.1017/S1574019624000142
Pozen DE (2016) Constitutional bad faith. Harv Law Rev 129(4):885–955
Roznai Y (2023) Clownstitutionalism: making a joke of the constitution by abuse of constituent power. Jurídica Anuario del Departamento de Derecho de la Universidad Iberoamericana 15:51–98. https://doi.org/10.48102/ji.15.220
Schnieders AK, Strickrodt S (2025) Good Faith in German Constitutional Law. In: Podkowik J, Chmielarz-Grochal A, Stębelski M, Sułkowski J (eds) Gleams of good faith in constitutional law, Springer Nature, Cham
Stănescu LS (2025) Good Faith in Romanian Constitutional Law. In: Podkowik J, Chmielarz-Grochal A, Stębelski M, Sułkowski J (eds) Gleams of good faith in constitutional law, Springer Nature, Cham
Tokson M, Gentithes M (2023) The reality of the good faith exception. University of Utah College of Law Research Paper, No. 546
Tur Ausina R (2025) Good faith in Spanish constitutional law. In: Podkowik J, Chmielarz-Grochal A, Stębelski M, Sułkowski J (eds) Gleams of good faith in constitutional law. Springer, Cham
Vidal-Naquet A, Magnon X (2025) Good Faith in French Constitutional Law. In: Podkowik J, Chmielarz-Grochal A, Stębelski M, Sułkowski J (eds) Gleams of good faith in constitutional law, Springer Nature, Cham
Whittington K (2023) A typology of constitutional crises. Hoover Institution Working Paper
Young EA (2007) The constitution outside the constitution. Yale Law J 117(3):408–473
Ziółkowski M (2020) Constitutionally shameful judgement in bad faith (Abortion case before the polish constitutional tribunal). Available at: https://blogs.eui.eu/constitutionalism-politics-working-group/constitutionally-shameful-judgement-in-bad-faith-abortion-case-before-the-polish-constitutional-tribunal/

Inspirations

Good Faith in Public Law and the European Legal Tradition

Grzegorz J. Blicharz

Abstract The concept of *bona fides* is an indigenously ancient Roman invention. Roman *bona fides* – the notion of private law – was linked to Roman *fides* widely present in the public sphere, which permeated its culture and influenced the Roman state to become one of the most resilient mega-organizations in the world. *Fides* embraced trust and trustworthiness, i.e. keeping one's word also in non-equal relationships, and even among enemies. *Bona fides* in the realm of private law went much further also preventing against the deceit and abuse, and motivating to respect tacit obligations as referred to the basic goods to be realized in a given polity. Not surprisingly, in the *ius commune* it was *bona fides* that was proclaimed as the basis of commercial transactions (*lex mercatoria*), and in modern times *fides* and *bona fides* was invoked as the foundation of international law called by the rebranded Roman name *ius gentium*. Not only modern doctrine, but also the European legal tradition allows to argue for two statements. *Bona fides* is not just a technical concept of private law, but is the foundation of the legal order in general. To understand the purpose and use of *bona fides* in the public law sphere, centuries of private law reflection on Roman *bona fides* should be a constant source of inspiration. After all, the public and private spheres are linked by human person and the moral framework as reflected in the constitutional order.

1 Introduction

The concept of *bona fides* is an indigenously ancient Roman invention. It is often expressed by the English phrase good faith, and in other languages by respective formulas, like *dobra wiara*, *bonne foi*, *buona fede*, *goede trouw* or more distant *Treu*

G. J. Blicharz (✉)
Faculty of Law and Administration, Jagiellonian University, Cracow, Poland
e-mail: grzegorz.blicharz@uj.edu.pl

J. Podkowik et al. (eds.), *Gleams of Good Faith in Constitutional Law*, Ius Gentium: Comparative Perspectives on Law and Justice 132,
https://doi.org/10.1007/978-3-032-06486-8_2

und Glauben. As a result of the development of European legal tradition good faith became a modern notion well known even without a reference to Roman roots. Can it be, however, fully grasped and used nowadays without embedding it into the original context? In 2024 in the case *Trump v. Anderson* the US Supreme Court quoted Senator Jacob Howard's opinion from the time the XIV Amendment to the US Constitution was framed (i.e. in 1866) that its Section 5 (i.e. enforcement clause) should be understood in such a way that it: "casts upon Congress the responsibility of seeing to it, for the future, that all the sections of the amendment are carried out in good faith".[1]

We came a long way from ancient Roman institution of private law to the US constitutional law jurisprudence. The entire volume is exactly about applying good faith to constitutional law. This chapter, however, tries to unfold how historical development of good faith may inform constitutional law and public law in general. Reading European legal tradition together with Roman legal framework of *bona fides* may shade light on importance of good faith also in public law. From the perspective of the application of *bona fides* in the public sphere, examples of the considerations of Roman jurists that influenced the European legal tradition will supplant the analysis of this chapter, one of them being the Roman case of Barbarius Philippus transmitted by Ulpian (D. 1.14.3),[2] i.e. a slave who was elected praetor by the citizens unaware of this fact, which centuries later was commented by the medieval jurist Baldus de Ubaldis from the point of view of *bona fides*.

2 Why *Bona Fides*? Sources of Inspiration

Bona fides formed the basis of Roman private law, and as such it was inherited and is still used today especially in civil law tradition. It also reaches out, however, to common law tradition, i.e. more than fifty provisions of the US Uniform Commercial Code refer to the duty of good faith.[3] Also, Far East countries inspired by Western legal tradition introduced good faith as a foundational principle of civil law, like recently in the art. 7 of the Chinese Civil Code.[4]

Fides, however, was, according to Cicero, the foundation of justice – *Fundamentum autem est iustitiae fides* (Cic. *De Off.* 1.7.23), so it underlies all law, thus, including public law. Some claim that *bona fides* was privatized so it originally came from *fides* in public law[5] or even *fides* in a "pre-law" sense,[6] or that initially it

[1] *Trump v. Anderson*, 601 US 100 (2024), 109.

[2] D. – *Digesta Iustiniani*. English versions of Roman legal sources follow Alan Watson's translation of Justinian's Digests (from 2009), unless otherwise noted.

[3] Pozen (2016), p. 890.

[4] Wang (2024), p. 42; Pichonnaz (2024), p. 81.

[5] D'Alvia (2018), p. 344.

[6] Valsan (2017), p. 84.

was only another face of *fides* as applied to private law,[7] but over time was given a separate and special meaning in private law which could even "reverse the original meaning of *fides*" as proposed by Cicero.[8] Be as it was, ancient Romans were known for their *fides*. An ancient Greek historian Diodorus of Sicily (first c. BC) referred to more generic figure of Roman *fides* invoked in international context when reporting "that the Romans, harping as they did on the word *fides*, certainly ought not to protect assassins who had shown the greatest contempt for good faith"[9] – Ῥωμαῖοι δέ, θρυλλοῦντες τὸ τῆς πίστεως ὄνομα, παντελῶς οὐκ ὀφείλουσι τοὺς μιαιφόνους, μάλιστα πίστεως καταφρονήσαντας (Diod. Sic. *Bib. hist.* 23.1.4). An ancient Roman rhetor and educator Quintilian (first c. AD) explained that "*fides* is the supreme bond of human affairs, and is sacred between enemies" – *fides supremum rerum humanarum vinculum est, sacra inter hostes* (Quintil. *Decl. min.* 343.12). Cicero when putting *fides* at the foundations of *iustitia* defined it as "the reliability and truthfulness of promises and agreements" – *dictorum conventorumque constantia et veritas* (Cic. *De Off.* 1.7.23). The correlation and possible developments between *fides* and *bona fides* are a matter of constant debates, but what we know is that *bona fides* was developed in Roman private law as a specific technical concept which became the subject of reflection for many generations of jurists, creating a stock of meanings that can be used by contemporaries. As a general principle it influenced not only private law but also international law and its origins confirms that it is justifiable to refer to good faith also in public law. One should be reminded that *fides* was present in ancient Rome at the public square. The temple of *Fides* – deity which protected honesty and fidelity in performing obligations – was placed on the Capitol just next to the Jupiter's temple.[10] Its prominent position was to remind citizens that "a solemn promise given as before God as one's witness is to be sacredly kept. For the question no longer concerns the wrath of the gods (for there is no such thing) but the obligations of justice and good faith" – *quod autem adfirmate quasi deo teste promiseris, id tenendum est: iam enim non ad iram deorum quae nulla est, sed ad iustitiam et ad fidem pertinent* (Cic. *De Off.* 3.29.104). As Fritz Schulz explains: "to guarantee bona fides now no longer only means to keep one's word, but also to act as honest persons do, to keep faith fairly and in accordance with custom".[11]

According to Schulz "fidelity led to the two important rules" related to the doctrine of legal sources, so in the realm of public law. First, that "[t]he magistrate who issues an edict is bound by it" which is somehow depicted also in the Pontius Pilate's reply: "What I have written, I have written", and second, that laws have no retroactive force.[12] In Roman times both were not absolute, neither are today, although they

[7] Fiori (2008), p. 249.

[8] Prescendi et al. (2006).

[9] Sierksma-Agteres (2024), p. 629.

[10] Schulz (1936), p. 224.

[11] Schulz (1936), p. 224.

[12] Schulz (1936), p. 229.

constitute in fact obvious emanations of good faith which are considered as separate principles. It seems that *bona fides* may say more than that for public law purpose. This is already evidenced by the Swiss Constitution, which states in Article 5.3 that *Staatliche Organe und Private handeln nach Treu und Glauben* ("State institutions and private persons shall act in good faith"), which goes further than the principle of legality or non-retroactivity. The importance of good faith has also been confirmed in European Union law,[13] or as we have seen also in US constitutional law,[14] where good faith is an object of scholarly discussion or is sometimes a nicety to be found in courts jurisprudence.

3 Legal Meanings of *Bona Fides*

Words have their proper meaning, although sometimes, as has been the case in good faith, attempts are made to understand them completely out of context. As Bruce Frier highlights referring to Roman law: "*bona fides* is, in this respect, an aggressive concept, more far-reaching than the corresponding concept of *good faith* in Anglo-American law".[15]

It is not just the case that *bona fides* because it is in Latin may sound foreign and bombastic, or erroneously be considered in English a plural form, and thus "good faith" sounds like linguistically more preferred option.[16] Frier explains *bona fides* further: "Not only does it require that parties abstain from deceit and fraud, it also requires, to some extent, that they actively cooperate with one another; and it often does so by imposing duties that the parties may not have envisaged in forming their agreement".[17] These two understandings are commonly approximated in civil law tradition as two "versions" of good faith: subjective and objective. In Roman law both uses of *bona fides* were known, but ancient jurists never distinguished them or conceptualized them. It was the product of *ius commune* which started to uncover pluralistic nature of *bona fides*, but eventually as András Földi argued subjective-objective distinction set the stage thanks to Carl Georg von Wächter in 1871.[18] The subjective one "refers to the state of a party's knowledge (honesty and fairness in mind)" which allows to protect a person acting under a justified mistake,[19] when there was no intention to cause damage or invade someone's rights. It is best known for bona fide acquisitions, such as when the buyer was unaware of the sellers' lack of right. Sometimes this subjective good faith even holds different name, e.g. in

[13] De Baere and Roes (2015).

[14] McCanse Wright (2018).

[15] Frier (2021), p. 10.

[16] Garner (2011), p. 116.

[17] Frier (2021), p. 10.

[18] Földi (2014), p. 312.

[19] Halberda (2020), p. 313.

German it is called *gutter Glaube*, not *Treu und Glauben*.[20] The objective good faith works as a safety valve which is related to protection against the abuse of rights, and allows: "to assess the parties' conduct from the perspective of a specific extra-legal model based on such intangibles as fairness, honesty, and decency".[21]

While usually the former understanding is clearly accepted also in common law tradition, the latter should not be entirely excluded from its significance outside civil law tradition, even in English law, as highlighted recently Jan Halberda.[22] Moreover the objective understanding at least meaning the prohibition of the abuse of rights perhaps even was on Senator Howard's mind in the commentary to the XIV Amendment cited above. After claiming that "all the sections of the amendment are carried out in good faith" he added "and that no State infringes the rights of persons or property". This wider version of good faith may require more active cooperation between public bodies in order to reach the end of law. Such concept of good faith would pose a question whether duties and rights can be implied in public law when they are not specifically regulated, which perhaps may sound controversial knowing how strictly public law is usually construed.

James Gordley when analyzing medieval *ius commune* pointed to yet broader context of good faith. Among three well known meanings of good faith for medieval jurists he included: "keeping one's word, avoiding deceit and overarching, and respecting obligations that were implicit in the transaction in which one is engaged".[23]

He claims that Baldus de Ubaldis added yet another development. In a positive sense *bona fides* means: "the observation of that to which the parties are committed according to natural equity and the ordination of law".[24]

Baldus identifies this natural equity with *quod quis non locupletetur cum aliena iactura* – which allows Gordley to conclude that Baldus: "identified a critical principle of equity or good faith: no one should be enriched at another's expense".[25]

This principle underlies abovementioned three meanings of good faith. According to Gordley it allowed to place the limit on keeping one's word, ie. that is was required only when there was *causa* in terms of "either liberality or the exchange of things of equivalent value".[26] Moreover, it explained the remedy against fraud, and duty to honor tacit obligations arising from a contract. Baldus unlike other medieval jurists linked his reflection both with Roman legal texts and with philosophy of Aristotle and Thomas Aquinas. For Baldus good faith required equity, and was justified by the principle "no one should be enriched at another's expense". This principle was based on the development of Roman legal thought. There, however,

---

[20] Földi (2020), p. 738.

[21] Halberda (2023), p. 236.

[22] Halberda (2023), p. 236.

[23] Gordley (2000), p. 114.

[24] Gordley (2000), p. 109.

[25] Gordley (2000), p. 114.

[26] Gordley (2000), p. 114.

according to Pomponius this principle was based on *aequitas*, not on *bona fides*, and originated from natural law: "By the law of nature it is just that no one become richer by the loss and injury of another" – *Iure naturae aequum est neminem cum alterius detrimento et iniuria fieri locupletiorem* (D. 50.17.206). *Bona fides* for Roman jurists was not entirely equated with *aequitas*. There must have been however a correlation between *bona fides* and *aequitas*, just like there was between *iustitia* and *fides*. Compilators of Justinian's Digest placed in the same title as the abovementioned principle of Pomponius, the fragment of the Roman jurist Gaius who explains that "Good faith does not allow the same thing to be claimed twice" – *Bona fides non patitur, ut bis idem exigatur* (D. 50.17.57) which seems to rely on the principle that "no one should be enriched at another's expense" which Pomponius related to *ius naturale* and *aequitas*, where later Baldus equated with *naturalis aequitas* as the basis of *bona fides*. As Wojciech Dajczak concluded *bona fides* allowed to correct legal order from within, and did not serve to criticize law from the outside,[27] not always leading to the same results as *aequitas*.[28] It fits with Franz Wieacker approach that for example in German law *Treu und Glauben* clause plays the role of praetorian law which in ancient Rome constituted an element of legal order and which "in the public interest the praetors have introduced in aid or supplementation or correction of the *ius civile*".[29] The same praetors used procedural clause *ex fide bona* to legal actions which gave rise to *actiones bonae fidei* – *bonae fidei iudicia* – and developed the technical concept of *bona fides* in private law. This clause allowed judge greater discretion in interpreting and adjudicating legal relationships which did not belong to strict law, like famous *stipulatio*. One may say that *stipulatio* – formal verbal promise – originated from ancient oath and was based on Roman *fides* to keep one's word regardless of consequences. Transactions lacking that formal character, were more flexible, and usually available also to foreigners required to remind parties about acting with *bona fides* and respecting tacit duties. The public interest was thus at the bottom also of this praetor's practice. One should not overlook, however, that for example praetorian *actio iniuria aestimatoria* contained a formula which allowed similar discretion of a judge but framed as *quantum (…) bonum et aequum*. Nevertheless it was rather *ius commune* that merged *bona fides* with *aequitas*, leaving reflection on *bona fides* in the area of acquiring property, e.g. *bona fide* purchase. Perhaps, as Wim Decock suggested, *bona fides* conceived as a mutual trust was too obvious to discuss it in the culture permeated by Christianity.[30] Good faith was taken for granted as the moral basis for all legal relationships especially from the point of view of canon law. The same Baldus explained that with regards to canonical equity (*aequitas canonica*) "all contracts in this world are of good faith" – *quod de aequitate canonica omnes contractus mundi sint bonae fidei*[31] which did not cause any change in the distinction between *actiones stricti*

[27] Dajczak (1998), p. 159.

[28] Longchamps de Bérier (2013), p. 125.

[29] Zimmermann and Whittaker (2000), p. 24, fn. 88.

[30] Decock (2013), pp. 617–618.

[31] Decock (2013), p. 279.

iuris and *bonae fidei* which remained in civil law realm. It led to highlight that in *bonae fidei* actions *bona fides* is expected to the highest degree which was coined as *bona fides exuberans.*[32] Perhaps it is not a coincidence that Baldus referred to the text of Roman jurists Tryphoninus who wrote: "in contracts *bona fides* requires maximum justice" – *Bona fides quae in contractibus exigitur aequitatem summam desiderat* (D. 16.3.31pr.). In the *principium* the text shows that *bona fides* may be differently interpreted with regards to *ius naturale* and *ius gentium*. With regards to *ius naturale*, it would be enough to give back 100 sesterces to a man who deposited it with you although he was deported and his estate forfeited to the state; and differently with regards to *bona fides* in the light of *ius civile* and *legum ordinem:* it should be given directly to the state. Whereas in the first paragraph (D. 16.3.31.1) the Roman jurist, just like Dajczak suggested, shows that *bona fides* may require to keep one's word, so give back a thing to a person who deposited it with me even though its owner claims it from me. *Totius rei aequitatem* (the full justice) would require, however, to consider other people affected by our contract of deposit, ie. to give it back to the owner who claims it: *hanc esse iustitiam, quae suum cuique ita tribuit.* Here one may grasp a difference that *bona fides* operates within a given relationship, whereas *aequitas* or *iustitia* serve to transgress that internal relationship for the sake of common good.

It was in medieval *lex mercatoria* – the body of rules of international commerce – that *bona fides* shined as a foundation of legal order. Again it was Baldus who wrote: *bonam fidem valde requiri in his, qui plurimum negotiantur* (good faith is much required of those, who trade most).[33] Later in 1707 Giuseppe Lorenzo Maria Casaregis coined the famous phrase that: *Bona fides est primum mobile ac spiritus vivificans commercii* – "good faith is the prime mover and lifegiving spirit of commerce".[34] *Bona fides* and *fides* retained its principled position also as the basis of "new" *ius gentium* developed as international public law, to which Hugo Grotius referred multiple times. Referring to Cicero and Aristotle he famously stated that "If good faith has been taken away, all intercourse among men ceases to exist" – *Fide enim non tantum respublica quaelibet continetur ut Cicero dicit, sed et maior illa gentium societas: Hac sublate ut vere Aristoteles ἀνῄρηται ἡ πρὸς ἀλλήλουσ χρεία τῶν ἀνθρώπων, tollitur quod inter homines est commercium (For not only is every state sustained by good faith, as Cicero declares, but also that greater Society of States. Aristotle truly says that, if good faith has been taken away, 'all intercourse among men ceases to exist').*[35,36] In this reflection one may find how *bona fides* connects both international trade and international relations between the states. On the verge of both areas also Roman *fides* and *bona fides* was developed and distinguished ancients Romans from other nations and legal orders.

[32] Földi (2014), pp. 314–315.

[33] Zimmermann and Whittaker (2000), p. 18.

[34] Zimmermann and Whittaker (2000), p. 18.

[35] O'Connor (1991), p. 56.

[36] de Groot [1625] (1939), p. 877.

The Romans were guided by a belief in the existence of basic goods primary to the law. Wanting to avoid arbitrariness in interpreting what good faith means, it is always worth reaching for the cultural context, which for us is constituted within the European legal tradition. There one may find persuasive arguments for today's challenges when asking about good faith not only in private, but also in public law, and in both spheres of European legal tradition: civil law and common law. Law does not work without and apart from culture, in our case, the Western culture. Legal thinking was grounded in and shaped by Roman law, so even the Christian Roman Empire also adopted the ancient pre-Christian understanding of good faith which fueled European legal tradition.

Analyzing European legal tradition one can uncover the basic role of *bona fides*: it provides for the completion of to the legal order where explicit statutory regulations or contractual provisions are lacking, or where such existing provisions require interpretation. *Bona fides* does so in two ways. First, it implies basing the legal order on ethical grounds, such that all legal actions should be performed with *bona fides*, and therefore presuppose the sincerity of the parties and mutual trust. Thus, *bona fides* is understood to refer and to protect the moral foundations of law – *iuris praecepta* (precepts of law) – expressed by Roman jurist Ulpian (D. 1.1.10 pr.–1): to live honorably (*honestum vivere*), not to harm any other person (*neminem laedere*), to render to each his own (*ius suum cuique tribuere*).[37] From jurists was required prudence, ie. awareness of God's and men's affairs (*divinarum atque humanarum rerum notitia*), which is how Ulpian defined notion of *iurisprudentia* (D. 1.1.10.2). Violation of *bona fides* will always be a deceitful (*dolus*) and dishonest action (*non omne quod licet honestum est*). This reference to moral foundations is also present in the Cicero's explanation of *fides*. According to him it is wrong to cause harm to another to obtain a benefit. Cicero considers the law of nations to be the juridical embodiment of nature (*natura, id est iure gentium*). For him, the *ius gentium* oscillated between the two great coordinates of human justice set down by the Greek philosophers and refined by the Roman jurists: *natura* and *fides*.

Secondly, *bona fides* is used as an opportunity to relax the letter of the law when justice, the legitimate interest of the parties, the nature of the act in question or the public interest requires it. In a technical sense, in Roman law, it meant granting discretion to the judge in assessing damages in the case of contracts of good faith (*bonae fidei contractus*) according to the circumstances and, above all, depending on the degree of the violation of *bona fides*, thus also taking into account the deceitfulness of (*dolus*) or the fault or negligence (*culpa, imperitia*) of the parties to the legal relationship. The opposite was that the judge was bound by the letter of the contract between the parties – following strict law, from which he could not deviate on his own, which occurred in agreements protected by *actiones stricti iuris*. Even then, however, the praetor was allowed to grant *exceptio doli* to cripple a claim based on fraud and abuse. Therefore, it is not surprising that in the *ius commune* it was *bona fides* that was promulgated as the basis of commercial transactions (*lex*

---

[37] Dajczak (2012), p. 39.

mercatoria), and in civil law it led to a broadening analysis of the parties' duties and rights in the execution of contracts.

4 *Bona Fides* Applied in Public Law: From Ulpian to Baldus

An example will allow us to see the application of *bona fides* to a Roman case from the sphere of public law which is of most interest to this volume. The famous representative of the commentators Baldus de Ubaldis refers to *bona fides* when analyzing the Roman case of Barbarius Philippus transmitted by Ulpian (D. 1.14.3),[38] i.e. a slave who was elected praetor by the citizens unaware of this fact and for some time issued decisions in individual cases. The situation eluded legal regulation and required recourse to something beyond the letter of the law in order to settle whether such acts issued by *falsus* praetor should be considered valid.

D. 1.14.3 Ulp. 38 ad Sab.

> Barbarius Philippus cum servus fugitivus esset, Romae praeturam petiit et praetor designatus est. sed nihil ei servitutem obstetisse ait Pomponius, quasi praetor non fuerit: atquin verum est praetura eum functum. et tamen videamus: si servus quamdiu latuit, dignitate praetoria functus sit, quid dicemus? quae edixit, quae decrevit, nullius fore momenti? an fore propter utilitatem eorum, qui apud eum egerunt vel lege vel quo alio iure? et verum puto nihil eorum reprobari: hoc enim humanius est: cum etiam potuit populus Romanus servo decernere hanc potestatem, sed et si scisset servum esse, liberum effecisset. quod ius multo magis in imperatore observandum est.

> Barbarius Philippus, while he was a runaway slave, stood as a candidate for the praetorship at home and became praetor designate. His servile status was no kind of obstacle, says Pomponius, to his being praetor; as a matter of fact he did perform the functions of the praetorship. But let us consider: if a slave, so long as his status was unknown, exercised the praetorian responsibilities, what are we to say? That the edicts and decrees he issued would be null and void? Would that be to the benefit of those who had sued in his court either on statutory grounds or by some other right? The truth, I think, is that none of these edicts, decrees, and so forth, would be deemed nullities. For this is the more humane view. For the Roman people certainly was competent to have conferred this power on a slave, but, of course, if it had known he was a slave, it would have set him free. The right to do so then must all the more be held valid in the case of the emperor.

The slave who often abandoned his owner (*servus fugitivus*) became praetor probably during the time of the second triumvirate.[39] For a fairly long time, no one realized that he was a slave: in ancient Rome, however, such situations were widespread. The questions Ulpian asks present a characteristic of extraordinary situations in which the jurist must arrive at a just and flexible solution, when the rules posed by the legislature usually do not offer a clear answer. Thus, here the question that arises is whether all acts that had been performed during praetor's magistracy should be

[38] This section is based on a broader analysis in Blicharz (2016), pp. 335–352.

[39] Trisciuoglio (2022), p. 2027.

considered null and void or retain their validity. Ulpian's asks whether these acts should be valid by reason of the utility of all those who performed acts in the face of the "false" praetor. Ulpian's solution is simple: all acts of the false praetor are valid, because this is *humanius*. This formula: *humanius est* is further explained: the Roman people accepted the person of Philippus, so the formal issue becomes less important-the people's competence was not diminished by the fact that the praetor was a slave because he could be freed through the same people. This specific case was very delicate because it touched on the retroactivity of annulment and a limitation of the existence of concrete legal acts, especially court proceedings in front of the praetor. Therefore, a flawed act could be validated for reasons of *utilitas* and *humanitas*. Thus, *humanis esse* or *humanitas* was a criterion of the interpretation and evaluation of legal acts-those of the praetor – both a true and a false praetor. Although, from the perspective of the laws Barbarius could not be a praetor, and he violated the legislation which should end up with proper punishment, the acts he produced were judged from the standpoint of *humanitas*.

As Guido Rossi has proven extensively the leading medieval jurist Baldus builds on the case of Barbarius the concept of the relationship between public office and public officer which introduces the difference between agent and office.[40] In discussing the case of Barbarius, Baldus cites the example of the election of a prelate whose invalidity remains undisclosed. It is in this passage that, according to Rossi "[t]he difference between internal and external validity of agency is particularly evident":

> Verius credo quod valeant gesta, si est in possessione, et communis error et publica vtilitas hoc suadent. Hoc probo. Prelatus est obligatus subditis ad faciendum eis iustitiam, et potest ad hoc cogi, in Auth. de quaestore § super hoc. Item est obligatio realis. Nam ipsa dignitas est obligata subditis ad hoc, et sic ex hoc resultat ius reale. Igitur quasi possidetur hoc ius ab uniuersitate subditorum. [...] Ex hoc concludo quod ista quasi possessio subditorum iustificat processum in eorum favorem propter eorum bonam fidem, dato quod prelatus habeat malam fidem, dico etiam quod istud ius possidet vniuersitas subditorum, non singuli, quia sic infinite essent possessiones [...].[41]

> I rather think that the deeds are valid if [Barbarius] is in possession, and the common mistake and public utility both argue for this. I prove it this way. A prelate is bound to his subjects to render them justice, and may be compelled to do as much [...] This is an obligation in rem [realis], for the dignitas itself is bound to its subjects to do as much, and that amounts to a real right. So it is as if the collectivity of the subjects had quasi possessio of this right [...] Hence I argue that this possession of the subjects justifies the legal proceedings in their favour because of their good faith, given that the prelate was in bad faith. The subjects possess this right as a collectivity, not as individuals, otherwise there would be infinite possessions [Rossi translation].[42]

Baldus expands the Ulpian's argument from *humanitas* and includes *bona fides – propter eorum bonam fidem*, to protect subjects acting in trust of the public office.

---

[40] Rossi (2019), p. 454.

[41] Rossi (2018), p. 120.

[42] Rossi (2019), p. 454.

One should note, that decisions and acts delivered by *falsus praetor* were considered effective in order to protect the core values of legal order. Baldus invokes both the public utility which resembles Ulpian's *utilitas*, it refers to common mistake (*error communis*) already seen in this fragment by Accursius,[43] but also, and most importantly for our purpose, appeals explicitly to the good faith of the people. As Rossi explains:

> [t]he simple possession of the office (instead of de iure entitlement) suffices as to its valid exercise because of the good faith of the people (which triggers public utility). But the validity is only towards the commonwealth (external validity) and not to the agent (internal validity), who has no entitlement to the office, and so no right to it.[44]

Quite interestingly, however, these acts and decisions were delivered in a manner that was not contrary to justice or expectations which can lead us to conclusion that not only *bona fides* of people but also effective and proper performing of the office by the *falsus praetor* was necessary to keep these acts and decisions valid, as Baldus put it in the formula *si est in possessione* – if he is in possession of the office. This points to Baldus' idea that people have their own right vis-à-vis the public office – the real right (*ius reale*) – which protects them from any internal flaws in public structures and allows to preserve the rule of law.

5 Conclusion

Roman *bona fides* – the notion of private law – was linked to Roman *fides* widely present in the public sphere, which permeated its culture and influenced the Roman state to become one of the most resilient mega-organizations in the world. *Fides* embraced trust and trustworthiness, i.e. keeping one's word also in non-equal relationships, and even among enemies. *Bona fides* in the realm of private law went much further also preventing against the deceit and abuse, and motivating to respect tacit obligations as referred to the basic goods to be realized in a given polity. *Bona fides* in the European legal tradition occurs in the so-called unregulated sphere. Looking at the legal order as a whole, *bona fides* concerns the morality and sincerity of the intentions of the subjects of the law, who are called not to abuse their powers. In the case of private law, it entails not only the prohibition of abuse of right and deceitful actions, the protection of actions taken in the belief of their legality, but also rules concerning the proper performance of a contract, especially where certain rights and obligations do not arise directly from the contract, but must be assumed or implied in view of the parties' unexpressed will, the nature of the relationship and transaction and the requirements of custom and fair dealing. Not only modern doctrine, but also the European legal tradition allow to argue for two statements. *Bona fides* is not just a technical concept of private law, but is the foundation of the legal

[43] Trisciuoglio (2022), p. 2027.

[44] Rossi (2018), p. 121.

order in general. In order to understand the purpose and use of good faith in the public law sphere, centuries of private law reflection on Roman *bona fides* should be a constant source of inspiration. After all, the public and private spheres are linked by human person.

References

Blicharz G (2016) Giudicare una decisione del pretore: la relazione tra diritto e fatto nel passo di Paolo (D. 1,1,11) e nel caso di Barbarius Philippus (D. 1,14,3). Seminarios Complutenses de Derecho Romano 29:335–352

D'Alvia D (2018) From public law to private law: the remarkable story of *bona fides*. In: Heidemann M, Lee J (eds) The future of the commercial contract in scholarship and law reform. Springer, Cham, pp 343–368

Dajczak W (1998) Zwrot bona fides w rozstrzygnięciach dotyczących kontraktów u prawników rzymskich okresu klasycznego. Wydawnictwo UMK, Toruń

Dajczak W (2012) The nature of the contract in reasoning of civilian jurists. Wydawnictwo Naukowe UAM, Poznań

De Baere G, Roes T (2015) EU loyalty as good faith. Int Comp Law Q 64(4):829–874

de Groot H [1625] (1939) In: de Kanter-van Hettinga Tromp BJA (ed) De iure belli ac pacis. Brill, Leiden

Decock W (2013) Theologians and contract law: the moral transformation of the ius commune (ca. 1500–1650), Legal History Library 9, Studies in the History of Private Law 4. Martinus Nijhoff, Leiden

Fiori R (2008) Fides e bona fides. Gerarchia sociale e categorie giuridiche. In: Fiori R (ed) Modelli teorici e metodologici nella storia del diritto privato 3. Jovene, Napoli, pp 237–259

Földi A (2014) Traces of the dualist interpretation of good faith in the ius commune until the end of the sixteenth century. Fundamina 20(1):312–321

Földi A (2020) "False Friends" and some other phenomena reflecting the historical determination of the terminology of Hungarian private law. Int J Semiot Law 33:729–747

Frier BW (2021) A casebook on the Roman law of contracts. Oxford University Press, New York

Garner BA (2011) Garner's dictionary of legal usage. Oxford University Press, New York

Gordley J (2000) Good faith in contract law in the medieval ius commune. In: Zimmermann R, Whittaker S (eds) Good faith in European contract law. Cambridge University Press, Cambridge, pp 93–117

Halberda J (2020) The principle of good faith and fair dealing in English contract law. Pravovedenie 64(3):312–325

Halberda J (2023) Winds of change in common law jurisdictions: the concept of good faith and fair dealing in the performance of contracts. In: Griffiths C, Korporowicz ŁJ (eds) English law, the legal profession, and colonialism: histories, parallels, and influences. Routledge, London, pp 234–257

Longchamps de Bérier F (2013) L'abuso del diritto nell'esperienza del diritto privato romano. Giappichelli, Torino

McCanse Wright A (2018) Constitutional good faith. NY Univ Law Rev 93:41–49

O'Connor JF (1991) Good faith in international law. Aldershot, Hants, England; Brookfield, Vt., USA, Dartmouth

Pichonnaz P (2024) Comparative perspectives on the general part of the Chinese Civil Code. In: Bussani M, Cardillo I, Infantino M, Jun X (eds) The Chinese Civil Code in the global legal order: inner and outer perspectives. Brill, Leiden, pp 71–91

Pozen DE (2016) Constitutional bad faith. Harv Law Rev 129(4):885–955

Prescendi F, Schiemann G, Büchli J (2006) Fides. In: Brill's New Pauly Online. Brill. Available via BRILL https://doi.org/10.1163/1574-9347_bnp_e411430
Rossi G (2018) Baldus and the limits of representation. Leg Hist Rev 86(1–2):55–122
Rossi G (2019) Representation and ostensible authority in medieval learned law. Vittorio Klostermann, Frankfurt am Main
Schulz F (1936) Principles of Roman law. Oxford University Press, Oxford
Sierksma-Agteres S (2024) Chapter 7: Pistis, charis, and dynamis: faith as transjuridical and trans-ethnic bond of trust. In: Paul and the philosophers' faith. Brill, Leiden, pp 569–691
Trisciuoglio A (2022) Dalla lex Barbarius (D. 1.14.3) al principio error communis facit ius. In: Fasolino F (ed) Ius hominum causa constitutum. Studi in onore di Antonio Palma, vol 3. Giappichelli, Torino, pp 2025–2032
Valsan R (2017) Fides, bona fides, and bonus vir: relations of Trust and Confidence in Roman Antiquity. J Law Relig State 5(1):48–85
Wang L (2024) Highlighting the significance of the Chinese Civil Code. In: Bussani M, Cardillo I, Infantino M, Jun X (eds) The Chinese Civil Code in the global legal order: inner and outer perspectives. Brill, Leiden-Boston, pp 31–50
Zimmermann R, Whittaker S (2000) Good faith in European contract law: surveying the legal landscape. In: Zimmermann R, Whittaker S (eds) Good faith in European contract law. Cambridge University Press, Cambridge, pp 7–62

Good Faith in International Law

Marcin Kałduński

Abstract Good faith has long been recognized in international law. Yet, there is an ongoing debate on its relevance, normativity and scope of application. Thus, this chapter will examine the position that good faith can play in international law. In so doing, it will appraise whether good faith has a normative or rather descriptive character in the ecosystem of international rules, processes and actors. Against this background, this chapter will analyze good faith as a conception governing international law. The analysis will primarily rely on the dogmatic method and the review of basic sources of international law, including treaties and case law. Also, the historic approach will be employed to achieve the purpose of the chapter highlighted above.

Through these lenses, the chapter will reveal that good faith is a legal norm and has a non-derogable place in the decentralized international legal order, which bases the creation and performance of international obligations on the will of its subjects. This is a principle governing international law which ensures its coherence and systemic organization, as it both creates and justifies the consistency and effectiveness of international obligations. This contribution will show that good faith creates meaningful relations between various norms of international law. It seems impossible to imagine the efficient existence of international law without good faith. The validity of good faith stems directly from the very essence of international law.

This chapter will also show that although good faith is not derived from the will of States, it has a primordial character in relation to that will – it governs it and ensures its fulfillment in accordance with the intentions of parties and the letter and purpose of the obligation(s). While good faith is too general in its nature to impose concrete normative requirements on States, it lays the foundations for other more concrete and specific norms. Therefore, this chapter will identify good faith as a general principle within the meaning of Article 38 (1) (c) of the Statute of the International Court of Justice.

M. Kałduński (✉)
Faculty of Law and Administration, Nicolaus Copernicus University, Toruń, Poland
e-mail: mmk@umk.pl

J. Podkowik et al. (eds.), *Gleams of Good Faith in Constitutional Law*, Ius Gentium: Comparative Perspectives on Law and Justice 132,
https://doi.org/10.1007/978-3-032-06486-8_3

1 Introduction

Good faith is one of the most often debated rules in international law. It is a concept which is ambiguously interpreted in the context of ethics and morality and which is intertwined with numerous – apparently different – legal norms. Good faith exists in various normative forms, sometimes as an independent principle of law and sometimes as a constituent of another norm, such as the principle of fulfilling obligations in good faith. Additionally, there is an objective and subjective side to good faith, where the former generally is often presented in the form of a legal principle, which is independent of the qualification of the inner (mental) state of the subject of law, whereas the latter is equated with the subject's inner conviction that their actions are in conformity with law the opposite of which is bad faith. Consequently, defining and describing good faith poses serious difficulties. Some scholars even warn about an attempt to search for definitions.[1] Additionally, there has been a dispute going on for years concerning the normative status of good faith in international law. It combines a debate on the bases and sources of international law, the law of treaties, international responsibility and mechanisms concerning the creation and fulfilment of international obligations. The discussion also centers on whether good faith has a normative or rather descriptive character in the decentralized ecosystem of international rules, processes and actors.

It is a truism to say that the principle of good faith remains an area of interest for the science of international law. The analysis of the literature shows that it is very scattered and refers to good faith in the context of individual principles and rules of international law, usually without a general and wider reflection. For the most part, the literature is diversified, and at times even superficial as regards the merits. Only in very few instances, the principle of good faith was the subject of deeper analysis. Most of all, three books by Zoller (1976), Kolb (2000) and O'Connor (1991), where an attempt at a comprehensive study of good faith was made, should be mentioned here. Noteworthy is also a book by Cheng (1951) devoted to the general principles of law[2] and a treatise by Müller (1971) concerning the principle of trust in international law. The same can be said about articles of certain scholars, such as Cot (1968), Lachs (1977), Mik (2011), Sperduti (1952), Verdross (1952), and White (1994). Significant are also books on the law of treaties, among which monographs by Elias (1974), McNair (1961), Reuter (1985), and Rosenne (1989) as well as commentaries to the Vienna Convention on the Law of Treaties of 23 May 1969 (hereinafter: VCLT) stand out.[3] Last but not least, noteworthy are also commentaries to Article 2(2) of the UN Charter.[4] Valuable material includes the works of the ILC, in particular as regards international responsibility and the law of treaties. The

[1] Lachs (1966), p. 33, para. 17.

[2] The second part of the book is devoted to the principle of good faith (at 105–160).

[3] The Vienna Convention on the Law of Treaties of 23 May 1969, 1155 UNTS 331. *The Vienna Conventions on the Law of Treaties: A Commentary* (2011).

[4] Kolb and Müller (2002).

documentation of the United Nations Conference on the Law of Treaties of 1968 and 1969 is of the same significance. Separate material includes the works of experts in international law. All those elements constitute an abundant and sufficient cognitive source and important illustration of research reflection.

This piece submits that good faith is a legal norm and has a non-derogable place in the decentralized international legal order, which bases the creation and performance of international obligations on the will of its subjects (States). This is a principle governing international law which ensures its coherence and systemic organization, as it both creates and justifies the consistency and effectiveness of international obligations. This contribution also shows that good faith creates meaningful relations between various norms of international law. It seems impossible to imagine the efficient existence of international law without good faith. The validity of good faith stems directly from the very essence of international law.

The second submission is that good faith is a meta-principle (meta-norm) of international law, being part of general principles of law within the meaning of Article 38(1)(c) of the Statute of the International Court of Justice (hereinafter: ICJ).[5] It is assumed here that a meta-principle is superior norm, norm on norms. Given this understanding, a meta-principle does not determine concrete rights and obligations of the subject of law. A meta-principle determines when the subjects, through their conduct, may lead to the creation (generation, formation), change or termination of original rules. Therefore, without meta-principles it is impossible to explain other norms of legal order and legal obligations. They are rules of law that have an inherent or necessary validity, without which no system of law can exist or be originated.[6] The particular purpose of a meta-principle is to infuse the basic values (*e.g.*, peace and justice) or regulatory ideas (e.g. State sovereignty) into the international legal order, as well as to implement and disseminate such values (using its subordinate norms). Meta-principles, being general and abstract norms, may also crystallize in other norms, for which meta-principles form a basis for validation or from which the other norms will be derived (constituting their emanations). Thus, a meta-principle is of a structural and organizational character and explains the relationship between legal norms.

2 The ICJ Case Law

A good area for researching the relationship between potential (meta-)principles and other norms of international law is the case law of international courts and tribunals. More generally, the International Court of Justice has recalled on a number

[5] The Statute of the International Court of Justice of 26 June 1945, 33 UNTS 993.

[6] Pauwelyn (2003), p. 125; Koskenniemi (2000), p. 372; Fitzmaurice (1958), p. 164. Fitzmaurice, and not using the term “meta-principle” writes about: “rules of law that have an inherent and necessary validity, in whose absence no system of law can exist or be originated.”

of occasions that good faith is "a well-established principle of international law."[7] However, from the above perspective, of more relevance remains the dictum of the Court that the *pacta sunt servanda* is based on good faith.[8] In those cases, the ICJ declared that: "[o]ne of the basic principles governing the creation and performance of legal obligations, whatever their source, is the principle of good faith. ... just as the very rule of *pacta sunt servanda* in the law of treaties is based on good faith, so also is the binding character of an international obligation assumed by unilateral declaration." In addition, the World Court further explained that good faith: "is not in itself a source of obligation where none would otherwise exist."[9] Therefore, good faith is neither a rule that matters for the purpose of establishing the Court's jurisdiction *ratione materiae* nor a rule that if a State, in bad faith, alleged that another State has breached substantive obligations vis-à-vis the former State, this would not in itself constitute a violation of those substantive obligations.[10]

Other examples of possible meta-principles can be identified in the case law. In its first dispute, the ICJ assumed that the obligation of notification of the existing minefields in time of peace and warning the approaching vessels of inevitable danger are based on three general and well-known principles: (1) elementary considerations of humanity (the Martens clause), (2) the freedom of maritime communication, and (3) every State's obligation not to allow knowingly its territory to be used for acts contrary to the rights of other States.[11] The Court used the last principle to derive the principle of prevention, as it found that this norm – as a customary rule – has its origins (*trouve son origine*) in the due diligence that is required of a State in its territory.[12] This translates into an obligation to perform environmental impact assessment under general international law to undertake an environmental impact assessment where there is a risk that the proposed industrial activity (e.g. an industrial or mining one) may have a significant adverse impact in a transboundary

---

[7] *Land and Maritime Boundary between Cameroon and Nigeria (Cameroon* v. *Nigeria)*, Preliminary Objections, Judgment, 11 June 1998, I.C.J. Reports 1998, 38.

[8] *Nuclear Tests* (Australia v. France), Judgment, 20 December 1974, I.C.J. Reports 1974; *Nuclear Tests* (New Zealand v. France), Judgment, 20 December 1974, I.C.J. Reports 1974, 46, 49.

[9] *Border and Transborder Armed Actions (Nicaragua* v. *Honduras)*, Judgment, 20 December 1988, I.C.J. Reports 1988, 94.

[10] *Allegations of Genocide under the Convention on the Prevention and Punishment of the Crime of Genocide (Ukraine v. Russian Federation)*, Preliminary Objections, Judgment, 2 February 2024, I.C.J. Reports, 142; "[E]ven if the Russian Federation had, in bad faith, alleged that Ukraine committed genocide and taken certain measures against it under such a pretext – which the Respondent contests – this would not in itself constitute a violation of obligations under Articles I and IV of the Convention."

[11] *Corfu Channel (United Kingdom of Great Britain and Northern Ireland v. Albania)*, Merits, Judgment, 9 April 1949, I.C.J. Reports 1949, 22.

[12] Since it is the obligation of each state to prevent its territory from being used for acts contrary to contrary to the laws of other states. *Pulp Mills on the River Uruguay (Argentina* v. *Uruguay)*, Judgment, 20 April 2010, I.C.J. Reports 2010, 101 (referring to the *Corfu Channel* case).

context.[13] In Military and Paramilitary Activities in and against Nicaragua, the ICJ took the view that the rules enshrined in Article 3 common to all four Geneva Conventions of International Humanitarian Law of 12 August 1949 constitute basic fundamental general principles of humanitarian law and reflect elementary considerations of humanity.[14] Yet in another case, the ICJ held that the rule of State immunity derives from the principle of sovereign equality of States,[15] which for some internationalists means that this principle forms the basis for other norms and may be classified as a meta-principle of international law.[16]

3 Origins of International Good Faith

Bona fides has an extra-positivist origin, for it stemmed from religious and moral *fides* and natural law, the concept and essence of which was derived from Greek philosophy. Hence, it has moral, ethical, logical and legal dimensions. It mandated fidelity and loyalty to one's partner and required diligent and honest behaviour. *Bona fides* was seen as an objective basis that secured trust in the given word (passive element) and demanded its observance (active element). The declared behaviour of the subject gave rise to an expectation of behaviour in accordance with the declaration. The basis of this expectation was good faith. *Bona fides* also meant the subjective belief that one was acting in accordance with the law. The fathers of the law of nations framed good faith as: (1) a principle underpinning promises and treaties, without which there would be no relations between nations, and (2) a standard for assessing the conduct of states in implementing and interpreting obligations entered into. Particular emphasis was placed on honouring treaties and pledges, with which the hope of maintaining peace and justice between nations was linked. The classic writers focused on the active side of good faith, emphasising the necessity of keeping faith. They further noted that removing good faith from the law of nations would amount to its abolition. The certainty and reciprocity of relations between people always depended on good faith, and thus the functioning of the law of nations also depended on good faith. Therefore, philosophers and jurists referred to Roman jurisprudence, drew on natural law and Christian doctrine, and thus invoked the principle of good faith in the law of nations. This was done by, among

[13] *Pulp Mills* (2010), 204; *Construction of a Road in Costa Rica along the San Juan River (Nicaragua v. Costa Rica)*, Merits, Judgment, 16 December 2015, I.C.J. Reports 2015, 104.

[14] *Military and Paramilitary Activities in and against Nicaragua (Nicaragua* v. *United States of America)*, Merits, Judgment, 27 June 1986, I.C.J. Reports 1986, 218.

[15] *Jurisdictional Immunities of the State (Germany* v. *Italy: Greece intervening)*, Judgment, 3 February 2012, I.C.J. Reports 2012, 57.

[16] See Kläger (2013), p. 155.

others, de Vattel,[17] van Bynkershoek[18] andWolff.[19] It is important to emphasise here that it was the horizontal nature of international law, as opposed to vertical domestic law, that determined the importance attached to good faith and placed it at the centre of the law of nations, treating it as the basis of contracts and promises, which determines the effectiveness and durability of obligations. This was of particular importance in view of the international practice of the time abounding in acts of faithlessness, which was deplored by those eminent writers. With this in mind, too, they underlined the need to perform and interpret agreements in good faith.

4 The Content and Classification of Good Faith: Its Relations with Other Legal Rules

A distinction needs to be made between the objective and subjective good faith.[20] They can be described as follows:

1. Objective good faith (*bonne foi objective*, *Treu und Glauben*) – it does not depend on the psychological states of the subjects of the law. It is a principle which, on the passive side, implies trust in the given word and, on the active side, the fulfilment of the expressed will (keeping the given word, keeping faith), fidelity and loyalty to the other party and honest, diligent and reasonable conduct, with the consequent protection of legitimate expectations. Objective good faith ensures the durability and effectiveness of obligations. It regulates the creation, application and termination of obligations and constitutes a principle that is a rationale for other norms (meta-principle). This understanding of good faith makes it possible to distinguish two approaches:
    a. Positive good faith safeguards the effectiveness and permanence of international obligations by virtue of regulating their creation, performance and termination. This best reflects its essence, that is, faith and trust in international relations. Accordingly, good faith is the basis for the principle of honouring obligations (*obligationes sunt servandae*) and, consequently, the principles of: (1) *pacta sunt servanda*, (2) *consuetudo, sicut ius accepta, servanda est*, (3) *acta sunt servanda*, (4) estoppel, and (5) acquiescence. It is of particular importance in the law of treaties;
    b. Negative good faith safeguards the effectiveness and permanence of obligations by demanding fidelity and loyalty to the other party and the honest,

[17] de Vattel (1758), book II, ch. XII, XIV, XV, XVII.

[18] van Bynkershoek (1737), book II, ch. X.

[19] Wolff (1764), ch. IV.

[20] See Ferrari Bravo (1964), pp. 314–321; Gialdino (1960), pp. 431–434; Kolb (2000), pp. 111–153; Kałduński (2017), pp. 137–141. In particular, Kolb distinguishes between and thoroughly explains the concepts of objective, subjective and objective-subjective good faith.

diligent and reasonable performance of obligations. An entity is entitled to expect its partner to perform the obligation correctly. The negative principle of good faith opposes the exercise of a right or the satisfaction of a claim when the subject's conduct does not deserve legal protection. This may result from an unreasonable exercise of a right (prohibition of abuse of a right) or from dishonest and negligent behaviour (doctrine of clean hands). Accordingly, good faith prevents the taking of advantage in a situation where the behaviour of the subject and the satisfaction of his demand would strike at the legal order and strain the protection it provides. In other words, granting legal protection would strike at the faith and trust necessary in international relations.

To sum up, negative good faith consists in not doing what is contrary to good faith, while positive good faith is when the subject's conduct produces legal effects by creating, modifying or extinguishing an obligation

2. Good faith in the subjective (psychological) aspect (*bonne foi subjective*, *guter Glaube*) – it denotes a real and internal state of consciousness consisting of a (mistaken) belief in the existence or correct exercise of a certain right, competence or legal relationship, and consequently in the legal consequences of a given situation. Consequently, an actor acting in subjective good faith engages in conduct that may not be protected by international law. Its opposite is bad faith, which is also an internal and subjective state of consciousness;
3. Objective-subjective good faith (*bonne foi semi-objective*) – it combines both aspects of good faith in the performance and interpretation of obligations. It thus prescribes fidelity and loyalty to the other party, the honest and diligent performance of the obligation (objective element) and implies the subject's inner conviction that he or she is acting in accordance with the obligation, which includes the intention to perform the obligation (subjective element). It therefore constitutes a criterion for the ethical and moral assessment of the manner in which a party to an obligation performs and interprets it and, at the same time, outlines a pattern of conduct for that party.

In this classification, good faith comes in two forms: active and passive. In the first form, it is a question of the fulfilment of the will expressed by a certain behaviour (keeping one's word, keeping faith). In its passive form, good faith refers to the trust and confidence (*confiance réciproque*, *confiance légitime*, *Treu und Glauben*, *Vertrauensschutz*) that the latter entity places in the behaviour of the former. This means that the "placing" of faith and trust in the behaviour of the first subject (confiding, trusting the word) leads to the formation of legitimate expectations. Their content will be what the behaviour of the first subject says. It should be clear, unambiguous, unconditional, irrevocable, attributable to the first subject and known to the second.

Moreover, the classification thus developed made it possible to distinguish the concept of legitimate expectations. These are the expectations created by the behaviour of a State, expressing its will as to the behaviour of that State in the future, entering into the area of legal interests of the other State, who took note of this behaviour and subsequently trusted it. Legitimate expectations are therefore the result of the second State's trust in the conduct of the first State. In order for legitimate expectations to arise, it is necessary that on the basis of the behaviour of the first State, it is possible to determine its unambiguous and concrete future behaviour which is subsequently contained in the legal obligation. What is protected here is passive and not active good faith. Accordingly, for the creation of a legitimate expectation the following elements are necessary:

(1) The clear and unconditional behaviour of the first State, expressing its will towards the second State and entering into the sphere of its interests;
(2) Acknowledgement by the second State of this behaviour;
(3) The trust of the second State in this behaviour (passive good faith);
(4) Conduct of the second State in good faith.

The features of the protection of legitimate expectations so understood are:

(1) Ensuring consistency of declared and actual behaviour; unity of words, deeds and intentions with subsequent words, deeds and intentions;
(2) The promotion of constancy, consistency and permanence of behaviour and to oppose variability and vacillation in the conduct of subjects of the law;
(3) Ensuring predictability, stability and legal security.

The creation of legitimate expectations is not influenced by the subjective feelings of a State. This is in consonance with the general trend of international law to objectify all law. Consequently, the consciousness of the organs of a State (the psychological element, if any) and its intentions are examined through the external manifestations of the activities of the organs of that State. The internal intentions of States and the feelings of their representatives are irrelevant. Hence, the creation and performance of obligations cannot be based on the subjective attitude of a party to an obligation (that is, on what the party considers to be good faith conduct), but on objective, external criteria.

The above theoretical matrix, based at least to some extent on the ICJ case law, leads to the following conclusions. Good faith implies, first and foremost, trust in one's word and an obligation to keep it, so it is the basis for justifying the principle of honouring international obligations (*obligationes sunt servandae*) regardless of their source (Article 2(2) of the UN Charter), and thus the principle of good faith is the rationale that justifies the following five norms: (1) *pacta sunt servanda*, (2) *consuetudo, sicut ius accepta, servanda est*, (3) *acta sunt servanda*, (4) estoppel and (5) acquiescence. It is worth noting in this regard that it is one of the bases, while others may be principles of equity and reciprocity. In turn, these five legal rules determine the binding force of obligations. There is a close connection between those norms and good faith, as the latter integrates and centres those norms around itself through its externally derived content and its values. This is a material and axiological link. It is also possible to argue that the fact that good faith is recognised as a general principle of law necessary for the operation of international law entails recognition of the norms required for its effective implementation. On this basis, and in line with the ICJ case law, it can be concluded that international law should be viewed as an organised and structured set of legal norms between which there are meaningful relationships. It is a legal order that resembles a system of law, rather than a random and chaotic set of norms. In the light of the relationship between good faith and the norms determining the binding force of obligations, it needs to be emphasised that good faith is the basis justifying the durability (stability) and effectiveness of obligations irrespective of their source. It fosters the perception of international law as a compact and coherent whole governed by certain principles.

Therefore, good faith is not a "source norm" of States' obligations, but a "source norm" of obligations. It is structural in nature. It allows one to think about international law in a systemic way. Thus, it is not possible to understand the mechanisms of that law without good faith. For these reasons, good faith may be referred to as a principle about principles, i.e. a meta-principle. It is therefore a kind of "second-order rule" (*i.e.*, a rule that does not create specific rights and obligations) in general international law. It makes this law capable of being defined as a normative order. The principle thus understood is characterised by three properties:

(1) It does not depend on the will (or discretion) of States. It is an objective element of the legal order;
(2) It is too general in nature to impose specific normative requirements on States, but nevertheless lays a strong foundation for other more specific norms that may regulate the conduct of subjects of law;
(3) It is primary in nature and logically precedes the consent of States.

International law in its essence must presuppose the validity of certain objectively valid principles that are independent of the will of States at all times and in all places. This is necessary because otherwise it would be possible to assume that a legal system could be in force without the protection of trust in the given word and the obligation to keep it, or that States could change this obligation at will. Such a legal order is untenable. In view of this, good faith as a legal principle must derive its normativity from the essence of that law, be logically primary to the consent of States and justify the law-making effects of the will of the subjects of the law. A norm can be shown to be a legal rule if it is derived from a recognised source, being an expression of the will of states, or if, by virtue of its own unique characteristics, it should be in force to ensure peace and justice.[21] As already noted, good faith, through its ethical and moral content, ensures that international law can be in force and function properly. For this reason, good faith must be permanently embodied in the structure of international law.

The relationship of good faith with other norms outlined above can best be described using the example of *pacta sunt servanda* and treaty law as a whole. Good faith is the basis justifying the *pacta sunt servanda*, which, according to ICJ case law, makes treaties legally binding on their parties. At the same time, good fiath indicates the limits beyond which the validity of *pacta sunt servenda* ends, as exemplified by the *rebus sic stantibus* clause. Good faith governs the conclusion, application and termination of treaties. Their formation is understood as a process of the

[21] Thirlway (2014), p. 15.

parties reaching consensual statements of intent, which the principle of good faith transforms into an agreement. A party takes note of the counterparty's statement of intent, trusts it and expresses its will to be bound by the contract, thus creating a legal bond between the parties. The partners thus acquire a legitimate expectation of mutual word-keeping, fidelity and loyalty and of future diligent, honest and reasonable performance of the treaty. According to good faith, the form in which an agreement is concluded is irrelevant. Hence, a declaration of intent made even tacitly or impliedly can produce legal effects.

Good faith controls treaty negotiations when these involve the settlement of an international dispute or when the parties are bound by a *pactum de negotiando* or a *pactum de contrahendo*. In addition, good faith provides a rationale for the obligation not to defeat the object and purpose of a treaty prior to its entry into force. More importantly, good faith governs the implementation and interpretation of treaties. In this context, it transforms and functions as an objective-subjective standard and becomes part of other norms, being an accessory and complementary component thereof. Only in conjunction with a given obligation can it impose additional obligations on the parties – such as obligations of cooperation and information – necessary for the proper performance of the obligation. In doing so, the objective aspect of good faith prescribes a minimum level of fidelity and loyalty to the other party as well as diligence and honesty of conduct. It implies an obligation on the part of the parties to cooperate and exchange information. On the other hand, the subjective aspect relates to the subject's state of consciousness, namely, the conviction to act in accordance with what the obligation requires, involving an intention to perform it correctly.

Hence, the standard has a regulatory function in that it prescribes a course of action for the performance of an obligation that corresponds to what the parties actually intended to achieve. The intentions of the parties, the purpose and the letter of the obligation are relevant. The standard applies to any obligation, regardless of its origin or nature. It protects general, reasonable expectations regarding the manner of performance of the obligation and the parties' cooperation in the area of performance, as well as specific reasonable expectations that depend on the content and nature of the obligation in question. Consequently, many rules (e.g. efficiency and proportionality) as well as a holistic approach to the interpretation of the law can be justified by good faith.

Last but not least, good faith also governs the termination of treaties. It binds together the vast majority of rationales for the termination of treaties, as these are either anchored on the consensual will of the parties, which is secured by good faith, or derive from an objective rule (e.g. the *rebus sic stantibus* clause). Hence, it should be concluded that good faith is a fundamental principle of treaty law. Consequently, removing good faith from international law will remove the basis for which treaties are to be respected and properly enforced. There would be no point in concluding them. Good faith ensures the security and stability of treaty relations and safeguards the effectiveness and durability of contractual provisions. It protects the sanctity of treaties and defends them against attempts to unilaterally revise the agreement. In doing so, it demands honest and diligent conduct, without ulterior motives, falsehood or deception.

5 Conclusion

All above aspects of good faith come together to form a comprehensive concept of good faith governing the system of international law as a legal rule occupying a non-derogable place in the decentralised international legal order, which bases the creation and performance of obligations on the will of States. Absent good faith, it is impossible to think of a well-functioning international law. Its validity derives from the essence of the law itself. Although good faith does not derive from and is primary to the will of States, it controls that will and ensures that it is fully implemented in accordance with the intentions of the parties and the purpose and letter of the obligation. Good faith is too general in nature to impose specific normative requirements on States, but it nevertheless lays the foundations for other more specific norms. It gathers and integrates legal norms around it, binding them together content-wise and axiologically. Using Redslob's metaphor, it can be said to be like a source around which geometrical figures gather.[22] Accordingly, good faith is a principle that has a structural character and allows one to think about international law as a system of law. It is not a "source norm" of States' obligations, but a "source norm" of obligations. It explains and justifies the permanence and effectiveness of legal obligations by protecting legitimate expectations. It endows international law with an axiological dimension, since it reveals and implements the values that inspire that law, ultimately constituting its – not the only one – basis and making it a normative system. It should therefore be seen as a meta-principle of international law, included in the catalogue of general principles of law. At the same time, since good faith is a structural norm, it cannot be considered an *jus cogens* norm, as only substantive legal norms can enter the catalogue of peremptory norms.

General principles of law encompassed by Article 38(1)(c) of the ICJ Statute include principles that do not in themselves constitute the source of specific rights and obligations of the subjects of international law, but justify other legal rules and determine when subjects, through their behaviour, can create, change or terminate the primary rules. They take place logically primary to the consent of States (they are independent of their will) and reveal the values that inspire the legal order as a whole, ultimately underpinning it and making it a normative system. They can be referred to as meta-principles. A very good contender to the group of such norms is good faith, as it is a rule of legal reasoning and a principle derived from the general concept (idea) of law, ensuring the functioning of the international order. Being a principle of a general nature, it can find concretisation (emanation) in individual rules of international law. It governs the creation, performance and interpretation of

[22] Redslob (1923), p. 42.

obligations. In itself, however, it does not constitute their source. Without good faith, legal obligations cannot be explained. It forms the basis for the justification of certain norms such as *pacta sunt servanda* or the prohibition of abuse of rights.

Lastly, it is worth noting that good faith draws its content from morality and ethics, thus making international law based on ethical and moral values such as loyalty, diligence, honesty, fidelity and trust. In this context that, through such content, good faith evaluates the conduct of actors and indicates which is ethical and moral and which is not; which is reprehensible and which safeguards the two core values of international law, which are peace and justice. This links harmoniously with the primary function of the principle of good faith, which is the maintenance of international peace and security. Its other functions are formative, regulatory, tempering formalisms, reinforcing legal reasoning and avoiding *non-liquet*.

References

Cheng B (1951) General principles of law as applied by International Courts and Tribunals. Cambridge University Press, Cambridge

Corten O, Klein P (eds) (2011) The Vienna Conventions on the law of treaties: a commentary. Oxford University Press, Oxford

Cot JP (1968) La bonne foi et la conclusion des traités. Revue belge de droit international 14:141–159

de Vattel E (1758) Le droit des gens, ou Principes de la loi naturelle. Apud Liberos Tutior

Elias TO (1974) The modern law of treaties. Oceana Publications, Dobbs Ferry

Ferrari Bravo L (1964) Diritto internazionale e diritto interno nella stipulazione dei trattati. Morano, Napoli

Fitzmaurice GG (1958) Some problems regarding formal sources of international law. In: Verzijl JHW, van Asbeck FM (eds) Symbolae Verzijl: présentées au Professeur J. H. Verzijl à l'Occasion deson LXX-iè Anniversaire. Martinus Nijhoff, La Haye

Gialdino AC (1960) Imputazione giuridica e buona fede nella conclusione dei trattati. Rivista di Diritto Internazionale 43:427–448

Kałduński M (2017) The principle of good faith in international law [Zasda dobrej wiary w prawie międzynarodowym]. C.H. Beck, Warszawa

Kläger R (2013) Fair and equitable treatment. In: International Investment Law. Cambridge University Press, Cambridge

Kolb R (2000) La bonne foi en droit international public. Contribution à l'étude des principes généraux de droit. Presses Universitaires de France, Paris

Kolb R, Müller JP (2002) Article 2 (2). In: Simma B (ed) The Charter of the United Nations. A commentary. Oxford University Press, Oxford

Koskenniemi M (2000) General principles: reflexions on constructivist thinking in international law. In: Koskenniemi M (ed) Sources of international law. Routledge, London

Lachs M (1966) 849. Meeting of the ILC, 11 May 1966, 1966 YILC (I)(2)

Lachs M (1977) Some thoughts on the role of good faith in international law. In: Akkerman RJ et al (eds) Declaration on principles: a quest for universal peace. Springer

McNair A (1961) The law of treaties. Oxford University Press, Oxford

Mik C (2011) The Principle of fulfillment the obligations in good faith. An Introduction to the theory of international Obligations [Zasada wykonywania zobowiązań w dobrej wierze. Wstęp do teorii zobowiązań prawnomiędzynarodowych. Zarys problematyki]. In: Galicki Z et al (eds) Manfred Lachs - the world's pre-eminent lawyer [Manfred Lachs – wybitny prawnik świata]. Warsaw University Press, Warsaw, pp 115–172

Müller JP (1971) Vertrauensschutz im Völkerrecht. Carl Heymanns Verlag, Cologne and Berlin
O'Connor JF (1991) Good faith in international law. Dartmouth Publishing Company, Aldershot
Pauwelyn J (2003) Conflict of norms in public international law. Cambridge University Press, Cambridge
Redslob R (1923) Histoire des grands principes de droit de gens. Rousseau, Paris
Reuter P (1985) Introduction au droit des traités. Presses Universitaires de France, Paris
Rosenne S (1989) Developments in the Law of Treaties 1945–1986. Cambridge University Press, Cambridge
Sperduti E (1952) Il principio della buona fede et l'ammissione di nuovi membri alle Nazioni Unite. 7 La Comunità internazionale
Thirlway H (2014) The sources of international law. Oxford University Press, Oxford
van Bynkershoek C (1737) Quaestionum juris publici libri duo. Johannes van Kerckhem
Verdross A (1952) La bonne foi comme fondement du Droit international public. Revue Hellénique de Droit International 17(1–2):17–21
White G (1994) The principle of good faith. In: Lowe V, Warbrick C (eds) The United Nations and principles of international law: essays in memory of Michael Akehurst. Routledge, London
Wolff CF (1764) Ius gentium methodo scientifica pertractatum, in quo ius gentium naturale ab eo, quod voluntarii, pactitii et consuetudinarii est, accurate distinguitur. Societatis Venetae
Zoller E (1976) La bonne foi en droit international public. A. Pédone

Good Faith in European Union Law

Marcus Klamert

Abstract European Union law is characterized by the existence of a number of closely related manifestations of good faith obligations. Firstly, good faith has been applied by the European Courts in the manner familiar from public international law. Secondly, the duty of sincere cooperation in Article 4(3) Treaty on European Union is the source of a variety of rules of cooperation, compliance and conflict resolution. Finally, a principle of solidarity exists in EU law that has been applied to appeal to ideas of fairness between the Member States of the Union.

1 Introduction

The nature of the European Union as a legal system is famously ambiguous. EU law has its "its own legal system" but is at the same time "an integral part of the legal systems" of the Member States.[1] The EU is not a state, thus it is not a federal state, but it has been associated with legal federalism and political confederalism, called a *Staatenverbund*, and a composite constitution (*Verfassungsverbund*).[2]

At the same time, EU law on Treaty change, among others, remains deeply rooted in public international law.[3] Moreover, Article 3(5) TEU requires the EU to contribute to "the strict observance and the development of international law",

[1] See Case C-26/62, *Van Gend,* ECLI:EU:C:1963:1, and Case 6/64, *Costa/ENEL,* ECLI:EU:C:1964:66.

[2] See Klamert (2024a), paras 10–11, with further references.

[3] See de Witte (2011), p. 19.

M. Klamert (✉)
Faculty of Law, University of Graz, Graz, Austria
e-mail: marcus.klamert@uni-graz.at

J. Podkowik et al. (eds.), *Gleams of Good Faith in Constitutional Law*, Ius Gentium: Comparative Perspectives on Law and Justice 132,
https://doi.org/10.1007/978-3-032-06486-8_4

thereby obliging Union institutions to observe international law in its entirety, including customary international law and general international humanitarian law.[4]

This ambiguity also affects the legal principles applicable in EU law. Some principles are clearly inspired by national (constitutional) law. This mainly concerns the fundamental rights regime of the EU, as set out under Article 6 TEU. Other principles have their roots in public international law. In addition, public international law principles apply in EU law as public international law.[5]

This legal "cacophony" can very well be illustrated by the principle of good faith in EU law. In the following, I will discuss the role of good faith as public international law principle in EU law, the role of the principle of loyalty as a "hybrid" between public international law and constitutional law principle, and the role of solidarity, which is a manifestation of good faith quite specific to the EU.

2 Sources of Inspiration

2.1 Introduction

Several good faith-related concepts exist in EU (constitutional) law, entailing prescriptions of varying intensity. In its strongest and probably most idiosyncratic form, these concepts compensate for a comparable lack of a clear-cut division of competences and the absence of more robust means of ensuring the compliance of the Member States with their obligations under Union law. Good faith takes the forms of good faith in the traditional public international law sense, as principle of loyalty, and as principle of solidarity, all discussed in the following. These concepts of good faith clearly differ from manifestations in especially European private law, which are generally addressed to relations between private actors, not to the Member States of the Union.[6]

2.2 Good Faith

The public international principle of good faith or *pacta sunt servanda* embodies the logic that an actor should not act contrary to its own commitment to certain objectives and their realisation.[7] According to the General Court of the EU, "the principle of good faith is a rule of customary international law whose existence is recognized

[4] Compare Neframi (2016), p. 208.

[5] Castellarin (2019), p. 131.

[6] See, e.g., Reich (2014), p. 189.

[7] See Klamert (2022), p. 118 with further references.

by the International Court of Justice and is therefore binding on the Community".[8] Thus, in a number of cases where the EU acted on the international plane such as through agreements with international organisations, good faith was not applied as a general principle of EU law, but was applied as a source of public international law.

However, even vis-à-vis third states, these good faith obligations may be more pronounced. When Great Britain withdrew its membership in the EU, Union law remained applicable during a transition period. During that period, the UK technically was a third state, but its legal alignment with the EU warranted a stronger good faith standard than with other third states. Thus, Article 5 of the Withdrawal Agreement with the United Kingdom[9] that sealed "Brexit" contains a clause modelled on Article 4(3) TEU on loyalty but is entitled "good faith". Against the background of the continued application of Union law in the United Kingdom during the transition period, Article 129(3) of the Agreement provides: "In accordance with the principle of sincere cooperation, the United Kingdom shall refrain during the transition period from any action or initiative which may harm the interests of the Union, in particular in the context of international organisations, agencies, conferences or fora to which the United Kingdom is a contracting party in its own right".

In some instances, the Court has essentially claimed that this international principle of good faith is analogue in its functions with Article 4(3) TEU discussed below. Thus, in the case of the interpretation of the Montego Bay Convention, to which the EU is a party, the European Court of Justice (ECJ) referred to the Marpol Convention 73/78, to which the EU is not a party, as a standard of interpretation. It held that "In view of the customary principle of good faith, which forms part of general international law, and of Article 4(3) TEU, the Court is to interpret the provisions by taking account of the Marpol Convention 73/78 (…)".[10]

2.3 Loyalty

An obligation of loyalty has been contained both in the European Coal and Steel Treaty in Article 86 ECSC as well as in the later Treaty on the European Economic Community in Article 5 EEC. Most likely, it was inspired from both the above mentioned public international principle on the one hand and by the German constitutional law principle of federal fidelity (*Bundestreue*) on the other hand.[11]

A certain relation to the above-mentioned principle of good faith becomes apparent in case law of the ECJ, where he refers to "the principle of cooperation in good faith laid down in Article 4(3) TEU", which would require the EU Member States

[8] Case T-115/94, *Opel Austria v Council*, ECLI:EU:T:1997:3, para 90; Case C-366/10, *Air Transport Association of America and Others*, ECLI:EU:C:2011:86, para 101.

[9] Agreement on the withdrawal of the United Kingdom of Great Britain and Northern Ireland from the European Union and the European Atomic Energy Community, OJ 2019 C 384I, 1.

[10] See Case C-15/17, *Bosphorus Queen Shipping*, ECLI:EU:C:2018:557, paras 46 ff.

[11] See Klamert (2014), pp. 9, 41; de Baere and Roes (2015).

"to nullify the unlawful consequences of a breach of European Union law, and that such an obligation is owed, within the sphere of its competence, by every organ of the Member State concerned".[12] The wording of Article 4(3) TEU does not contain such mention of good faith.

However, Article 4(3) TEU and the obligations derived from it differ significantly from good faith in international law.[13] It has been suggested that this is because loyalty in EU law commits all actors, ie the Member States and the Union organs, to the "higher" purpose of ensuring the functioning of the EU legal order.[14] A good example for this is the method of interpretation most commonly associated with EU law and the Court of Justice, viz. *effet utile*. This approach often seeks to realise the maximum effect of Union law.[15] This higher purpose also entails that EU Member States are under a whole set of obligations ensuring compliance with EU law. A third reason, why good faith cannot be the same in EU law and in international law is the very different role of individuals. In EU law, they are as a rule empowered to secure their rights stemming from EU law and loyalty provides the necessary rationale to impose obligations on national authorities to this end.[16]

The other source of inspiration for loyalty in the EU is derived from national constitutional law. The German Federal Constitutional Court (BVerfG) has held that it would be in accordance with the federal principle that all entities in the federation are bound by a mutual constitutional duty to be loyal and to cooperate (*Bundestreue*).[17] This has also included financial aspects such as concerning the safeguarding of the budgetary balance between the *Länder* and the German federal state,[18] or duties of financial support among the *Länder*.[19] Especially the latter prescription recalls good faith discussed above. However, it is submitted that the federal angle that is added here has more to do with competences than good faith has in international law. A principle such as the *Bundestreue* is more important in Germany than in the equally federally organized Austria, because in contrast to Germany, Austrian constitutional law does not foresee competing competences of the federal and the state level.[20] The Austrian Constitutional Court (VfGH) has introduced a so-called principle of consideration (*Berücksichtigungspflicht*) for dealing with contradictory yet validly

[12] Case C-73/23, *Chaudfontaine Loisirs*, ECLI:EU:C:2024:734, para 53 and the case law cited.

[13] Klamert (2022), p. 130.

[14] Eckes (2018), pp. 46, 72.

[15] See Potacs and Mayer (2014), p. 17.

[16] Klamert (2024b), paras 65–66.

[17] 2 BvH 2/52 *Wohnungsbauförderung* [1952] BVerfGE 1, 299, 314; see Gamper (2011), pp. 257, 258.

[18] Case 2 BvG 1/54 *Besoldungsgesetz von Nordrhein-Westfalen* [1954] BVerfGE 4, 115; Case 2 BvQ 1/53, 2 BvQ 2/53 *Weihnachtsgeld* [1953] BVerfGE 3, 52.

[19] Case 1 BvF 2/51 *Finanzausgleichsgesetz* [1952] BVerfGE 1, 117, 130–131, which however refers to the federal principle (*bundesstaatliches Prinzip*) and not to the *Bundestreue*).

[20] Case KII-4/79 Sammlungsgesetz [1982] VfSlg. 9337.

enacted provisions by the federal state and the provinces, respectively.[21] Similar to the *Bundestreue*, this principle equally seems to have its roots in the federal principle, among others.[22]

If we would want to compare the EU with either Germany or Austria for the present purposes, it arguably is closer related to Germany. The existence of the category of shared competences shows that there is no strict division of competences in the EU. I have discussed elsewhere that the fact that there are often no clear boundaries of competences in Union law explains the importance of the principle of loyalty in the Union.[23] This concerns especially those duties of (sincere or loyal) cooperation that I have considered to be a subcategory of a more general principle of loyalty and which are relevant for more technical, procedural matters of the relations between the EU and its Member States.[24]

2.4 Solidarity

Solidarity has for a long time been absent from the Treaties. It has however featured prominently in the Schuman Declaration of 9 May 1950 where it was recognised that "Europe will not be made all at once, or according to a single plan. It will be built through concrete achievements which first create a de facto solidarity". Notably, the EEC Treaty did not contain any reference to solidarity.

Solidarity in public international law has been associated with matters as diverse as financial assistance, military assistance, and the prohibition of discrimination.[25] Article 42(2) TEU on mutual defence certainly has drawn its inspiration from Article 5 of the NATO Treaty, and EU migration law has, at least in theory, clear roots in the solidarity-based international refugee law. Beyond that, there is no indication that the principle of solidarity in EU law is rooted in public international law.

It most likely was a political slogan in the beginning without any clear legal meaning. However, solidarity was at a very early stage referred to in connection of unilateral acts by Member States. In a case from 1969, the Court held that powers of authorization or intervention of the Community institutions conferred by the Treaties "would be otiose if the Member States were free, on the pretext that their action related only to monetary policy, unilaterally to derogate from their obligations under the provisions of the Treaty and without being subject to control by the institutions", and that solidarity would be at the basis of these obligations as of the

[21] Case G 5/80 *Wr. Behindertengesetz* [1980] VfSlg. 8831; Case G 81/84, 82/84 *Jagdrecht/Forstrecht* [1984] VfSlg. 10.292.

[22] Klamert (2014), p. 58.

[23] Klamert (2014).

[24] Klamert (2014), p. 33; Neframi (2010), p. 325.

[25] Klamert (2022), p. 120.

whole of the Community system.[26] In 1973, the Court held that "unilaterally breaking, according to its own conception of national interest, the equilibrium between advantages and obligations flowing from its adherence to the Community" would be a "failure in the duty of solidarity accepted by Member States by the fact of their adherence to the Community" which "strikes at the fundamental basis of the Community legal order".[27]

This case law has since then only been revisited by the Court after the Treaty of Lisbon in the course of the rule of law-crisis.[28] It clearly recalls both good faith in public international law and federal fidelity in constitutional law, as mentioned above. Thereby, it also recalls loyalty. The idea is that the interests of the Member States are intertwined as part of a great "bargain", which cannot allow cherry-picking.

There is other case law especially under the ECSC Treaty, which referred to solidarity in the context of undertakings and producers in one Member State owing solidarity to undertakings in other Member States. For a very long time, it was only in this case law that the Court spoke regularly of a "principle of solidarity".

Moreover, there is another, comparably more recent line of case law which relies on considerations of "financial solidarity" between nationals of different EU Member States in order to require one EU Member State to give a student from another Member State access to certain benefits.[29]

This arguably shows that solidarity as a legal concept has developed in a fairly unsystematic and piecemeal manner in EU law, without clear sources of inspiration in either national or international law. What seems to underlie these strands of case law is a very general idea of the need for solidarity in the EU, as it has been expressed in the Schuman Declaration. Only recently, the legal contours of this concept have become clearer, as I will discuss below.

3 Legal Basis

3.1 Introduction

While loyalty has a clear anchor in Article 4(3) TEU, this is not the case for solidarity, whose appearances in the Treaties are heterogeneous and scattered. Thus, while Article 4(3) TEU is seen as an expression of an underlying general principle of EU law, the general meaning and nature of solidarity has been more difficult to

---

[26] Joined Cases 6/69 and 11/69, *Commission v France (Rediscount rate)*, ECLI:EU:C:1969:68, para 15.

[27] Case 39/72, *Commission v Italy (Premiums for slaughtering cows)*, ECLI:EU:C:1973:13, paras 24–25; see also Case C-128/78, *Commission v United Kingdom (Tachographs)*, ECLI:EU:C:1979:32, para 9.

[28] Case C-123/22, *Commission v Hungary*, ECLI:EU:C:2024:49, para 117.

[29] Case C-184/99, *Grzelczyk*, ECLI:EU:C:2001:458; Case C-209/03, *Bidar*, ECLI:EU:C:2005:169.

understand. Loyalty has had a prominent role in especially the early stages of the "constitutionalisation" of EU law, different from solidarity, which only recently plays a more pronounced role. With both principles, their understanding has clearly evolved and is still evolving, especially concerning solidarity. Both principles play a role as guidance for the interpretation of (secondary, derived) EU law. Neither loyalty nor solidarity have so far been defined or concretised in a general manner through acts of secondary law. However, both principles underpin a large number of legal acts enacted by the Union organs.

3.2 *Loyalty*

Article 4(3) TEU contains the "principle of sincere cooperation" comprising three separate indents. Firstly, the Union and the Member States are required, in full mutual respect, to assist each other in carrying out tasks which flow from the treaties. Furthermore, the Member States must take appropriate measures, general or particular, to ensure fulfilment of the obligations arising out of the treaties or resulting from the acts of the institutions of the Union. Finally, the Member States must facilitate the achievement of the Union's tasks and refrain from any measure that could jeopardise the attainment of the Union's objectives. Loyalty also applies to the relations between Union institutions under the principle of institutional balance, which the Treaty of Lisbon now explicitly provides in Article 13 TEU.

Loyalty is one of the principles the Court has qualified as "inherent" in the Union legal order,[30] respectively a principle "underlying" what is today Article 4(3) TEU.[31] Many provisions in the EU Treaties (TEU, TFEU) can be considered specifications of this inherent principle of loyalty.[32] Thus, the ECJ has often ruled that Article 4(3) TEU would yield to another Treaty provision as *lex specialis*.[33]

Loyalty has furthered the development of EU law through gap-filling.[34] It has played a central role in leading judgements of the ECJ since the 1960s. Because this role of loyalty has long been neglected in the prevailing discourse on the development of Union law,[35] the understanding of loyalty has clearly evolved over time. Moreover, the ECJ initially claimed that the predecessor provisions of Article 4(3) TEU (which had nearly identical wording) could not provide a basis for obligations on the part of the Member States due to their abstract nature and the discretion they

[30] Joined Cases C-46/93 and C-48/93, *Brasserie du Pêcheur*, ECLI:EU:C:1996:79.

[31] Case C-404/97, *Commission v Portugal*, ECLI:EU:C:2000:345, para 40; Case C-2/88 Imm. *Zwartveld*, ECLI:EU:C:1990:440.

[32] See Klamert (2024a), para 34.

[33] E.g. Joined Cases C-332/92, C-333/92 and C-335/92, *Eurico Italia*, ECLI:EU:C:1994:79, para 22; CaseC-459/03, *Commission v Ireland*, ECLI:EU:C:2006:345, para 169 ff.

[34] Klamert (2014), pp. 63–83.

[35] Klamert (2014), pp. 68 ff.

granted the Member States.[36] This view has also informed the view of the literature, especially in Germany.[37] However, in judgements since the late 1980s, the ECJ has repeatedly ruled that Member States have violated Article 4(3) TEU – and in some cases only Article 4(3) TEU – in particular with regard to cooperation obligations in the context of infringement proceedings.[38] Ireland has been found in violation of its obligations under the principle of loyalty by instituting dispute resolution proceedings before an international arbitral body without first informing and consulting with the competent EU institutions.[39]

The principle of loyalty has not been defined as such in an act of secondary law. However, in the absence of a general codification of the cooperation or coordination mechanisms in the administrative network of the EU and the Member States, these are many acts of secondary legislation providing co-operation mechanisms or notification obligations in a variety of areas. All these must be seen as concretisations of loyalty and Article 4(3) TEU.

3.3 Solidarity

As mentioned, solidarity appears in many places and many different contexts in the EU Treaties. According to Article 2 TEU, solidarity is one of the values that are "common to the Member States in a society in which pluralism, non-discrimination, tolerance, justice, solidarity and equality between women and men prevail". Article 3(3) TEU lists solidarity among Member States in the context of the promotion of economic, social, and territorial cohesion as an objective of the EU. Article 24(2) and (3) TEU, on the EU's common foreign and security policy, refers to "mutual political solidarity" among Member States. Article 42(2) TEU does not mention solidarity, but is widely seen against this background, as mentioned above.

Article 67 TFEU on the area of freedom, security, and justice calls on the Union to "frame a common policy on asylum, immigration and external border control, based on solidarity between Member States". Article 80 TFEU says that the policies of the Union in this field shall be "governed by the principle of solidarity and fair sharing of responsibility, including its financial implications, between the Member States". Article 80 TFEU is the only place where the Treaties mention a "principle" of solidarity. In Article 122(1) TFEU, a mandate is given to the Council to decide, "in a spirit of solidarity between Member States", upon measures addressing severe difficulties in the supply of certain products, notably in the area of energy.

[36] Case 9/73, *Schlüter*, ECLI:EU:C:1973:110, para 39; 78/70,Case *Deutsche Gramophon*, ECLI:EU:C:1971:59, para 5; Case 2/73, *Geddo*, ECLI:EU:C:1973:89, para. 4.

[37] Klamert (2014), p. 32.

[38] Case C-82/03, *Commission v Italy*, ECLI:EU:C:2004:433; Case C-22/20, *Commission v Sweden*, ECLI:EU:C:2021:669; Case 272/86, *Commission v Greece (Olive oil)*, ECLI:EU:C:1988:433, paras 30–2; Case C-65/91, *Commission v Greece (List D)*, ECLI:EU:C:1992:388, paras 12–17.

[39] Case C-459/03, Commission v Ireland.

Article 194 TFEU states that Union policy on energy shall aim to attain certain objectives such as ensuring security of energy supply in the Union and promoting energy efficiency and energy saving and the development of new and renewable forms of energy "in a spirit of solidarity between Member States". The "solidarity clause" of Article 222 in Part V of the TFEU, on the external action of the Union, mandates that "[t]he Union and its Member States shall act jointly in a spirit of solidarity if a Member State is the object of a terrorist attack or the victim of a natural or man-made disaster".

Finally, solidarity is the heading of Title IV of the Charter of Fundamental Rights, which includes provisions on "social rights" such as labour rights and protections for individuals on health care and consumer matters.

In recent case law, the Court seems to argue for the existence of an (unwritten) principle of solidarity claiming that "the principle of solidarity is one of the fundamental principles of EU law".[40] The spirit of solidarity between Member States, mentioned in Article 194 TFEU, would constitute "a specific expression, in the field of energy, of the principle of solidarity, which is itself one of the fundamental principles of EU law".[41] The Court recalled all the references to solidarity in the Treaties mentioned above, from which it would follow that "the principle of solidarity underpins the entire legal system of the European Union".[42] The principle of solidarity would entail rights and obligations "both for the European Union and for the Member States, the European Union having an obligation of solidarity towards the Member States and the Member States having the same obligation between themselves and with regard to the common interest of the European Union".[43]

As with loyalty, no act of secondary law lays out the meaning of this principle in general terms. However, a number of legal acts that were enacted recently based on the economic policy competence of Article 122 TFEU to deal with the COVID-19-crises invoke solidarity at least in their preambles. Among them are Regulation (EU) 2020/672 establishing a European instrument for temporary support to mitigate unemployment risks in an emergency (SURE) following the COVID-19 outbreak,[44] Regulation (EU) 2020/2094 establishing a European Union Recovery Instrument to support the recovery in the aftermath of the COVID-19 crisis,[45] Regulation (EU) 2022/1854 establishing an emergency intervention to address high

[40] Case C-123/22, *Commission v Hungary*, para 116.

[41] Case C-848/19 P, *Germany v Poland (OPAL)*, ECLI:EU:C:2021:598, para 38.

[42] Case C-848/19 P, *Germany v Poland (OPAL)*, para 39–41.

[43] Case C-848/19 P, *Germany v Poland (OPAL)*, paras 43 and 46.

[44] Council Regulation (EU) No 2020/672 of 19 May 2020 on the establishment of a European instrument for temporary support to mitigate unemployment risks in an emergency (SURE) following the COVID-19 outbreak, OJ 2020 L 159/1.

[45] Council Regulation (EU) No 2020/2094 of 14 December 2020 establishing a European Union Recovery Instrument to support the recovery in the aftermath of the COVID-19 crisis, OJ 2020 L 433 I, 23.

energy prices,[46] and Regulation (EU) 2022/2578 establishing a market correction mechanism to protect against excessively high gas prices.[47] Also the Union budget and Article 322(1)(a) TFEU have been qualified by the Full Court as "one of the principal instruments for giving practical effect, in the Union's policies and activities, to the principle of solidarity, mentioned in Article 2 TEU".[48]

4 Constitutional Practice

4.1 Introduction

Loyalty and increasingly also solidarity appear in many, often very important judgements by the European courts. Both loyalty and solidarity have only recently shown that they can be invoked directly to review the legality of acts by the Union institutions in disputes between them and Member States. Solidarity has been discussed as allowing for broader implications than in the narrow field of energy policy where this has occurred to date. Solidarity also played a more indirect role with restrictions on fundamental rights.

4.2 Loyalty

I have shown elsewhere that what is now Article 4(3) TEU has played a central role in leading judgements of the ECJ since the 1960s.[49] In *Costa/ENEL,* the ECJ recognised in what is probably the central passage that the primacy of Union law is necessary for Union law to apply equally in all Member States, as otherwise the achievement of the objectives of the Union, as stated in the predecessor provision of the current Article 4(3) TEU (Article 5(2) EEC Treaty), would be jeopardised.[50] Apart from the prohibition of discrimination (then in Article 7 EEC Treaty), this was the only Treaty provision that the ECJ invoked. In *ERTA,* the ECJ explained why the then EEC must always have exclusive external competence when it lays

[46] Council Regulation (EU) No 2022/1854 of 6 October 2022 on an emergency intervention to address high energy prices, OJ 2022 L 261 I, 1.

[47] Council Regulation (EU) No 2022/2578 of 22 December 2022 establishing a market correction mechanism to protect Union citizens and the economy against excessively high gas prices, OJ 2022 L 335, 45.

[48] Case C-157/21, *Poland v EP and Council (Conditionality mechanism),* ECLI:EU:C:2022:98, para 147; Case C-156/2, *Hungary v EP and Council (Conditionality mechanism),* ECLI:EU:C:2022:97, para 129; see also Case C-409/05, *Commission v Greece,* ECLI:EU:C:2009:782, para 55; C-38/06, *Commission v Portugal,* ECLI:EU:C:2010:108, para 67.

[49] Klamert (2014), pp. 71–83.

[50] Case 6/64, *Costa/ENEL,* 594.

down "common rules".[51] The ECJ argued with reference to the objective of a common transport policy (then in Article 3 EEC Treaty) and Article 5 EEC Treaty (now Article 4(3) TEU). The fact that loyalty was the main argument in *ERTA* is demonstrated by subsequent decisions.[52] Reference can also be made to the role of the current Article 4 (3) TEU in the case law on the direct applicability of directives[53] as well as in the case law on state liability.[54]

Loyalty can, albeit rarely, provide guidance for the interpretation of secondary law.[55] It would certainly guide the interpretation of such legal acts that are concretisations of the duty of sincere cooperation, mentioned above. Moreover, recent case law has suggested that Article 4(3) TEU could be a standard of legality for EU secondary law.[56] This concerned a duty of care of the European Commission when drafting secondary legislation. Until now, however, no act of Union law has been invalidated on its basis. If such function of loyalty would be confirmed, it would strengthen the "reverse" vertical duties imposed on the Union institutions in view of the fact that the overwhelming duties derived from loyalty have so far been imposed on the Member States.

4.3 *Solidarity*

Under Article 80 TFEU on asylum policy, the Council of the EU is required to give effect to the principle of solidarity and fair sharing of responsibility, including its financial implications, between the Member States, when adopting measures.[57] The ECJ expressly referred to the principle of solidarity mentioned in Article 80 TFEU in coming to the conclusion that, in essence, Member States had failed to fulfil certain of their obligations under EU law on border controls, asylum and immigration.[58] The Court has recently also relied on solidarity in this context to justify imposing a particularly severe financial penalty on a Member State for failing to

[51] Case 22/70, *ERTA*, ECLI:EU:C:1971:32.

[52] Case C-467/98, *Commission v Denmark*, ECLI:EU:C:2002:625, para. 110 f; Case C-523/04, *Commission v Netherlands*, ECLI:EU:C:2007:244, para74 ff.

[53] Case 190/87, *Moormann*, ECLI:EU:C:1988:424, para 24.

[54] Joined Cases C-6/90 and C-9/90, *Francovich and Bonifaci*, ECLI:EU:C:1991:428, para 36.

[55] See Case C-38/14, *Gobierno en Gipuzkoa*, ECLI:EU:C:2015:260, para 25; Case C-176/15, *Guy Riskin Timmermans*, ECLI:EU:C:2016:488; Case C-116/11, *Bank Handlowy*, ECLI:EU:C:2012:739.

[56] Case C-677/18, *Amoena*, ECLI:EU:C:2019:1142, para 56; compare also Joined Cases C-36/97 and C-37/97, *Kellinghusen*, ECLI:EU:C:1998:499, para 30 et seq.

[57] See Joined Cases C-643/15 and C-647/15, *Slovak Republic and Hungary v Council (Relocation quotas)*, ECLI:EU:C:2017:631, para 252.

[58] Joined Cases C-643/15 and C-647/15, *Slovak Republic and Hungary v Council (Relocation quotas)*, para 291; Joined Cases C-715/17, C-718/17 and C-719/17, *Commission* v *Poland, Hungary and Czech Republic (Temporary mechanism for the relocation of applicants for international protection)*, ECLI:EU:C:2020:257, paras 80 and 181.

comply with standards for the reception of applicants for international protection in the EU.[59]

In an annulment case concerning a legislative decision by the European Commission, the Court held that acts adopted by the EU institutions, including by the Commission under the EU's energy policy, must be interpreted, and their legality assessed, in the light of the principle of energy solidarity, even if there is no express reference to that principle in the secondary legislation applicable.[60] The Commission had, when enacting the decision concerned, not taken sufficient consideration of the interests of Poland. This was the first case where the Court derived such strong implications from a violation of solidarity, even when the omission by the Commission was largely procedural. It has been discussed whether solidarity could also have such implications outside energy policy. Unlike the energy case, in the cases mentioned above in the area of asylum policy, the secondary law concerned had all made express reference to solidarity.

Moreover, solidarity has guided the interpretation of secondary law based on Article 67 TFEU and Article 122 TFEU, respectively, which both make reference to solidarity.[61]

Finally, solidarity has played a role with the fundamental (market) freedoms under EU law (which are also covered by the Charter of Fundamental Rights of the EU) and has recently played an even more pronounced and highly controversial role in curtailing the right of Member States to award national citizenship and thus, as a consequence, Union citizenship.[62]

5 Conclusion

EU law is pervaded with good faith. It comes in different guises but the common thread in theory is that the interests of all actors in this complex constitutional arrangement must be duly considered. In practice, it is most often the case that the EU's Member States must yield to the interests of the Union, and more concretely the acts of the Union's institutions. There is a logic in this because without this good faith, solidarity, loyalty, fairness in other words, a construction such as the EU could not properly function. Until now these principles have proven sufficiently persuasive. It is to be hoped that they will continue to do so in an ever more polarised world.

---

[59] Case C-123/22, *Commission v Hungary*, para 114.

[60] Case C-848/19 P, *Germany v Poland (OPAL)*, paras 43 and 46.

[61] Klamert (2022).

[62] Case C-192/05, *Tas-Hagen*, ECLI:EU:C:2006:676, para 35; Case C-437/09, *AG2R Prévoyance*, ECLI:EU:C:2011:112; Case C-181/23, *Commission v Malta*, ECLI:EU:C:2025:283.

References

Castellarin E (2019) General principles of European Union law and general international law. In: Andenas M et al (eds) General principles of law and the coherence of international law. Brill, pp 131–148

de Baere G, Roes T (2015) EU loyalty as good faith. Int Comp Law Q 64(4):829–874

de Witte B (2011) The European Union as an international legal experiment. In: Weiler J, de Búrca G (eds) The worlds of European constitutionalism. Cambridge University Press, Cambridge, pp 19–56

Eckes C (2018) EU powers under external pressure. Oxford University Press, Oxford

Gamper A (2011) Koordination im Bundesstaat: Ein "ungeschriebenes" Verfassungsprinzip? In: Rosner A, Bußjäger P (eds) Im Dienste der Länder: Im Interesse des Gesamtstaates: Festschrift 60 Jahre Verbindungsstelle der Bundesländer. Braumüller, Vienna, p 257 ff

Klamert M (2014) The principle of loyalty in EU Law. Oxford University Press, Oxford

Klamert M (2022) Loyalty and solidarity as general principles. In: Ziegler K, Neuvonen P, Moreno-Lax V (eds) Research handbook on the general principles of EU Law. Edward Elgar, Cheltenham, pp 118–135

Klamert M (2024a) Commentary on Article 1 TEU. In: Kellerbauer M, Klamert M, Tomkin J (eds) The EU Treaties and the Charter of Fundamental Rights – a commentary. Oxford University Press, Oxford

Klamert M (2024b) Commentary on Article 4 TEU. In: Kellerbauer M, Klamert M, Tomkin J (eds) The EU Treaties and the Charter of Fundamental Rights – a commentary. Oxford University Press, Oxford

Neframi E (2010) The duty of loyalty: rethinking its scope through its application in the field of EU external relations. Common Mark Law Rev 47(2):323–359

Neframi E (2016) Customary International Law and Article 3(5) TEU. In: Eeckhout P, Lopez-Escudero M (eds) The European Union's external action in times of crisis. Hart Publishing, Oxford, p 208

Potacs M, Mayer C (2014) Effet utile as a method of interpretation. In: Tichý L, Potacs M, Dumbrovský T (eds) Effet utile. Charles University, Prague, p 17

Reich N (2014) General principles of EU Civil Law. Intersentia, Cambridge

Good Faith in the European Convention on Human Rights

Aleksandra Kochman

Abstract The chapter examines how the principle of good faith permeates the Convention for the Protection of Human Rights and Fundamental Freedoms. It departs from good faith as an instrument underlying international law. Using mainly doctrinal approach, it delves into reading of the Convention and the case law of the European Court of Human Rights. First, the chapter traces the good faith of States within substantive rights and freedoms in the Convention. Later, it looks at States' procedural obligation to cooperate with the Court as a prerequisite for international adjudication. As a whole, the chapter proposes a systematics of and a reflection on understanding the principle of good faith in the Strasbourg system of fundamental rights protection.

1 Introduction

The principle of good faith takes a prominent place in international law, functioning as a meta-norm.[1] It underlies the principle of *pacta sunt servanda* and serves as a directive for treaty interpretation. As such, it has been codified in the Vienna

The original version of the chapter has been revised. A correction to this chapter can be found at https://doi.org/10.1007/978-3-032-06486-8_18

The views and opinions of the author expressed herein are personal and do not necessarily reflect those of the European Commission or other EU institutions.

[1] Kałduński (2025).

A. Kochman (✉)
European Commission, Brussels, Belgium
e-mail: aleksandra.kochman@ec.europa.eu

J. Podkowik et al. (eds.), *Gleams of Good Faith in Constitutional Law*, Ius Gentium: Comparative Perspectives on Law and Justice 132,
https://doi.org/10.1007/978-3-032-06486-8_5

Convention on the Law of Treaties (VCLT).[2] In the context of international cooperation, good faith denotes doing so in an honest and loyal manner. While objective good faith is independent from psychological state and ensures effectiveness of obligations, subjective good faith refers to internal consciousness and as such is the opposite of bad faith.[3]

The European Convention on Human Rights (ECHR, Convention)[4] forms part of international law. The Court has been relying on the rules of execution and interpretation codified in the VCLT, notably in its Preamble, Articles 26–27 and 31–33. Although the VCLT postdates the ECHR, the European Court of Human Rights (ECtHR, Court) has explained that it must take into account VCLT's provisions in so far as they codify pre-existing international law.[5] That observation seems to prevail to most, if not all, VCLT norms.[6] However, the nature of a human rights treaty equipped with a Court sets a specific context for compliance and interpretation. The ECtHR has explained that the Convention differs from classic international treaties insofar as it "comprises more than mere reciprocal engagements between Contracting States. It creates, over and above a network of mutual, bilateral undertakings, objective obligations that, in the words of the Preamble, benefit from a 'collective enforcement'".[7] This indicates that all States are liable towards each other for the compliance with the ECHR as a means to uphold the European public order. It also suggests that the treaty obligation of good faith in the ECHR is addressed to States and consists in loyalty towards each other, through the execution of the Convention, including, ultimately, through securing rights and freedoms to persons in their jurisdiction, creating a complex relationship.

To support the collective enforcement, the Court has developed a sophisticated system of application and interpretation, with the main principles of effectiveness and subsidiarity.[8] It can be said that effectiveness permeates and animates the substantive and interpretive principles of the Convention.[9] Notably, in relation to

---

[2] The Vienna Convention on the Law of Treaties of 23 May 1969, 1155 UNTS 331.

[3] Kałduński (2025), in this volume 6–7.

[4] Convention for the Protection of Human Rights and Fundamental Freedoms of 4 November 1950, ETS 5.

[5] *Stichting Mothers of Srebrenica and Others v. the Netherlands* (dec.), 11 June 2013, no. 65542/12, § 144.

[6] See *Golder v. the United Kingdom*, 21 February 1975, no. 4451/70, § 29.

[7] *Mamatkulov and Askarov v. Turkey* [GC], 4 February 2005, nos 46827/99 and 46951/99, § 100.

[8] Gerards (2019). Beyond the many interpretative principles developed in the Court's case law, Gerards points also at references to meta-values of the Convention, such as democracy and pluralism, see 59–67.

[9] Serghides (2017), pp. 14–15. At the same time, even with a strong place of effectiveness in the Court's reasoning, it cannot be said that the result of the case will point out at effective human rights protection as primary consideration, see e.g. *N.D. and N.T. v. Spain* [GC], 13 February 2020, nos 8675/15, 8697/15.

prohibition of abuse of rights, good faith and effective protection might be overlapping in content.[10]

Specifically, regarding good faith, it is not referenced *verbatim* in the Convention itself, Statute of the Council of Europe (CoE statute)[11] nor Rules of Court. However, Article 3 CoE statute makes reference to sincere and effective cooperation with relation to the aim of CoE. This aim is realised in the maintenance and further realisation of human rights and fundamental freedoms, as enunciated in Article 1b CoE Statute.

This shows that an inquiry into the Court's case law is necessary. Altogether, the overarching aim of this chapter is to reflect on understanding the principle of good faith in the Strasbourg system of fundamental rights protection and to propose a systematics to the Court's references and interpretations of good faith. The analysis will explore its importance, especially given the existing universe of principles governing Convention's interpretation. It will also check whether the Court takes a negative approach and define what is not done in good faith by State authorities, for example, through references to bad faith.

To fulfill this aim, the chapter follows the structure of the Convention: primarily encompassing vertical relations between State and individuals and, to support the protection granted, regulating procedural aspects of international cooperation. Hence, Sect. 2 analyses the case law on substantive rights of the Convention. First, it presents the Court's passing references to good faith. Second, it takes a look at the references to arbitrariness and bad faith, which is most frequently recalled by the Court in Article 5 context[12] and under Article 18 analysis.[13] Next, Article 18 jurisprudence and its terminology disallowing misuse of powers are presented. Finally, the section draws attention to a negative assessment of authorities' intentions in cases where the Court uses Article 18 language without its application.

Section 3 demonstrates that the interpretation of Convention's procedural provisions points to the need for sincere cooperation in the effective realisation of the treaty through the right to application, cooperation in investigations and execution of Court's judgements. Breaches of procedural obligations frequently have more objective characteristics, yet, as it will be shown, it is not uncommon that they coincide with the doubts as to intentions in the substantive assessment of the case. Section 4 concludes.

[10] Serghides (2017), p. 13.

[11] Statute of the Council of Europe of 5 May 1949, ETS 1.

[12] E.g. *S., V. and A. v. Denmark* [GC], 22 October 2018, nos 35553/12 et al.

[13] *Khodorkovskiy,* § 260.

2 Deciphering Good Faith Among the "Rights and Freedoms" of the Convention

2.1 Passing Reference to Good Faith

It is not uncommon for the Court to require good faith from the applicant.[14] Examples are cases concerning freedom of expression, where journalists are granted wide protection subject to their good faith compliance with journalistic ethics[15] or protection of whistle-blowers.[16]

A search through the HUDOC database suggests that this is less evident towards States, where the references seem to be made in passing, without justification. Notably, in the context of a trial of a dead person, the Court noted that such action "runs counter to the object and purpose of Article 6 of the Convention, as well as to the principle of good faith and the principle of effectiveness inherent in that Article".[17] However, this was not accompanied by any additional comment concerning good faith by the Court. A more recurring example can be found when the Court undertakes the assessment of Articles 8 to 11. There, occasionally the ECtHR demarcates its scrutiny with the view on the margin of appreciation by explaining that it goes beyond "ascertaining whether the respondent State exercised its discretion reasonably, carefully and in good faith". This is mentioned as part of the test on the necessity of a restriction in democratic society,[18] or indicated as a general principle for the assessment.[19] Whatever the alternative, it seems that the Court's analysis goes beyond a good faith review, but the meaning of such a review is left unexplained. Hence, an initial consideration might be that good faith carries limited value in the Court's analysis. The referred cases leave an impression that good faith is merely superficially recalled in the assessment of authorities' actions. However, as it will be shown below, notably under Articles 5 and 18 ECHR the Court has managed to use this notion in a more consistent and slightly less obscure manner.

[14] As a separate category from abuse of the right of application prohibited by Article 35 § 3 (a) ECHR and of abuse of rights under Article 17 ECHR. In the context of Article 17 ECHR, it is worth noting that inasmuch as it prohibits States from abusing Convention rights, the case law is almost exclusively focused on interpreting this prohibition towards the remaining addressees of the provision, namely individuals and groups.

[15] E.g. *Radio France and Others v. France*, 30 March 2004, no. 53984/00, § 37.

[16] There, in assessing an applicant's good faith, the Court verifies, in each case brought before it, whether he or she was motivated by a desire for personal advantage, held any personal grievance against his or her employer, or whether there was any other ulterior motive for the relevant actions, see *Guja v. Moldova* [GC], 12 February 2008, no. 14277/04, §§ 77 and 93.

[17] *Magnitskiy and Others v. Russia*, 27 August 2019, nos 32631/09, 53799/12, § 281.

[18] E.g. *Mouvement raëlien suisse v. Switzerland* [GC], 13 July 2012, no. 16354/06, § 48.

[19] E.g. *Zhdanov and Others v Russia*, 16 July 2019, no. 12200/08 et al., § 141.

2.2 Arbitrariness and the Emergence of Bad Faith

The notion of good faith accompanies the Court's assessment of detention under Article 5 ECHR. Notably, for detention to avoid being branded as arbitrary, it must be carried out in good faith.[20]

Arbitrariness, named by the Court the negation of the principle of the rule of law,[21] has been left undefined by the Court. One can say that the protection against it is inherent to the Convention[22] and it is closely related to procedural safeguards under the requirement of lawfulness, or the wider reasonableness, of an interference.[23] Yet arbitrariness might accompany restrictions that are lawful under national law. This inherent fight against arbitrariness might indicate the meta-presence of good faith in the Convention system.[24]

The notion of arbitrariness can vary between the types of detention.[25] Among the factors to consider, the ECtHR established that detention will be arbitrary "where, despite complying with the letter of national law, there has been an element of bad faith or deception on the part of the authorities".[26] Consequently, the concept of bad faith in ECtHR jurisprudence has emerged in connection with the assessment of authorities' actions under Article 5 of the Convention.[27] However, the Court did not explain what is the meaning of bad faith in this context. There exist other, non-cumulative criteria for arbitrariness, such as genuine conformity between order and execution of the detention, and its purpose permitted by the Convention, a reasonable suspicion[28] and necessity of the detention. Altogether they point to a rather contextual assessment of the case. Lack of reasonable suspicion for detention might bring the Court to observe that the authorities failed to demonstrate that they acted in good faith towards the applicants,[29] but it does not define bad faith within the meaning of Article 5.

Çalı noted that before the Court began applying Article 18, finding arbitrariness was likely the closest to a reflection on abuse of powers.[30] However, this standard

---

[20] *Saadi. v. the United Kingdom* [GC], 29 January 2008, no. 13229/03, § 74.

[21] *Al-Dulimi and Montana Management Inc. v. Switzerland* [GC], 21 June 2016, no. 5809/08, § 145.

[22] *Ibid.*

[23] Gerards (2019), pp. 200, 212–214; it is important to note that given its proximity with lawfulness the scrutiny of arbitrary restrictions has also been present under other Convention articles.

[24] Tsampi (2020), p. 146.

[25] *Kavala v. Turkey*, 10 December 2019, no. 28749/18, § 133.

[26] *Saadi*, §69; *Mooren v. Germany* [GC], 9 August 2009, no. 11364/03, § 78

[27] E.g. *I.E. v. the Republic of Moldova*, 26 May 2020, no. 45422/13.

[28] Two aspects to the "reasonable suspicion" requirement are separate but overlapping: a factual aspect (facts at issue had actually occurred and were attributable to the persons under suspicion) and an aspect concerning the classification as criminal conduct, *Sabuncu and Others v. Turkey*, 10 November 2020, no. 23199/17, §§ 145–147.

[29] *Ibrahimov and Mammadov v. Azerbaijan*, 13 February 2020, no. 63571/16 et al., § 154.

[30] Çalı (2023), p. 188.

does not explicitly include an evaluation of (il)legitimate motives of authorities,[31] as it was also demonstrated above through the rather superficial reference to bad faith in the context of Article 5.

2.3 Application of Article 18 ECHR with the View on Ulterior Purposes and Misuse of Power

Article 18 ECHR appears to be the most straightforward area to search for good faith in the Convention. It reads "The restrictions permitted under this Convention to the said rights and freedoms shall not be applied for any purpose other than those for which they have been prescribed", making a literal reference to subjective intentions.[32] In its context the Court has reiterated that the whole structure of the Convention rests on the general assumption that public authorities act in good faith yet that such a presumption is rebuttable.[33]

The article originates in the drafters' experience that the totalitarian regime creeps up in a disguise of legality[34] and in the shared concern that the core of rule of law must be protected.[35] *Travaux préparatoires* to Article 18 hint on the fact that it prohibits the misuse of powers by State authorities,[36] which in its likely origin of French administrative law requires a definition of a measure's ulterior purpose by the reviewing authority.[37] Therefore Article 18 connects the essence of democracy with some evidentiary challenges.

Article 18 was a dormant provision until in *Gusinskiy*[38] the Court finally found its violation in conjunction with Article 5 ECHR. Finding only five violations of this article until *Merabishvili* judgement in 2017, the Court explained that it "finds a violation of Article 18 of the Convention when it concludes that the whole legal machinery of a State is misused *ab initio*, which is an indication that from beginning to end the authorities have acted in bad faith and in blatant disregard of the Convention".[39] The presumption of good faith could have been firmly rebutted through a presence of a "hidden agenda" of public policy or individual measures at stake, following a very high evidentiary standard burdening the applicant. This

---

[31] *Ibid.*

[32] As noted by the Court itself, see *Tymoshenko v. Ukraine*, 30 April 2013, no. 49872/11, Joint concurring opinion of Judges Jungwiert, Nussberger and Potocki.

[33] *Rasul Jafarov v. Azerbaijan*, 17 March 2016, no. 69981/14, § 153; *Khodorkovskiy v. Russia*, 31 May 2011, no. 5829/04, § 255; *Lutsenko v. Ukraine*, 3 July 2012, no. 6492/11, § 106; *Ilgar Mammadov v. Azerbaijan*, 22 May 2014, no. 15172/13, § 137.

[34] *Ukraine v. Russia (re Crimea)*, 25 June 2024, nos. 20958/14 and 38334/18, § 1334.

[35] See Mortier (2023) and the references included therein.

[36] Heri (2020), pp. 45–49.

[37] Tsampi (2020), p. 139.

[38] *Gusinskiy v. Russia*, 19 May 2004, no. 70276/01.

[39] *Khodorkovskiy*, § 260.

threshold meant that even if authorities were driven by "improper motives", without convincingly showing their continuity "from beginning to end" of the right's restriction Article 18 would not have been violated.[40] In general, Article 18 is autonomous but only applied in conjunction with other Convention articles that do not have to be violated as a prerequisite.[41] However, practice shows that the Court usually finds first a violation of the standard provisions. The natural consequence is that Article 18 has a qualified character, requiring the conviction of the Court that such a separate violation might be at stake. It might also provoke a reflection on subsidiarity, since international tribunals are not democratically legitimised to find misuse of powers within a State nor in the best position to access the necessary evidence.

Merabishvili brought a clarification of the initial standard, laying the foundation for more frequent use of Article 18. It marked an evolution from "bad faith *ab initio*" in earlier case law towards the predominant ulterior purpose test. The Court self-reflected that the binary divide between good faith and bad faith does not carry any distinctive meaning for the interpretation of Convention rights as such.[42] Indeed, as hinted on in Sect. 2.1, one might wonder what meaning and added value of examining State's good faith in a concrete case of alleged violation of human rights are. This question seems more pertinent if good faith understood as under international law is concerned. However, there is no clear indication to assume that it should be understood in a more constitutional sense, e.g. as a democratic principle. Thus, instead of proving bad faith, which has not been defined by the Court, the Court can find "hidden aim" as a proxy.[43] Notions of "ulterior purpose", "ulterior motives", or "hidden agenda" and "hidden aim" are interchangeably used by the Court. The ECtHR provided a textbook definition of the ulterior purpose as "a purpose not prescribed by nor permissible under the Convention, involving misuse of power".[44] It explained that "'bad faith' and 'ulterior purpose' are related notions, but the Court does not consider them necessarily equivalent in each case".[45] Ulterior purpose goes beyond the lack of legitimate aim that might be established, albeit infrequently,[46] during the examination of explicit restriction clauses of Articles 8 to 11. Even at

[40] *Khodorkovskiy and Lebedev v. Russia*, 25 July 2013, nos. 11082/06 and 13772/05, § 908.

[41] *Merabishvili v. Georgia* [GC], 28 November 2017, no. 72508/13, §§ 265, 271, 288.

[42] *Merabishvili*, § 283.

[43] *Merabishvili* clarified that the burden of proof shall not lay on the applicant but instead follow the general rules in this regard i.e. that the burden is not borne by any of the parties because the Court examines all available material before it and can ask for evidence out of its own initiative, § 311.

[44] *Ukraine v. Russia (re Crimea)*, § 1356. Meaning that is different from the one proclaimed by authorities, see ECtHR, Guide on Article 18 of the Convention, updated 31 August 2024, § 31.

[45] *Merabishvili*, § 283.

[46] It is uncommon for ECtHR to not find any legitimate aim of the contested measures whatsoever. Similarly, there were very few cases where it found a violation of the Convention specifically due to absence of a legitimate aim, see *Merabishvili*, § 296. Even when the Court has doubts as to the existence of any legitimate aim, it prefers to emphatically channel the critical findings through the test of necessity in a democratic society; see with the example of cases concerning rule of law and judicial independence *Baka v. Hungary* [GC], 23 June 2016, no. 20261/12, §§ 156–57; *Żurek v. Poland*, 16 June 2022, no. 39650/18, § 217.

such occasion,[47] the Court does not delve into considerations of authorities' intentions, nor directly point out a lack of good faith in the action of State authorities.

In *Merabishvili* the Court has come to a conclusion that proving bad faith might indeed be problematic, if not impossible, for the applicants and for the Court. Instead, ulterior purpose should provide a more objective standard to indicate a misuse of power. Its predominance depends on all circumstances of the case, but the Court should take into account the nature and degree of reprehensibility of the ulterior motive and the underlying values of the Convention.[48] Heri[49] suggested that the reprehensibility has thus become the new "bad faith" but it should be noted that the Court used this criterion only in some of the Article 18 cases that followed.[50] Hence, when considering a violation of Article 18 of the Convention, the absence of a legitimate aim is not sufficient to establish a violation, it is necessary to find a (predominant)[51] ulterior purpose. Indeed, one of the many criticisms of this test is that the illegitimate purposes can freely exist alongside legitimate ones.[52]

As ulterior purposes rarely come with direct evidence, to meet the standard of proof (beyond reasonable doubt), the Court looks at a combination of relevant case-specific facts, such as the sequence of events or personal references to the applicant by members of the government, and other circumstantial evidence, such as NGO/IGO reports on the situation at hand. Depending on the case, the ECtHR might reflect on a pattern in applicant's treatment or a systemic pattern of treating social group to which the applicant belongs.[53] From this perspective the Court's adjudication under Article 18 might be seen as an interplay between individual and contextual, likely systemic considerations.

Article 18 violations were found in cases concerning political pluralism, opposition politicians, human rights activists, and recently judges. More than 20 of them were decided after *Merabishvili* and, consequently, took into account the new evidentiary regime. Frequently the core of the alleged Article 18 violation is the applicant's persecution for their role in democratic society, for example as an opposition politician, and not as a private person.[54] The Court sees this argument through the

---

[47] See e.g. cases concerning LGBT rights restrictions: the legislative ban on "propaganda of non-traditional sexual relations aimed at minors" (*Bayev and Others v. Russia*, 20 June 2017, nos 67,667/09 and 2 others) and the suspension of children's fairy tale book publication depicting same-sex relationships and its subsequent labelling as harmful to children (*Macatė v. Lithuania* [GC], 23 January 2023, no. 61435/19). In both cases the measures did not pursue any legitimate aim and were "incompatible with the notions of equality, pluralism and tolerance inherent in a democratic society" (*Bayev,* § 83; *Macatė* § 215) but the Court did not delve into intentions of the legislator.

[48] *Merabishvili,* § 307.

[49] Heri (2020), p. 31.

[50] On this inconsistency and solutions see Mortier (2023).

[51] Finnerty (2023), p. 11.

[52] See *ibid.*, Heri (2020).

[53] See e.g. *Aliyev v. Azerbaijan*, 20 September 2018, nos 68762/14, 71200/14, §§ 223–224.

[54] *Natig Jafarov v. Azerbaijan*, 7 November 2019, no. 64581/16, § 69; *Navalnyy v. Russia* [GC], 15 November 2018, nos 29580/12 et al., § 174.

prism of impact on democracy, highlighting the systemic aspect. Thus defined, the ulterior purpose of persecution of actors driving democratic discourse reaches significant gravity and affects the very essence of democracy to which the Convention refers.[55]

Similarly, in the first-ever violation of Article 18 in an inter-state case, *Ukraine v. Russia*[56] the ECtHR observed that "Russian authorities ultimately sought to suppress that political pluralism which forms part of 'effective political democracy' governed by 'the rule of law'. (…) For that reason, the Court attaches the utmost importance to the chilling effects of the impugned restrictions." Overall, it seems that grand formulas are used, especially in relation to the systemic impact of the restrictions, but it remains difficult to see a clear-cut definition of misuse of power or absence of good faith in the Court's optics.

It is worth signaling that application of the doctrine of chilling effect, prominently developed under Article 10, is obviously insufficient by itself to infer bad faith or find a violation of Article 18. In *Ahmet Hüsrev Altan* the Court found violations of Articles 5 § 1 and 10, and concluded that the measures against the applicant lacked a legitimate aim and created a chilling effect.[57] However, despite no legitimate aim,[58] the Court did not establish an ulterior one. Hence, first, the chilling effect seems to be too broad of a category to infer bad faith and could result in a clash between effects-based approach normally taken by the Court and examination of intentions. Second, as mentioned earlier, absence of a legitimate aim is insufficient as such to find a misuse of power. Thus, while the chilling effect is insufficient to trigger Article 18 application and violation, Article 18 violation always entails some chilling effect.

Article 18 judgements point to a threshold in undemocratic practices aimed at its essential components: political pluralism, rule of law, judicial independence protected by the Convention. They might refer to the presumption of good faith on authorities' part and use very strong wording to condemn the situation on top of Article 18 as a qualifier. They point out ulterior motives of authorities but depart from the direct qualification as "bad faith", perhaps given its unclear denomination under the Convention. However, the article's growing use and evolving interpretation (e.g. through loosened evidentiary regime) demonstrates the Court's engagement in discourse on motives of public powers to defend the core Convention values. In addition, as pointed out by Çalı,[59] this enhanced use of Article 18 as a shield against anti-democratic practices can be seen as a driver for the development of an evidentiary standard for bad faith conduct in international law.

[55] *Ibid.*

[56] *re Crimea,* § 1379.

[57] *Ahmet Hüsrev Altan v. Turkey*, 13 April 2021, no. 13252/17. See also the partly dissenting opinion of Judge Kūris.

[58] *Ahmet Hüsrev Altan,* § 240.

[59] Çalı (2023), pp. 186–187.

2.4 Ulterior Motives Beyond Article 18

As explained above, as a rule the Court analyses ulterior purposes and, hence, the authorities' malicious intentions under Article 18, given its special character. However, attention should be paid to the practice of assessment of authorities' intentions outside its scope. Using Article 18 language, that is a reference to ulterior motives and the "qualified" disregard of the Convention, without applying Article 18, seems to be a novelty in the ECtHR jurisprudence.

One might suppose that despite the principle *iura novit curia*, given the continuously rather extraordinary character of Article 18 it would be unlikely that the Court conducts own-initiative assessment under Article 18. In addition, as mentioned earlier, even when applicants claim ulterior purposes, it is not a given that the Court will find it necessary to conduct a separate analysis on top of earlier violations found. Yet, the Court might still want to demonstrate the observation of systemic antidemocratic tendencies that emerge from facts of the case and other sources of evidence. In this respect, using firm language can prove useful to send "warning signs" without any direct consequences of using Article 18, such as potential accusations of judicial activism.

The Polish rule of law crisis saga offers an example to the above. The first (2021) cases concerned the election of judges to the Constitutional Court (*Xero Flor*),[60] premature termination of mandates of presidents of ordinary courts (*Broda and Bojara*)[61] and appointment of judges to the Supreme Court (*Reczkowicz*).[62] Finding violations of Article 6 § 1 ECHR, the Court noted that the "very essence" of the right to "a tribunal established by law" was undermined and that these cases presented grave irregularities. However, a few months later the value judgments of the Court became accompanied by its assessment of the intentions of executive and legislative powers. In *Dolińska-Ficek and Ozimek*[63] the Court observed that the actions towards appointment of Supreme Court judges "demonstrated an attitude which can only be described as one of utter disregard for the authority, independence and role of the judiciary".[64] Those actions were "clearly taken with the ulterior motive of not only influencing the outcome of the pending court proceedings but also preventing the proper examination of the legality of the resolution that recommended candidates for judicial posts and, in consequence, rendering judicial review of the resolution meaningless".[65] This reasoning was repeated in *Advance Pharma.*[66] Both judgements concluded that the President "-by deliberate actions disregarding a binding judicial decision and through f*aits accomplis*, interferes with the course of justice,

[60] *Xero Flor w Polsce sp. z o.o.*, 7 May 2021, no. 4907/18.

[61] *Broda and Bojara v. Poland*, 29 June 2021, nos 26691/18, 27367/18.

[62] *Reczkowicz v. Poland*, 22 July 2021, no. 43447/19.

[63] *Dolińska-Ficek and Ozimek v. Poland*, 8 November 2021, nos. 49868/19, 57511/19.

[64] *Dolińska-Ficek*, § 330.

[65] *Ibid.*

[66] *Advance Pharma sp. z o.o v. Poland*, 3 February 2022, no. 1469/20, § 333.

in order to vitiate and render meaningless a pending judicial review of the appointment of judges, [what] can only be characterised as blatant defiance of the rule of law".[67] These constatations, directly referring to blatant disregard of Convention principles and ulterior motives, seem to correspond to the findings under Article 18. Other cases concerning Polish judges pointed at the general trend of undue influence on judiciary by the other two state powers[68] and chilling effect,[69] following Article 18 tendencies described earlier. However, they do not refer directly to good or bad faith of the authorities.

In *Juszczyszyn*[70] the Court finally found Article 18 violation in conjunction with Article 8. The ulterior purpose was to sanction the applicant and to dissuade him from assessing the status of newly appointed judges in accordance with relevant legal standards.[71] The Court's observations, consolidated through earlier cases, as well as individual circumstances and external context (e.g. findings of the European Court of Justice related to the applicant) made it possible. Although there seems to be a connection between Article 18 violations and such democratic principles as separation of powers,[72] the Court at times judges the intentions of authorities without the explicit use of Article 18. This seems to concern the situations where some grave democracy concerns are at stake, going beyond the effectiveness of protection of a single applicant's rights.[73]

In addition, in *Juszczyszyn* the ECtHR noted that the national Constitutional Court attempted to prevent execution of ECtHR's judgements through its own adjudication. In this context, it observed that States cannot invoke their domestic law to justify their failure to abide by international law, as enunciated in Article 27 VCLT.[74] This brings the question of procedural obligations incumbent upon States to act in good faith and comply with the Convention.

---

[67] Do*lińska-Ficek,* § 338*; Advance Pharma* § 334.

[68] *Grzęda v. Poland* [GC], 15 March 2022, no. 43572/18, § 348.

[69] *Żurek,* § 227.

[70] *Juszczyszyn v. Poland.* 6 October 2022, no. 35599/20.

[71] *Juszczyszyn*, § 337.

[72] See Tsampi (2023).

[73] See *Wałęsa v. Poland,* 23 November 2023, no. 50849/21 as a potential coda to the Polish rule of law cases where the Court initiated a pilot-judgement procedure to end systemic violations of Article 6 § 1.

[74] *Juszczyszyn*, §§ 207–209.

3 Searching for Good Faith in Procedural Obligations of States Under the ECtHR

Ensuring effectiveness of the Strasbourg system goes beyond the Court handing down its judgements. It involves the cooperative attitude of States from individual applications to evidence gathering, to compliance with a final judgement. The need to cooperate with the Court,[75] as a facet of good faith in execution of the treaty, appears thus as a natural consequence of adhering to the Strasbourg protection system. It is also growingly explicit throughout the history of the Convention system, given the nuancing of obligations and their execution over time.

3.1 Effective Exercise of the Right to Application and the Duty to Cooperate with the Court

On top of the *erga omnes* obligations concerning individual rights and freedoms, some of the procedural provisions, further refined in the Rules of Court, require State parties to act in a specific way or refrain from action. Article 34 ECHR forbids hindering in any way the right to effective individual application. A breach of this provision originates from lack of compliance with Rule 39, allowing the Court to indicate interim measures[76] or other hindrance of the effective right to application, e.g. through influence on correspondence or impossibility to meet the applicant's lawyer.[77]

In applying Article 34 the Court rarely refers to good faith but instead points to the need for overarching effectiveness of the Convention and the States' duty to cooperate. This is seen by the wording used by the Court: a State is in breach of its obligations or has failed to comply with its obligation and only occasionally has violated a Convention provision.[78] The more objective character has been stressed by the Court: "the intentions or reasons underlying the acts or omissions in question are of little relevance when assessing whether Article 34 of the Convention was complied with (…) What matters is whether the situation created as a result of the authorities" act or omission conforms to Article 34′.[79]

---

[75] It is worth to note that with regard to procedural obligations, States are also required to "cooperate with each other, exhausting in good faith the possibilities available to them" as the Court noted in the context of the procedural limb of Article 2 and of international cooperation in investigation. *Güzelyurtlu and Others v. Cyprus and Turkey* [GC], 29 January 2019, 36925/07, § 235.

[76] *Mamatkulov and Askarov,* §§ 102, 125.

[77] *Rasul Jafarov,* §186; see also European Agreement relating to Persons Participating in Proceedings of the European Court of Human Rights of 5 March 1996, ETS 161.

[78] Schabas (2015), p. 747.

[79] *Paladi v. Moldova* [GC], 10 March 2009, no. 39806/05, § 87.

This objective approach can be seen to different extent in cases alleging violation of Article 18 where non-compliance with Article 34 was found. In *Ecodefence*[80] which concerned imposing on NGOs and their directors a "foreign agent" status and subsequent requirements related to it, Russia dissolved one of the applicant NGOs, thus disregarding the interim measure issued by the ECtHR. Ignoring interim measures for whatever reasons seems sufficient to find a breach of Article 34. Another approach can be discerned from *Khodorkovskiy and Lebedev*. There, the first applicant suggested that the question of real intent of authorities posed under Article 18 applies also to disciplinary and other measures against his lawyers, alleging violation of Article 34 for this reason.[81] In response, the Court reiterated the existence of legitimate aim under Article 18 but found that the aim of actions against lawyers was not evident and primarily aimed at their intimidation to pursue the case.[82] This case might be an example that the ECtHR's *dictum* from *Paladi* that intentions are of little importance does not always hold true.

Article 38 bears similarities to Article 34, and in respect to individual applications can be considered its *lex specialis.* It requires that States "shall furnish all necessary facilities for the effective conduct of an investigation" by the Court. The requirement to submit requested evidence is concretised in the Rules of Court (Rules 44A-C). The Court uses the same qualification of "not complying with obligation" rather than a violation, hinting on its more objective, procedural character. This obligation, required to ensure effective observance of the ECHR, makes the Court refer to *pacta sunt servanda* and good faith observance of treaties under Articles 26 and 27 VCLT, stressing that the Convention must be performed by the States in good faith and consequently, they must comply with the duty to submit requested information.[83]

[80] *Ecodefence and Others v. Russia*, 14 June 2022, nos 9988/13 et al. This is one of the cases where the Court used its discretion to accept a legitimate aim, channel the analysis on the necessity in democratic society and discard any potential considerations under Article 18, despite pleadings in this respect by some applicants. However, the strong condemnation of such anti-democratic legislation was further seen in *Kobaliya and Others v. Russia*, 22 October 2024, nos. 39446/16 et al. where the Court said "The legislation examined in this case goes even further [than *Ecodefence*] and bears the hallmarks of a totalitarian regime", § 86.

[81] *Khodorkovskiy and Lebedev*, § 929.

[82] *Khodorkovskiy and Lebedev*, §§ 930–933.

[83] *Janowiec and Others v. Russia* [GC], 21 October 2013, nos. 55508/07, 29520/09, § 211; *Al Nashiri v. Poland*, 24 July 2014, no. 28761/11, § 366; *Husayn (Abu Zubaydah) v. Poland*, 24 July 2014, no. 7511/13, § 358.

3.2 Execution of Judgements

Article 46 § 1 ECHR requires defender States to abide by the final judgements. The Court has seen it as a "specific formulation of the general principle *pacta sunt servanda*".[84] As mentioned in Sect. 2.3, the assumption that authorities act in good faith, following the obligations endorsed in the VCLT, underlies the whole structure of the Convention. This presumption extends to ECHR's execution mechanism, coordinated by the Committee of Ministers. As explained by the Court, a failure to implement judgement leads to ineffectiveness of the protection offered by the Convention and a lack of execution of final judgement likely leads to a situation incompatible with the principle of rule of law.[85]

The repetitive argument of effectiveness lied at heart of the explanatory report to Protocol 14 which added the possibility for the Court to declare non-compliance with its judgement under Article 46 § 4.[86] Since its entry into force 2010, it has been used twice, unsurprisingly, in cases that involved protracted deprivation of liberty and earlier both Article 5 and Article 18 violations. The Committee of Ministers brought the infringement proceedings to exert political pressure in the most blatant cases where misuse of power was found, as a last resort to side with continuously detained applicants.[87] In these cases the Court stressed that the execution should be done in good faith and in a manner compatible with the "conclusions and spirit" of the judgement[88] and found violations of Article 46 § 4. It underlined that there is a special need to comply in good faith with the judgement if earlier the Court has found a violation of Article 18.[89] Indeed, the Court implied that it is impossible for a State to act in good faith in execution of a judgement if abusive detention of the applicants continues after Article 18 violation has vitiated any charges against them. It reiterated that judgement compliance is required by international law and embodied notably in Article 26 VCLT.[90]

Although the Court does not differentiate between objective and subjective good faith, it clearly acknowledges the binary divide between good and bad faith under the Convention. The urgency to demonstrate good faith following an earlier misuse

---

[84] Schabas (2015), p. 866; *Verein gegen Tierfabriken Schweiz (VgT) v. Switzerland (no. 2)* [GC], 30 June 2009, no. 32772/02, § 87.

[85] *Ilgar Mammadov v. Azerbaijan (infringement proceedings)* [GC], 29 May 2019, no. 15172/13, §§ 214–215; *Kavala v. Türkiye (infringement proceedings)* [GC], 11 July 2022, no. 28749/18, § 170.

[86] Explanatory Report to Protocol No. 14 to the Convention for the Protection of Human Rights and Fundamental Freedoms, amending the control system of the Convention of 13 May 2004, CETS 194.

[87] On the exceptional character of the procedure see *ibid.* §§ 99–100. On execution of other Article 18 judgements see notably 2023 Annual Report of the Committee of Ministers, April 2024, 26–29 and a thematic factsheet from October 2024 prepared by the Council of Europe's Department for the Execution of Judgments of the European Court of Human Rights.

[88] *Mammadov (infringement)*, § 214; *Kavala (infringement)*, § 169.

[89] *Ibid.*

[90] *Mammadov (infringement)*, § 152.

of powers found by the Court is an example of a plea for "restitution of trust" on top of the wider attempt to reinforce the effectiveness of the execution mechanism. In addition, there is less automatism in the assessment of execution of a judgement compared to other procedural considerations described in Sect. 3.1.

4 Conclusion

First, it seems clear that the understanding of good faith in the ECHR remains obscure. Despite this, the chapter distinguished two dimensions where good faith is manifesting itself. Such perspective takes into account the Convention's character of an international obligation of collective enforcement of human rights: both its special role to safeguard rights and the characteristics of a more "traditional" international law instrument of bi- and multilateral cooperation.

From a vertical perspective, good faith seemingly permeates the substantive rights, including preventing misuse of power vis-à-vis individuals and upholding the values of the Convention. Consequently, it exists also in the subjective opposition to bad faith. However, at times it is also referenced in passing, without an independent meaning, suggesting limited value for the interpretation of Convention rights. In addition, States benefit from a presumption of acting in good faith.

From a horizontal perspective, there is not only a presumption but also a corelated procedural duty to cooperate for the effective functioning of the Convention system, which might have more objective character, as it is the case for Articles 34 and 38, and, consequently, appear significantly more straightforward to assess than under substantive articles of the Convention. The Court refers to good faith's presence in international law and, specifically, in the VCLT, to insist on States' procedural obligations and on the binding force of Strasbourg judgements.

The two perspectives are intertwined, as exemplified e.g. by the relation between Article 18 judgements and Article 46 § 4 procedure or the right to an effective application in a situation of alleged misuse of powers. In both alternatives there is proximity between good faith and effectiveness. In that sense the gap between effects-based approaches taken towards human rights violations do not contradict considerations on good faith, which can also have an objective character. This means, first, that good faith is implicitly included in the Convention and the review under its scope and second, that the default violations of ECHR can be seen as good faith violations, because, as a rule, the Court does not examine good faith of the authorities.

Second, the Court has discretion in channeling its analysis to focus on the aims and categorising where doubts as to authorities' intentions, and notably ulterior purposes emerge. This analysis has shown that the absence of legitimate aims does not point to the absence of good faith, nor necessarily does arbitrariness. However, the opposite notion of bad faith, incorporated at times as part of the arbitrariness assessment under Article 5, was also used by the Court under Article 18 ECHR which prohibits misuse of State powers. The ECtHR clarified the evidentiary regime in this respect notably in *Merabishvili* and uses a category of predominant ulterior purpose (called also illegitimate aim, hidden agenda, hidden aim) to prove a misuse of powers. Departing from *verbatim* references to authorities' bad faith as a rebuttal of the good faith presumption, Article 18 is growingly used to point out measures denying the core democratic principles of the Convention. With this special role, it serves as part of the "nuclear arsenal" of this treaty.[91]

Third, the rising consideration of ulterior purposes' grave negative effects on democracy, rule of law and separation of powers under this article bears some similarities with the usual effects-based approach of the Court, merging the intentions with the impact. The ECtHR also points to an important systemic role carried by Article 18. In addition, as brought up with the example of the Polish rule of law saga, the indicators of bad faith can be more linguistic than considering a violation of Article 18. The discussed cases allowed condemning the authorities' intentions through essentially the same notions of ulterior motives and blatant disregard of Convention, without resorting to formal qualification under Article 18 or *verbatim* references to good or bad faith.

Fourth, the perception of good faith by the Court has been indirectly substantiating over years. This was demonstrated through Article 18 and related jurisprudence but also the sharpening of the Convention's execution mechanism. The use of Article 46 § 4 to date has shown the urgency of the State's demonstration of good faith where a misuse of powers was previously found by the Court. Other obligations of cooperation, such as those related to an effective application and evidence gathering, imply good faith and benefit from Court's references to VCLT to stress the duties of honest participation in the Convention system.

Finally, the analysis of the two dimensions suggests that while in procedural terms the meaning of good faith is uncontestably related to international law, in substantive dimension of the Convention this is far from clear, and potential constitutional understanding could be further explored. It might be that in *Merabishvili* the Court insisted on a shift from authorities' bad faith to ulterior purposes not only for evidentiary reasons. Article 18 concerns democratically impermissible situations, where the emphasis should be put at the state of national democracy and situation of individuals therein, and not at State's relationship with the Court and other States, where good faith operates directly. Altogether, although the principle of good faith is not expressly included in the Convention, it seems present across its governing principles, provisions and interpretation techniques. At the same time, for it to provide a more useful matrix for analysis, further clarification, substantiation and organisation by the Court would be much appreciated.

---

[91] O'Leary (2023), p. 10.

References

Çalı B (2023) Proving bad faith in international law: lessons from the Article 18 Case law of the European Court of Human Rights. In: Kajtár G et al (eds) Secondary rules of primary importance in international law: attribution, causality, evidence, and standards of review in the practice of International Courts and Tribunals. OUP, Oxford, pp 183–201

Finnerty J (2023) When is a state's 'hidden agenda' proven? The role of the Merabishvili's three-legged evidentiary test in the Article 18 Strasbourg Case Law. Eur Conven Hum Rights Law Rev 4(4):447–472

Gerards J (2019) General principles of the European Convention on Human Rights. Cambridge University Press, Cambridge

Heri C (2020) Loyalty, subsidiarity, and Article 18 ECHR: how the ECtHR deals with mala fide limitations of rights. Eur Conven Hum Rights Law Rev 1(1):25–61

Kałduński M (2025) Good faith in international law. In: Podkowik J et al (eds) Gleams of good faith in Constitutional Law

Mortier T (2023) Reprehensible or legitimate aims?: a proposal for a new approach to Article 18 ECHR in light of its predominance test. Eur Conven Hum Rights Law Rev 4(2):133–178

O'Leary S (2023) The challenged, challenging but very necessary European Convention on Human Rights. Speech delivered at the Institute of International and European Affairs, Dublin, 15 March 2023

Schabas WA (2015) The European Convention on Human Rights: a commentary. OUP, Oxford

Serghides G (2017) The principle of effectiveness in the European Convention on Human Rights, in particular its relationship to the other convention principles. Hague Yearb Int Law 30:1–16

Tsampi A (2020) The new doctrine of misuse of power under Article 18 ECHR: is it about the system of contre-pouvoirs within the State after all? Neth Q Hum Rights 38(2):134–155

Tsampi A (2023) Article 18 ECHR as a new pillar of judicial independence and separation of powers. Eur Rights Liber 1(7):369–381

Perspectives

Good Faith in French Constitutional Law

Ariane Vidal-Naquet and Xavier Magnon

Abstract The purpose of the article is to test the relevance of the requirement of good faith in the application of the Constitution. Starting from the observation that the requirement of formal regularity is not sufficient to avoid the instrumentalization of the Constitution, it envisages supplementing it with a substantive requirement of good faith in the execution of the constitutional provisions. The latter would make it possible to cover a whole range of situations that are formally regular but which, in reality, aim to circumvent the constitutional provisions in force.

In the first instance, the article seeks to objectivize the requirement of good faith, abandoning the use of generic categories of values or general quality of behavior, tinged with a strong axiological dimension, to identify categories of specific behaviors likely to concretize the requirement of good faith execution in the Constitution.

In the second instance, the article aims to test, by means of a practical test, the relevance of resorting to good faith. The latter appears difficult to mobilize objectively in, what we will call, "border cases". Above all, it raises the question of the subjectivity of the assessment of the actors of constitutional law as well as that of the establishment of mechanisms for sanctioning respect for good faith which can result in a transfer of political subjectivity from the organs of power to the judge.

From our point of view, the requirement of a good faith execution of the Constitution illustrates the limits of the juridicisation of virtuous action.

1 Introduction

Should the good faith execution of constitutional law be imposed to resolve the difficulties generated by "abusive constitutionalism"? "Abusive constitutionalism", as popularized by David Landau, refers to "the use of the Constitution, or more

A. Vidal-Naquet (✉) · X. Magnon
Louis Favoreu Institute, Aix-Marseille University, Aix-en-Provence, France
e-mail: a.vidal-naquet@univ-amu.fr; xavier.magnon@univ-amu.fr

J. Podkowik et al. (eds.), *Gleams of Good Faith in Constitutional Law*, Ius Gentium: Comparative Perspectives on Law and Justice 132,
https://doi.org/10.1007/978-3-032-06486-8_6

precisely of the mechanisms of constitutional revision, to undermine democracy".[1] How, in fact, is it possible to prevent *regular* constitutional revisions from being *instrumentalized* to keep a head of state in power, for example, by removing the constitutional provision limiting the number of terms? How can we prevent a change in the electoral system for the selection of representatives just few months before legislative elections to mitigate an unfavorable result expected from such an election?

The requirement of regularity does not capture behaviors that circumvent the general requirements of power limitation linked to the rule of law, constitutionalism, and political liberalism. Power instrumentalizes the Constitution, either by embedding its actions within the silences of the Constitution (for example, in France, the method for electing members of the National Assembly is not specified by the Constitution, nor is the duration for appointing the Prime Minister after the election of the National Assembly), or by modifying it to better circumvent the demands it imposes (such as the limitation on the number of presidential terms in Russia). In both cases, the Constitution is distorted as a tool for limiting power. Certainly, it is always possible, based on explicit constitutional norms, either to strictly frame certain practices that were not previously considered within the Constitution (such as the method of voting or the duration for appointing a Prime Minister), or, through "eternity clauses", to prevent constitutional revisions on sensitive electoral matters (such as limiting the number of presidential terms). Introducing a requirement of good faith in the application of the Constitution would ensure a general limitation on what we might call its *instrumentalization*, adapting to the different situations that might constitute such instrumentalization. Compliance with the law would thus incorporate, beyond the mere strict adherence to regularity, a requirement for the application of good faith. Good faith would therefore be integrated into positive law and would complement the requirement for strict formal regularity.

The requirement of good faith in the application of the Constitution adds to the obligatory nature of constitutional respect another axiological requirement, which allows, beyond formal regularity, to assess, based on certain values, how the Constitution is applied. It is not enough to respect the Constitution solely in the prescriptions it imposes, but to introduce additional requirements into positive law, immediately linked to general values, mandating a certain way of respecting the Constitution in its application. "Regularity" would no longer only be *formal*, in the sense we have maintained until now, but also *substantive*; it would incorporate a

[1] Landau (2013), p. 191: "Abusive constitutionalism involves the use of the mechanisms of constitutional change – constitutional amendment and constitutional replacement – to undermine democracy." In their book, R. Dixon and D. Landau take a broader definition of abusive constitutionalism, with constitutional abuses including formal amendment and replacement of the Constitution, sub-constitutional change through the adoption of new laws, and informal methods of change such as judicial reinterpretation (Dixon and Landau 2021, pp. 25–31); for a broader view of abusive constitutionalism, incorporating not only constitutional revision but also sub-constitutional legislative changes, jurisdictional interpretations and political practices, see Petrov (2024), p. 196 – see also and from a slightly different perspective Levinson (2021), pp. 14–21.

general axiological dimension in order to sanction a problematic goal pursued by the author of the revision. A constitutional revision could then be formally regular, particularly if it respects the material limits on the power of revision, but it could substantively reflect a problematic behavior in terms of power limitation because, for example, it would allow someone to remain in power in the future who would not be authorized to do so under the current constitutional text. This situation goes beyond constitutional revision cases alone to encompass all regular applications of the Constitution that translate into its instrumentalization.

However, as we will return to, the state of formal positive constitutional law does not demonstrate a consecration of good faith as a condition for the application of the Constitution. To find significant traces of good faith, we must first turn to public international law and the fundamental rule *pacta sunt servanda*. In its conventional formulation, Article 26 of the Vienna Convention of 23 May 1969 on the Law of Treaties stipulates that: "Every treaty in force is binding upon the parties to it and must be performed by them in good faith". Pacta sunt servanda thus imposes both the binding nature of treaties and their performance in good faith. The latter is added to the former, thus enriching the regularity of a substantive approach when it comes to adopting conduct to comply with the rule. In the same perspective, EU law uses another term, that of "loyalty", to require States and, more broadly, the Union, according to a generic formulation, an obligation of honest conduct in the application of European Union law.[2] This consecration, which was originally essentially jurisprudential,[3] is taken up by Article 4 § 3 of the Treaty on European Union, according to which "pursuant the principle of sincere cooperation, the Union and the Member States shall, in full mutual respect, assist each other in carrying out which flow from the Treaties". More broadly, the rule of good faith performance appears in contractual relations. Article 1104 of the French Civil Code thus provides that "Contracts must be negotiated, formed and performed in good faith".

Unilateral decisions then seem to escape the requirement of good faith. The latter would be linked to contractual relations and undoubtedly, if the reason for this area of application must be identified, because compliance with contractual relations depends solely on the attitude of the parties, and because it remains largely under the sole gaze of the parties, it cannot be easily sanctioned. Imposing good faith performance would thus make it possible to hold the parties accountable even though their contractual relationship is not necessarily visible or even always seizable by law and therefore punishable when contractual obligations are ignored. Good faith would compensate for the difficulty in sanctioning non-compliance with contractual constraints. The contract appears as a particular standard that is imposed, in principle, on a small number of people. To put it another way, it is a decentralized mode of production of law, which must be contrasted with general standards such as the law, regulations or decisions of constitutional courts, which are visible, less

[2] See in this regard Magnon (2011), pp. 245–251.

[3] See the leading judgment, which refers to "reciprocal duties of loyal cooperation": ECJ, 10 February 1983, *Luxembourg v. European Parliament*, Case C-230/81, ECR, 255, paragraph 37.

numerous, which reflect a centralized mode of normative production and which are more easily punishable. A decentralized mode of production undoubtedly requires greater individual accountability of the producers of standards to guarantee their execution, which depends only on them, than a centralized mode of production whose execution concerns a whole group of people and which refers to a collective responsibility for its application and compliance.

The contractual dimension could be considered from a constitutional perspective with the fiction of the social contract. However, this transposition does not seem entirely relevant. The social contract is a contract between citizens by which they intend to limit the action of some of them, their representatives, the holders of power. The contractual relationship exists between citizens and not, at least directly,[4] between citizens and the holders of power. The holder of power is not registered in a contractual relationship; this only exists between citizens. In this regard, Article 20 of the German Basic Law of 23 May 1949 establishes different rights and obligations for the powers and for the people. If "The legislature shall be bound by the constitutional order, the executive and judiciary by the law and justice"; "(4) All Germans shall have the right to resist any person seeking to abolish this constitutional order if no other remedy is available". The power must respect the Constitution and, more broadly, the law; the people must be able to resist any attempt that would affect the social contract. The government must respect the social contract: the people have the right to resist anything that would call this social contract into question. The contractual dimension thus only appears for the people and not for the government.

In the extension, most often, Constitutions do not impose, in general, an obligation to respect them, whether on the public authorities and/or citizens, which is the case in France, any more than they enshrine the manner in which they should be applied. Broadly speaking, Constitutions do not formalize the requirement for their respect, nor the modalities of this respect, to the extent that one can think that the obligatory nature of the standards results from their prescriptive formulation and thus relates to their ontology. Any affirmation of the obligatory nature would be in some way superfluous.

In such a context, the constitutional reference to good faith remains rare without, however, being absent from the constitutional texts in force: whether it is a question of generically enshrining in the Preamble a general framework for the application of the Constitution,[5] of imposing through an oath of office an action of good faith,[6] of imposing on public officials[7] or on public action[8] a certain way of fulfilling their

---

[4] It can be considered that citizen representatives are contracting citizens and thus have an indirect contractual relationship.

[5] Preamble of the Constitution of Thailand, which mentions "constitutional conventions that are appropriate to the situation and nature of Thai society, which include the principles of good faith, human rights, and good governance."

[6] Section 13 of the Thai Constitution, Article 94, §4 of the Chilean Constitution.

[7] Article 266 of the Portuguese Constitution.

[8] Article 8, §5 of the 2023 Chilean Constitution draft.

function, of imposing on all a fair application of the Constitution,[9] of sanctioning the responsibility of the Head of State who would not execute the Constitution in good faith,[10] of explaining the abuse of fundamental rights,[11] of acting to protect disadvantaged people,[12] such as those affected by discrimination or, finally, of granting the President being prosecuted a means of defense because he would have acted in good faith.[13]

Among all these illustrations, the oath, in its symbolic scope, fits perfectly into the logic of good faith. It imposes on a public authority a moral obligation to "loyally" apply the Constitution, beyond the mere formal respect for it. The collective dimension of respect for the law is reinforced by an individual and moral dimension thanks to the oath. In France, the requirement to apply the Constitution in good faith is totally absent from formal positive constitutional law. At most, one can note a jurisprudential requirement, based on Articles 6 of the Declaration of the Rights of Man and of the Citizen of 26 August 1789 and paragraph 1 of Article 3 of the Constitution of 4 October 1958,[14] of « clarity and sincerity of the parliamentary debate » which appears to echo a substantial approach to regularity. This requirement allows, beyond the regularity of parliamentary procedure, to sanction abusive uses of the powers entrusted to the government or to parliamentarians in the practice of this procedure. The strong political dimension that the conduct of parliamentary procedure presents seems to justify the introduction of a requirement linked to the quality of its use to avoid abuses. It is still possible to add another illustration of good faith with the oath of the members of the Constitutional Council, provided for by Article 3 of the Ordinance of 7 November 1958 relating to the organic law on the Constitutional Council, who must swear "to perform their functions well and faithfully". This intuition of a substantial axiological complement which is added to compliance with the formal requirements of regularity to cover a whole set of situations which are certainly formally regular, but which nevertheless appear to circumvent the constitutional provisions in force, deserves to be put to the test by explaining the general meaning of the application of the Constitution in good faith. While it is a question of respecting an axiological requirement, it may seem difficult to objectively identify what does or does not materialize a good faith application of the Constitution. It is necessary to recall the principle of non-cognitivism in the ethical field, according to which, to retain only one formulation: "it is futile to try to find a just and valid standard of behavior in an absolute manner on the basis of a rational

[9] Article 37, §1 of the 2023 Chilean Constitution draft, Article 83 of the Colombian Constitution, Article 5, §3 of the Swiss Constitution.

[10] Article 98 of the Zimbabwean Constitution.

[11] Article 55 of the Moldovan Constitution, Article 57 of the Romanian Constitution, Article 17 of the Mongolian Constitution.

[12] Part 2 of the Human Rights Act 1992, New Zealand.

[13] Article 98, §4 of the Zimbabwean Constitution.

[14] CC, n° 2005–526 DC, 13 octobre 2005, *Résolution modifiant le règlement de l'Assemblée nationale*, cons. 5.

See on this concept Brunessen (2011); See more broadly on sincerity: Barque (2009).

enterprise, that is to say a standard excluding the possibility that contrary behavior could be considered just".[15] We will undertake a necessarily relative approach of objectivization of this requirement (2). This relativity deserves to be put to the test by analyzing the cases likely to fall under the definition of this requirement. From this angle, one can only note a concrete subjective testing of the meaning of good faith in the reading of institutional practices (3).

2 A Relative Objectivization of the Meaning of Good Faith in the Application of the Constitution

The integration of an axiological dimension to formal regularity is attractive but it raises a difficulty regarding its formalization. While it is a question of requiring behavior that conforms to a value, necessarily relative, the question of the minimal objectivization of this value arises. Indeed, the value must not introduce a strong subjectivity, under penalty of introducing a large part of discretion, or even arbitrariness, when assessing the conformity of behavior to a value. To establish the meaning of good faith, it is possible to subscribe to two different perspectives. First, it is possible to refer to generic categories of values, of general quality of behavior. This first path suggests too large a part of discretion in the objective assessment of what could or could not be behavior adopted in good faith (2.1). We can therefore prefer an objectivization of the meaning of the latter through more precise generic behaviors, an undertaking which does not, however, appear to be totally convincing either (2.2).

2.1 Objective Assessment of What Could or Could not be Behavior Adopted in Good Faith

The integration of good faith into formal regularity adds a qualitative dimension to the way of applying the constitution from the perspective of the behavior to be accomplished. It is not enough to respect the formal regularity of the constitutional provision, it is appropriate to make an application of it in good faith. This refers to the requirement aimed at avoiding a circumvention of the rule in a way that had not been envisaged by this rule and which results in behavior that, if not prohibited by it, nevertheless amounts to betraying the behavior that it intends to prescribe.

[15] Kelsen (1953), p. 89. To put it another way, "The problem of values is first and foremost the problem of conflicts of values. And this problem cannot be resolved with the means of rational knowledge. The answer to this question is always a judgment that, ultimately, will be determined by emotional factors and, for this reason, will be highly subjective. In other words, it is a judgment valid only for the judging subject and is, in this sense, relative" (34).

Article 8 of the French Constitution provides that "the President appoints the Prime Minister". However, it does not set any deadline for doing so, either because the constituents did not think of doing so, assuming that it was obvious that this appointment would take place immediately after new legislative elections, or because they did not want there to be a delay, no doubt relying on the same assumptions. It cannot be thought that the constituents implicitly accepted an appointment within too long a period. However, there is nothing to be certain of this and this is the heart of the difficulty when it comes to objectively resorting to the intention of the constituent. However, because the constituents did not provide for anything and if we stick to strict compliance with formal regularity, any deadline for appointment will be deemed regular. However, can we accept a deadline of 6 months for doing so which, if it is not prohibited, nevertheless raises formidable difficulties with regard to the functioning of the institutions[16]? There would be little difficulty here in recognizing the bad faith of a President who would wait 6 months to appoint the Prime Minister after the election of the National Assembly.

The requirement of application in good faith would compensate for the limits of formal regularity by imposing a certain way of applying the Constitution. Formal regularity is coupled with a psychological-ethical dimension, referring to the conscience of the person who is supposed to apply the Constitution by imposing a moral obligation on him. In addition to the generality of the obligation to apply the rule, there is a personal dimension regarding the responsibility for applying the rule. The creation of an individual and moral obligation reinforces, if not compensates for, the general obligation to respect the rule. Good faith thus presents a "psychological element, intrinsically linked to the individual and [a] moral element that is detached from it, relating more to the values of society than to individual morality.[17]"The formal collective dimension of respect for the law, which is prescriptive by nature, is coupled with an individual psychological-moral dimension.

More broadly, good faith has two very different relationships with respect to compliance with the rule: either, positively, it allows one to challenge someone who acts in bad faith even if they have complied with the rule, or, negatively, it allows one to exonerate someone who has acted in good faith while violating the rule. Good faith can thus be "honest behavior" or an "erroneous belief.[18]" In addition to these subjective dimensions, there is a more objective dimension that refers to "keeping one's word,[19]" which refers more or less directly to compliance with the rule.

---

[16] In France, following the dissolution on June 9, 2024, and the subsequent election of deputies to the National Assembly on June 30 and July 7, the President appointed the Prime Minister on September 5 and the rest of the government on September 21, more than 2 months after the elections.

[17] Lefevbre (1996), p. 324.

[18] Roland, Boyer (1999), p. 40, respect. 70 and 67. See also for a distinction that seems well-established today: Cornu (1996), p. 105; Zoller (2003), p. 143; Kolb speaks of "false representation of the facts", Kolb (2017), p. 22.

[19] Cordeiro (1996), p. 230.

Of these three dimensions, we will only consider the subjective dimension of good faith, whether it is invoked positively or negatively. In both cases, identifying what constitutes good faith raises the same difficulties. The question of good faith is part of a reflection on the possibility of supplementing a formal requirement of regularity with a substantial requirement of an axiological nature to guarantee greater effectiveness of the constitutional rule.

It is therefore necessary to set aside its objective dimension of "respect for the given word", which does not seem to add anything to the requirement of respect for the rule, the latter imposing this respect.[20] It would then have a redundant, even tautological, character, even if we can agree that it adds a psychological-moral dimension to the legal obligation. In any event, in this situation, the violation of the rule as well as the attack on good faith overlap, so that the same behavior will be deemed to disregard both formal regularity and good faith, the latter only reinforcing the former from a psychological-moral perspective. Formal irregularity is sufficient to sanction the behavior. The situation that interests us lies in another situation, that in which formal regularity is respected but the application of bad faith raises a difficulty. Formal compliance with the rule is no longer sufficient; it is also appropriate not to divert it.

This dimension of misappropriation refers to the honest behavior expected of those who are constrained by the rule. In a negative formulation, good faith can be seen as "an absence of malicious intent" or "an absence of guilty intent.[21]"The subjective dimension raises questions of proof of intent. From this perspective, the existence of a psychological element appears to be the most difficult, if not impossible, to demonstrate in practice. It is probably appropriate, moreover, when it comes to the law requiring an application of good faith, to set aside any psychological dimension in order to focus solely on the moral element. The fact that the President waited 6 months to appoint the Prime Minister constitutes a lack of respect for good faith, with regard to the moral dimension alone, without there being any need to identify a psychological element, namely malicious intent. It matters little whether the President's choice is based on an honest or dishonest intention; what poses a problem is the length of time he took to appoint the Prime Minister. The behavior is decisive, not the intention. This difficulty having been set aside, another remains, just as decisive: what are the behaviors that reflect a dishonest attitude? It is useless here to develop with words other than that of honesty, which would only shift the problem of identifying what materializes good faith: loyalty, "qualified loyalty[22]", "legitimate trust[23]", fidelity, sincerity…[24] It seems however necessary to

[20] In this sense, see the analysis by Kelsen (1951), p. 89. On this subject, see Kolb (2017), p. 40.

[21] Roland, Boyer (1999), pp. 70 and 72.

[22] Kolb (2017), p. 30.

[23] *Ibid.*

[24] For E. Zoller, "good faith is […] a moral quality. To be in good faith is to demonstrate a loyal, honest spirit; it is to be faithful to one's word; it is to keep promises. Understood in this way, good faith opposes fraud and deceit; it excludes any malicious intent" (Zoller 2003, p. 143).

extend the reflection and to categorize in an objective manner the situations in constitutional law likely to be covered by good faith.

2.2 *Objectivization of the Meaning Through more Precise Generic Behaviors*

To escape the subjectivity of the approach linked to the assessment of honest behavior, it is possible to identify three generic categories of behaviors likely to concretely affect this requirement: immediate personal benefit, distortion or misappropriation of the normative system and abuse of rights.

Immediate personal benefit reflects what others have described as the instrumentalization of the Constitution.[25] While the rule is intended to be general, the holder of power mobilizes the rule not only in the context of his function but for his personal benefit. The action of power is guided not by the function but by the personal interest of its holder. The application of the rule is personalized, it does not refer to the general exercise of the function. The most significant example of this situation lies in the constitutional revisions initiated to allow the holder of a function to remain in power, for example, by modifying clauses limiting mandates. The rule is modified for the immediate and personal benefit of the future candidate, who could not be so under the current Constitution and not for the general interest of the office. The benefit is indeed personal and immediate. In our example, we assume that the constitutional revision is regular, but that it reflects a dishonest exercise of power. In a manner that is completely opposite to the example of the personalized constitutional revision, it is appropriate here to mention the constitutional revision of September 24, 2000 in France which institutes the 5-year term, thus reducing the mandate of the President of the Republic from 7 to 5 years. This constitutional revision is made at the initiative of the Head of State, Jacques Chirac, on the occasion of what is then only his first term, and it will apply to him for his second term. There is no personalization of the constitutional revision here while it is potentially unfavorable to its instigator from the perspective of the duration of the exercise of his second term.

The concept of "*dénaturation*" (*distortion*) or "*détournement*" (*misuse*) of the normative system refers to the general equilibrium that can be drawn from a constitutional system, either based on its general values (in the first case) or based on the system's norms (in the second). The approach is not entirely subjective; it does not refer to the spirit of the system, nor to its purpose or object according to a constructive functional logic, but rather to more objective balances regarding the general values of the system (*distortion*) or the behaviors allowed, prohibited, or required as resulting from the entire set of norms within the legal system (*misuse*).

[25] See Diop and Robles (2025).

From the angle of *misuse*, an appointment of the Prime Minister 6 months after the election of the National Assembly affects the balance of the normative system of the Fifth Republic: it is no longer possible to submit bills, draft finance and social security financing laws, the government can no longer intervene in the legislative procedure… The incriminated behavior blocks the normative system as a whole. The same would apply if the President appointed a Prime Minister from a parliamentary minority. Of course, the President has no obligation regarding the political origin of the Prime Minister, but if he does not appoint a Prime Minister supported by a parliamentary majority, the latter could not remain in place and, a fortiori, govern. Such regular behavior would nevertheless affect the entire normative structure in its very possibility of functioning.

More subjectively, with the *distortion*, the general values to which legal systems are attached, when they are formalized by the Constitution, can also constitute markers of the challenge to the normative system. In France, according to Article 1 of the Constitution, the Republic is indivisible, secular, democratic and social. Anything that would affect one of these qualifiers, without being irregular, could constitute an application of the Constitution in bad faith. We can also think of Article 20 of the German Basic Law which defines Germany as a federal, democratic and social state. These qualifiers are removed from the competence of the power of constitutional revision by virtue of Article 79 of this same Basic Law. In addition, the forfeiture of fundamental rights, as captured by Article 18 of the German Basic Law, is part of this logic while this forfeiture is subordinate to the abusive exercise of certain freedoms in order to "combat the free democratic bases order". The use of fundamental rights is regular but considered abusive because it aims to distort the values of the system.

Abuse of rights refers to a better-known concept even if it receives variable definitions.[26] The general idea that can be retained from this concept is that it prohibits one from being able to claim a right because this claim would not have as its object the benefit of the exercise of this right, but exclusively that of limiting the exercise of rights or freedoms recognized to others. The use of individual rights is only there to limit the exercise of the rights and freedoms of others. Hence the idea that we often find of fraudulent intent, of the intention to harm, in abuse of rights. In its reference judgment,[27] the Court of Cassation uses three elements to establish the existence of an abuse of rights: the usefulness of the use of the right for the person claiming it, the harmful nature of the use with regard to third parties and the absence of protection of a legitimate interest in the use. Article 55 of the Portuguese Constitution requires, to identify an abuse of rights, the absence of good faith and the case of violation of the rights and freedoms of other beneficiaries. The European Convention on Human Rights, in its Article 17, distinguishes two situations: the destruction of rights and freedoms and the limitation of the rights of third parties beyond what is permitted by the text, in other words when the use of the right results

[26] See in particular: Eck (2010); Guilbert (2023); Kohl (2024); Lemey (2021); Markovitch (1936).

[27] Cass., req., 3 août 1915, *Coquerel contre Clément-Bayard*, n° 00–02378.

in disregarding other rights and freedoms as guaranteed by the Constitution. The logic pursued by the Convention is objective in this second element. If the use of a right or freedom affects another right or freedom beyond what is permitted by the text of the Convention, it constitutes an abuse of rights. The delimitation is objective: an abuse of rights is the use of a right or freedom by a holder that leads to affecting another right or freedom of a third party beyond the limits authorized by the law. The abuse of rights is thus constituted by an irregular infringement, following the exercise of a right or freedom, of other rights and freedoms that are also constitutionally protected.

These three generic categories seem to allow a certain objectivization of good faith. They must, however, undergo the test of their practical application.

3 A Concrete Subjective Test of the Meaning of Good Faith in the Reading of Institutional Practices

The proposed conceptualization of good faith must be tested against its practical application. From this perspective, one can only observe the limitations that the mobilization of good faith in constitutional law encounters. Good faith appears to be difficult to mobilize objectively in what we will qualify as extreme cases (3.1). This raises the question of the subjectivity of the assessment by the actors of constitutional law, as well as the establishment of mechanisms to sanction the respect of good faith, which may lead to a transfer of the political subjectivity of the organs of power to the judge (3.2), which can prove to be a dangerous transfer of power from the political power to the jurisdictional power.

3.1 Extreme Cases

The previously described attempt to objectivize behaviors related to good faith encounters practical difficulties that mark the return of subjectivity in the concrete assessment of such behaviors. The testing of various attempts at objectivization through the generic value of honest behavior, as well as the three generic categories of behaviors – namely, immediate personal benefit, distortion or misuse of the normative system, and abuse of rights – particularly illustrates this in extreme cases. Therefore, it is essential to identify two main extreme cases from which the reflection will be conducted.

The first refers to a situation encountered in French positive law, which involved altering the electoral system from a majority vote to a proportional vote before new legislative elections, which the majority knew they would lose, in order to mitigate the foreseeable defeat. The second is more general, while finding illustrations in American positive law. It pertains to the appointment by the head of state of members of a constitutional court or a supreme court, tasked with centralizing judgments of constitutional regularity of the law, who share the same values as the appointing authority.

In both cases, the honesty of the behaviors can be questioned, as can the three proposed generic situations. From the perspective of honest behavior, both extreme cases raise questions. If one considers that the goal of any political party, as well as any individual holding a political office, is to gain power, maintain it, and implement the policies for which they were elected – this precisely constitutes the logic of political maneuvering – then the two identified cases appear as methods of governance. Mitigating a political defeat to preserve one's majority in the National Assembly is not a means of maintaining power within the limits of legal respect? Appointing a judge who shares the same values as the appointing authority does not enable the latter to pursue the policies for which they were elected with fewer obstacles?

Certainly, the judge is merely the guarantor of the respect of the law, but this law, particularly constitutional law, offers judges a margin of appreciation due to its indeterminacy. Appointing a judge who upholds the values of the power allows that power to benefit from the margin of appreciation granted by constitutional law in a manner favorable to its policies. In both cases, the boundary between political opportunity and the honest nature of the behavior remains blurred.

Regarding immediate personal benefit, despite the precautions taken to clarify, as best as possible, the behaviors likely to fulfill this criterion, concrete assessment remains difficult. Is it, more specifically, in the two cases considered a personal benefit or a benefit for the elected parliamentary majority? It is not so much a matter of personal exercise of power, but rather a way of governing by obtaining a majority in the National Assembly or by appointing judges in favor of a given policy.

The difficulty identified with this first criterion still needs to be tested based on a range of behaviors that a head of state might exhibit when, although unable to run for office under positive law, he would modify that law to enable such a run. The assessment certainly seems obvious in the case of a president who would amend the Constitution to be able to stand for re-election immediately after it is prohibited by the Constitution. The case seems slightly more delicate for a president who, while having initiated the revision, would not immediately run for a new term but would do so later. Even more subtle, as occurred in France, is the case of a president who would initiate an organic law reversing the order of parliamentary and presidential elections to have the latter precede the former, a reversal from which he would derive a real benefit, as it would allow him to consolidate his grip on Parliament and capture the parliamentary majority for his own benefit, without it having been truly anticipated or desired by him. Depending on the means mobilized, the identification of personal benefit is therefore not always evident.

Regarding the distortion or misuse of the normative system, assessment can also be difficult. It first requires establishing "values inspiring the normative system" to which the behavior of the perpetrator of the behavior or act could be related, which is not always evident from reading various Constitutions, even when the realization of these values offers a wide margin for interpretation. In the two benchmarks we have considered, can we, for example, argue that the democratic character of the Republic, enshrined in Article 1 of the Constitution, is affected by a change in the electoral system? As long as the people have the final say, the democratic demand is preserved. Does the appointment of a judge who defends the values of the one who appointed him pose difficulties in terms of guaranteeing rights, without which, according to Article 16 of the Declaration of the Rights of Man, there is no Constitution? The guarantee of rights does not seem affected as long as the judge, as we have assumed, only intervenes within the margin of appreciation allowed by constitutional norms, in the indeterminate part they offer to power. From the perspective of affecting the system's norms, neither of the two situations seems to affect them. The change in the electoral mode, like a personal appointment of a judge, does not hinder the functioning of the normative system; at most, they affect its general orientation.

With the third case considered, the abuse of rights, the same difficulties arise. In the first situation, with the change in the electoral mode, one could see a reduction in the rights of the opposition to access power. Is there, however, an abuse? There is no right to access power; it is for the people to decide. Mitigating the possible effects of an alternation does not affect the possible existence of an alternation, as was the case in 1986 with François Mitterrand's change to the voting system. The presidential majority lost the elections, and proportional voting merely mitigated the extent of the defeat. With the personal appointment of a judge, it is difficult to identify a right benefiting third parties that would be affected. In fact, despite the desire to identify objective elements for assessing good faith and generic categories, testing these generic categories reveals a highly subjective moral assessment. It can moreover be assumed that, with the exception of a few clear situations allowing the identification of bad faith in the exercise of power, such as amending the Constitution to remain in power, subject to the reservations already mentioned, most situations liable to fall under the absence of good faith remain highly debatable.

3.2 Subjectivity

In borderline cases, the assessment of good faith refers to a considerable subjectivity on the part of the evaluator of the behavior. Regularity, by requiring the observance of good faith, indirectly incorporates a question of legitimacy and presents a dimension related to political opportunity. In this context, the question that may arise is what mechanisms are capable of sanctioning such behaviors. Again, the concrete implementation of the sanction for the respect of good faith raises difficulties.

Going beyond the respect for mere constitutional regularity, evaluated through the objective determination of the meaning of constitutional statements,[28] tends to integrate a dimension of legitimacy, even political opportunity, into the assessment of the behaviors of political bodies. As we have seen, good faith necessarily implies, in practice, a degree of subjectivity that may, in borderline cases, lead to the assessment of the political opportunity of a behavior.

In such a context, the issue of procedures and especially the body responsible for sanctioning the respect for good faith comes into question. Is it within the judge's role, as a third party to the parties in a dispute tasked with resolving it based on the law, to incorporate elements of political opportunity into their assessment? This precisely marks the boundary between the political aspect, and therefore the opportunity of choices, and the law, namely the respect for the general rules that bind those choices. While the first dimension pertains to the creator of the norms, the second belongs to the one who controls the regularity of their actions in light of superior norms. We are familiar with the formula of the Constitutional Council, which states that "the Constitutional Council does not have a general power of appreciation and decision of the same nature as that of Parliament."[29] The integration of good faith into regularity tends to challenge this boundary by incorporating a dimension of political opportunity into constitutional judgment. It may disrupt the relationships between constitutional bodies by generating, in choices that pertain to political opportunity, a certain subordination of the political to the judicial, as the latter assesses the political opportunity of the former's behavior.

Lastly, it may be useful to illustrate these difficulties through the decision of the Constitutional Council regarding the pension reform,[30] by considering how it applied the principle of clarity and budgetary sincerity. The elasticity of this constitutional requirement is such that the constitutional judge, when faced with the same behaviors, may justifiably accept either the irregularity or the regularity of the behavior. The boundary is so blurred that the sanction thus refers to political opportunity. In the politically problematic context in which the pension reform was

---

[28] We assume here that it is possible to "know" the objective meaning of a statement, regardless of the degree of indeterminacy of the statement. The meaning can be established even if it reveals a wide margin of discretion concerning behaviors that are permitted, prohibited, or made mandatory by the norm. When Article 11 of the Declaration of the Rights of Man and of the Citizen allows for a limitation of the freedom of communication only in cases of "abuse" in the exercise of this freedom, it is possible to establish an objective meaning of the term "abuse," namely, a behavior that exceeds the average of tolerated behaviors, even though, when concretely identifying a behavior that would fall under this definition, it is always possible to objectively discuss what constitutes or does not constitute abuse.

[29] For a recent illustration: CC, n° 2024-1115 QPC, 13 décembre 2024, *M. Olivier D. [Plafonnement de la déductibilité de la contribution sociale généralisée acquittée au titre de certaines plus-values mobilières]*, § 14.

[30] CC, n° 2023–849 DC, 14 avril 2023, *Loi de financement rectificative de la sécurité sociale pour 2023.*

introduced, with unprecedented union mobilization[31] and clear public hostility toward the reform,[32] the decision to either censor or not censor the government's actions would align the judge with either the people or the government. The situation thus reveals where the constitutional judge stands whether as a defender of the people or a protector of social order.

This blurred boundary becomes apparent upon reading the decision. The complaints related to the violation of the clarity and sincerity requirements of parliamentary debate and the right to amend are numerous: the procedure followed by the National Assembly to select the motion to submit the bill to referendum, the government's opposition to the examination of certain sub-amendments not submitted to the committee examining the substance of the bill, the use of the blocked vote, the closure of debates, the prioritization of certain amendments, the examination of the admissibility of amendments, the documents attached to the bill, 40 paragraphs of the decision are dedicated to these points. All of these complaints demonstrate that the government significantly and repeatedly used its various powers to control the legislative process. Under each complaint, the constitutional judge's assessment is measured by the description of the government's actions in question, and each of these complaints is rejected. At most, we can note a harsh description of the government's behavior, yet the complaint is not upheld: "The fact that certain ministers may have made initially incorrect estimates regarding the amount of pensions to be paid to certain categories of insured individuals, during their speeches in the National Assembly and in the media, does not affect the procedure for adopting the law referred, since these estimates were open to debate."[33] Therefore, the lies told by some ministers have no impact on the legislative process as long as the issue surrounding the lie was discussed. Bad faith is forgiven as long as it leads to parliamentary deliberation.

More than the discussion of each individual complaint, it is perhaps the overall one – the cumulative application of several procedures provided by the Constitution and the regulations of the assemblies that deserves particular attention. It raises a question of threshold, abuse, honest behavior, and therefore good faith on the part of the government in exercising its powers to control the parliamentary procedure. The applicants' argument is as follows: "While the use of each of the procedures implemented in this case to expedite the adoption of the referred law could be seen as compliant with the Constitution, their cumulative use had the effect of hindering

[31] Ten strike call days were organized, not including spontaneous gatherings (January 19, January 31, February 7, February 11, February 16, March 7, March 8 and 9, March 15, March 16, March 23, and March 28, 2023), gathering millions of people in the streets.

[32] According to an IFOP poll for the *Journal du Dimanche* on March 5, 2023, 68% of French people are against the pension reform, 74% of those under 35, and 85% in the public sector (source).

According to an Elabe poll for BFM TV on March 20, 2023, 68% of French people are against the reform, 68% are in favor of adopting a motion of censure, 65% approve of the mobilization, 58% support the blockade, 67% want the mobilization to continue, and 68% of French people believe the reform will be maintained (https://elabe.fr/reforme-retraites-2023-10/)

[33] CC, n° 2023–849 DC, 14 avril 2023, *Loi de financement rectificative de la sécurité sociale pour 2023, préc.*, § 65.

the full exercise of the right of amendment by parliamentarians, in violation of the requirements of clarity and sincerity in parliamentary debate."[34]

It is indeed undeniable that the government made use of all available means, not only to ultimately control the adoption of the pension reform law by inserting it into an organic law concerning the financing of social security, which increases the government's control over the legislative process,[35] but also to shorten parliamentary deliberation. This forceful approach is all the more glaring as it responds to strong political opposition within the National Assembly, unfavorable public opinion, and unprecedented social movements. These objective elements, however, did not lead the Constitutional Council to censor the cumulative use of procedural control instruments by the government. Its response is significant: "While the combined use of the procedures implemented was unusual, in response to the conditions of the debate, it did not result in the legislative procedure being contrary to the Constitution."[36] The unusual nature is linked to the conditions of the debate, thus it is the parliamentary circumstances that explain this unusual use. The government reacts, regardless of the provocation posed by a desire to reform without consulting social partners and pushing ahead in an expedited manner before Parliament. The Constitutional Council sided with the government, not Parliament or the people.

The constitutional judge could, however, just as well have censored the text without it appearing as a political censorship. Ultimately, it positioned itself from the perspective of political opportunity, to limit its control, in the face of a generic requirement of positive law for the government to use in good faith the tools at its disposal in the conduct of the parliamentary process.

---

[34] *Loc. cit.*, § 67.

[35] There are several advantages for the government in adopting a social security financing law procedure compared to the ordinary legislative procedure: there is no limitation on the use of Article 49(3), which allows the government to take responsibility for the vote on a text (this can only be used once per session for an ordinary law); the examination before the Assembly focuses on the text as proposed by the government (Article 42 of the Constitution, and not on the text adopted by the committee examining the substance); the deposit of the text, the social security financing bill, is made first before the National Assembly (Article 39 of the Constitution, as the deposit cannot be freely made before either the National Assembly or the Senate); there is no 6-week delay between the deposit and the discussion in the first reading before the first assembly, and no 4-week delay before the other assembly between transmission and discussion (Article 42 of the Constitution); finally, if the National Assembly has not decided within 20 days of the deposit, the government refers the matter to the Senate, which must rule within 15 days (Article 47–1 of the Constitution), and the joint committee may be convened after the first reading if there is no agreement (Article 45 of the Constitution).

[36] CC, n° 2023–849 DC, 14 avril 2023, *Loi de financement rectificative de la sécurité sociale pour 2023*, *préc.*, § 70.

4 Conclusion

While it is possible to establish an objective meaning for the requirement of good faith, the practical implementation of this requirement in constitutional law reveals too much uncertainty and subjectivity. It therefore does not seem entirely convincing to supplement, in positive law, the requirement of formal regularity with an obligation of good faith application. In a democratic system, it is probably up to the voters, ultimately, to sanction the lack of good faith in the practices of political actors. The assessment of political opportunity is likely too subjective to entrust it exclusively to anyone other than the source of power in a democratic system, that is, the people.

References

Barque F (2009) La sincérité de l'action publique. Son contrôle par les juges constitutionnel et administratif. Dissertation, Atelier national de reproduction des thèses, Université de Lille 3, Lille-thèses

Brunessen B (2011) L'exigence de clarté et de sincérité du débat parlementaire. Étude sur un concept régulateur de la procédure législative sous la Ve République. RDP 2:431 et ss

Cordeiro M (1996) La bonne foi à la fin du vingtième siècle. RDUS 26:225–245

Cornu G (1996) Vocabulaire Juridique. Association Henri Capitant, 5th edn. PUF, Paris

Diop S, Robles J (2025) La régularité de l'usage personnalisé du pouvoir. Le concept de normes constitutionnelles individualisées. In: Regards sur l'actualité juridique: les temps forts 2023/2024 - Journée des doctorants du 6 juin 2024, coll. Droits. Pouvoirs et Sociétés, PUAM. (in press)

Dixon R, Landau D (2021) Abusive constitutional borrowing: legal globalization and the subversion of liberal democracy. Oxford University Press, Oxford

Eck L (2010) L'abus de droit en droit constitutionnel. L'Harmattan, Logiques juridiques, Paris

Guilbert J (2023) Essai sur le concept d'abus de droit fondamental. LGDJ, Bibliothèque constitutionnelle et de science politique 167

Kelsen H (1951) The law of the United Nations. Stevens and Sons Limited, London

Kelsen H (1953) Qu'est-ce que la justice ? and (1960) Droit et morale. Preface by Lasserre V (2022). Markus Haller, Geneva

Kohl B (2024) L'abus de droit. Anthemis, Commission Université-Palais, Limal

Kolb R (2017) Good faith in international law. Hart Publishing, Oxford

Landau D (2013) Abusive constitutionalism. Univ Calif Davis Law Rev 47:189–260

Lefevbre B (1996) La bonne foi notion protéiforme. RDUS 26(2):321–354

Lemey M (2021) L'abus de droit en droit international public. LGDJ, Bibliothèque de droit international et de l'Union européenne 135

Levinson S (2021) Assessing "abusive constitutionalism" in a complex political universe. Can J Comp Contemp Law 7:14–21

Magnon X (2011) La loyauté : aspects institutionnels. In: Picod F, Sousse F (eds) Dossier spécial: La loyauté en droit de l'Union européenne. RAE 2, pp 245–251

Markovitch M (1936) La théorie de l'abus des droits en droit comparé. Dissertation, Lyon

Petrov J (2024) How to detect abusive constitutional practices. Eur Const Law Rev 20(2):191–221

Roland H, Boyer L (1999) Adages du droit français, 4th edn. Litec

Zoller E (2003) Bonne foi. In: Alland D, Rials S (eds) Dictionnaire de la culture juridique. Lamy-PUF, p 143

Good Faith in German Constitutional Law

Ann Kathrin Schnieders and Simon Strickrodt

Abstract Does the concept of good faith exist in German constitutional law? The following essay aims to clarify this. It is therefore dedicated to the origin of the concept in public law and attempts to discuss connecting factors for the legal principle of good faith (Treu und Glauben) on both a horizontal and vertical level. Using the examples of loyalty to the federal government (Bundestreue) and loyalty to the Constitution (Verfassungsorgantreue), it is shown why the use of a general legal principle, especially in constitutional law, carries more dangers than benefits, and why recourse to constitutional standards may be the only sensible way forward.

1 Introduction

The principle of good faith is a central component of German private law. Constitutional law, on the other hand, has no equivalent that can be derived directly from the constitutional text. Nevertheless, various attempts have been made over the decades to derive duties of good faith and loyalty as legal concepts in the constitutional state. The aim of this article is to shed light on the conceptual origins, to reduce the various existing concepts to a common denominator and, finally, to examine the question of the necessity of a good faith principle in constitutional law.

A. K. Schnieders · S. Strickrodt (✉)
Faculty of Law and Economics, University of Bonn, Bonn, Germany
e-mail: schnieders@uni-bonn.de; strickrodt@uni-bonn.de

J. Podkowik et al. (eds.), *Gleams of Good Faith in Constitutional Law*, Ius Gentium: Comparative Perspectives on Law and Justice 132,
https://doi.org/10.1007/978-3-032-06486-8_7

2 Good Faith as a Category of Constitutional Law?

General principles of law are an expression and reflection of the modern legislative state.[1] They can be described as the general principles and guiding ideas that unite and internally hold together the standardized legal principles, which the legislator has not always incorporated into a specific legal norm.[2] Thus, at all levels of the legal system and in all areas of law, they have the role of reflecting fundamental values and acting as fundamental norms of legal ethics.[3] Their impact and their general character serve several functions: Filling gaps, harmonizing the law, aiding argumentation and, finally, optimizing in the case of conflicting interests.[4] This is why it is also referred to as "dynamic law".[5]

The principle of "good faith" (Treu und Glauben) is a fundamental legal principle that, together with "good morals" (Gute Sitten), has sparked lively debate in legal theory and practice.[6] Good faith has its roots in Roman law, where it was known as "bona fides" and "aequitas" (Schubert 2022, BGB § 242 Rn. 32). The principle had two effects: It established the law and it controlled and supplemented the content of legal relationships and the interpretation of contracts (Schubert 2022, BGB § 242 Rn. 32). The German Civil Code (BGB) is based on this in § 157, 242 BGB. It transfers the old commercial custom from Roman law to German civil law as follows: The debtor is required to perform in a manner that is in accordance with the standards of good faith and custom (*Der Schuldner ist verpflichtet, die Leistung so zu bewirken, wie Treu und Glauben mit Rücksicht auf die Verkehrssitte es erfordern.*). Everyone must act in good faith when exercising their rights and obligations. There must also be an appropriate relationship of trust between the contracting parties (Krebs 2021, BGB § 242 Rn. 1). In civil law, the general principle of law is a cornerstone of judicial development[7]. It can therefore be stated that the general legal principle of good faith in civil law has found a "special expression" in written law[8] and thus is firmly established in this legal field. The question now arises as to how far this principle has been incorporated into public law, and in particular, whether constitutional law has adopted it.

This issue was highly controversial in public law literature, but has been clarified[9]. In a landmark decision on the revaluation of public law claims from 1926, the civil court (Reichsgericht) unequivocally stated that the principle of good faith applies across all areas of law, irrespective of its legal standardization (RGZ 113,

[1] Barczak (2021), p. 1.

[2] Ibidem, 2.

[3] Ibidem.

[4] Ibidem.

[5] Baumann (1952), p. 1.

[6] Ibidem, 18.

[7] Sutschet (2024).

[8] Bauer (1992), p. 245.

[9] Baumann (1952), p. 51; Sutschet (2024).

24). Other courts built on this, and the Hamburg Administrative Court ruled that the principle of good faith was the expression of a general moral law that applied without further ado in public law.[10] As a result, the principle's applicability in public law was significantly influenced by case law.[11] The literature largely accepted and assumed its validity. *Smend* was the first to identify the existence of unwritten constitutional law in the monarchical federal state and to establish the legitimacy of the principle of good faith in public law.[12] The theory of integration, developed by him, is based on one unwavering principle: loyal cooperation. This is the only way to achieve state unity and cooperation.[13] *Heller's* work and subsequent literature both attest to this idea.[14]

It is important to note that the general legal principle of good faith, which in German law cannot be used synonymously with the concept of "guter Glaube" (Section 932 (1) sentence 1 HS. 2 and (2) BGB), has therefore also gained significance in constitutional law over 100 years ago. The legal principle in public law is valid and accepted by literature as well as case law.

3 Good Faith Conceived Vertically: Federal Loyalty (Bundestreue) as Incorporation of the Principle of Good Faith?

The principle of loyalty to the federal government (Bundestreue) has always been closely linked to the concept of good faith. It has shaped the relationship between the federal government and the federal states in the German constitutional system from the very beginning and has since been a significant factor.

The first duties of loyalty are clearly defined by *Smend*. In his 1916 treatise on unwritten constitutional law in the monarchical federal state, he established the legal rediscovery of the doctrine of unwritten constitutional law.[15] He highlighted the distinctive nature of the imperial constitution at that time, which encompassed constitutional law that had either not been formally documented or had been documented in a particularly ambiguous manner.[16] *Smend* argued in favor of supplementing constitutional law with unwritten principles, which he initially saw as being tailored only and exclusively to the monarchical federal state. However, he later

---

[10] Hamburgisches Verwaltungsgericht, JW 1927, S. 2948 Nr. 4.

[11] BVerwGE 19, 188, 190 = VerwRspr. 1966, S. 292; BVerwGE 35, 159, 162 = NJW 1970, S. 1564; BVerfGE 32, 305, 308.

[12] Smend (1968), p. 51.

[13] Lorz (2001), p. 36.

[14] Heller (1963), p. 228.

[15] Smend (1968), p. 40.

[16] Schröcker (1966), p. 137.

abandoned this restriction to monarchical federal state law.[17] He outlined the peculiarities of the imperial constitution and the characteristics of the principle of Bundestreue. He made it clear that the rights of the individual states vis-à-vis the empire and the duties and restrictions of the individual states vis-à-vis the imperial state were of particular importance.[18] In the turbulent years that followed his publication, unwritten constitutional law was clearly rendered ineffective and insignificant as the republic gave way to dictatorship. It is therefore surprising that from the very beginning of its existence, the Federal Constitutional Court (Bundesverfassungsgericht) took up the doctrine developed at the time in its established case law and based its decisions on the principle of Bundestreue in the relationship between the federal government and the federal states. In a decision from 1961, for example, the Bundesverfassungsgericht explicitly referred back to *Smend's* approach and stated:

> The entire constitutional relationship between the German federal state and its constituent parts, as well as the constitutional relationship between the constituent parts, is governed by the unwritten constitutional principle of the reciprocal duty of the Federation and the Länder to behave in a manner that is friendly to the Federation.[19]

It also refers to various early decisions that further define the principle of Bundestreue and provide it with a framework. The Bundesverfassungsgericht has made it clear that the constitutional principle arises in a number of situations. For instance, when a law requires cooperation between the federal government and the federal states, it establishes an increased duty to cooperate between the parties involved.[20] Similarly, when the exercise of legislative powers affects the area of the federal states, the state legislature must take into account the interests of the federal government or the other federal states.[21] Furthermore, the court has established a significant number of specific legal obligations that extend beyond the constitutional obligations explicitly outlined in the federal constitution.[22] The constitutional literature has followed the Bundesverfassungsgericht's case law and recognized the principle of Bundestreue as an important component of the federal order. Different conceptual formulations (federal-friendly conduct, federal bona fides, federal loyalty requirement, etc.[23]) have been used to describe this principle over time.[24] According to *Sauer*, the necessity of such a concept could hardly be disputed. The interdependence of the federal government and the federal states due to the federal structure posed a clear and present danger of mutual blockades or inhibitions that could and would thwart effective

---

[17] Ibidem, 138.

[18] Smend (1968), pp. 40, 45.

[19] BVerfGE 12, 205, 254.

[20] BVerfGE 1, 299, 315.

[21] BVerfGE 4, 115, 140.

[22] BVerfGE 1, 117, 131; 6, 309, 328 u. 361 f.; 8, 122, 138.

[23] Bauer (1992), p. 254.

[24] Sauer (2008), p. 374.

cooperation.[25] The principle of Bundestreue should be upheld for "the benefit of national cohesion".[26] It is the duty of the federal government and the federal states to behave in a considerate and cooperative manner. This is about more than just the exercise of constitutionally delegated powers. It is about the cooperation of the two players in a federal multi-level system.[27]

However, the existing necessity of federal loyalty for mutual cooperation does not address its normative origin. It is therefore crucial to determine the source of the principle of Bundestreue, a question that has been particularly important in German public law literature.

It is clear from an examination of both the Weimar Constitution (Weimarer Reichsverfassung) and the Constitution (Grundgesetz) that there is no explicit mention of the principle of Bundestreue. The Bundesverfassungsgericht states that the essence of the federalist principle, along with other principles, determines the character of the Federal Republic of Germany.[28] In contrast, various derivation approaches have emerged in the literature.[29]

There are two distinct approaches to deriving the principle: one from general legal principles, and another starting with the original written principles themselves. On the one hand Bundestreue is indisputably linked to good faith. This principle provides a compelling legal foundation, and it can be argued that Bundestreue is best understood as a specific manifestation of the overarching legal principle.[30] *Bauer's* work on Bundestreue is a primary source of this view, which goes back to the unwritten constitutional law found by *Smend* in the monarchical federal state. The principle of good faith is a general principle of law that is valid in all areas of law and is independent of (partial) codification.[31] All public law is governed by this principle, which can be given a specific character when considered in conjunction with the express provisions of the Basic Law.[32]

However, on the other hand, this derivation is negated and Bundestreue is linked to the principle of the federal state in Article 20 para. 1 GG.[33] *Isensee* is aware that the concept of Bundestreue "can only be determined from the positive legal context of the Basic Law, by taking into account the relevant individual norms".[34]

In this respect, he asserts that there is no need to refer back to a general legal principle from which other principles should also arise.

---

[25] Ibidem, 375.

[26] Ibidem.

[27] Ibidem, 374.

[28] BverfGE 1, 299, 315.

[29] Sauer (2008), p. 376.

[30] Bauer (1992), pp. 243–253.

[31] Ibidem, 245.

[32] Ibidem, 252.

[33] Isensee (2001), p. 730.

[34] Ibidem.

This normative derivation appears to make sense for several reasons. The principle of Treu und Glauben is primarily tailored to relationships under private law, where it acts as a regulatory between two equal parties. Therefore, as long as a more concrete derivation can be found, which can also be linked to normative principles, recourse to a general legal principle is superfluous and even carries the risk of conflicts being inappropriately legalized. Furthermore, the nature of general legal principles speaks in favor that the principle of Bundestreue cannot be derived from them. General principles of law are broadly defined, vague, and indeterminate.[35] This means that they are left to the discretion of the person applying the law. Therefore, an interpretation of the Constitution renders recourse to general legal principles unnecessary here.

The differentiated structure of tasks and competences expressed in Art. 20 para. 1 GG and Art. 83 ff. GG require cooperation between the federal and state governments in the interests of the state as a whole.[36] From a logical point of view, pro-federal conduct is therefore not only laid down in Art. 20 para. 1 GG in terms of positive law, but is also incorporated in the constitution and ultimately presupposed.

To return to the initial question: The Bundestreue, which is enshrined in the German constitution, is not an incorporation of the principle of good faith, but an original legal principle that was shaped by the literature, but in particular by the early case law of the Bundesverfassungsgericht.

4 Good Faith in the Horizontal Dimension

While the concept of Bundestreue has long been a significant factor in the relationship between the federal government and the federal states, the question of duties of loyalty in the horizontal relationship between the constitutional bodies has played a subordinate role for a long time.[37] The concept of Bundestreue is limited to the federal structure.[38] However, the question of unwritten constitutional requirements for the exercise of competences between the constitutional bodies with equal rights is obvious, as there is a very substantial potential for conflict in a constitutional state characterized by the separation of powers.

The legal literature has developed requirements for the conduct of state bodies towards each other under various topoi. For example, the concept of Bundestreue was not interpreted as an isolated concept. Rather, it was understood as an expression of a general principle of loyalty that encompasses the entire state structure and therefore enables the derivation of corresponding duties of conduct at the horizontal

[35] Bauer (1992), p. 251.

[36] Grzeszick, 2024, GG Art. 20 Rn. 132; Sommermann, 2024, GG Art. 20 Rn. 45.

[37] Poscher (2021), § 3 Rn. 124; Schenke (1977), p. 22.

[38] Lorz (2001), p. 34.

level.[39] Similar approaches can be found under the concepts of inter-organ respect[40] and inter-organ loyalty[41] as well as a general requirement of consideration.[42] The numerous overlaps make it even more challenging to differentiate between these concepts.[43]

Schenke's 1977 monograph on the duties of loyalty between federal bodies (Verfassungsorgantreue) is the central text on this subject.[44] The choice of term was already aimed at expressing the conceptual connection with the principle of Bundestreue.[45] Verfassungsorgantreue is also known as the "younger sister of Bundestreue".[46] *Schenke's* goal was not to create an entirely new concept of constitutional law. Rather, he sought to synthesize a multitude of existing approaches to describing the obligations of constitutional bodies in their mutual dealings.[47] To prevent state disintegration, for example through subversive behavior by individual constitutional bodies, *Schenke* formulates a wide variety of applications in which he summarizes unwritten duties of loyalty, consideration, and fidelity under the concept of the Verfassungsorgantreue.[48] The sheer diversity of potential duties of loyalty, which can only be determined on a case-by-case basis, makes it even more challenging to attempt an abstract definition of the Verfassungsorgantreue.[49]

The Bundesverfassungsgericht also laid the foundations for a corresponding concept immediately after its constitution. This was prompted by the debate on the status of the Constitutional Court, whose position in the structure of the young Federal Republic had not yet been consolidated.[50] In its non-procedural memorandum, the Bundesverfassungsgericht stated the following:

> However, it is clear that the coordination of the constitutional bodies is not limited to their mutual dependence within the framework of the constitution. It is legally untenable to assume that the relationship between the constitutional bodies is governed by a legal vacuum in which only the good will of the constitutional bodies and the rules of political morality matter. The coordination of the constitutional bodies requires, as a matter of course, that they cooperate harmoniously in the exercise of their constitutional activity and refrain from anything that could damage the reputation of the other constitutional bodies and thus jeopardize the constitution itself. A constitutional body violates its constitutional obligations if, based on its own authority, it disparages another constitutional body in

[39] Kloepfer (1974), p. 52; Kaufmann (1966), p. 14.

[40] Lorz (2001); Schulze-Fielietz (1997), p. 27.

[41] Schneider (1970), p. 422.

[42] Lepa (1974), p. 403.

[43] Sommermann, GG Art. 20 Rn. 225.

[44] Schenke (1977).

[45] Ibidem, 20.

[46] Poscher (2021), § 3 Rn. 124.

[47] Schenke (1977), p. 19.

[48] Ibidem, 53.

[49] Lorz (2001), p. 41.

[50] Masing (2021), § 15 Rn. 37.

> public. This includes words and actions that show a lack of respect for the other constitutional body. Every constitutional body has a legal right to this respect.[51]

The Bundesverfassungsgericht was quick to view the exercise of its powers in a considerate manner, along with the prohibition of obstruction, as a legal obligation under the Constitution, not merely a matter of political style. In addition to the constitutionally determined order of competences, there is a general requirement of "harmonious cooperation", which must be observed in the exercise of competences in individual cases. The Bundesverfassungsgericht established the fundamental principles (not limited to the relationship between the federal government and the federal states) for duties of loyalty and fidelity in the constitutional state, paving the way for future literature to build upon. The court did not just position itself as a constitutional body. It also marked a denial of this position by other constitutional bodies as a violation of the constitution.

In subsequent case law, the Bundesverfassungsgericht has repeatedly used corresponding approaches to define the outer limits of the exercise of competences without going into any normative basis in greater depth. It recognizes the loyalty of a constitutional body (Organtreue) as an unwritten constitutional principle from which it derives a general requirement of consideration.[52] This allows the constitutional judges to have a sufficiently abstract catchword at their disposal that can be referred to in different contexts. In substance, the Bundesverfassungsgericht has also accepted the concept of Verfassungsorgantreue.[53]

While there has been considerable conceptual diversity over the years, there is broad agreement on the substance. In a constitutional state that recognizes the separation of powers as a fundamental principle, the ability of the state as a whole to function requires that the bodies obliged to act in the public interest do not use the powers conferred on them for extraneous purposes, for example to harm another body.[54]

The legislative process at federal level serves as an illustrative example of the need for cooperation between constitutional bodies. In addition to the legislature, the Bundesregierung, as the highest executive body, also has the right to initiate legislation (Art. 76 para. 1 GG). The Bundesrat is involved in the legislative process as the representative of the interests of the federal states. In the event of substantive concerns, the Bundesrat can request the appointment of a mediation committee (Art. 77 para. 2 GG). The entry into force of a law also presupposes that it has been signed by the Bundespräsident (Art. 82 para. 1 sentence 1 GG), who, according to the prevailing view, even has the right not to have to sign laws that are at least evidently unconstitutional.[55]

---

[51] JÖR N.F. 6 (1957), S. 194 (206 f.).

[52] BVerfGE 143, 101, 144; 90, 286, 337; 89, 155, 191; 45, 1, 39; 35, 193, 199.

[53] BVerfGE 134, 141, 201; 159, 26, 34 f.

[54] BVerfGE 1, 208, 248 f.; 3, 383, 393 f.; 4, 31, 36, 40; 6, 84, 92; 6, 104, 118 f.

[55] Butzer, 2024, Art. 82 Rn. 115 ff., 159.

It is clear that the fathers and mothers of the Basic Law (Grundgesetz) assumed cooperative collaboration in this interplay of powers.[56] This rules out fundamental obstruction by a state body.[57] From the structure of powers in the constitution itself, we can derive a general principle. It is – in *Schenke's* words:

> the necessary correlate of a state organization which, as a consequence of the doctrine of the separation of powers, has several constitutional bodies at the head of the state, each of which has equal rights in relation to the competence to which it is entitled […].[58]

This is a constitutional necessity whose derivation – the same applies to the principle of Bundestreue – does not require recourse to the principle of good faith.

Once we have established the principle of loyalty at the horizontal level of the state, we will examine a further development of this approach that has been widely overlooked in the literature to date – its applicability to intra-organizational relationships.[59]

The German constitutional system inevitably leads to a situation in which the bodies respectively the members of the bodies normally have a mutual interest in working together constructively, simply due to their political affinity. In the German parliamentary system of government, the Bundesregierung is dependent on a majority in the Bundestag – the possibility of a minority government (cf. Art. 63 para. 4 GG) has never been realized to date. All state governments currently include representatives of the same parties that govern at federal level. This political reality is far more effective at preventing obstruction of "one's own people" than any legal principle could ever be.

However, these regulating forces of political solidarity have no bearing when the exercise of authority concerns a political actor with whom no political cooperation exists and is not sought. While the government consisting of the Federal Chancellor (Bundeskanzler) and his ministers are united by the joint coalition, so that the concept of intra-governmental loyalty is likely to be of little relevance here, there is an increased risk of abusive exercise of competences towards the parliamentary opposition. In the history of the Federal Republic (Bundesrepublik), the entry of new political actors into the Bundestag has repeatedly caused conflicts, as its majority has also used its position of power to disadvantage the new political adversary – not necessarily in an illegal way – within the parliamentary structures.[60]

While these initial phenomena regarding the (last government composition 2021 – 2025) party "Alliance 90/The Greens" and the left wing "Party of Democratic Socialism" (later "The Left") have subsided with their establishment, the right wing "Alternative for Germany" (AfD) has been met with substantial and persistent rejection within the political landscape. The majority in the Bundestag reacted to this new political movement with changes to the rules of procedure of the Bundestag,

[56] Sachs, 2021, GG Art. 20 Rn. 82.

[57] Poscher (2021), § 3 Rn. 124.

[58] Schenke (1977), p. 27.

[59] Lorz, (2001), p. 92.

[60] BVerfGE 70, 324; 96, 264; 112, 118.

the partial refusal to elect its deputies to Bundestag offices, and wide-ranging political isolation.[61] The Bundestag's long-standing tradition of appointing the oldest member of parliament in terms of age to preside over the first constituent sitting of parliament is an obvious example of this.[62] In the 19th legislative period, this would have been a (controversial) representative of the Alternative for Germany, whereupon the Bundestag broke with tradition and now appoints the so-called "Alterspräsident" according to the length of parliamentary membership.[63]

In one of its first decisions, the Bundesverfassungsgericht established the principle of fair and loyal application of the Rules of Procedure (Geschäftsordnung) of the German Bundestag.[64] This is based on the assumption that an unfair or disloyal application of the internal parliamentary rules by the parliamentary majority towards the opposition would be abusive and unconstitutional. In subsequent case law, the Bundesverfassungsgericht has repeatedly used this concept as a barrier to abuse, for example to label the use of the speaking order to prevent a parliamentarian from contributing to a debate[65] or the one-sided composition of parliamentary committees as inadmissible.[66] This principle therefore has the potential to substantially influence the application of internal parliamentary rules, the political style in general[67] and thus restrict the Bundestag's autonomy of procedure.[68]

Is it permissible to break with decades-old conventions and traditions to keep a political opponent out of office? What binding force does unwritten parliamentary law have? Can a new party rely on its continued validity?

The existing proceedings provide ample opportunity to further substantiate this principle.[69] One example is the election of the chairs of the Bundestag committees, which in parliamentary tradition are (also) distributed among the opposition groups.[70] This tradition was partially broken in the 20th legislative period of the Bundestag – not a single committee chairmanship was held by representatives of the Alternative for Germany, although according to the traditional rule, it is entitled to three chairmanships. Furthermore, the provisional chairmanship of these committees is the responsibility of the respective deputy, all of whom in the committees concerned come from the governing parliamentary groups.[71] In addition to the question of misuse of the Rules of Procedure, there is also the question of compliance with democratic proportionality.

[61] Schönberger, Schönberger (2018), p. 105; Darsow (2019), p. 1013.

[62] Schwarz (2024), GG § 1 GOBT Rn. 22 ff.

[63] Klein and Schwarz (2024), GG Art. 39 Rn. 50.

[64] BVerfGE 1, 144, 149.

[65] BVerfGE 10, 4, 13; BVerfGE 80, 188, 229.

[66] BVerfGE 70, 324, 340; BVerfGE 96, 264, 282 f.

[67] Schulze-Fielitz (1984).

[68] Schneider (1970), p. 637.

[69] Huber (2024), p. 119.

[70] Austermann (2024), GG § 58 GOBT Rn. 2, 5.1.

[71] Ritzel et al. (2021), § 12 1. d.

5 Enforceability of an Exercise of Authority Based on the Principle of Good Faith

Actual or alleged violations of the principle of Organtreue can be challenged before the Bundesverfassungsgericht (Art. 94 para. 1 no. 1 GG). This procedure enables the federal bodies to submit measures or omissions of another body for review as long as they are legally relevant.[72] A similar procedure is in place for disputes between the federal government and the federal states (Art. 94 Para. 1 No. 3 GG). If an applicant can be found – the Bundesverfassungsgericht cannot act ex officio[73] – acts in breach of trust can be comprehensively reviewed.

The crux of the matter is that the effective enforcement of such a principle already presupposes that the respective federal body at least recognizes the authority of the Bundesverfassungsgericht even without traditional means of coercion: In its judgement the Court is limited[74] to the mere declaration of the unconstitutionality of a measure or omission.[75] If, for example, a Federal President were to use his power not to block laws that are evidently unconstitutional but to prevent laws that are constitutional and merely politically unpalatable to him, the Court may very well determine that act unconstitutional. However, it could not force the Federal President to comply by imposing a penalty payment or by other measures. To a certain extent, concepts of loyalty and inter-organ respect presuppose themselves for their enforceability.[76]

6 Dangers of a General Good Faith Dogma

The compilation of the conceptualizations in literature and case law points in the direction of the central problem of such a constitutional principle: its dogmatic and linguistic lack of precision. As has already been noted in the context of federal loyalty, such a principle is at risk of becoming a "super legal source" and a general clause that can be used to achieve any desired result on a case-by-case basis.[77]

This also harbors a manifest problem concerning the rule of law. Such elastic terms with an exaggerated tendency, which can mean everything and nothing, give the Bundesverfassungsgericht comprehensive access to the exercise of competences by other constitutional bodies without clear limits. Invoking the principle of Organtreue as a judicial tactic inevitably risks conflict with the separation of

[72] Bethge (2023), BVerfGG § 64 Rn. 26.

[73] von Coelln (2023), BVerfGG § 23 Rn. 3

[74] Hillgruber, Goos (2020), Rn. 535.

[75] Section 67 sentence 1 BverfGG.

[76] BVerfGE 6, 257, 266.

[77] Stettner (1983), p. 406; Walter (1967), p. 625.

powers.[78] This potential danger is further amplified by the fact that corresponding duties of loyalty defy abstract definition due to their dependence on the individual case.[79]

This problem is particularly evident when viewed through the lens of its interparliamentary application. The Bundestag is entitled to autonomy of procedure in accordance with its pre-constitutional legacy, Art. 40 para. 1 sentence 2 GG.[80] Over the decades, a detailed and complex parliamentary procedure has developed, fed by legislation and customary law.[81] Potential requirements for this parliamentary process crafted by the Constitutional Court interfere with this autonomy and are themselves in need of justification.[82] The Bundesverfassungsgericht therefore emphasizes that its standard of review for these questions is limited.[83] The Bundestag is the body responsible for determining how a fair parliamentary procedure should be structured. It is not the role of a court that is not involved in the political process to make this determination.[84] Judicial overreach in the service of a diffuse principle of loyalty would expose itself to the accusation of a disloyal behavior.

It therefore seems preferable for the Bundesverfassungsgericht to only find conduct contrary to good faith, for example through an abuse of powers, in extraordinary and obvious cases. The Bundesverfassungsgericht recently made this clear by requiring an "evident" breach, albeit in an equally vague manner.[85] The assumption of a general duty of loyalty between constitutional bodies alone is insufficient for legal subsumption. It must be actualized in connection with the relevant norm.[86] The specific structure of the competency structure must be examined whether and to what extend a duty of consideration or restraint can be derived from it. Such an approach, which takes into account the specific constitutional text, cannot be replaced by retreating to an abstract, unspecific principle of good faith. The former approach leads the discussion away from a general clause with dubious legal stringency and back to the established method of interpreting the meaning and purpose of a provision.[87] For example, the specific structure of the legislative procedure and the time frames within the bodies must fulfill their responsibilities indicate that the constitutional bodies must take into account the constitutionally required participation of other bodies. A breach of the duty of consideration can be inferred if a body

[78] Zeh (1978), p. 622.

[79] Unger (2024), GG Art. 44 Rn. 41.

[80] Arndt (1966), p. 18.

[81] Morlok (2015), GG Art. 40 Rn. 8.

[82] BVerfGE 160, 368, 388 ff.

[83] Meinel (2019), p. 169.

[84] BVerfGE 80, 188, 220.

[85] BVerfGE 160, 368, 390.

[86] Butzer (2024), GG Art. 82 Rn. 212 f.

[87] Zeh (1978), p. 622.

misuses its powers to obstruct or prevent the constitutionally required participation of another body.[88]

7 Conclusion

Principles of cooperative collaboration, which are discussed under the term "good faith", can be derived directly from the constitution, for example from the principle of Bundestreue or the presupposed ability of the state to function. Recourse to the principle of good faith has a long tradition in Germany. However, there is no need for such a principle in constitutional law; on the contrary, it paves the way for a concept that is lacking in precision and delivers the desired subsumption results without sufficient reference to the constitutional text.

References

Arndt KF (1966) Parlamentarische Geschäftsordnungsautonomie und autonomes Parlamentsrecht. Duncker& Humblot

Barczak T (2021) Rechtsgrundsätze – Baupläne für die normative Einheits – und Systembildung. JuS 61:1

Bauer H (1992) Die Bundestreue, Zugleich ein Beitrag zur Dogmatik des Bundesstaatsrecht und zur Rechtsverhältnislehre. J.C.B. Mohr (Paul Siebeck)

Baumann M (1952) Der Begriff von Treu und Glauben im öffentlichen Recht, Ein Beitrag zur Lehre von den obersten Rechtsgrundsätzen. Juris-Verlag

BeckOK BGB/Sutschet, 70 Ed. 1.5.2024, BGB § 242 Rn. 2 f., 11

BeckOK GG/Austermann, 58. Ed. 15.6.2024, GOBT § 58 Rn. 2, 5.1

BeckOK GG/Schwarz, 58. Ed. 15.6.2024, GOBT § 1 Rn. 22 ff

Darsow T (2019) Über die Grenzen des Gutgemeinten – zum Wahlgeschehen eines Vizepräsidenten des Deutschen Bundestags. NVwZ 38:1013

Dreier/Morlok, 3. Aufl. 2015, GG Art. 40 Rn. 8

Dürig/Herzog/Scholz/Butzer, 104. EL Januar 2024, GG Art. 82, Rn. 115 ff., 159, 212 f

Dürig/Herzog/Scholz/Grzeszick, 104. EL Janaur 2024, GG Art. 20 Rn. 132

Dürig/Herzog/Scholz/Klein/Schwarz, 104. EL Janaur 2024, GG Art. 39 Rn. 50

Heller H (1963) Staatslehre. Sijthoff-Verlag

Herdegen/Masing/Poscher/Gärditz/Masing, Handbuch des Verfassungsrechts, 2021, § 15 Rn. 37 ff

Herdegen/Masing/Poscher/Gärditz/Poscher, Handbuch des Verfassungsrechts, 2021, § 3 Rn. 124 ff

Hillgruber C, Goos C (2020) Verfassungsprozessrecht. Verlagsgruppe Hüthig Jehle Rehm

Huber B (2024) Die AfD – Facetten aktueller Rechtsprechung. NVwZ 3:119

Huber/Voßkuhle/Sommermann, 8. Aufl. 2024, GG Art. 20 Rn. 45, 225

Huber/Voßkuhle/Unger, 8. Aufl. 2024, GG Art. 44 Rn. 41

Isensee J (2001) Der Bundesstaat – Bestand und Entwicklung. In: Dreier H, Badura P (eds) Festschrift 50 Jahre Bundesverfassungsgericht. J.C.B. Mohr (Paul Siebeck)

Kaufmann E (1966) Bericht zum Beratungsgegenstand "Die Grenzen der Verfassungsgerichtsbarkeit". In: Veröffentlichungen der Vereinigung der deutschen Staatsrechtslehrer. De Gruyter

[88] Schneider (1970), p. 422; BVerfGE 165, 206, 240 ff.,166, 304, 330 ff.

Kloepfer M (1974) Vorwirkung von Gesetzen. C.H. Beck'sche Verlagsbuchhandlung
Lepa G (1974) Das Bundesverfassungsgericht im Schnittpunkt von Politik und Recht. DVBl:399
Lorz RA (2001) Interorganrespekt im Verfassungsrecht, Funktionenzuordnung, Rücksichtnahmegebote und Kooperationsverpflichtungen. In: Eine rechtsvergleichende Analyse anhand der Verfassungssysteme der Bundesrepublik Deutschland, der Europäischen Union und der Vereinigten Staaten. J.C.B. Mohr (Paul Siebeck)
Meinel F (2019) Selbstorganisation des parlamentarischen Regierungssystems, Vergleichende Studien zu einem Verfassungsproblem der Bundesrepublik Deutschland. Mohr Siebeck
MüKoBGB/Schubert, 9. Aufl. 2022, BGB § 242 Rn. 32
NK-BGB/Peter Krebs, 4. Aufl. 2021, BGB § 242 Rn. 1
Richter des Bundesverfassungsgerichts (1957) Bemerkungen des Bundesverfassungsgerichts zu dem Rechtsgutachten von Professor Richard Thoma. In: Jahrbuch des öffentlichen Rechts der Gegenwart. Mohr Siebeck
Ritzel/Bückner/Schreiner, Handbuch für die parlamentarische Praxis, § 12 1. d), Sachs/Sachs, 9. Aufl. 2021, GG Art. 20 Rn. 82 ff
Sauer H (2008) Jurisdiktionskonflikte in Mehrebenensystemen, Die Entwicklung eines Modells zur Lösung von Konflikten zwischen Gerichten unterschiedlicher Ebenen in vernetzten Rechtsordnungen. Springer
Schenke WF (1977) Die Verfassungsorgantreue. Duncker& Humblot
Schmidt-Bleibtreu/Klein/Bethge/Bethge, 63. EL Juni 2023, BVerfGG § 64 Rn. 26
Schmidt-Bleibtreu/Klein/Bethge/von Coelln, 63. EL Juni 2023, BVerfGG § 23 Rn. 3
Schneider H (1970) Der Niedergang des Gesetzgebungsverfahrens. In: Ritterspach T, Geiger W (eds) Festschrift für Gebhard Müller zum 70. Geburtstag des Präsidenten des Bundesverfassungsgerichts. Mohr
Schönberger C, Schönberger S (2018) Die AfD im Bundestag. JZ 73:105
Schröcker S (1966) Ungeschriebenes Verfassungsrecht im Bundesstaat: zum 100. Gründungsjahr des deutschen Bundesstaates, Der Staat 5(3):315–340
Schulze-Fielitz H (1984) Der informale Verfassungsstaat, Aktuelle Beobachtungen des Verfassungslebens der Bundesrepublik Deutschland im Lichte der Verfassungstheorie. Duncker& Humblot
Schulze-Fielietz H (1997) Das Bundesverfassungsgericht in der Krise des Zeitgeists: Zur Metadogmatik der Verfassungsinterpretation. AöR 122:1
Smend R (1968) Staatsrechtliche Abhandlungen und andere Aufsätze. Duncker& Humblot
Stettner R (1983) Grundfragen einer Kompetenzlehre. Duncker& Humblot
Walter H (1967) Unlauterer Wettbewerb unter Bundesländern? DÖV 20:622
Zeh W (1978) Buchbesprechung "Die Verfassungsorgantreue". Der Staat 17:620

Good Faith in Polish Constitutional Law

Monika Florczak-Wątor

Abstract This chapter examines the concept of good faith within the Polish legal system, focusing on its interpretation in legislation, case law, and academic literature. It traces the development of good faith as a legal principle, outlining its sources of inspiration, legal basis, and constitutional practices. Although the Polish Constitution does not explicitly mention or define good faith, the Constitutional Tribunal upholds it as a fundamental principle, assuming its existence as inherent to a democratic state governed by the rule of law (Article 2 of the Constitution). The Constitutional Tribunal anchors this principle in the idea of citizens' trust in the State and its laws, while the Supreme Court associates it with the protection of good customs and principles of social coexistence. The analysis demonstrates that the commitment to protecting good faith is reflected across various fields of law, influencing both legislative development and enforcement practices. While some scholars argue for a coherent interpretation of good faith across legal contexts, such unification appears impractical. Nevertheless, there is a consensus that good faith remains essential to promote trust, legal certainty, and predictability, requiring respect for the rights of third parties and the legitimate interests of individuals in legal transactions.

This chapter has been prepared as part of the research project funded by the Priority Research Area Heritage under the program Excellence Initiative—Research University at the Jagiellonian University in Cracow.

M. Florczak-Wątor (✉)
Faculty of Law and Administration, Jagiellonian University, Cracow, Poland
e-mail: m.florczak-wator@uj.edu.pl

J. Podkowik et al. (eds.), *Gleams of Good Faith in Constitutional Law*, Ius Gentium: Comparative Perspectives on Law and Justice 132,
https://doi.org/10.1007/978-3-032-06486-8_8

1 Introduction

The concept of good faith is frequently invoked within the Polish legal framework. It is enshrined in numerous pieces of legislation and, as a result, is also reflected in judicial decisions and the legal literature.

The principle of the protection of good faith, which has constitutional status, upholds the values of trust, certainty, and predictability in the actions of various private and public entities, thereby ensuring the security of individuals and legal transactions.[1] This principle also prohibits the infringement of the rights of third parties and requires that the legitimate interests of the parties to legal transactions be respected.

At the core of the principle of the protection of good faith is the assumption that people are inherently good, honest, and decent. This presumption is based on an optimistic view of human nature. However, the Constitutional Tribunal emphasizes that: "the protection of good faith always requires a statutory basis".[2]

Consequently, this principle does not protect everyone in all possible circumstances. The law explicitly defines who is entitled to benefit from legal outcomes arising from actions undertaken in good faith, along with the specific conditions under which such protection apply.

The presumption of good faith within the Polish legal system is rebuttable, meaning that it can be challenged by demonstrating that an individual acted in bad faith. The burden of proof lies with the party challenging the opponent's good faith or seeking to gain a favorable legal outcome by attributing bad faith to that opponent. The presumption of good faith is not negated merely by casting doubt; instead, such doubt must be resolved in favor of good faith. Thus, to rebut the presumption of good faith, it is necessary to present evidence demonstrating that the individual acted in bad faith.

2 Sources of Inspiration

The concept of good faith functions within Polish constitutional law across various contexts and meanings. It is applied to assess the behavior of individuals toward one another, as well as the actions of the state and its authorities toward individuals, and even the interrelations between state institutions. Good faith is attributed not only to natural persons but also to legal entities,[3] and, in the context of international law, to states as subjects bound by international legal obligations. Thus, the concept of

[1] See resolution of the Supreme Court of 6 December 1991, ref. III CZP 108/91.

[2] Judgment of the Constitutional Tribunal of 16 June 1998, ref. U 9/97; See Piasecki (2003), p. 91; Holocher and Krzyżewska (2021), p. 1149.

[3] Holocher and Krzyżewska (2021), p. 1150.

good faith operates in both private and public law and spans national and international legal domains.

In the Polish legal system, the most prevalent and extensively developed understanding of good faith is the civilian one that applies within horizontal relations – that is, the relations between private entities. Article 7 of the Civil Code establishes a presumption of good faith, according to which, where the statute makes legal consequences dependent on good or bad faith, the existence of good faith shall be presumed. This presumption, applicable throughout the Polish private law system,[4] reflects an optimistic perspective that individuals inherently act with good intentions and are predisposed to cooperate for mutual benefit. Furthermore, it implies that, as a rule, individuals do not intend to inflict harm or damage on others. Consequently, this presumption shifts the burden of proof to the party alleging that an individual is acting in bad faith, thereby necessitating the presentation of relevant evidence within civil proceedings.

This civilian understanding of good faith, as it pertains to relations between individuals, is firmly grounded in many statutory provisions, as well as in judicial decisions. Additionally, it can be derived from the Constitution of the Republic of Poland of 2 April 1997 (hereinafter referred to as the Constitution), in particular, Article 31(2), which establishes an obligation to respect the rights and freedoms of others, based on the aforementioned assumption that every individual exercises his or her rights and freedoms in good faith, without any intention to harm others by his or her behavior and actions. Accordingly, the exercise of individual rights and freedoms necessitates respect not only from the state and its organs but also from other individuals.

The literature indicates that the concept of good faith operates in two distinct senses: subjective and objective.[5] Good faith in the subjective sense refers to a person's state of mind, characterized by a mistaken yet justified belief regarding the existence or nonexistence of a particular right or legal relationship. An individual is thus considered to be in subjective good faith if they are mistakenly convinced of their entitlement to a certain right, provided this belief is justified – meaning that, even with the exercise of reasonable due diligence, they could not have known they were in error.

Good faith in the objective sense, on the other hand, functions as a general clause[6] allowing the court to assess the behavior of an entity based on extralegal (axiological) criteria, such as moral or ethical standards, principles of good customs, or social coexistence.[7] In this context, phrases such as "performing obligations in good faith" or "interpreting contracts in good faith" are used. When assessing good faith in this objective sense, both awareness of wrongful behavior

[4] Radwański and Olejniczak (2017), p. 63.

[5] Doliwa and Doliwa (2015), p. 85; Holocher and Krzyżewska (2021), pp. 1147–1148.

[6] See e.g. Stelmachowski (1965), p. 5; Safjan (1990), p. 48; Zieliński (1992), p. 195; Leszczyński (2016), p. 11; Radwański and Zieliński (2001), p. 11; Florczak-Wątor (2013), p. 49.

[7] Pilich (2007), p. 37.

(in light of the aforementioned standards) and ignorance of wrongdoing, which cannot be reasonably excused, are relevant.

The opposite of good faith is bad faith, which exists similarly in a subjective and objective sense. Thus, bad faith includes both the person who, objectively speaking, behaves in a morally or ethically unacceptable manner (e.g., performs obligations in bad faith) and the person who acts with knowledge that his or her behavior is wrong – that is, either knows this or would have known it had he or she exercised due diligence.[8]

The concept of good faith is found not only in private law, where it is used to evaluate the actions of individuals in horizontal relationships, but also in public law, where it serves to assess the actions of the state and its organs. In the relationship between the individual and the state, the value of the individual's trust in the state and its laws is particularly protected. From this trust arises the individual's good faith in acting with the expectation that they will not be unexpectedly disadvantaged by the state and that their actions will yield outcomes, as described by the relevant legal regulations. The principle of protecting good faith in this sense also has solid constitutional grounds, derived from the principle of trust in the state and the law, which itself is rooted in the principle of the democratic state ruled by law enshrined in Article 2 of the Constitution.

However, the significance of this principle differs in vertical (individual-to-state) relations compared to horizontal relations. In horizontal cases, good faith is presumed for both parties, requiring the party alleging bad faith to prove such allegations. In vertical relationships, however, such a strong presumption of good faith on the part of the state is less feasible, nor is it incumbent on the individual to prove every instance of alleged bad faith on the part of the state. Nevertheless, the complainant must establish a plausible case in which the state has acted unlawfully and initiate an appropriate procedure through which to raise this allegation. This mechanism underpins proceedings before the Constitutional Tribunal, where the presumption of constitutionality applies – namely, the presumption that, in enacting a statute and giving it specific content, the parliament acted in good faith. The burden of challenging the presumption of constitutionality rests with the one who claims that the statute is unconstitutional.[9] Thus, for instance, a citizen bringing a constitutional complaint before the Constitutional Tribunal must specify the alleged unconstitutionality and provide supporting evidence.

In public law, the requirement to act in good faith also applies to relations among state organs. This requirement is grounded in the principle of cooperation between authorities, as articulated in the Preamble to the Constitution.[10] Within the executive branch, this principle is specifically addressed in Article 133(3) of the Constitution, which stipulates that the President of the Republic of Poland, in foreign policy matters, should cooperate with the Prime Minister and the relevant minister. Although

[8] Przybyłowski (1970), pp. 17 et seq.

[9] Jamróz (2014), pp. 65–66; Grabowski and Dębowska (2021), p. 877.

[10] Witkowski (2009); Brzozowski (2010).

this kind of presumption of good faith pertains to relations between state organs, it is conceptually similar to the presumption of good faith in both horizontal and vertical relations involving individuals. This implies an obligation for state organs to engage with one another in a constructive manner that is oriented toward the achievement of intended objectives, fostering a spirit of cooperation rather than unhealthy competition.

3 Legal Basis

Polish law does not provide a legal definition of good faith, despite the concept's presence in the legislation, judicial decisions, and legal literature. Conversely, bad faith is defined within the context of the Act on Land and Mortgage Registers and Mortgages. The Civil Code invokes a presumption of good faith when assessing the effects of the facts and legal relationships within which it is relevant, but also does not define this concept.

The good-faith clause is strongly anchored in constitutional principles,[11] especially those enshrined in the 1997 Constitution of the Republic of Poland, which refer to the notion of "the good." The Preamble to the Constitution identifies four universal values uniting the Polish Nation – truth, justice, beauty, and goodness – and underscores the importance of culture rooted in the Christian heritage of the Nation and universal human values. The concept of "good" further appears in multiple contexts throughout the Basic Law. The Constitution envisions the Republic of Poland as "the common good of all citizens" (Preamble, Article 1), thus imposing upon citizens the duty to "care for the common good" (Article 82).[12] It also provides for Poland's cooperation with other nations "for the good of the Human Family" (Preamble) and its cooperation with churches and religious associations "for the good of man and the common good" (Article 25(3)).

Additionally, the Constitution mandates the application of its principles "for the good of the Third Republic" (Preamble) and instructs state authorities to consider "the good of the family" in social and economic policies (Article 71(1)). It guarantees the right to the protection of a "good name" (Article 47) and the freedom to enjoy "cultural goods" (Article 73), while obliging Polish authorities to foster conditions for the dissemination of and equal access to cultural resources (Article 6(1)). The Constitution also permits the limitation of the right to strike for the "public good" (Article 59(3)), and includes in the oaths of deputies and senators the duty to act "for the good of the citizens" (Article 104(2)). In the oaths of the President of the Republic, the Prime Minister, and members of the government, the "good of the Fatherland" and citizen welfare are elevated as the "supreme imperative" (Articles

[11] Holocher and Krzyżewska (2021), p. 1151.

[12] On the meaning of "common good" see e.g. Lipowicz (2017), p. 17; Granat and Granat (2019), pp. 23–24.

130 and 151). Finally, the Constitution provides for the possibility of excluding the publicity of Sejm sittings on the grounds of the "good of the State" (Article 113). These numerous references to "good" in various meanings and contexts underscore it as one of the Constitution's most central axiological categories.

The justification for protecting good faith may also be derived from constitutional provisions reflecting an optimistic concept of human nature. These include, foremost, those provisions that place human dignity and freedoms at the center of thinking about human rights, mandating public authorities to protect these values (Articles 30 and 31(1)), and obliging all individuals to respect them (Article 31(2)). Furthermore, the protection of good faith finds support in constitutional norms safeguarding property rights (Articles 21 and 64) and freedom of contract (derived from Articles 31(1) and (2) of the Constitution) (Holocher and Krzyżewska 2021, p. 1151). However in case law, good faith is frequently regarded as an integral component of good customs.[13]

Article 2 of the Constitution is also pivotal for the protection of good faith, as it articulates the principle of a democratic state governed by the rule of law, from which the principle of protecting citizens' trust in the state and its laws emerges. The Constitutional Tribunal regards this principle of protecting citizens' trust as the normative basis for safeguarding good faith within the Polish legal system. This principle of trust in the state and its laws rests upon legal certainty – that is, such a set of features vested in the law that ensure legal security to individuals, enabling them to determine their actions with a full understanding of the prerequisites for the actions of state bodies and the legal consequences their actions may entail. Individuals must be able to foresee the consequences of particular behaviors and events based on laws in force at a given time and expect that the legislator will not change them arbitrarily. The legal security afforded by the certainty of the law thus facilitates predictability in state actions and allows individuals to plan their conduct accordingly.[14]

In the jurisprudence of the Constitutional Tribunal, numerous examples can be given of cases in which the principle of protection of good faith has been derived precisely from the principle of protection of citizens' trust in the state and the laws. To illustrate this thesis, two judgments are worth mentioning.

In the judgment of 28 February 2016 (ref. P 13/05), which examined the constitutionality of provisions concerning the delivery of official correspondence to citizens, the Constitutional Tribunal asserted:

> The principle of the individual's trust in the State and the laws requires that the delivery of documents in proceedings conducted by public authorities be regulated such that an individual, acting in good faith and with due diligence, is not surprised by the negative consequences of a document's delivery in situations where, through no fault of their own, they were unable to acquaint themselves with its content.

[13] See e.g. the judgments of the Supreme Court of 3 February 2006, ref. I CSK 297/05; of 13 June 2012, ref. II CSK 515/11; and of 16 October 2014, ref. III CSK 302/13.

[14] See judgment of the Constitutional Tribunal of 14 June 2000, ref. P 3/00.

Similarly, in the judgment of 18 October 2016 (ref. P 123/15), which reviewed the constitutionality of a provision enabling the Agricultural Property Agency to demand high remuneration from individuals in possession of state treasury agricultural property without legal title, the Constitutional Tribunal held that the provision was consistent with the Constitution: "to the extent that it applies to holders of real property in bad faith".

The Court elaborated as follows:

> The principle of protecting trust in the State and its laws (...) applies generally to those who act in good faith and observe the laws in force (...). The disputed provision, however, pertains to entities that utilize public property for economic gain without legal title and (...) are in bad faith, as they refuse to surrender the property upon request by the Agricultural Property Agency; they are, therefore, fully aware that they lack legal title to the property. These entities thus either abuse the law or operate outside its scope. Constitutional protections for such entities must necessarily be weaker than those for entities that act 'within the law' and possess legal title to the property. (...) It cannot be argued that those who abuse the right (the rights of the owner of the property) have a constitutionally justified expectation that the state of infringement caused by them (non-contractual use of agricultural property) will be respected by the legislator. Nor can they reasonably expect that legislators will permit them to continue their unlawful occupation of public property and derive economic benefits from it under preferential, existing terms.

The protection of the good faith of individuals is established by numerous laws within the current legal framework of the Republic of Poland. The Polish electronic legal information system (LEX) identifies 98 laws containing at least one provision referring to the concept of good faith. These laws span various fields of law, including civil law, family law, labor law, cultural property protection law, financial law, press law, and many others. The concept of good faith also appears in numerous sub-statutory acts. Consequently, it can be regarded as a frequently used concept in the Polish legal system, although at the same time, different meanings are ascribed to it on the grounds of various legal acts in different contexts of its application.

Referring to the notion of good faith in statutory legislation has a tradition exceeding 100 years. The first statutes recognizing the protection of persons acting in good faith already appeared in Poland during the inter-war period. For instance, the Tobacco Monopoly Act of 1 June 1922 established criminal liability for tobacco farming and allowed for the confiscation of tobacco and related farming tools, even if they were already in the possession of a third party – unless the third party had acquired these items in good faith. The latter stipulation thus served to protect third parties who had no knowledge of the unlawful use of the items they had purchased.

Following the Second World War, the principle of good faith was first addressed in the Decree of 12 November 1946 on General Provisions of Civil Law, subsequently in the Act of 18 July 1950 on General Provisions of Civil Law, and finally in the Act of 23 April 1964 on the Civil Code, which remains in force today. The 1946 Decree stipulated that: "Private rights should be exercised in accordance with their content, in a manner consistent with their social purpose and the requirements of good faith" and that "Actions contrary to this cannot be considered as the exercise of a right and do not enjoy protection" (Article 5). Additionally, it asserts, "Where the statute makes legal consequences dependent on good or bad faith, the existence of good faith shall be presumed" (Article 8). The 1950 Act reiterated this provision, reinforcing the presumption of good faith and specifying that "Anyone alleging bad faith shall prove it" (Article 5). Similarly, the current Civil Code enshrines a presumption of good faith in alignment with the aforementioned framework (Article 7) and extends protection to a party who has entered into a legal transaction in good faith with an unauthorized party (Article 92 § 2). Moreover, it safeguards the good-faith holder of an item vis-à-vis the item's rightful owner, establishing specific rules for the reimbursement of expenses incurred by such holders (Articles 224–231).

The principle of good faith is especially significant in laws regulating real estate transactions and land and mortgage registers. Article 5 of the Act of 6 July 1982 on Land and Mortgage Registers and Mortgages provides for the warranty of public credibility of land and mortgage registers, ensuring that, in cases where discrepancies arise between the registered legal status of a property and its actual legal status, the contents of the register resolve in favor of the person who acquired ownership or another right *in rem* through a legal transaction with a person listed as entitled in the register. However, this warranty does not protect transactions conducted with a purchaser in bad faith. When an entry in the land and mortgage register is necessary for a transaction, the timing of the application for entry is decisive for determining the purchaser's good or bad faith. Article 6 of this Act defines bad faith, specifying that "A person is in bad faith if they are aware that the content of the land and mortgage register is inconsistent with the actual legal status, or if they could easily have become aware of this inconsistency." This last premise, known as the premise of gross negligence of the purchaser, raises some doubts in practice, as it is difficult to provide a single objectified standard of the "ease of becoming aware" of the inconsistency of the contents of the register with the actual legal state. Scholars argue that each case must be individually assessed, guided by principles of life experience and particular circumstances.[15]

Irrespective of the attempts made in the more recent literature to interpret the concept of bad faith in an objective manner, approximating the "ease of becoming aware" criterion to the requirement of "due diligence"[16] prevailing views in jurisprudence and doctrine maintain that the assessment of bad faith should remain case-specific, taking subjective criteria into account.[17]

The concept of good faith is also very often referred to in international agreements to which the Republic of Poland is a party. Both bilateral and multilateral agreements often contain a directly expressed obligation of states that are party to these agreements to act in good faith, particularly in fulfilling their international legal obligations. The Vienna Convention on the Law of Treaties, which has bound the Republic of Poland since 1990, underscores in its preamble that the fundamental principles guiding states that are party to the Convention are those of free consent,

[15] See Mysiak (2002), pp. 82 et seq; Gładyszowski (1983), p. 13.

[16] See the resolution of the Supreme Court of 5 May 1993, ref. III CZP 52/93, and the case law cited by Majewski (2007), pp. 52 et seq.

[17] See, inter alia, the decision of the Supreme Court of 16 April 1964, ref. II CR 336/63, as well as Rudnicki (2002), 8–9; Holocher and Krzyżewska (2021), p. 1154.

good faith, and *pacta sunt servanda*. Under the Convention, every treaty is to be "performed in good faith" (Article 26) and should also be "interpreted in good faith" (Article 31). Furthermore, if a treaty is later deemed invalid, acts conducted in good faith under that treaty before the declaration of invalidity "shall not become unlawful by reason of the invalidity of the treaty itself" (Article 69(2)(b)). The concept of good faith is cited in over 100 international agreements to which the Republic of Poland is a party, establishing a strong foundation and justification for the principle of good-faith protection in international law.

4 Constitutional Practice

In the jurisprudence of the Constitutional Tribunal and the Supreme Court, there are numerous references to the concept of good faith, although this concept itself is seldom subjected to in-depth legal analysis. The Constitutional Tribunal assumes that it is a so-called stagnant concept – that is, a concept with content explained and established in the doctrine of law and judicial decisions, which thereby removes the obligation to define its meaning in detail.

Over nearly 40 years of Constitutional Tribunal activity, the concept of good faith has appeared in approximately 200 judgments, with over 100 of these issued at the merits review stage. Notably, the notion of good faith does not always appear in the Tribunal's legal deliberations; sometimes, it appears in the historical part of the reasoning of the judgment, in which the views presented by the initiator of the proceedings and its participants are reported. However, according to the Tribunal's database of judgments available on its website, the concept of good faith is cited in the legal reasoning – the section containing the Tribunal's findings on the applicable regulations – in 55 judgments, 47 of which were issued after the 1997 Constitution came into effect.

It is worth noting that the Tribunal referred to the notion of good faith in its first historic ruling, issued on 28 May 1986 (ref. U 1/86). In this case, it declared the regulations increasing fees for citizens' use of state-owned real estate unconstitutional. In the final part of the reasoning of this ruling, the Tribunal addressed complaints and letters it had received from citizens regarding the case, stating:

> Among the complaints from citizens are those from residents of Poland's western and northern regions. These complaints bear fundamental significance. They reflect positively on society's legal consciousness by demonstrating an attachment to the principle of protecting good faith among individuals obtaining subjective rights (…). The Constitutional Tribunal draws a key conclusion from the citizen complaints and letters in this case: that there is a need for the active development of legal culture, both in the law-making activities of state bodies and in the application of law. This observation extends equally to the Tribunal's role in safeguarding the rule of law in the legislative process.

The Tribunal has most frequently cited the concept of good faith in cases reviewing the constitutionality of regulations related to land and mortgage registers and the acquisition of real estate. An in-depth examination of this issue is contained in its judgment of 20 April 2009 (ref. SK 55/08), where the Tribunal upheld the constitutionality of the institution of the warranty of public credibility of land and mortgage registers, already mentioned above. In this case, the Tribunal concluded that a person acting in good faith could be considered:

> a purchaser who, in light of the surrounding circumstances, had no reason to doubt the legal status of the real property and based his conviction in this respect on the contents of the land and mortgage register.

The Tribunal reasoned that:

> the purchaser cannot be expected – after verifying the legal status of the property in the land and mortgage register and becoming acquainted with the state of possession of the real estate – to undertake additional investigations. There must be additional, special circumstances that would justify doubts as to the legal status disclosed in the land and mortgage register, but even then, the purchaser cannot be required to conduct laborious or costly inquiries (…). The mere existence of doubts does not justify a presumption of bad faith if addressing those doubts would entail undue difficulties or require efforts beyond what would be considered ease of finding out.

The Tribunal has also examined the relevance of the presumption of good faith in the allocation of the burden of proof. In its judgment of 20 April 2009 (ref. SK 55/08), it noted that the presumption of good faith arising from the Act on Land and Mortgage Registers and Mortgages places the burden of proving bad faith on the party seeking to negate the warranty's effect:

> The demonstration of the purchaser's bad faith rests with the party demanding the exclusion of the warranty's operation. If bad faith cannot be demonstrated, it follows that the purchaser is presumed to remain in good faith.

Furthermore, in its decision of 9 October 2013 (ref. Ts 53/12), the Tribunal clarified that the presumption of good faith under the Civil Code:

> is rebutted if the circumstances surrounding the transfer and delivery of the item should have raised doubts regarding the legitimacy of such a belief. The purchaser's good faith is thus negated not only by awareness that the vendor is not authorized to transfer the item, but also by circumstances where this lack of awareness results from negligence or a failure to exercise reasonable diligence.

The principle of protecting good faith is also referred to by the Tribunal in tax cases, recognizing that lawmaking and law-enforcing authorities must not surprise taxpayers who act in good faith, relying upon existing legal provisions. In its judgment of 25 November 1997 (ref. K 26/97), the Tribunal asserted:

> It is not the constitutional duty of the legislator to establish tax reliefs or exemptions related to housing investments, nor is it their duty to extend these reliefs or exemptions beyond a single tax year. However, once the legislator has introduced such a regulation, it is impermissible to withdraw it without providing adequate protection to citizens who, acting in good faith, have made commitments under this regulation.

The concept of good faith is additionally invoked by the Constitutional Tribunal in the context of the duty of cooperation among state authorities. In its decision of 20 May 2009 (ref. Kpt 2/08), the Tribunal stated:

> The Preamble to the Constitution obliges the authorities of the Republic to co-operate. This directive requires them to mutually respect the constitutional responsibilities of state organs, their competencies, and furthermore to honor the dignity of offices and their holders, demonstrating mutual loyalty, good faith, timely communication of initiatives, and a readiness to collaborate, agree, observe, and execute reliably (…). The alignment of objectives, as an expression of the idea of cooperation, is a consequence of the fundamental constitutional principle set out in Article 1 of the Constitution, namely, that 'the Republic of Poland is the common good of all citizens.' State constitutional organs are thus required to act in a manner that realizes the systemic directive contained in Article 1 of the Constitution.

This perspective was reaffirmed by the Constitutional Tribunal in its judgment of 5 June 2012 (ref. K 18/09), in a case concerning the duty of cooperation between the President of the Republic of Poland and the National Council of the Judiciary in the procedure for the appointment of judges.

In the jurisprudence of the Constitutional Tribunal, the concept of good faith is also applied to the actions of public officials, indicating an expectation of conduct that is honest, responsible, and decent, and that demonstrates respect for the law and the rules in force. In its judgment of 21 April 2016 (ref. K 2/14), the Tribunal found that the provision defining the scope of substantive immunity for deputies and senators, including: "other activities inherent in the exercise of the mandate", referred to in Article 6(2) of the Act of 9 May 1996 on the exercise of the mandate of deputies and senators, was constitutionally valid. In clarifying this provision, the Tribunal referred to a resolution of 16 February 1994 (ref. I KZP 40/93) in which the Supreme Court held that actions covered by immunity must be closely related to the MP's specific parliamentary duties and responsibilities, constituting a form of parliamentary mandate execution. The Supreme Court also stressed that:

> inherent in this mandate – held by an MP on behalf of and at the election of the Nation – is the requirement for decent methods of conduct that do not breach the principles of good faith towards the public in relation to the officeholder.

This view has been upheld in recent Supreme Court case law (see the judgments of the Supreme Court of 13 April 2007, ref. I CSK 31/07 and of 21 September 2011, ref. I CSK 754/10) and was referenced by the Constitutional Tribunal in the aforementioned judgment of 21 April 2016 (ref. K 2/14), further clarifying the meaning of good faith within the scope of parliamentary immunity.

In jurisprudence, as previously noted, the concept of good faith frequently arises, particularly in cases concerning the rights of the holder of real property. However, it is worth noting that the courts' understanding of good faith has evolved since the Second World War.[18] Initially, good faith, in this context, was commonly understood as the belief of a property holder, justified by circumstances, in his or her right to exercise that right. In the mid-1950s, a more liberal approach emerged, positing that good faith could be assumed when a person reasonably believed, given the circumstances, that his or her actions did not harm others. This interpretation, however, was limited to cases involving holders who had developed someone else's real

[18] See the decision of the Supreme Court of 8 September 2006, ref. II CK 3/06.

property, and remained in effect for only a short period. After the Civil Code came into force, a return to a stricter, traditional understanding of good faith occurred, framing it as a justified but erroneous belief in the existence of a right. In this sense, good faith signifies an erroneous yet reasonably justified belief that one is entitled to exercise a right.[19] Nonetheless, judicial decisions have also sustained an alternative view, wherein good faith is equated with the belief – based on objective grounds derived from the relationship underlying the situation – that the right is exercised without infringing upon another's rights.[20]

In recent jurisprudence, the Supreme Court has defined good faith as:

> the mental state of a person (a specific legal entity) manifesting as an erroneous but justified belief in the existence of a certain right, legal relationship, or legally relevant situation, even though the actual legal state, objectively assessed, is different.[21]

The Court further emphasized that good faith, in this context: "is excluded by the emergence of circumstances that would cause serious doubts in an average person as to their right to use a thing in its previous scope".[22]

Therefore, the determination of the existence of good faith relies on an assessment of the state of consciousness of a given person regarding legally significant premises, which, although erroneous, is recognized by the law in certain cases in favor of that individual because it is justified by the specific circumstances of the case.[23]

Good faith is also defined negatively, with the principle that:

> one is not in good faith who exercises a right knowing that they are not entitled to it, nor is one in good faith if they exercise a right without this awareness, yet could have ascertained the actual legal status by exercising due diligence.[24]

In summary, there is no single, established, and widespread understanding of good faith within court jurisprudence. The interpretation of good faith varies depending on the specifics of different cases and legal provisions. At times, the courts emphasize the subjective aspect of good faith, while in other instances, they stress the importance of an objective approach in its assessment. Judicial jurisprudence in this area is extensive and has evolved over several decades. When assessing the constitutionality of provisions related to good faith, the Constitutional Tribunal primarily relies on the interpretation established in judicial decisions, especially those of the Supreme Court, and only infrequently attempts to independently define the concept.

---

[19] See e.g. the resolutions of the Supreme Court of 11 December 1975, ref. III CZP 63/75 and of 24 March 1980, ref. III CZP 14/80.

[20] See the resolution of a panel of seven judges of the Supreme Court of 25 May 1955, ref. I CO 14/55.

[21] Judgment of the Supreme Court of 13 January 2010, ref. II CSK 374/09.

[22] Ibidem.

[23] See the decision of the Supreme Court of 12 April 2019, ref. I CSK 501/18.

[24] See the resolution of the Supreme Court of 20 November 2015, ref. III CZP 76/15.

5 Conclusion

The concept of good faith has long been established in Polish constitutional law. Although it is neither explicitly mentioned in the Constitution nor defined in legislation, both legal doctrine and the jurisprudence of the Constitutional Tribunal and the Supreme Court affirm the principle of protecting good faith and the resulting presumption of its existence. The Constitutional Tribunal derives this principle from the broader concept of citizens' trust in the state and its laws, which itself arises from a democratic state ruled by law (Article 2 of the Constitution). Similarly, the Supreme Court (and, by extension, other courts) bases the principle of protecting good faith on the protection of good customs and the principles of social coexistence.

Polish legal doctrine indicates that the principle of protecting good faith is firmly rooted in the Constitution, supported by various constitutional principles and human rights provisions. Examples from the jurisprudence of the courts and the Constitutional Tribunal illustrate that the principle of protecting good faith also has practical implications for the processes of lawmaking and law enforcement. The concept of good faith appears in numerous legal provisions, taking on different meanings depending on the context of specific laws. Although a scholarly proposal exists to unify these interpretations across legal provisions,[25] such unification appears impractical. Nevertheless, there is a broad consensus that good faith should be respected and protected, as it underpins essential values such as trust, certainty, and predictability in the actions of legal entities. This principle entails a prohibition against infringing upon the rights of third parties and imposes an obligation to respect the legitimate interests of the parties in legal transactions.

References

Brzozowski W (2010) Współdziałanie władz publicznych [Cooperation between public authorities]. Państwo i Prawo 2:3–16

Doliwa K, Doliwa A (2015) Zasada słuszności i dobra wiara a prawo pozytywne (na przykładzie polskiego prawa cywilnego) [The principle of equity and good faith versus positive law (based on the example of Polish civil law)]. Studia Prawnoustrojowe 30:85–94

Florczak-Wątor M (2013) Kontrola konstytucyjności klauzul generalnych [Review of the constitutionality of general clauses]. Przegląd Sejmowy 4:49–64

Gładyszowski J (1983) Uwagi o rękojmi wiary publicznej ksiąg wieczystych na tle ustawy z dnia 6 lipca 1982 r. o księgach wieczystych i hipotece [Remarks on the warranty of public credibility of land and mortgage registers in the light of the Act of 6 July 1982 on Land and Mortgage Registers and Mortgages]. Palestra 7:10–15

Grabowski A, Dębowska A (2021) Domniemanie konstytucyjności ustawy [Presumption of constitutionality of a statute]. In: Florczak-Wątor M, Grabowski A (eds) Argumenty i rozumowania prawnicze w konstytucyjnym państwie prawa. Komentarz [Legal arguments and reasoning in a constitutional state of law. Commentary]. Księgarnia Akademicka Publishing House

[25] Holocher and Krzyżewska (2021), p. 1160.

Granat M, Granat K (2019) The Constitution of Poland. A contextual analysis. Hart Publishing
Holocher J, Krzyżewska B (2021) Domniemanie i ochrona dobrej wiary [Presumption and protection of good faith]. In: Florczak-Wątor M, Grabowski A (eds) Argumenty i rozumowania prawnicze w konstytucyjnym państwie prawa. Komentarz [Legal arguments and reasoning in a constitutional state of law. Commentary]. Księgarnia Akademicka Publishing House
Jamróz L (2014) The Constitutional Tribunal in Poland in the context of constitutional judiciary. Temida 2. Publishing House
Leszczyński L (2016) Generalne klauzule odsyłające - ujęcie teoretycznoprawne [General referencing clauses - A legal theoretical approach]. Annales UMCS 2:11–26
Lipowicz I (2017) The common good. Ruch Prawniczy, Ekonomiczny i Socjologiczny 3:17–31
Majewski A (2007) Możliwość dowiedzenia się z łatwością o niezgodności treści księgi wieczystej z rzeczywistym stanem prawnym, jako przesłanka złej wiary nabywcy [Possibility to easily find out about the inconsistency of the content of the land and mortgage register with the actual legal status as a prerequisite for bad faith of the purchaser]. Rejent 3:48–60
Mysiak P (2002) Pojęcie złej wiary w odniesieniu do instytucji rękojmi wiary publicznej ksiąg wieczystych [Concept of bad faith in relation to the institution of the warranty of public credibility of land and mortgage registers]. Rejent 9:79–87
Piasecki K (2003) Kodeks cywilny. Księga pierwsza. Część ogólna. Komentarz [Civil code. Book one. General part. Commentary]. Zakamycze Publishing House
Pilich M (2007) Zasady współżycia społecznego, dobre obyczaje czy dobra wiara? Dylematy nowelizacji klauzul generalnych prawa cywilnego w perspektywie europejskiej [Principles of social coexistence, good morals or good faith? Dilemmas of amending general clauses of civil law in a European perspective]. Studia Prawnicze 4:37–57
Przybyłowski K (1970) Dobra wiara w polskim prawie cywilnym (ogólne uwagi o pojęciu) [Good faith in Polish civil law (general remarks on the concept)]. Studia Cywilistyczne 15:3–30
Radwański Z, Olejniczak A (2017) Prawo cywilne – część ogólna [Civil law - general part]. C.H. Beck
Radwański Z, Zieliński M (2001) Uwagi de lege ferenda o klauzulach generalnych w prawie prywatnym [De lege ferenda remarks on general clauses in private law]. Przegląd Legislacyjny 2:11–33
Rudnicki S (2002) Dwa problemy rękojmi wiary publicznej ksiąg wieczystych [Two problems of the warranty of public credibility of land registers]. Przegląd Sądowy 6:8–9
Safjan M (1990) Klauzule generalne w prawie cywilnym (przyczynek do dyskusji) [General clauses in civil law (contribution to the discussion)]. Państwo i Prawo 11:48–59
Stelmachowski A (1965) Klauzule generalne w kodeksie cywilnym (Zasady współżycia społecznego — społeczno-gospodarcze przeznaczenie prawa) [General clauses in the Civil Code (Principles of social coexistence - socio-economic purpose of the law)]. Państwo i Prawo 1:5–20
Witkowski Z (2009) Dyrektywa "współdziałania władz" jako element organizujący życie wspólnoty państwowej w świetle Konstytucji RP z 2 kwietnia 1997 r. [The directive of "cooperation of authorities" as an organising element of the life of the state community in the light of the Constitution of the Republic of Poland of 2 April 1997]. In: Wawrzyniak J, Laskowska M (eds) Instytucje prawa konstytucyjnego w dobie integracji europejskiej. Księga jubileuszowa dedykowana Prof. Marii Kruk-Jarosz [Constitutional Law Institutions in the era of European integration. anniversary book dedicated to Prof. Maria Kruk-Jarosz]. Sejm Publishing House
Zieliński T (1992) Klauzule generalne w demokratycznym państwie prawnym [General clauses in a democratic state ruled by law]. Studia Iuridica 23:195–210

Good Faith in Romanian Constitutional Law

Lucian-Sorin Stănescu

Abstract With strong roots in Roman private law and a genealogy that transcends all branches of Romanian positive law, good-faith is today an undeniable normative reality, whose conceptualization is far from being completed and requires an interdisciplinary approach from an epistemological point of view. The corollary of the penetration of good faith into Romanian public law is its enshrinement as a constitutional norm as an obligation incumbent on Romanian citizens, foreign citizens and stateless persons in the exercise of their constitutional rights and freedoms, on the one hand, and on the other hand, on the Romanian State in its activity of fulfilling the obligations it undertakes in the treaties to which it is a party. Contrary to the ubiquity of the principle of good faith in private law, where this obligation is incumbent on all participants in legal relations, it is noted that this condition of participation in constitutional legal relations is not imposed by the fundamental law on the powers of the state or public authorities.

In this context, the present study aims to analyze whether the state powers are subject to the obligation of good faith in the activity of realizing their constitutional prerogatives and attributions in accordance with their constitutional mission. For this purpose the study will use the method of semantic analysis of good-faith in relation to constitutional loyalty in the activity and relations between the state powers. At the same time, the study will seek to identify the forms of manifestation of good-faith in the specific activities of the legislative, executive and judicial powers, according to the method of content analysis.

In our opinion, if, in private law legal relations, good faith presupposes the concomitant presence of its structural elements, namely probity, prudence, order and temperance, our study will examine whether they are identical in constitutional law or whether undergo certain transformations through the action of subjects of law distinct from those of private law and in accordance with their specific competences or rights as outlined by the Romanian Constitution.

L.-S. Stănescu (✉)
"Stephen the Great" University of Suceava, Suceava, Romania
e-mail: lucian.stanescu@fdsa.usv.ro

J. Podkowik et al. (eds.), *Gleams of Good Faith in Constitutional Law*, Ius Gentium: Comparative Perspectives on Law and Justice 132,
https://doi.org/10.1007/978-3-032-06486-8_9

1 Introduction

Good-faith was defined by Cicero by the traits of "sincerity in words" *(veritas)* and "fidelity in commitments" *(constantia)*.[1] Over time, the content of the notion of good faith, in the sphere of private law, has been enriched with several other traits such as: loyalty, cooperation, tolerance, consistency, patience, sincerity and perseverance.[2] In 1994, with a premonitory clairvoyance, Professor I. Muraru (1938–2021), former president of the Constitutional Court of Romania between 1995 and 1998, established that the fundamental rule for the efficiency and viability of the young democratic Constitution of Romania was the respect for authority even by the public authorities legitimized by the fundamental law, which had: "the obligation to correctly receive the structures and functions of the constitutional order in which they will act".[3]

In the view of the first president of the Constitutional Court of Romania, the *sine qua non* condition of a correct constitutional behavior, as a guarantee of the effectiveness of the fundamental law, would have been such as to attest: "the certain will to create the rule of law, based on the balance and cooperation of public powers".[4]

After 15 years of these observations and 19 years of political and constitutional practice, another author assessed that:

> the normative order must be protected from abusive practices of political, social, institutional or individual actors, while the supremacy of constitutional rules must be guaranteed within a constitutional democracy. We cannot have a genuine democracy if constitutional rules are violated.[5]

Today, it is a certainty that good faith has acquired a constitutional dimension,[6] reflected in the obligation of all Romanian citizens, foreigners and stateless persons alike, to exercise their constitutional rights and freedoms in good faith, without infringing the rights and freedoms of others. According to this view, the meaning of the exercise in good faith of the rights and freedoms guaranteed by the Constitution is to realize them in order to ensure the full participation of all members of society in social life.[7]

In the matter of loyalty to the country, declared sacred, the Romanian Constitution lays down the obligation for a narrower category of persons, namely those who fulfill public functions and the military, to faithfully fulfill their obligations, in which sense they shall take the oath provided by law. At the same time, Article 11, para. 1, that in the field of international law, the Romanian State has the obligation

---

[1] Gherasim (1981), p. 7.

[2] Floare (2019), p. 9.

[3] Muraru (1995), p. 25.

[4] Muraru (1995), p. 25.

[5] Dima (2009), p. 4.

[6] Dogaru (2002), p. 4.

[7] Dogaru (2002), p. 4.

"to fulfill its obligations under the treaties to which it is a party, in good faith and to the letter and in good faith."

Therefore, the civil obligation of good faith in the exercise of subjective rights by Romanian citizens, the honesty of public institutions and authorities in their constitutional and international activity up to the limit of abuse of power, the faith, as a synonym or species of loyalty to the country or public office, as well as the fullness of good faith as such in the exercise of the subjective rights of Romanian citizens and non-citizens, are the theoretical premises that we have identified in the early constitutional literature developed under the Romanian Constitution in force, and they can be the starting point in determining the specific content of the concept of "good faith" in Romanian constitutional law.

Given these coordinates, the stake of our research lies in analyzing the forms in which good-faith manifests itself in Romanian constitutional law, where we find individual subjects, but also public authorities, the mechanism of transfer of a private law concept into public law, and we will align ourselves with the cognitive effort to offer new perspectives for defining this meta-legal concept. Even from a metaphorical perspective, this initiative entails reconstructing the Roman road that the idea of good faith traveled from *fides* to *bona-fides*. (Pop 2019, p.58).

2 Genealogy of the Idea of Good Faith from Roman Law to Romanian Private Law

In Roman antiquity, the mutual obligation of *fides* was born in man's relationship with the divinity and had the meaning of ritual observance of the ancestral religion, loyalty to friends and the city and the faithful fulfillment of promises made to the gods in exchange for their goodwill towards human activities.[8]

Initially, this ritualistic practice accompanied private law legal relations, in contracts, pacts or fidejusiones since: "every human act implies a sacred side".[9]

In Roman legal practice *fides* will receive the meaning of "oath, obedience" and will form the civil legal institutions *fiducia, fideicommisium, fideipromissio* and *fideiussio,* institutions *stricti iuris,* as opposed to the attributes *fidus* (sure, trustworthy), *fidelis* (faithful), fiducia (trust, trust), *fiducia* (trust, trust), *confidere* (trust), which remain in the ethical sphere.[10]

From the second century BC onwards, the archaic *fides, which* had become a general ethical value, was to impose itself in Roman law as *bona fides*. The metamorphosis of this value proper to the sphere of private social life and its penetration into the public sphere as a moral ideal or general value is due to a constant tendency

[8] Pop (2019), p. 59.

[9] Pop (2019), p. 58.

[10] Pop (2019), p. 59.

of Roman legal thought: "to define behaviors and to transpose into theory some rules",[11] empirically drawn from the social practices of the time.

In the context of Romanian private law, this Roman conceptual heritage profoundly influenced the way in which good faith was integrated into the modern legal system, especially through the fanariote codifications (Code Calimah – 1817, Caragea Legislation – 1818), in the context in which Romanian written law was traditionally based on Byzantine sources.[12] These codifications, influenced by Byzantine law and the Roman tradition, took over certain provisions related to *good faith,* applicable especially in the sphere of obligations and contracts. Fully inspired by the Napoleonic Civil Code, the Romanian Civil Code of 1864 reflected the desire for legal modernization and alignment with Western values, but maintained the essence of Romanesque principles, including the concept of *good faith* as the foundation of legal fairness and stability.

The new Romanian Civil Code, which entered into force in 2011, has taken this principle and extended it by including it in the text of Article 14, which states that "rights must be exercised and obligations fulfilled in good faith", which is an adaptation to the needs of contemporary society, where good faith is no longer just a principle applicable to contracts, but also a general standard of legal behavior in all areas of private law.

3 Structure and Forms of Good Faith in Romanian Private Law

The entropic tendency of law in general to define behaviors is concretized by the creation of normative models of the ideal type. The premises of these models of legal relations or patterns of behavior are knowledge and human will. The relationship between the two notions is that honesty manifests itself in human behavior in social relations, "dealing with life in and for itself", regardless of whether these will take the form of legal relations or not.[13] By comparison, good faith, a quasi-legal concept, but *sine qua non,* in some private law legal relations (such as contracts), constitutes: "a social aspect which requires a different criterion of appreciation than the strictly individual".[14]

Thus, if the virtues of honesty, as the essential foundation of good faith, are loyalty (or probity), prudence, order and temperance, the structure of the legal concept of good faith is made up of the following elements: right intention, as a result of loyalty and probity; diligence, corresponding to the moral value of prudence, which determines the performance of acts or deeds with the foreseeing of their result

[11] Pop (2019), p. 59.

[12] Bob (2015), p. 88.

[13] Gherasim (1981), p. 8.

[14] Gherasim (1981), p. 10.

circumscribed within the limits of the law; lawfulness, i.e. the legal hypostasis of order as a moral value and refraining from harming or causing harm to another, which derives from the moral value of temperance and is equivalent to the Ulpian precept: *alterum non laedere*.[15]

Therefore, good-faith implies an axiological dimension as well as a cognitive one. As a subjective attitude, good-faith depends on the possibility and limits of cognition oriented towards the idea of the Good. However, this attitude is not a random one, but it presupposes a permanent conscious and intentional involvement in the meaning of the action or act of good-faith, concomitant with the rejection of the diametrically opposite, negative attitude, that is, of what expresses bad-faith.[16]

Likewise, the moral foundation of the legal concept of good faith requires that the choice of this subjective attitude is not only the result of free will, but also the concretization of a general positive obligation, which is incumbent on all parties in civil legal relations, regardless of whether they are concerned with a particular legal situation or a particular action.[17] The consequence is that good faith, as a subjective element, becomes both the object of a general positive obligation, hence its current status as a general principle of civil law.[18]

From this perspective, *good faith* is not a legal norm in the strict sense of the formal definitions ubiquitous in the general theory of law, but it is a moral-legal concept that has always been present in Romanian civil law, which has now reached the status of a general principle of the most important branch of private law. The problem that arises from this point is how a legal institution of private law transcends the limits of the branch of law in which it was formed, as well as the avatars that it receives in the sphere of the branches of public law.

4 The Mechanism of Transfer of Good Faith from Private to Public Law

As it follows from its historical development, good faith is a legal concept that has traditionally been formed and belongs to the private civic space and private law.[19] Recent civil legal doctrine, the legal rules governing the private space form a closed normative order.[20] Of course, this assertion could have an autarchic connotation, in the sense that the sphere of private legal relations would be completely isolated from the sphere of public legal relations. But the two regulatory spheres are in constant communication and interaction.

---

[15] Gherasim (1981), p. 10.

[16] Stoica (2020a), p. 18.

[17] Stoica (2020a), p. 18.

[18] Stoica (2020a), p. 18.

[19] Stoica (2020b), p. 2.

[20] Stoica (2020b), p. 2.

The difference lies in the fact that the public legal space is regulated primarily by rules containing commands and prohibitions and, in a subsidiary, limited way, by permissions.[21] By comparison, the legal relations that are established in the private legal space are equivalent due to the equal position of the parties and are regulated by numerous dispositive rules, with commands and prohibitions being the exception and permissions being the rule. In this sense, it has been rightly asserted that in the private legal space everything that is not prohibited is permitted.[22]

However, it is not the conceptual delimitation of the two branches of law that is of interest here, but rather the fact that, as component parts of the legal system, they influence each other. One of the most striking legal phenomena that has been manifest in legal systems for at least 100 years is the influence of public law on private law.

Today we would say that this phenomenon constitutes a functioning law of legal systems due to the "hard law" character public law, with its corollary in the last 50–60 years in Europe and in the world of constitutional democracies, namely the constitutionalization of systems of law. This legal phenomenon occurring within the systems of law has at least two visible consequences, namely, the very transformation of law in the sense of ensuring the supremacy of the Constitution and the conformity of the entire system of law with the supreme law of a state[23] and even a real normative unification.

On the other hand, however:

> let us not conclude, however, from these divisions and ramifications that the separation is well characterized and that in private law we shall find only provisions of special, particular utility, and in public law only provisions concerning society considered in itself, as a whole. In fact, we often find provisions of public law in private law and vice versa.[24]

In other words, in the process of interaction of types of norms and branches within the system of law, the reverse phenomenon, i.e. the influence of public law by private law, is also recorded, all the more so since even the first attempts at doctrinal study of public law were made by means of private law concepts: "which are already ready worked out since Roman times".[25]

But the reverse process of influencing public law through private law rules or institutions is not identical with the rational imposition of "hard" law in the face of the flexible law of the world of individuals, i.e. that: "space of freedom of the individual and the community in which the free will of private individuals is sufficient to carry out the various forms of conduct".[26]

A distinctive feature, however, of the conceptual borrowings that public law has received from private law is a certain epistemic subtlety that is embodied in a

---

[21] Stoica (2020b), p. 2.

[22] Stoica (2020b), p. 2.

[23] Lupu (2020), p. 10.

[24] Dissescu (1915), p. 35.

[25] Djuvara (1930), p. 137.

[26] Stoica (2020b), p. 2.

specific morphology meanings or functions that the legal institutions or concepts transferred are recorded in relation to the subject matter, method of regulation and principles of each field of activity. In other words: "private law concepts have a different meaning in public law".[27]

In this sense, Martin Loughlin, argues that the mix of public and private law rules is desirable and represents a: "normative architecture that combines legal rules, ethical principles and control mechanisms to protect citizens' rights and prevent institutional slippage".[28]

5 The Premises of the Analysis of Good Faith in Romanian Constitutional Law

In terms of its ability to adapt to any legal environment, i.e. to any field of regulation, it has been stated in our recent civil doctrine that good faith is protean, which is why it gives rise to new conditions of existence[29] under which we will have to identify it in public law.

A first observation is that good-faith is not a general principle of constitutional law, but a constant in legal doctrine, regardless of the authors or approaches inventoried for this purpose.

Secondly, good-faith is enshrined at the level of the constitutional norm with regard to the obligation of the Romanian State to "fulfill its obligations under the treaties to which it is a party", according to Art. 11, para. 1 of the Romanian Constitution and in the obligation of all Romanian citizens, as well as foreigners and stateless persons, to exercise their constitutional rights and freedoms, without infringing the rights and freedoms of others. In the form of its structural element, as fidelity, good faith is also included in the oath of persons occupying positions of public dignity and of the military, according to art. 54 of the Romanian Constitution. By therefore, in relation to the subjects of constitutional law, the obligation of good faith is incumbent only on individual subjects (Romanian citizens, foreigners and stateless persons) and, among the collective subjects of constitutional law, only on the Romanian State, but only in the performance of its external function. Surprisingly or not, this obligation is not laid down either for the public authorities constituted as powers of the state or for the political parties or political formations engaged in the competition for power and the exercise of governance.

What could be the rational explanations for these findings? Are they merely epistemic shortcomings of Romanian constitutional law treatises or should they be sought in the features and particularities of constitutional law, as a fundamental and constitutive branch of public law, reflected in its general principles and in the

[27] Djuvara (1930), p. 137.

[28] Loughlin (2003), p. 87.

[29] Stoica (2020a), p. 29.

distinct features of its norms, subjects and sanctions, in relation to which we could also understand the different configuration of good-faith in this branch of law.

6 Features and Particularities of Constitutional Law

A classical characterization of constitutional law, as a branch of public law, is very useful in the parsimonious context of our work: "constitutional law is, within public law, the discipline that deals with the knowledge of the rules that establish and constitute the state, that organize and define its institutions".[30]

All democratic constitutions are characterized by a unity of normative content, which regulates with normative value the following principles: national sovereignty, representation, separation of powers in the state, cooperation and relations between them, the fundamental values that define the identity of a nation; the form of government, state structure and political regime; the rights of citizens and their duties; the relationship between domestic and international law, the manner of adoption and amendment of constitutional provisions,[31] but also newer ones, such as the principle of non-retroactivity of the law (except for more favorable criminal or contravention law), provided by art. 15, para. 2 of the Romanian Constitution. To these we can add the principle of proportionality, extracted by way of interpretation from the general principles of the law of equity and justice,[32] which is useful in analyzing the forms of manifestation of good faith in constitutional law, with emphasis on the incidence and applicability of the concept in question in the area of separation and balance between the powers of the state.

The subjects of constitutional law are of interest from the point of view of their classification according to the criteria of their individual or collective character and their politico-legal nature. As regards the situations in which individuals, as citizens, aliens and stateless persons, appear in their own name in legal relationships under constitutional law, no further mention is necessary here, except for the obligation of good faith incumbent on them in the exercise of constitutional and civil rights and freedoms.

On the other hand, in addition to the classic questions on the essence and nature of political power, the relationship between power or powers and the law, why it is necessary to institutionalize power and others,[33] in our case, the focus is on the relationship between powers, on the need to limit powers and the remedies to effectively limit their action.

The definitions of power are multiple and reflect a plurality of constitutive factors and forms of expression, but among these we will retain as representative:

---

[30] Constantinesco and Pierre-Caps (2022), p. 33.

[31] Andreescu and Puran (2022), p. 36.

[32] Andreescu and Puran (2022), p. 57.

[33] Deleanu (2006), p. 27.

abusive extension, coercion, domination[34] and even irrationality.[35] Given these intrinsic features of power, the concept of constitution of the modern era appears as a rational normative product reactive to a social phenomenon that had already been experienced as arbitrary, suffocating and with totalitarian tendencies or precisely:

> so that political power does not remain wild, spontaneous and unpredictable, to be used rationally and according to criteria of efficiency and efficiency according to the will of society (…), it will have to be legitimate, to be controlled by civil society, to take an institutionalized form, to be complemented by authority.[36]

In order to achieve this aim, constitutional law has normativized the principle of the separation of powers in the State, following the model conceived by Montesquieu, *"pouvoir arrette pouvoir"*, thus contrasting the unpredictable and expansionist nature any power with another power or other powers having the same characteristics. The specific way of distributing the powers of the powers in the state in order to ensure their balance is achieved through the judicious distribution of powers and equipping each of them with effective means of control over the others, thus preventing the inherent tendency to exceed their own limits and powers.[37] In this area, the constitutional norms are intended to establish the procedural framework for the lawful exercise of power and authority of state bodies, the consequence of non-compliance with the rules of constitutional rank in the manner of exercising their powers outlined by the fundamental law of the state being the nullity of their acts and decisions.[38]

A specific mention should be made regarding the characteristics of justice as a state power, whose genesis and the principles on the basis of which it was established are different from those of the other two powers. The political powers: "are repelled by that which restrains them, that is, natural law, the unwritten laws, the general principles of law, the rule of reason",[39] whereas justice has a mixed origin, revealed and civil, which exempts it from the primordial irrationality of the phenomenon of power. However, its institutionalization and the granting of the power of jurisdiction, even its role as a regulating valve of confrontation between the state and civil society[40] and its interaction with the other powers in the state within constitutional democracy give it the status of a collective subject of constitutional law.

In this context, the regulation of social relations of power is specific to the creation of imperative legal norms (onerative and prohibitive), dispositive norms being the exception. In other words, the public legal space is regulated primarily by commands and prohibitions, and secondarily, in a limited way, by permissions.[41] Thus,

---

[34] Dănişor (2007), p. 493.

[35] Stoica and Aligică (2009), p. 85.

[36] Iovan (2013), p. 83.

[37] Andreescu and Puran (2022), p. 66.

[38] Ionescu (2019), p. 44.

[39] Dănişor (2007), p. 445.

[40] Dănişor (2007), p. 447.

[41] Stoica (2020b), p. 3.

the most difficult problem of constitutional law is to induce the representatives of the state (especially if they are public authorities constituted as powers – *o.e.*) to constrain themselves by such normative commands.[42]

The constraint of a power by the other powers of the state is a consequence of the constitutional normativization of the principle of separation of powers in the state and consists in the creation of procedures of mutual checks and control between them, and the essence of this system is to assign the exercise of each power to a separate organ of the state, which is prohibited to cumulate functions, and to control each other.[43]

Moreover, in order to bring to order a state power that exceeds the limits of its competence set by the Constitution, the reaction of the other two powers is activated, but a simple reaction or opposition on their part has been considered insufficient in constitutional law. The solution in constitutional law, following the Kelsenian conception,[44] was to create a jurisdictional type of body that could impose the constitution as supreme law on the state powers, namely the Constitutional Court.

7 Good Faith, a Private Law Concept and Its Morphology in the Sphere of Constitutional Law Relationships

Therefore, good faith, with its moral and private law roots, is not a constitutional principle, nor could it have been as long as constitutions have been centered on the general normative framework of state organization and the establishment, exercise and transmission of power.[45]

In the meantime, the definition of constitutional law has become more complex, as it is both a law that constitutes the state itself, which limits the autonomy of the state structure, and a law of reconciliation between freedom and authority, in which the protection of human rights predominates. Thus, the new constitutional law starts from the idea that law is: "more than positive law",[46] and the focus of the constitution shifts from the pillar of the separation of powers in the state to the system of guarantees of civil and human rights and freedoms. More specifically, the organization of political powers is based on principles and rules that prevent the misuse or overreach or non-exercise or improper exercise of the powers granted,[47] being, therefore, a "constraining order" as in the Kelsenian conception.[48]

[42] Dănişor (2007), p. 8.
[43] Dănişor (2007), p. 8.
[44] Rigaux (1998), p. 326.
[45] Ionescu (2019), p. 39.
[46] Dănişor (2007), p. 6.
[47] Stoica (2020b), p. 3.
[48] Rigaux (1998), p. 330.

The principle of the separation of powers in the state, which has remained the only effective remedy for rationalizing power and its obedience to the law since the beginnings of modern constitutionalism, is regulated by technical rules (which we have called rules of constitutional control), which establish the strict powers of each of the three powers, as well as the ways of verifying and limiting each other, and are contained in a real: "charter of the limitation of power".[49]

The technical rules regulating the principle of power-sharing have a prohibitive nature of the type "everything that is not allowed is forbidden" or, in other words, commands and prohibitions are the main forms of regulating the acts, abstentions and activities of public authorities, and they must do or not do only what the law commands or prohibits them to do.[50] Thus, one cannot speak of permissions granted generically to state powers, so that the authorities do not enjoy *weak permissions*, and *strong permissions* are conferred only in the form of the judgment of expediency. The consequence of this is that in public law *strong prohibitions* are those that expressly prohibit certain acts provided for in legal norms.[51]

In other words, such entities, presumed to be sociopathic in the absence of effective mechanisms of coercion, could only form the subject of regulation by a hard law, because: "hard law imposes obligations on the entities within its regulatory domain, and if the entities violate their obligations, sanctions are provided *ex ante*".[52]

Therefore, the tendenational features of political powers imposed, in the first place, the regulation of their organization and powers exclusively through imperative and prohibitive rules, having an effective ability to limit the actions of political powers through powers of verification and control granted to other powers on the basis of a principle of equality between powers.

Secondly, the contemporary Constitutions have introduced the settlement of disputes of competence between the powers of the state by means of constitutional jurisdiction, whose decisions have, as a rule, general binding and definitive effect, which is also the solution of the Romanian Constitution. These solutions, rules and instruments of constraint undoubtedly belong to hard law, and constitutional law, as an instrument of legal constraint of the political powers, which have become subjects of constitutional law, has patented them as a response to their intrinsic nature.

Our conceptual dilemma is whether the action of the powers can be guided and accompanied by a certain freely chosen subjective attitude of the public authorities as powers of the state, which determines good faith in its subjective sense. Hans Kelsen excludes any:

> existing human sentiment which would introduce a factual element into the operation of legal rules in connection with the activity of a legal person, (...) which would corrupt the purpose of a legal order with metaphysical privileges.[53]

---

[49] Deleanu (2006), p. 63.

[50] Stoica (2020b), p. 3.

[51] Stoica (2020b), p. 3.

[52] Stoica (2020b), p. 3.

[53] Rigaux (1998), p. 331.

Good faith, in its classical sense, presupposes a voluntary act on the part of the subject of the law to respect the legal and moral limits imposed by the law. In the sphere of relations between the political powers, this premise is eroded by their abusive nature with which good faith cannot be associated.

The Romanian Constitution follows this logic, at least in its part that deals with the organization and optimal functioning of political powers according to the principle of separation of powers in the state (according to art. 1, para. 4) for which the concept of good faith is rather an exception than a normative rule. The main function of good faith in private-law legal relations, that of a "lubricating mechanism" for converging legitimate interests, is replaced in relations between the powers by the instruments of the "hard-law" system, which are designed to impose clear and effective legal constraints.

The same is not the case with "good-faith" in the exercise of foreign functions of the Romanian state, where it acquires the character of a positive legal obligation. According to the topography of the structure of the Romanian Constitution, *good faith* in the exercise of the external sovereignty of the Romanian State is part of the general principles of our fundamental law. The explanation lies in the fact that the source of the positive legal obligation that the Romanian state assumes in the field of international relations is to be found in public international law, which has a dual nature, both "soft-law" and "hard-law".

The term "soft law" has emerged and developed in the context of international law due to the flexible nature of its rules, such as *gentlemen's agreements* or *memorandum of agreement*,[54] where negotiation is the predominant method of establishing rules, according to the principle of availability of the parties. In an instrumental vision, soft law has been defined as the set of instruments aimed at modifying or guiding the behavior of their addressees, requiring their voluntary adherence. This is the normative framework in which good faith can coexist with "soft-law" legal rules and instruments, the flexible rules of *ius gentium* making it possible to express the good will of the parties and to comply bilaterally with positive obligations.

To summarize, when the State is regarded as a State power in the performance of its external functions and objectives, constitutional law admits the existence of a "subjective" will directed towards the fulfillment of just ends in relation to the international order, which is positivized by the obligation of good faith in the performance of the treaties to which it is a party.

[54] Duțu (2015), p. 181.

8 Transformations in Constitutional Law: Impact on the Forms of Manifestation of Good Faith in Constitutional Law

In its current sense, constitutional law is the result of the pressure exerted by citizens to obtain recognition of their individual freedoms and to participate in the exercise of power, so that its definition as a "technique of authority" becomes obsolete in favor of a broader meaning, as an expression of the balance between the protection of the individual and the general interest of the community.[55] The paradigm shift is reflected in the meaning of the contemporary notion of constitution, which now becomes more a "constitution-guarantee of rights" than a "constitution-separation of powers", as well as in a more pronounced axiological dimension, which is manifested in the increased permissiveness of constitutional law towards moral values in the area of rules guaranteeing the sphere of subjective rights of the individual.[56] At the same time, the free market economy and a society in which individuals are able to make free choices, cooperate and associate, encourages the tendency to apply in the field of public law rules and institutions specific to private law, such as the "social contract"[57] or even the good faith.

In the Romanian Constitution, good faith is a positive legal obligation incumbent on Romanian citizens, foreigners and stateless persons in the exercise of constitutional rights and freedoms. Apparently, this regulation at the level of the constitutional norm would have the meaning of a reduction of the general principle of good faith in civil law to the sphere of rights and obligations incumbent on private persons, as subjects of legal relations under constitutional law. In reality, however, the consecration of a general principle of civil law to the rank of constitutional norm is nothing other than the logical effect of the constitutionalization of the entire Romanian law, and on the other hand, the recognition of the autonomy of civil society from the state in which legal relations are regulated by rules of the type: "everything that is not forbidden is allowed"[58] and where the intervention of state authority is minimal.

In this private legal space, the free will of private individuals is sufficient to carry out the various forms of conduct or this is the framework in which the role of good faith becomes decisive in the exercise of rights and obligations under the law and morality because it is complementary to the civil obligation not to harm anyone.[59] Consequently, what constitutionalized the fundamental law of Romania was one of the oldest principles of the world of persons, with ritual and social roots.

---

[55] Dănişor (2007), p. 4.

[56] Dănişor (2007), p. 6.

[57] Balan (2015), p. 120.

[58] Stoica (2020b), p. 3.

[59] Stoica (2020a), p. 35.

The second vector of transformation of constitutional law is the process of institutionalization and democratization of political power in society. *In statu nascendi*, power tended to be exercised in a conflictual, conjunctural and arbitrary manner by individuals taken separately. The formalization of power through legal norms of constitutional law was an extremely complex process, which involved the manner of appointment of rulers, the nature and content of their mandate, the functional and territorial division of power, the separation of powers, mutual control and balance of powers, competences and decision-making procedures.[60]

While the institutionalization of political powers as public powers dates back to the classical period of modern constitutionalism and is characterized by the patenting of conventional mechanisms of control between and over public powers, the complexification of contemporary society has developed new control mechanisms, some institutionalized, and others born from new social and political practices.

These new mechanisms, which are part of a more vague process of "influencing the powers",[61] as opposed to the process of controlling the powers, are the result of the establishment of auxiliary bodies of the various public authorities (Legislative Council, Supreme Council for the Defense of the Country, Superior Council of Magistracy, Constitutional Court, Court of Accounts, Ombudsman). This process of multiplication of decision-making factors and dissuasive forms of control leads to the formation of a new civic conduct of the public authorities constituted as state powers, which has the effect of a certain "depoliticization" of the powers in favor of the amplification of their "civility" features.[62]

Seen as subjects of law:

> the three powers must be considered as three moral persons that complement and subordinate each other, being the beneficiaries of a simple division of powers, according to the principle of division of labor.[63]

With the common features of their status as subjects of law, legal relations under public law follow the same structure as private law. The difference lies in the specific form of manifestation of legal capacity depending on the branch of law in which the subjects of law enter into specific legal relations. More specifically, in relation to the form of the subjects of law, legal capacity in civil law, belonging to a natural or legal person, is transformed into competence in the case of state organs or authorities or into sovereignty, if it is the state itself.[64]

To the extent that: "the constitution is no longer a mere concept, but a real contract",[65] and public authorities are increasingly detached from their original status of irrational and abusive powers under the action of the rules and mechanisms of constitutional democracy, returning to their roots as "moral persons", we witness a

---

[60] Deleanu (2006), p. 29.

[61] Deleanu (2006), p. 186.

[62] Deleanu (2006), p. 37.

[63] Deleanu (2006), p. 57.

[64] Andriuţă (2017), p. 43,

[65] Stoica and Aligică (2009), p. 86.

complete translation of the content and object of civil law legal relationship into the content of the constitutional law legal relationship. Within the latter, the exercise of the subjective rights and the fulfillment of the correlative obligations of private persons become special and binding prerogatives of the public authorities. Unlike private individuals, however, public authorities do not have the freedom to do whatever they wish, their acts having to fall strictly within the scope of the powers granted to them.[66] Thus, the mutations undergone by the substance of political power through its institutionalization in the form of public authorities, with an effect on the conduct shaped by constitutional norms in terms of ensuring the supremacy of the constitution and the normative pre-eminence of human rights, raise the question of a certain "subjectivity" of these authorities.

We can speak of the modeling of a constitutional conduct that accompanies and is reflected in the ways of fulfilling the prerogatives granted by the fundamental law in a similar way to the instrumental obligation of good faith, which, in the civil legal relationship is complementary to the civil obligation not to harm anyone. This conduct, which is about to become a necessary feature of the public authorities provided for in the Romanian Constitution, is most often referred to as "loyalty" in Romanian constitutional doctrine and, sometimes, "good faith" in the case law of the Romanian Constitutional Court.

9 Loyalty and Good Faith in Constitutional and Electoral Doctrine and Jurisprudence in Romania

In the Romanian constitutional doctrine, the principle of loyalty has been accepted as it has been invoked and exemplified in the jurisprudence of the Romanian Constitutional Court, in which sense we will adhere to the observation that: "the line of evolution of the principle of constitutional loyalty in our law follows the line of constitutional jurisprudence".[67]

Following the jurisprudential construction of this concept, the doctrine has commented on various decisions of the Constitutional Court of Romania that have referred to constitutional loyalty in its different stages of development. For example, an opinion states that the jurisprudence of the Constitutional Court of Romania has revealed the existence of three areas of manifestation of the principle of constitutional loyalty, namely: loyal behavior of public authorities towards the Constitution, loyal reciprocal behavior of public authorities in institutional relations and loyal behavior of public authorities called upon to carry out the popular will.[68] The author observes that in Decision no. 356 of April 5, 2007, concerning a legal conflict of a constitutional nature between the Prime Minister and the President of Romania

[66] Stoica (2020b), p. 3.

[67] Nae (2013), p. 5.

[68] Nae (2013), p. 5.

regarding the exercise of powers specific to each branch of the two branches of the Romanian executive, the Constitutional Court referred to the phrase "constitutional framework of loyalty and cooperation", creating a bridge between the two concepts, without granting them the status of "constitutional principles".[69]

Through a series of decisions in 2012, the Constitutional Court has enriched the conceptual content of good-faith (sometimes in relation to constitutional loyalty, sometimes dissociating them) and has gradually changed their epistemological status. Thus, by Decision no. 51 of January 25, 2012, constitutional loyalty is elevated to the rank of "constitutional principle", referring to the corollary of the principle of separation of powers, i.e. the relations of cooperation between them, which: "must be realized in the spirit of the rules of constitutional loyalty".[70]

By Decision No 209 of 7 March 2012, the Constitutional Court raises the issue of the loyal conduct of public authorities towards the Constitution of Romania, and the interpretation of the rules establishing their powers "must be made in good faith". In this context, loyalty to the Constitution implies compliance with its provisions, and the interpretation of the constitutional rules governing them must be made in "good faith". In other words: "the relationship between good faith and the loyalty of public authorities to the fundamental law is a relationship as from means or instrument to end or interest".[71]

In Decision No. 682 of 27 June 2012, the Constitutional Court establishes the obligation of the Romanian Parliament to carry out the sovereign will of the people expressed by referendum (even if of a consultative nature), reasoning that "this interpretation is also based on the principle of constitutional loyalty (…), a principle which requires that the authorities with decision-making powers in the areas concerned by the issue subject to referendum take into account, analyze and identify ways to implement the will expressed by the people".

The importance of the decision lies in the establishment of an obligation of loyalty to the people, as the holders of national sovereignty, which is incumbent on Parliament.[72]

In the recitals of Decision No. 727 of July 24, 2012, the Court already refers to the "obligation of constitutional loyalty" incumbent on all public authorities, which implies both respect for the supremacy of the Romanian Constitution and the obligation of the authorities to operate within the limits of the powers assigned by the fundamental law, without interference in the powers and functioning of the other powers of the state, but also in the spirit of cooperation between them.[73] In Decision No. 972 of November 21, 2012, the Court expresses the importance for the functioning of the rule of law of the collaboration between the powers of the state, which

[69] Nae (2013), p. 5.
[70] Nae (2013), p. 5.
[71] Nae (2013), p. 8.
[72] Nae (2013), p. 9.
[73] Nae (2013), p. 9.

must be carried out in the spirit of the rules of constitutional loyalty, which receives the status of: "guarantee of the principle and balance of powers in the state".[74]

In another view, constitutional loyalty can be characterized as a "value-principle" intrinsic to all constitutions, without which no constitution could function optimally.[75] In a comprehensive formulation, the authors define constitutional loyalty as:

> attachment to constitutional values, respect for the Constitution in its letter and spirit, fulfillment in good faith of the obligations and respect for the rights that the Constitution provides for, compliance with the limits of competence established by the constitutional texts and respect for the competence regulated for all public authorities, cooperation, collaboration, consultation in the fulfillment of concurrent competences.[76]

Analyzing the jurisprudence of the Romanian Constitutional Court in this matter, the authors have drawn the following concrete contents of constitutional loyalty depending on the legal situations that have been claimed. First of all, good faith was invoked as a rule of interpretation of the procedural rules relating to the internal activity of the Parliament in order to avoid bottlenecks that could occur in the work of the institution (the Court was asked to rule on the constitutionality of Parliament Decision No. 1 of February 9, 2012 on the granting of confidence in the Government).

Second, loyal constitutional behavior requires respect for the competence of public authorities, which derives from the letter and spirit of the Basic Law. Parliament is not permitted, on the basis of its own statutory provisions, to censure a final and irrevocable judgment which is res judicata. In resolving a legal conflict of a constitutional nature between the judicial authority, represented by the High Court of Cassation and Justice, and the legislative authority, represented by the Romanian Senate, the Constitutional Court ruled that constitutional loyalty must also be shown in Parliament's relations with the other public authorities, whose powers must also be respected. In this regard, the Court held that, by putting before the Senate plenary a final and irrevocable judicial decision, which found a senator to be incompatible, followed by a negative vote on the implementation of this decision:

> the Senate acted as a hierarchically superior court, which affects the fundamental principle of the rule of law, namely the principle of separation and balance of powers within the constitutional democracy, enshrined in Art. (4) of the Basic Law.[77]

The obligation of constitutional loyalty also requires the legislative authority not to adopt rules contrary to those decided by the Constitutional Court, with a view to adopting legislative solutions vitiated by unconstitutionality. By Decision No. 1018 of July 19, 2010, the Court held that constitutional loyalty requires that the interpretation and application of acts of Parliament be carried out in good faith, in compliance with the role of this authority in the rule of law.

---

[74] Nae (2013), p. 9.

[75] Toader and Safta (2011), p. 5.

[76] Toader and Safta (2011), p. 6.

[77] Toader and Safta (2011), p. 6.

In this sense: "the Parliament's judgment, like any legal act, must be interpreted and applied in good faith and in the spirit of loyalty to the fundamental law".[78]

The powers of the President of Romania and his obligation to behave loyally towards the Fundamental Law have been analyzed on the occasion of the legal conflicts of constitutional nature between the President of Romania and the Prime Minister of the Government. The Court ruled in this respect that "the institutional relations between the Prime Minister and the Government and the President of Romania must operate within the constitutional framework of loyalty and cooperation, in order to fulfill the constitutional attributions distinctly regulated for each of the authorities", while identifying some specific solutions in the spirit of these rules, as follows: (a) the procedure for appointing ministers presupposes loyal collaboration between the President of Romania and the Prime Minister, in the sense that the President of Romania, not having the right of veto, may ask the Prime Minister once only, with reasons, to make a new proposal for the appointment of another person to the post of minister, the reasons for the President's request not being open to censure by the Head of Government (Decision no.98 of February 7, 2008); b) The decision on Romania's representation at the European Council must be based on loyal cooperation between the President, the Prime Minister and the Parliament. The President of Romania participates in the meetings of the European Council as Head of State, but may expressly delegate this to the Prime Minister, the concrete assessment having to take into account a number of objective criteria. In this regard, in its decision no. 683 of June 27, 2012, the Court emphasized that:

> in carrying out their powers, the public authorities must be concerned with the proper functioning of the rule of law, and thus have a duty to cooperate in the spirit of the rules of constitutional loyalty.[79]

The principle of constitutional loyalty requires cooperation, constitutional dialogue and consensus in the procedure of signing or countersigning decrees of the President of Romania. The signing/countersigning of presidential decrees and the Court's ruling on the competences of the public authorities involved has led to new developments of the principle of constitutional loyalty.[80]

When asked about another legal conflict of a constitutional nature between the same authorities, by decision no. 284 of May 21, 2014, the Court developed the above-mentioned principle, noting that its application: "represents a bivalent legal operation, being equally opposable to the two public authorities involved in the procedure of issuing the decree (…)".[81]

In a more recent work, Professors Tudorel Toader and Marieta Safta have the merit of having found in the jurisprudence of the Constitutional Court of Romania the oldest decision in which the Constitutional Court refers to the idea of good faith, but whose major importance lies in raising its epistemic status to the level of a

---

[78] Toader and Safta (2011), p. 13.

[79] Toader and Safta (2011), p. 15.

[80] Toader and Safta (2011), p. 16.

[81] Toader and Safta (2011), p. 16.

"constitutional category" of general applicability, which is thus imposed on all subjects of law and legal relations, regardless of their nature.[82] At the same time, the authors also point out the extension of the conceptual scope of loyalty in constitutional law by coupling this trait of conduct incumbent on public authorities in their constitutional duties and on all public institutions operating in society to the concept of "constitutional normative order", defined as "the set of principles that establish the social, political and legal relations of a society" (Decision No 611/2017, Published in the Official Gazette No 877/2017).

Examining the jurisprudence of the Constitutional Court on the matter, the two authors note that there are close correlations between specific legal categories such as "constitutional normative order", "constitutional loyalty" and the old legal meta-category of "good faith", and these connections raise difficulties of conceptual delimitation when we refer to the conduct of collective subjects of constitutional law and in identifying the breach of the obligation of good faith and the legal effects it produces.[83]

In another opinion, the complex nature of the relations between the state authorities presupposes their proper functioning, regardless of whether or not they are mentioned in the Constitution, under the imperative of respect for the principle of its supremacy. With a view to ensuring this absolute principle, the jurisprudential interpretation carried out by the Constitutional Court after the 2003 revision of the Romanian Constitution has the role:

> to support the proper functioning of the public powers within the constitutional relations of separation, balance and mutual control between them, constituting a genuine work of law enforcement based on the interpretation of legal norms.[84]

In the authors' opinion, the constitutional obligation to behave constitutionally in loyalty to the normative content and purpose of the Constitution is also an expression of the requirement of legitimacy that must be fulfilled by both normative acts and governmental measures or provisions, in the sense that: "the legitimacy of a legal act (…) reveals the requirement that the act in question must correspond not only to the letter of the Constitution, but also to its spirit".[85]

Another expression of the loyal behavior of the authorities is also to be found in the proportionality ratio, which results from the institutional application of the fundamental principle of the separation of powers in the state. Considered to be the very foundation of constitutional democracy, this principle is an expression of the moderation and rationalization of state power. The conditions for achieving this goal of the principle of the separation of state powers are, on the one hand, the limitation of state power in relation to the fundamental rights and freedoms of citizens, and, on the other hand, the practical way in which the autonomy of public

[82] Toader and Safta (2024), p. 41.

[83] Toader and Safta (2024), p. 41.

[84] Andreescu and Puran (2022), p. 99.

[85] Andreescu and Puran (2022), p. 100.

authorities and the effective relations between them are conceived in order to prevent non-functional separatism.[86]

The concept of constitutional loyalty has received new connotations in the case law of the Constitutional Court of Romania assigned to the most recent elections for the election of the President of Romania. Thus, by Judgment No. 2 of October 5, 2024, on the resolution of a challenge to a candidacy filed for the office of President of Romania, constitutional loyalty implies the respect of all constitutional values, principles, standards, requirements and procedures by all subjects of law, who must not only value them, but also prove them through their conduct, this being "a real guarantee for the exercise of high dignities in the Romanian State".

All the more so, with regard to the persons who aspire to the highest dignity in the Romanian State, the Court particularizes their conduct in an axiological sense of respect for the Constitution, as "an obligation expressly enshrined in the Fundamental Law and reinforced by the oath of allegiance, as an expression of loyalty to the country". (Published in the Official Gazette, No. 1003 of October 8, 2024). At the same time, the process of individualizing the conduct of constitutional loyalty of the candidates for the office of President of Romania also consists in the fulfillment of an *ex novo* constitutional obligation, called "the defense of constitutional democracy", about which the Court states in the recitals of the Judgment that, together with the respect for the Constitution, they "are provided for by the Constitution, are accessible and foreseeable for all persons who express their intention to run for the highest office in the State".

According to the logic of legal liability, which presupposes the commission of an unlawful act, with guilt, the production of a socially negative result, a causal relationship between the unlawful act and the result and the examination of the causes that could remove the liability, the Court ruled that "the violation of constitutional values and unconstitutional propaganda by the candidate must be ascertained and sanctioned by specific means of constitutional law from the perspective of the right to be elected" and, at the same time, that it is the competent body to apply the sanction of invalidation of a candidacy for the supreme office in the state. There are, however, some legal injunctions in this judgment, which were pointed out in the separate opinion of one of the judges of the Court, but the legal nature of this sanction, the competence and the execution of the judgment are not the subject of this analysis.

However, from the perspective of this study, what is of interest is the enrichment of the concept of constitutional loyalty with an *ex novo* obligation, that of "defending constitutional democracy", as well as the fact that this judgment of the Constitutional Court sanctioned for the first time the violation of the fundamental duty of loyalty to the country, provided for by art. 54 of the Romanian Constitution, which was applied to a qualified subject of constitutional law, namely a candidate for the office of President of Romania.

[86] Andreescu and Puran (2022), p. 64.

10 Good Faith as a Principle of Judicial Authority

Unlike the other two powers of the state, whose antagonism is easier to understand,[87] the judiciary has a particular genesis, but also a particular status. Naturally, it does not have the same primordial features as political powers, i.e. a natural abusive tendency, coercion, domination or even irrationality. Both its mode of formation and its sources are distinct and, consequently, its principles of organization and functioning are different. In the Old Testament, where the need to constitute a body of judges arises, Moses is advised to choose his judges only from among: "righteous and God-fearing men who hate covetousness".[88]

Perfect objectivity, impartiality, non-partisanship, irrespective of the social rank of the person being judged, are qualities that every judge should possess.

It is not by chance that the new law on the Statute of Judges and Prosecutors in Romania, Law no. 303/2022, stipulates that "judges and prosecutors shall carry out their work in good faith and impartially, including by ensuring the appearance of impartiality". By comparison, in the previous law on the Statute of Judges and Prosecutors, Law No 303/2004, good faith was only a standard of conduct for magistrates in "relations at work and in society", having only the status of an ethical and deontological criterion.

From the perspective of this study, the genesis of good-faith as a principle of judicial authority presupposes, as implicit values, the honesty and impartiality of magistrates and equality before the law. If we add to this the biblical exhortation to just and lawful judgment: "judge and render just judgments in your parties; do not devise one against another without law, and do not love a crooked oath, for I hate all these things",[89] we are in practice in the presence of the primordial elements of good faith as it has been configured in private law, namely right intention, lawfulness and not harming another. Therefore, good faith, as a principle of activity of magistrates in the Romanian judicial system, appears under the name and its original meaning of *bona fides*, being common with that which is incumbent on all participants in legal relations.

Moreover, the filiation of good-faith, as a transcendent principle of law, is also extended to the different branches of the Romanian judicial process, having its own characteristics of the branch of substantive law that it processualizes according to the branch of public or private law to which they belong.

In Romanian civil procedural law, the parties are obliged to exercise their procedural rights in good faith, in accordance with the purpose for which they have been recognized by law and without violating the procedural rights of the other party, and they shall be liable for the material and moral damages caused by their abusive exercise. With regard to the conduct of the judge, whenever the law reserves to the judge the power of discretion or requires him to take into account all the

[87] Dănişor (2007), p. 424.
[88] Safta-Romano (1997), p. 38.
[89] Safta-Romano (1997), p. 42.

circumstances of the case, he shall take into account, inter alia, the general principles of law, the requirements of fairness and good faith, in accordance with Art. 22, para. 7 of the Code of Civil Procedure.

In Romanian procedural-criminal law, good-faith appears in the form of loyalty as a principle in the administration of evidence. The principle of loyalty in the administration of evidence involves three aspects: (a) the prohibition of the use of violence, threats, means of coercion, promises or inducements for the purpose of obtaining evidence; (b) the prohibition of the use of methods or techniques of eavesdropping that affect the person's ability to consciously and voluntarily remember and relate the facts that constitute the subject of the evidence; (c) the prohibition of provoking a person to commit or continue to commit a criminal act, for the purpose of obtaining evidence.[90]

Consequently, the judicial authority is the only one of the three powers of the state that has naturally embraced the idea of good faith as a genuine principle of organization, functioning and activity of the magistrates who compose it, not having to borrow or copy it from other social practices, because it is the very archetype on which it was established as an institutionalized power in the state.

11 Conclusion

The present study started from a rough observation that good faith is not currently a general principle of constitutional law, and the cause of this absence is to be found in the reactive nature of modern constitutions in relation to the original features of political power, which have required the finding of normative solutions belonging to hard law, namely rules of verification and control of an imperative nature. In principle, technical, mandatory rules, which regulate the organization and functioning of state powers as public authorities, are not compatible with good faith, as a model of conduct that presupposes a certain "subjectivity" of collective subjects of constitutional law, whose "good will" cannot be presumed but must be controlled.

As regards compliance with international treaties, where good faith is a positive legal obligation of the Romanian State, its source is public international law, whose flexible rules of *ius gentium* allow it to manifest itself when concluding and complying with mutual agreements.

However, the metamorphoses of contemporary constitutional law, which is no longer merely a law of the organization of the state and the powers, but a law of the reconciliation of authority and liberty, and constitutions are more "guarantees of rights" than "charters of the limitation of power", reduce the primordial incompatibility between the imperative norms of control of the powers and good faith as an instrumental norm of private law, which is why conceptual borrowings and even of legal institutions are becoming more permissive, particularly in the area of the

[90] Boroi and Neguț (2020), p. 194.

regulation of subjective rights. The constitutionalization of good faith as an obligation of individual subjects of constitutional law in the exercise of fundamental rights and freedoms is a direct reflection of this trend.

The absence of good-faith among the normative principles of constitutional law has been clarified by the praetorian construction of the constitutional dimensions of this concept through the case law of the Constitutional Court of Romania. In this sense, unlike the structural elements of good faith in civil law, i.e., right intention, lawfulness and abstention from causing any harm, in the Court's case law it has been defined by notions such as "loyal constitutional behavior", "collaboration and consensus between public authorities", "fidelity or loyalty towards the Constitution and the Romanian people", "respect for the Constitution in its letter and spirit", "real guarantee for the fulfillment of the functions of public dignity", "legal obligation", "proportionality", "normative order" and "defense of constitutional democracy".

It is certain that in this context, the epistemological status of good-faith is evolving, so that in a recent work it has been categorized as a constitutional value of a moral nature, along with the intangibility of human life, dignity, mental and physical integrity of man, justice, solidarity and equity, which "may be the result of one's own experiences, traditions or thinking, as a result of the organic development of spiritual, political and legal culture.[91]

We do not know whether good-faith will become a normative principle of constitutional law or will join the ranks of the supreme values of the Romanian state, along with those set out in Article 1, paragraph 3 of the Romanian Constitution, but it is already a democratic legal tradition, in the sense that it has belonged to people, as subjects of law, since ancient times. The force with which a civil law concept has penetrated the rigid sphere of public law rules, values and principles speaks of a true resurrection of private law and its effect on constitutional law is already spectacular.

References

Andreescu M, Puran AN (2022) Constitutional law. Philosophy of law and history. Studii şi eseuri, C.H. Beck Publishing House

Andriuţă E (2017) Aspecte generale cu privire la capacità juridică. Revista Naţională de Drept 198(4):43

Balan M (2015) Constitutional law and political institutions, General theory of state and constitution, vol I. Constituţia României în context European, Editura Hamangiu

Bob M (2015) In search of the roots of modern Romanian civil law. In: Popescu D, Popa I (eds) Liber Amicorum Liviu Pop. Reforma dreptului privat român în contextul federalismului juridi European. Universul Juridic Publishing House

Boroi A, Neguţ G (2020) Drept procesual penal, 2nd edn (revised and updated). Editura Hamangiu

Constantinesco V, Pierre-Caps S (2022) Constitutional Law (translated by Diana Dănişor). Universul Juridic Publishing House

[91] Varga and Benke (2021), p. 46.

Dănişor D (2007) Constitutional law and political institutions, Vol. I. Teoria generală. C.H. Beck Publishing House
Deleanu I (2006) Constitutional institutions and procedures - in Romanian and comparative law. C.H. Beck Publishing House
Dima B (2009) Conflictele juridice de natură constituţională dintre legislativ, executiv şi puterea judecătorească. Sfera Politica 141:3
Dissescu C (1915) Constitutional law. Socec & Co Publishing House
Djuvara M (1930) General theory of law. Drept raţional, izvoare şi drept pozitiv. ALL Beck Publishing House. (reprint 1999)
Dogaru I (2002) Et alii, Drept civil. Idei producătoare de efecte juridice. All Beck Publishing House
Duţu M (2015) The flexible law: complement, alternative or future of the law? Revista Dreptul 26(1):179
Floare M (2019) The role of good faith as a safety valve in contractual matters. In: Mangu F (ed) Probleme controversate în dreptul obligaţiilor. Universul Juridic Publishing House
Gherasim D (1981) Bona-credinţă în raporturile juridice civile. Editura Academiei
Ionescu C (2019) Tratat de drept constituţional contemporan. C.H. Beck Publishing House
Iovan M (2013) Power, authority and counteracting the abuse of power. Revista de Filosofie, Sociologie şi Ştiinţe Politice 163(3):74
Loughlin M (2003) The idea of public law. Oxford University Press
Lupu M (2020) Constitutionalizing law. Universul Juridic Publishing House
Muraru I (1995) Eficienţa şi valabilitatea Constituţiei. Revista de Drept Public 1
Nae B (2013) The principle of constitutional loyalty in Romanian Law - form without substance or metaphor of the rule of law? Revista ştiinţifică a studenţilor în drept
Pop C (2019) Aspecte privind evoluţia şi aplicabilitatea bune-credinţe în drept roman. Studia Universitatis Babeş-Bolyai Iurisprudentia 64(3):58
Rigaux F (1998) Hans Kelsen on international law. Eur J Int Law 9:325–343
Safta-Romano E (1997) Legal archetypes in the Bible. Polirom Publishing House
Stoica V (2020a) Consideraţii comparative privind noţiunile de bună-credinţă, diligenţă, eroare, dol, fraud, fraud, rea-credinţă, vinovăţie (intenţie şi culpă). Revista română de drept privat 4:13
Stoica V (2020b) Everything that is not forbidden is allowed or everything that is not allowed is forbidden? (The game of permissions, commands and contradictions in private and public law)
Stoica V, Aligică D (2009) Reconstruction of the Right: between the Western capitalist experiment and the Romanian national project. Humanitas Publishing House
Toader T, Safta M (2011) The principle of constitutional loyalty. In: Scientific Conference "20 years since the proclamation of independence of the Republic of Moldova", August 2011
Toader T, Safta M (2024) Good faith of public authorities in the interpretation and application of legal rules. In: Tăbăraş M, Maxim F, Dinu E (eds) Good faith in law. Good faith as the foundation of legal equity, Proceedings of the international conference of law, European studies and international relations, Bucharest, May 16–17, 2024, 12th edn. Universul Juridic Publishing House
Varga A, Benke K (2021) Perspective juridice asupra conţinutului valori înscrise în Constituţia României. In: Dorneanu V, Manole D, Benke K, Papuc T (eds) Patrimoniul constituţional şi valori democratice. Hamangiu Publishing House

Good Faith in U.S. Constitutional Law

Ethan J. Leib

Abstract The language of "good faith" and "bad faith" is rarely invoked directly with a specific legal meaning within the constitutional law of the United States. But it would be a mistake to ignore the work motivational analysis and faithfulness to role and the Constitution plays more broadly within constitutional law more capaciously conceived. Many domains of constitutional law interrogate the good faith or bad faith of government actors to test their compliance with constitutional norms – and constitutional practices routinely demand fidelity to the constitutional project itself. From the law of oaths and impeachments to the law of tiered scrutiny associated with the Equal Protection Clause under the Fourteenth Amendment among others, several features of U.S. constitutional law make important demands on public officeholders. More important, perhaps, than the pockets of direct enforcement of good faith norms to U.S. constitutional law, however, is the theory of public office they evince. That so often the Constitution of the United States demands as a primary rule of conduct that public officers act faithfully tells us that there is a fiduciary conception of office pervading the law even when it is not enforced directly as a rule of decision. That brings it closer to private law implementations of good faith than has thus far been appreciated.

> The task of legal theory is not simply to help decide (close) cases. Legal theory also seeks to illuminate the character of legal relations. It seeks, speaking a little loosely, to reveal the meaning of law. An account of good faith might therefore have great theoretical value even if it provides only limited assistance in deciding cases. An understanding of good faith thus does not so much help to decide cases as to understand what has been decided.[1]

[1] Markovits (2014), pp. 279–280.

E. J. Leib (✉)
Fordham Law School, New York, NY, USA
e-mail: ethan.leib@law.fordham.edu

J. Podkowik et al. (eds.), *Gleams of Good Faith in Constitutional Law*, Ius Gentium: Comparative Perspectives on Law and Justice 132,
https://doi.org/10.1007/978-3-032-06486-8_10

1 Introduction

The United States Supreme Court does not often overtly center "good faith" or "bad faith" in its constitutional doctrine. Indeed, in its recent watershed (and unprecedented) decision about the availability of presidential immunities from prosecution in *Trump v. United States*, the Court demeaned reliance on the "good faith" of prosecutors to sustain the right kind of separation of powers twice[2] and explicitly disallowed any interrogation of presidential motive.[3] One might agree, then, with a recent scholar who found a need to explain why the United States seems to suppress good faith discourse within constitutional law.[4] This chapter, instead, makes an effort to highlight the ways good faith actually is central to constitutional law, even as the apex Court seems only ambivalently committed to its ability to be useful in deciding cases.

Part II below tours the domains in which good faith and proper intent (and the avoidance of illicit motivation) matters to constitutional law. It also scopes outward to explain why these illustrative invocations of good faith ought to be seen to be doing more basic work at the root of constitutional law: setting a rule of conduct for officers empowered and entrusted by the Constitution even while signaling all the difficulties motivational inquiries can wreak upon courts. This strategy – of separating rules of decision from more basic rules of conduct – is a feature of domains of private law like fiduciary law; the constitutional system's fabric, in this way, draws on ideas from fiduciary governance. Part III reinforces why this makes sense, as concerns about conflicts of interest and structural opportunism triggered by power imbalances and the difficulty of monitoring pervade the U.S. constitutional system just like they do in areas of private law that use fiduciary duties to constrain powerholders. Even if the framers of the U.S. Constitution wanted to engage in institutional design to plan for devils at the helm and self-interested politicians contesting one another for power,[5] there still remain many strategies built into constitutional law broadly conceived that channel constitutional actors towards good faith conduct. All this speaks to a deeper conception of role and the requirement of faithfulness that underwrites the mechanisms of constitutional government.

2 Doctrines of Good Faith

It is hard not to start with the document itself. The President must under Article II, Section 1 take an oath to "faithfully execute the Office" and must under Article II, Section III "take Care that the Laws be faithfully executed." Lest one think it is only

[2] Trump v. United States (2024) 603 U.S., 37, 41.

[3] Trump v. United States (2024) 603 U.S., 18, 32.

[4] Pozen (2016).

[5] Gardbaum (2016), pp. 161–162.

the President who is obligated under oath to faithfulness, the oath of office commanded by Article VI to "Senators and Representatives" and "all executive and judicial Officers" to support the Constitution has been, by federal law, articulated to include a pronouncement of "true faith and allegiance" to the Constitution and a promise to "faithfully discharge" the office (5 U.S.C. § 3331). No one can be installed into an office under the Constitution without swearing or affirming faithfulness – and however courts seek to enforce such oaths and affirmations, they are part and parcel of a law of public office.[6] Indeed, even if one thought these oaths were ceremonial, they are a tool for norm internalization that draws rather prominently on faithfulness to the document and to office.

A closely related command to being faithful under the document is the emphasis on offices conceptualized as "trusts," a demarcation that appears four times in the short original Constitution – perhaps most famously in Article 1, Section 9's so-called Emoluments Clause.[7] That clause contains the Constitution's most explicit proscription against self-dealing, one that extends well beyond just the President who gets another prohibition from taking emoluments in Article II, Section 1; together they might be thought to support a more general "anti-corruption" principle that commands good faith.[8]

If one looked for law-as-rules-of-decision-applied-by-courts, there are just a handful of cases that seem to turn on the Constitution's description of offices as trusts.[9] But if one instead looked to legal impeachments throughout history (both articles of impeachment drawn in the House and subsequent trials in the Senate), the invocation of public office as a public trust is a dominant theme – revealing a powerful legal enforcement mechanism that suggests that the oath and the undertaking of office can have serious legal consequences for breach of trust and breach of faith: to wit, removal.[10] It is hard to deny that the mechanisms by which officers can lose their offices – and the associated legal standards therefor – are foundational to constitutional law and reveal a deep structure of the law of public office,[11] whatever pockets of judicial doctrine do or don't do to reinforce that picture. One of the recent House Reports impeaching President Donald Trump, for example, in citing the fiduciary theory of Article II of the U.S. Constitution,[12] wanted the President removed in part because he failed to "faithfully execute" his office by being "motivated" "in bad faith or with corrupt intent" to promote his "private self-interest" over the "public interest".[13]

---

[6] Leib and Kent (2021), Kent et al. (2019).

[7] Leib and Galoob (2019), pp. 306–308.

[8] Teachout (2009).

[9] Leib and Galoob (2019), pp. 305–306; Leib and Shugerman (2019), p. 487.

[10] Leib et al. (2013), pp. 715–717; Rogers and Young (1975).

[11] Leib (2023), p. 193.

[12] Kent et al. (2019).

[13] House Report (2019), pp. 34–35, 79.

Yet there are several corners of constitutional doctrine in the courts of law rather than courts of impeachment that do draw on conceptions of good and bad faith explicitly, as well. For example, good faith functions as a carve-out to protect public officials when they make a "reasonable mistake under the circumstances, including the good faith exception to the exclusionary rule, the good faith exception to a criminal defendant's guarantee of access to evidence, and, most broadly, the qualified immunity defense to civil actions".[14] Moreover, bad faith can be a factor in a range of decisional contexts: whether prosecutions are barred if a delay by the government was in bad faith; whether prior testimony can be used if a witness was deported by the government in bad faith; whether selective prosecution is unconstitutional because brought in bad faith, relying on race or religion; whether a retrial of a defendant is barred because of bad-faith conduct of the judge; and whether federal courts can enjoin state prosecutions undertaken in bad faith to interfere with federal constitutional rights.[15] Pozen warns us not to take these examples too seriously because it is hard to for a litigant to benefit from the high bars associated with bad faith.[16] But whether a litigant wins is a different question from the projection of the rules of conduct to constitutional actors subject to the relevant standards, including state officials who are also bound by oath to support the Constitution under Article VI.

Motivational analysis more generally – attempting to evaluate the constitutional validity of governmental action by rooting the inquiry in the motives of the state actors – can also be considered a law of good and bad faith. And these are abundant within the doctrines of U.S. constitutional law. Judges may and do look behind facially neutral laws to see if they are impugned by illicit motivations or discriminatory intent. Heightened scrutiny is used to smoke out race and sex discrimination in Equal Protection jurisprudence,[17] as well as religious discrimination or religious establishment in First Amendment jurisprudence that interrogates state purpose. Courts have found such discriminatory intent as a reason to invalidate state action in "conduct ranging from discrimination in employment to felon disenfranchisement, redistricting, and jury selection".[18] They have also focused on "penological purpose" and intent directly in cases under the Eighth Amendment's proscription on "cruel and unusual punishment".[19] And even when judges are supposed to be doing "mere" rational basis review rather than engaging in heightened scrutiny, they are supposed to be on the lookout for "animus",[20] a clear kind of bad faith review that looks for "malicious motives".[21] Again in these domains, hopeful litigants know

[14] Pozen (2016), p. 898.

[15] Pozen (2016), pp. 899–900.

[16] Pozen (2016), p. 900.

[17] Grutter v. Bollinger (2003) 539 U.S. 306, 326.

[18] Shaw (2019), pp. 1351–1352.

[19] Shaw (2019), pp. 1354–1355.

[20] MacMahon (2015), p. 2086.

[21] Pozen (2016), p. 903.

establishing malign intent will face formidable barriers – yet there is no question that these sorts of inquiries are part of the fabric of constitutional law doctrine, whatever their historical provenance[22] and whatever vocal critics of interrogating legislative intent for good or bad faith would prefer the law to be.[23] As Larry Sager wrote long ago, "[l]egislative bad faith is a constitutionally impermissible motive."[24]

Not everyone who knows the evidence about the roles good and bad faith and motive analysis play in the document and doctrines of constitutional law feels terribly impressed. Some would emphasize that it is very hard for courts to acknowledge that government actors actually are in bad faith or have discriminatory intent very often. They would argue that focusing on the most egregious cases of enforcement against bad faith governmental activity belies ordinary constitutional law where motive is not carefully interrogated nor is good faith particularly centered. More, courts also often explicitly distance themselves from motivational analysis not only in high-profile immunity cases about the President[25] but in more ordinary cases of, for example, potentially pretextual police work, undermining a core way courts could police the police.[26]

Courts are often refusing to look into the hearts and minds of government actors as mechanisms of control for at least two good reasons, too: First, by American tradition from *The Federalist No. 51,*[27] the American system is built for "ambition . . . to counteract ambition" rather than for "angels . . . to govern." Second, a standard set of institutional competence concerns (and the downstream chilling effects poor oversight could cause) leave courts tepid about combing other actors for evidence of motivations,[28] especially in legal domains where judges themselves could be accused of bad faith in using discretionary standards.[29]

Yet although these justifications for modest enforcement of good faith duties sound in constitutional considerations particularly, the divergence of the rhetoric of good faith from its actual judicial enforcement is not, however, distinctive to constitutional law. Rather, many other spheres of law actually reveal a similar pattern. Consider this study of good faith[30]:

> [I]n the real world of litigation, the application of [a duty of] good faith and fair dealing has generally fallen short of these demanding ideals. The case law is replete with judges expressing the need for caution, and courts have devised various restrictive doctrinal tests that make it difficult to establish a breach of the duty. When evaluating the defendant's performance, courts sometimes use deferential standards of review, akin to corporate law's

[22] Nelson (2008).

[23] Fallon (2016).

[24] Sager (1981), p. 77.

[25] Trump v. United States (2024) 603 U.S.

[26] Pozen (2016), p. 899.

[27] The Federalist No. 51 (1788).

[28] Pozen (2016).

[29] Levinson (2016), p. 170.

[30] MacMahon (2015), pp. 2052–2053.

> business judgment rule. In addition, courts often require plaintiffs to establish a bad motive, trickery, or some other form of particularly egregious conduct by the defendant. Another way that courts make it difficult to invoke the duty is to place challenging evidentiary burdens upon those claiming breaches. Further, in some contexts . . . many courts effectively refuse to apply the doctrine of good faith and fair dealing.

Sounds familiar, right? In trying to explain the pattern of cases in contract law's good faith jurisprudence, it has made sense to scholars to look back to constitutional law, where under-enforcement is the norm.[31]

In considering this pattern that spans private and public law in the United States, MacMahon insightfully draws upon the distinction between conduct rules on the one hand and decision rules on the other.[32] The core of the idea here is that the rule of good faith is directed to the parties governed by the norm – but that will plausibly (if awkwardly) sometimes diverge from the implementing law courts will have to use in accordance with their institutional competencies.[33] Although the conduct rules will furnish inspiration to the "judicially manageable standards," they are no "replacement" or substitution or equivalent.[34] This is the way we can see that although constitutional law assumes no angels, it still, as *Federalist No. 51*[35] concludes, must "oblige" constitutional actors "to control [themselves]" under good faith norms guided by a good faith law that comes rather shy of the grander norm.

However right or wrong MacMahon is about contract law's good faith jurisprudence, it is surely true of company or corporate law.[36] That makes sense especially for those who have emphasized that the Constitution is a kind of corporate charter.[37] We'd be hard-pressed to assume altruism among corporate directors and managers – and a body of law still tries to promote their good faith without overly micromanaging the deliberations of corporate actors. We use this careful calibration because judges lack relevant expertise or democratic authorization as other representatives do, but they also can't be too credulous. By refusing to "crowd out" intrinsic motivation by corporate and constitutional actors, an underenforced law of good faith might actually support rather than potentially undermine trust with those who have power over us.[38]

---

[31] Fallon (2006).

[32] Made famous by Dan-Cohen (1984).

[33] MacMahon (2015), p. 2055.

[34] MacMahon (2015), p. 2055.

[35] Federalist No. 51 (1788).

[36] Eisenberg (1993), Velasco (2012).

[37] Mikhail (2019).

[38] MacMahon (2015), p. 2102; Galoob and Leib (2018), pp. 123–125.

3 Holding Offices Faithfully Under the U.S. Constitution

This general picture of constitutional government and constitutional law has been developed in recent years by a growing group of "fiduciary constitutionalists".[39] Some pursue this work historically, arguing that constitutional actors are bound by fiduciary obligations (that would include good faith) because that is what the framers of the American Constitution encoded into the document. Others explore pockets of private fiduciary law to illuminate constitutional law since contemporary democracies and constitutional governance create conflicts of interest and the problem of how to guard guardians is one that private fiduciary law has struggled with for centuries. Irrespective of whether one takes a so-called "originalist" lens or a "living constitutionalist" lens to the work of constitutional interpretation, the challenge of public administration is a familiar one, all the same. Given that substantial power is invested in political actors who have widespread discretion that can render citizens vulnerable – and given that the stability and solidarity of a well-functioning polity hinges on at least some trust development between ruler and ruled – constitutional law should be infused with a foundation (1) that disincentives the worst kinds of self-dealing and opportunism; (2) that gives rulers room to breathe so they aren't second-guessed by a judiciary with its own potential conflicts of interest and imperfect accountability structures; and (3) that carefully calibrates its remedial regime[40] in a manner that develops constitutional rights and duties not to "crowd out" a healthy space for politics, dissent, and organic consilience with those governed thereunder. This is what constitutional-law-as-a-law-of-good-faith is poised to accomplish.

In light of irregular support for motivational inquiries on the current court – as evidenced by the recent immunity decision – it is perhaps somewhat surprising to be amplifying a good faith law that sits at the very foundation of U.S. constitutional law. Yet the conceptual core of what it means to serve in office under the Constitution is actually in plain view. Reinforced not only by installation oaths but also by a pervasive effort to require rulers not to self-deal, not to be (too) opportunistic, to take on a fiduciary role, to exercise fiduciary powers with care, to orient their work toward the public interest, and to police (even if only at the extremes) animus and illicit motivations is all of a piece. It points to the firmament of constitutional law in the United States as being about fidelity to the office and the document: a law of good faith.

To be sure, not all fiduciary constitutionalists will have the same prescriptions about how to realize good faith behavior by constitutional actors. Just like private law operates with general ideas of loyalty, care, confidentiality, best interests, and some no-conflict and no-profit rules in its fiduciary law – but then has to equilibrate and decide whether a purported misappropriation should be immunized on account of a disclosure, for example, so, too, constitutional law as a public fiduciary law will

---

[39] Lawson and Seidman (2017); Natelson (2004, 2007).

[40] Levinson (1999).

have similar problems to countenance. And seeing constitutional law as at root a law of good faith won't easily arbitrate among approaches. It can only give shape to the arguments and furnish a kind of grammar for them rather than adjudicate among them.

Linking these private law and public law subjects together is warranted for structural reasons but also for historical ones: there is suggestive historical evidence of the co-development of private and public fiduciary law and some of the private law's idea about the corruption of office may have had a part of its genesis in public law developments, even as public law theorizing and political theory was drawing on ideas about trust to fashion limits to exercising sovereign power.[41] To be sure, the historical connections between public and private offices – and their corollary juridical manifestations in public and private law – do not require full harmonization in the respective fiduciary laws that pertain to private and public law spheres. Even within private law spheres that draw from and contribute to fiduciary law – agency, partnership, trust law, corporate law – we do not expect perfect harmonization owing to differential implementation of the core duties of loyalty and care. Thus, pluralism of a sort reigns: context will do much to draw the contours of the legal regimes that apply fiduciary principles in different institutions and legal jurisdictions. And different ecologies in different domains will also help determine when non-enforcement is the law's best choice because the law might interrupt fiduciary morality that works better with a little room to grow without getting crowded out by micromanagement.[42] That is what we should expect of the law of good faith controlling many different kinds of fiduciaries, including constitutional officers.

This indeterminacy can be frustrating. Consider all the recent litigation under the Emoluments Clauses, with various litigants seeking to get courts to do something about the fact that President Trump had taxpayers and foreign governments funneling him money through stays at his local hotel properties in the District of Columbia. A fiduciary account of the presidency should plausibly render it unconstitutional as a rule of conduct for a President to accept monies through his private holdings from states and foreign sovereigns, a kind of conflict of interest that was close to the Framers' core cases of emoluments.[43] Yet by the time the cases got to the Supreme Court, the Court had various technical justifications sounding in the rules of standing and mootness to avoid the question – and rules of decision did not obviously align with the rules of conduct. For some, this might be seen as an abrogation of the role of the Court to enforce a fiduciary conception of office mandated by the Constitution (which could have led Trump to be permissive about accepting a very large gift of an airplane from Qatar and brazen about using the office to promote his cryptocurrency ventures); for others, it might be further evidence of fiduciarity, if one takes a more "systemic turn"[44] in fiduciary constitutional theory allowing for a

---

[41] Leib and Kent (2021).

[42] DeMott (2021).

[43] Teachout (2016).

[44] Ponet and Leib (2018).

constellation of fiduciary commitments by many different government actors that will routinely lead to under-enforcement.

Although emoluments litigation presented cases of first impression in the courts about that particular form of bad faith commitment to the public interest so the courts did not have occasion to elaborate there even about the rules of conduct, the whole apparatus of administrative law – a form of public law that controls constitutional officeholders bound by oath to the Constitution – is suffused with a fiduciary conception of office in which good faith is at the center. As Evan Criddle has most clearly argued[45]:

> To satisfy judicial review. .. agencies must show they exercised due care by furnishing a full, contemporaneous administrative record, explaining in detail the rationale for their decisions, and validating departures from past decisions. Agencies' explanations must address all salient aspects of a problem . . . and persuade courts that the final rule is not inconsistent with the empirical evidence before the agency. . . . The [law] thus provides that administrative agencies, like private fiduciaries, bear the initial burden to produce a record demonstrating that their decision was the product of reasoned decisionmaking.

This body of law can be considered a legal entailment of the oath of office administrators must undertake to "bear true faith and allegiance" to the Constitution and to "faithfully discharge" their offices (5 U.S.C. § 3331).

Consider the hypothetical discussion by the U.S. Supreme Court in *Judulang v. Holder* (2011). Suppose, the *Judulang* Court proposed, that an agency enacted a policy of adjudicating cases before it by flipping a coin. Utilizing such a mechanism to decide which removable persons are eligible for discretionary relief would be inconsistent with the norms of good faith administrative governance and would therefore be "reverse[d] in an instant"[46] because it would be based on factors that are arbitrary and not tied in a good faith manner to the broader purposes and concerns of the laws that the agency is charged with administering. Moreover, such a policy would be illegitimate even if the results generated by the mechanism could have been justified on "other, more rational bases"[47] because the method of deliberation would essentially be in bad faith and couldn't be cleansed. Good and bad faith aren't the concepts the Court draws upon directly here – but that clearly serves as the foundation.

Or consider the more recent case *Department of Commerce v. New York* (2019), which much more explicitly draws upon good and bad faith as the relevant legal standard in ordinary administrative law jurisprudence to hold constitutional officers to their oaths. A majority on the Court ultimately refused to agree that the Secretary of Commerce's decision to include a citizenship question on the constitutionally-mandated census was "arbitrary and capricious," the conventional standard of review under the Administrative Procedure Act. Although that kind of scrutiny is called "hard look review," courts rarely want to second-guess an expert agency if

[45] Evan Criddle (2006), pp. 153–154.

[46] Judulang v. Holder (2011) 565 U.S. 42, 55.

[47] Judulang v. Holder (2011) 565 U.S. 42, 55.

they can find some plausibility between the reasons the agency offers and the actions it ultimately takes. Thin as the rationale was that the Secretary offered, the Court was unwilling to tell the agency that it hadn't done its homework in responding to and rejecting career officials under the Secretary, who warned against the use of the citizenship question.

Still, a majority on the Court would not let the Secretary's decision about the citizenship question to stand with the administrative record the agency put before the Court. The Court added an overt motivational analysis: when a reason an agency proffers reads as "pretexutal," courts should invalidate agency action that rests on its basis.[48] Notwithstanding the Court's protestations that "further judicial inquiry into 'executive motivation' represents 'substantial intrusion' into the workings of another branch of government," and that "a court may not reject an agency's stated reasons simply because the agency might also have unstated reasons",[49] the Court still reached its conclusion about pretext by policing good and bad faith: it ultimately applied its "exception to the general rule against inquiring into 'the mental processes of administrative decisionmakers'" on a "strong showing of bad faith".[50] The Court emphasized that "contrived" reasons are not good reasons – and meaningful "disconnect between the decision made and the explanation given" undermines the good faith administrators are duty-bound both to exercise and to demonstrate.

From one perspective, one might see the co-called Census Case as exceptional. Indeed, the Court itself embraced the idea that this kind of direct motivational policing is only for the outlier case. The Court went out of its way to suggest that its particularly searching kind of good faith and bad faith oversight in the Census Case has to be rare, that institutionally the Court is not especially well-equipped to pursue questions of motivation on a regular basis. This has led at least one commentator to call this kind of review "harder look review," in contrast with the standard "hard look" standard.[51] To be sure, political reasons that get dressed up in some kinds of contrived technocratic expertise must be common in administration (both for strategic and legitimacy reasons)[52] – and it would be foolish to think courts are well positioned to supervise perfectly well all stated and unstated reasons, a form of review that would lead to ossification and tying up agencies in endless litigation and discovery.[53]

But however often the courts actually press agencies to furnish reasons that are not mere pretexts – the Census Case flows from at least one of the most canonical cases in the administrative law corpus[54] – much of mainline administrative law

[48] Department of Commerce v. New York (2019), 588 U.S. 752, 780.

[49] Department of Commerce v. New York (2019), 588 U.S. 752, 781.

[50] Department of Commerce v. New York (2019), 588 U.S. 752, 781.

[51] Walker (2019).

[52] Watts (2009), McGarity and Wagner (2019).

[53] Nou (2019).

[54] Citizens to Preserve Overton Park v. Volpe (1971), 401 U.S. 402.

keeps the motivations of administrative actors bound by oath to the Constitution in view, anyway. "Arbitrary and capricious" review as understood through the foundational *State Farm* case from 1983 works to oversee proper deliberation, conscientiousness, and good faith: such review still requires agencies to "articulate a satisfactory explanation" for a decision, requires them to "consider important aspects of the problem" they are seeking to address, and requires "explanation[s] . . . that [do not] run[] counter to the evidence".[55] Pretext analysis is surely more plainly motivation-focused and invokes the language of bad faith directly but it is hard not to see *State Farm* as often up to the task of rendering pretexts visible and invalidating agency actions taken for the wrong kinds of reasons, reasons proffered in bad faith.[56] Its orientation to police motive and good faith may be somewhat less transparent but "smoking out bullshit" has long been central to administrative law's animating spirit.[57]

4 Conclusion

This case study of the way good faith and bad faith matter to U.S. constitutional law broadly conceived started with some patent documentary and doctrinal components that are obviously a part of U.S. constitutional law. But rather than concluding there and then trying to solve a mystery about why it perhaps doesn't matter more in more pockets of doctrine more comprehensively with direct enforcement, the chapter aimed to develop several other ways that the theory of office that these documentary and doctrinal clues point toward actually do a lot more to structure the foundational norms governing how officers are expected to orient themselves under the U.S. Constitution. By developing links with the private law of fiduciary governance and the core of administrative law controlling constitutional officers bound by oath, this chapter shows that there really isn't much of a mystery to solve, after all: good faith in U.S. constitutional and public law looks rather similar to its role in private

[55] Motor Vehicle Mfrs. Assn. of United States, Inc. v. State Farm Mut. Automobile Ins. Co. (1983), 463 U.S. 29.

[56] The legislative history of the Administrative Procedure Act (1946) probably also makes it clear that pretext analysis is already prefigured in arbitrary and capricious review: "The required statement of the basis and purpose of rules issued should not only relate to the data so presented but with reasonable fullness explain the *actual* basis and objectives of the rule." S. Rep. No.752, at 201 (1945) (emphasis added); *see also* H.R. Rep. No. 1980, at 259 (1946). One might see Dept. of Homeland Security v. Regents of the Univ. of Calif. (2020), 591 U.S. 1. in this light, too: the Trump Administration's difficulty with reasoned explanations for its effort to rescind the Deferred Action for Childhood Arrivals program established during the Obama Administration ("DACA") is what led the Court there to invalidate the agency action on the more standard *State Farm* grounds that it was "arbitrary and capricious." The Court didn't need to reach for pretext but the Court was clearly probing whether the reasons proffered were made in good faith.

[57] Leib (2018), p. 276.

law. It serves as a rule of conduct but not nearly as often as a rule of decision. That careful calibration with judicial oversight is a feature rather than a bug of fiduciary law, whether public or private, and reveals the very foundations of constitutional government in the United States.

References

Criddle EJ (2006) Fiduciary foundations of administrative law. UCLA Law Rev 54:117–183
Dan-Cohen M (1984) Decision rules and conduct rules: on acoustic separation in criminal law. Harv Law Rev 97:625–677
DeMott D (2021) The domains of loyalty: relationships between fiduciary obligation and intrinsic motivation. William Mary Law Rev 62:1137–1185
Eisenberg MA (1993) The divergence of standards of conduct and standards of review in corporate law. Fordham Law Rev 62:437–468
Fallon R (2006) Judicially manageable standards and constitutional meaning. Harv Law Rev 119:1274–1332
Fallon R (2016) Constitutionally forbidden legislative intent. Harv Law Rev 130:523–589
Galoob S, Leib EJ (2018) Fiduciary loyalty, inside and out. South Calif Law Rev 92:69–126
Gardbaum S (2016) Comparing constitutional bad faith. Harv Law Rev Forum 129:158–165
House Report by the Judiciary Committee on the Impeachment of Donald Trump (December 2019), https://docs.house.gov/billsthisweek/20191216/CRPT-116hrpt346.pdf
Kent A, Leib EJ, Shugerman J (2019) Faithful execution and article II. Harv Law Rev 132:2111–2192
Lawson G, Seidman G (2017) A great power of attorney: understanding the fiduciary constitution. University Press of Kansas, Lawrence
Leib EJ (2018) Also, No. Tulsa Law Rev 53:267–277
Leib EJ (2023) Three modalities of (originalist) fiduciary constitutionalism. Am J Leg Hist 63:183–195
Leib EJ, Galoob S (2019) Fiduciary principles and public office. In: Criddle E, Miller P, Sitkoff R (eds) Oxford handbook of fiduciary law. Oxford University Press, Oxford, pp 303–322
Leib EJ, Kent A (2021) Fiduciary law and the law of public office. William & Mary Law Rev 62:1297–1348
Leib EJ, Shugerman J (2019) Fiduciary constitutionalism: implications for self-pardons and non-delegation. Georgetown J Law Public Policy 17:463–489
Leib EJ, Ponet D, Serota M (2013) A fiduciary theory of judging. Calif Law Rev 101:699–754
Levinson DJ (1999) Rights essentialism and remedial equilibration. Columbia Law Rev 99:857–940
Levinson S (2016) Trash talk at the supreme court. Harv Law Rev Forum 129:166–175
MacMahon P (2015) Good faith and fair dealing as an underenforced legal norm. Minnesota Law Rev 99:2051–2112
Markovits D (2014) Good faith as contract's Core value. In: Klass G, Letsas G, Saprai P (eds) Philosophical foundations of contract law. Oxford University Press, Oxford, pp 272–293
McGarity TOO, Wagner WE (2019) Deregulation using stealth "science" strategies. Duke Law J Vol. 68, pp. 1719–1803
Mikhail J (2019) Is the constitution a power of attorney or a corporate charter? Georgetown J Law Public Policy 17:407–440
Natelson RG (2004) The constitution and the public trust. Buffalo Law Rev 52:1077–1178
Natelson RG (2007) Judicial review of special interest spending: the general welfare clause and the fiduciary law of the founders. Texas Rev Law Polit 11:239–282
Nelson C (2008) Judicial review of legislative purpose. N Y Univ Law Rev 83:1784–1882

Nou J (2019) A place for pretext in administrative law?. SCOTUSBlog, At https://www.scotusblog.com/2019/06/census-symposium-a-place-for-pretext-in-administrative-law
Ponet D, Leib EJ (2018) Deliberative law. In: Bächtiger A, Mansbridge J, Warren M, Dryzek J (eds) Oxford handbook of deliberative democracy. Oxford University Press, Oxford, pp 612–624
Pozen DE (2016) Constitutional bad faith. Harv Law Rev 129:885–955
Rogers EM, Young S (1975) Public office as a public trust: a suggestion that impeachment for high crimes and Misdemeanors implies a fiduciary standard. Georgetown Law J 63:1025–1049
Sager L (1981) Foreword: constitutional limitations on congress's authority to regulate the jurisdiction of the Federal Courts. Harv Law Rev 95:17–89
Shaw K (2019) Speech, intent, and the president. Cornell Law Rev 104:1337–1400
Teachout Z (2009) The anti-corruption principle. Cornell Law Rev 94:341–413
Teachout Z (2016) Corruption in America: from Benjamin Franklin's snuff box to citizens united. Harvard University Press, Cambridge
Velasco J (2012) The role of aspiration in corporate fiduciary duties. William & Mary Law Rev 54:519–586
Walker CJ (2019) What the census case means for administrative law: harder look review?. Notice and Comment Blog, June 27, at https://www.yalejreg.com/nc/what-the-census-case-means-for-administrative-law-harder-look-review
Watts KA (2009) Proposing a place for politics in arbitrary and capricious review. Yale Law J 139:2–85

Good Faith in Spanish Constitutional Law

Rosario Tur Ausina

> *(…) I wanted to give you a word. The best of all.*
> *- Oh yeah? Which one is it?*
> *- Compassion. Which, as you know, is the ability to put oneself in the shoes of others.*
> *and to feel with the other what he feels.*
> *- Yes, I like it. But why do you say it's the best?*
> *- Because it is the only one of the great words that does not hurt,*
> *no torture, no imprisonment and no killing…*
> *On the contrary, avoid all this. There are very beautiful works of art:*
> *love, freedom, honour, justice… But all of them, absolutely all of them,*
> *can be manipulated, can be used as a weapon and can cause casualties.*
>
> *The Story of the Transparent King (2005) – Rosa Montero*

Abstract This study addresses the validity and progress of the Spanish constitutional system in the light of the principle of loyalty and from the complex configuration of the principle of division of powers, horizontal and vertical, after more than 45 years of democratic experience. And it does so without losing sight of two elements: firstly, the multilevel approach that constitutes, for the time being, a guarantee that the various powers can readapt and achieve the desired balances; and secondly, the mechanics of the counterpowers, sometimes invisible, but which can contribute to the correct functioning of the system. Territorial tensions have been an important legal-political destabilising factor in recent years. Added to this is the unstable coexistence between the gubernaculum and the jurisdictio, with significant strains on the rule of law. Observing these problems from the perspective of the principle of loyalty requires an in-depth conceptualisation, reflection on its elements – objective and subjective-, its placing in the context of good faith, and a search for the anchoring of this principle in the constitutional text. It is a question, therefore, of considering the regeneration of the democratic system on the basis of

R. T. Ausina (✉)
Miguel Hernández University of Elche, Elche, Spain
e-mail: charo.tur@umh.es

J. Podkowik et al. (eds.), *Gleams of Good Faith in Constitutional Law*, Ius Gentium: Comparative Perspectives on Law and Justice 132,
https://doi.org/10.1007/978-3-032-06486-8_11

the principle of loyalty, delving into its complex contours in order to demand greater activism in its configuration and implementation, which is the responsibility of public and private operators. This will serve to value and regenerate what has undoubtedly been the "happiest" stage – in the constitutional sense – of Spanish history since 1978.

1 The Conceptualisation of the Principle of Loyalty

The configuration of the political system based on the principle of constitutional loyalty should lead us, broadly speaking, towards the search for coherent balances between the different legal-political operators and the institutions.

It is indeed a matter of preventing rulers and institutions from undermining those who serve as their counterweight; but it is also a matter of preventing democracy from being reduced to the simple reception of the swings that come from citizen opinion, with a people who can do anything.

Although a political system may formally develop constitutional-democratic processes, it moves away from its initial objectives and becomes populist, not only, as is well known, when there is a reduction in political participation and a concentration of power with a loss of counterweights, but also when decision-making becomes overly dependent on the demands expressed by the people, who are "used" outside the institutions. In the latter case, power is consciously dragged along by a "public opinion" articulated through more or less democratically institutionalised instruments (electoral processes, freedom of expression in its most varied forms, demonstrations, social networks, associations, etc.), while institutional balances and levers are lost. For this reason, the aim of loyalty is to avoid an "all for the people without the people", but also an "all with the people and without balances between powers".

In both cases (tyranny of power or tyranny of the people, always at the service of a populist centre of power), loyalty acts to a certain extent as a "compensatory" mechanism in a constitutional-democratic regime that is expansive, without limits, unbridled, disorderly, and which causes chaos and licentiousness. The aim of the rule of loyalty is therefore to establish an authentic "militant" democracy that defends itself, with limits, adjusted to the democratic principle – in which it is integrated – , coherent, consistent and honest.

Undoubtedly, the very conceptualisation of the democratic principle in our political system has not favoured the configuration of constitutional loyalty, as the idea has prevailed that ours is not a militant democracy in that total reform of the Constitution is possible, there are in principle no express limits to constitutional reform,[1] and it is merely a procedural democracy. All this, among other factors, has prevented the idea of a serious commitment to that constitutional core – values,

[1] The Constitutional Court has ruled along these lines (see SSTC 48/2003 and 259/2015).

principles and rights – which constitutes a substantial part of democracy and without which the latter would lose all meaning. Loyalty, therefore, seems to have been reduced throughout this time to a weak political postulate referring to mere good governance.

Far from these theses, however, we maintain that Spanish democracy is clearly belligerent and by no means unarmed or defenceless, as it possesses an ideology impregnated with principles, values and fundamental rights shared in the sphere of European constitutionalism, and has the necessary levers to guarantee their defence and firm application, despite the fact that ideologies contrary to the Constitution itself are permitted. The fact that Spanish democracy is tolerant of ideological postulates contrary to the Constitution itself, and that it does not prosecute or prohibit them (unless they are criminal activities), does not imply that it gives up its defence of the constitutional order, since the political system must be protected by means of prevention and education, rather than repression.

However, the reality is that, in the more than 45 years of Spanish democracy since the Constitution was approved in 1978, it can be briefly observed that, to a certain extent, a very large part of legal-political life has been approached in black and white, with no grey areas, in such a way that conduct, actions or circumstances that do not fit in with the constitutional order are either manifestly unconstitutional or are presented in terms of exceptionality and, therefore, justifiable. There has not been much room, however, for the pedagogy mentioned in previous lines and for judging the lack of commitment to the constitutional pact, which needs to be observed in all its elements as an inseparable whole; nor for the possible deviations from the constitutional system, even if the literalness of the legal-constitutional order is apparently complied with and the great rules of the democratic game are not altered.

In the face of all this, we maintain that the principle of loyalty, in its legal-constitutional meaning, constitutes a good springboard for the defence of democracy, as it identifies for legal-political operators a commitment to act in the exercise of their own competences, taking into account their own institutional and personal development, avoiding populist behaviour, and taking into consideration the effects generated by their successive actions, both in terms of respect for the development of competences by other entities, and in terms of the rights that are at the basis of the political system and, in short, in the harmonious functioning of the constitutional-democratic model, which is anchored in the principles and values of our European multilevel system.

The principle of loyalty is thus based on three elements[2]: the very democratic principle in which loyalty is integrated, constitutional supremacy, which we interpret in a multilevel sense (since it is no longer possible to escape from European constitutionalism, which is our basic frame of reference), and the positivity that takes the Spanish Constitution (hereinafter EC) itself as the axis of this multilevel system. The socio-legal basis of this configuration of the principle of loyalty is,

[2] Álvarez Álvarez (2008).

therefore, the consideration of the State Constitution and European constitutionalism as legal-political commitments and movements that bring together great consensuses.

Loyalty implies, from the above parameters, a plus that must be added to respect for democratic processes and mere freedom in the exercise of institutional and personal freedom. Loyalty belongs, in this sense, within the more general duty of good faith towards the constitutional order, but it is something more than mere subjection to the rule, as it implies an attitude of marked prior and subsequent respect for the constitutional order, an attitude that is thoughtful and open to participation, but which, fundamentally, rejects interested and opportunistic interpretations and interventions of the constitutional order.[3] Loyalty is tolerance, respect, consideration and empathy, as well as firmness in the defence of democratic-constitutional postulates, for which it cannot lose sight of the four previous characteristics. This means, in short, that loyalty is, basically, coherence.

From this conceptualisation, the very nature of the institutions and the various legal-political operators, as well as their competences, are inextricably linked to the consequences they generate through their actions. They are not, therefore, separable elements, since the principle of loyalty serves the proper democratic-constitutional functioning of the system, its effective, coherent and harmonious development.

Despite the relevance which, in the light of the above considerations, this principle deserves, the Spanish Constitution does not use it literally, although, as we shall see later, it may be anchored in various parts of its text. And for its part, the Constitutional Court itself has used it in a collateral manner, but never to oblige the exercise of a system of competences in a certain sense, but basically to refer to subjection or compliance with the supremacy of the Constitution and the rules of the democratic game, avoiding an abusive use of the competences themselves (SSTC 122/1983 and 42/2014). Thus, the Court points out that "an inherent principle of collaboration and constitutional loyalty is deduced, which postulates the adoption of procedures for consultation, negotiation or, where appropriate, the search for prior agreement", which implies helping the central Government to be extremely zealous in reaching agreements with the Autonomous Communities, but without "these agreements having to be binding" (SSTC 217/2016, 13/2007 and 209/1990). In this way, the Court redirects the rule of loyalty to an exercise of territorial-institutional "good governance", urging, in those and other judgments, the public authorities to seek the greatest commitment to the constitutional order – through dialogue, through the State Pacts-; to work towards a rethinking of the territorial model that already requires responsible updating. And it also recalls the constituent process itself and the duty to respect it, even pointing to a possible constitutional reform and, in any case, to reforms and regulatory and political changes that deepen the most intense inter-territorial collaboration.

In the Spanish system, therefore, we have not reached the level of development of the principle of federal loyalty that we find in other countries. By way of

[3] Jiménez Campo (2003).

example, the German case, which has used the principle to configure a whole series of rights and duties of obligatory compliance for the different territorial entities, with the consolidation of a legal concept of loyalty that implies, on the one hand, the duty to abstain in the spheres of competence of other entities and, above all, a positive action to ensure the aims of the State as a whole.[4] And all this despite the fact that the Spanish territorial system presents a very high level of conflict and, for this very reason, may have a greater need for the principle of loyalty.

To a certain extent, the principle of constitutional loyalty seems to have remained an accessory or even, to a certain extent, decorative element, closer to the concept of good institutional behaviour or good government action and less to the democratic principle, where we believe, however, it has its place. Even so, we should not underestimate the Court's own pedagogical approach when, in its rulings on Catalan sovereignty, it alludes, without saying so, to loyalty by urging the political actors to resolve political problems through a State pact or constitutional reform, when it stresses the importance of using the appropriate legal-political instruments in the constitutional order, or when it warns of the need to avoid the judicialisation of political life. Rather, it evokes certain ethical and moral consequences that must be realised as a result of distorted behaviour on the part of juridico-political actors. It could therefore be said that, although it has not deduced a legal-constitutional principle of loyalty (or has not properly connected it, as a sub-principle, to the democratic principle), it has laid the foundations for it.

2 The Subjective Component of Loyalty

The principle of loyalty connects in a certain way with the concept of fraud of law, according to which a breach of the law is committed when a subject carries out an act under a legal framework, with the aim of achieving objectives that are contrary to the latter, so that the motivational component in this way of acting becomes a key element.

This invites us to ask ourselves, in a certain parallelism, whether the principle of loyalty is measured only by the effects and results of a measure – the objective element – and the consequences of disloyalty are sufficient, or whether the subjective element is also required, that is, the motivations and intentions underlying that conduct, indeed the breach of good faith, so that disloyalty would be close to the idea of fraud itself. Consequently, should a political and/or normative action be evaluated from the principle of loyalty by assessing the intentions of the issuing legal-political subjects, or are these absolutely indifferent or irrelevant in order to understand that there is disloyalty towards the constitutional system?

In our opinion, the concept of "constitutional fraud", which is at the basis of the principle of loyalty, implies the commission of an action that distances itself from

[4] Laso Pérez (2000).

truth or rectitude – in the words of the Dictionary of the Real Academia de la Lengua -, from good faith and, consequently, that would mean dispensing with the necessary interaction with the system of values and principles from which Spanish constitutionalism – in turn embedded in the European system – draws its inspiration. Thus, although apparently the action, measure or conduct carried out appears to be in accordance with mere formal legality, in constitutional fraud there is a relevant subjective element, a certain content of bad faith (or sometimes mere ignorance, which is still an "attenuated" bad faith, derived from the lack of diligence in the duty of understanding and knowledge of the constitutional system that is required of certain legal operators). In short, this would be a breach of good faith that these operators owe to their own political system. And it is obvious that those who violate the constitutional order in this way do so with the intention of manipulating and inclining the legal-political instrument towards their own interests or with a mere disregard for the "training in the Constitution" that they should have, to the detriment of the very nature of the Constitution and its core principles and values.[5] Whether consciously or unconsciously, through mere ignorance, carelessness or negligence, the principle of constitutional loyalty would be breached in any of these ways, since the consideration that an action has come to disrupt the desired harmony and the proper functioning of the system as a whole is paramount. In this way, the subjective element is of singular importance, although it is not required to have an exceptional or extraordinary quality, as requiring negligence or culpability would lead us to restrict the concept of loyalty and betray the very nature of this concept.

It is not possible, from the principle of loyalty, to compartmentalise the action of an institution from the intention of those who make it up, so it seems that we should not eliminate the subjective component of the action of an institution, which is made up of people and is not an isolated and neutral entity.

Legally speaking, this is a classic debate that is present above all in the discussion on the scope of the legislators' action: is it the written text that counts, or do the intentions behind it also count? A debate that puts us in the position of having to decide whether what we have to consider – what governs us – is the result expressed in the unfair measure, or whether the intentions are necessary or even sufficient to understand that the principle of loyalty has been violated.

There seems to be a certain consensus that the objective element – the mere will of the rule or measure itself – is the key element when we speak of fraud in the constitutional field. This element would therefore be essential, without the intention of the ruler alone being sufficient to legally address disloyalty. However, in the field of constitutional law there has been more reluctance to consider the intentional element[6]: what counts is the measure that is definitively acted upon, so it seems that a Court should not limit itself to ascertaining possible political exercises of simulative

[5] For example, Galvis Arenas, Rodríguez Delgado (2009), pp. 135–152, who in turn takes up the doctrine that has been profoundly elaborated by Professor Pedro de Vega.

[6] Simões Nascimento (2023).

democracy – intention – in order to determine the unconstitutionality of a rule or measure.[7]

Nevertheless, in our opinion, constitutional law must evolve and, therefore, we should not discard considering intentions – together with results – in order to measure the degree of disloyalty and contribute to implementing the principle of loyalty itself. In this sense, the subjective component is particularly valuable, in such a way that the principle of loyalty requires not merely the intention isolated from the results and effects, but the fact that the intention can be "objectified", "redirected" and "connected" with the final result. This is achieved, in short, by carrying out a joint reading of the emotional/intentional component with the objective effects/results that the decision generates in the system, in such a way that the principle of loyalty would oblige us to also consider any element (formal or informal) that serves to evidence disloyal motivations in the subject issuing the rule or measure – which we insist must necessarily be connected with the results of the measure to finally determine disloyalty.

The principle of loyalty, from this intense connection of the objective and subjective elements, thus comes to limit, subject or readjust the desires and room for manoeuvre of what we have traditionally called the "margin of political discretion/opportunity". Loyalty is based, in this sense, on the concept of "distortion of the Constitution", whereby certain constitutional norms would be given an interpretation and meaning different from what they would really have "in their spirit", which would result in a blatant distortion of constitutional law. The seriousness of this conduct could be so marked that it implies that at any given moment a non-formal reform of the Constitution itself could be taking place[8]; a mutation incompatible with the democratic principle.

By way of example, it seems that in principle it is not unreasonable to accept that a Government should make use of the figure of Decree-Laws[9] when it is not possible to reach the necessary agreements to pass a Law, it being understood that there is an extraordinary and urgent need that justifies it: the existing fragmentation in the parliamentary spectrum. Recourse to the Decree-Law in these circumstances thus becomes an instrument available in principle for the better efficacy/efficiency of government action (the intended result, which is to tackle a regulatory change that

---

[7] A debate which has emerged with force in the questioning of Organic Law 1/2024, of 10 June, on amnesty for institutional, political and social normalisation in Catalonia, since in a decision of such enormous significance as this one, it is essential to assess the context which favours it (and therefore, the intentions of the subjects who adopt it). See, for example, VVAA (2024b); and de Miguel Bárcena (2024).

[8] De Vega (1985).

[9] Art. 86.1 EC provides that

> In cases of extraordinary and urgent need, the Government may issue provisional legislative provisions which shall take the form of Decree-Laws and which may not affect the organisation of the basic institutions of the State, the rights, duties and freedoms of citizens regulated in Title I, the regime of the Autonomous Communities or general electoral law.

is extraordinary and urgent) and, furthermore, the material limits would not be infringed, so it does not appear that this regulatory instrument is being used outside the parameters of art. 86 CE. In fact, the dominant trend in recent years in the Spanish political system has been the profuse use of Decree-Laws given the "discomfort" generated by a fragmented Parliament, and where the technique of converting a validated Decree-Law into a Law has become widespread.[10] However, in our opinion, this way of using Decree-Laws alters the spirit of the Constitution and would not fit within the constitutional parameters of the principle of loyalty, since this principle demands, precisely, transcending art. 86 CE itself, that a "loyal" government action be capable of measuring the consequences that this way of acting has on the harmonious functioning of the system, without the Government's motivation being alien to a reading of art. 86 in the context of the parliamentary form of government. In effect, it is a question of evaluating the particular exercise of a competence (in this case the extraordinary regulatory power of the Decree-Law), from the context of the measure to be adopted and the effects that are generated, in such a way that loyalty would measure the contribution of that instrument in that specific case, to the coherence of the political system as a whole.

In effect, the result of this "fraudulent" way of acting is that what should be an extraordinary power of the Government (the Decree-Law itself) becomes an ordinary regulatory instrument, thereby altering the role that Parliament should play as the centre of coexistence of political pluralism, a privileged forum for negotiation and debate in the drafting of regulations with the status of law. Moreover, it turns the Government into something more than an institution for political leadership, which is responsible for promoting legislative action and does not assume the role of Parliament as an ordinary centre – even in urgent cases – for negotiation and debate of different interests. But there are more elements that cannot be accepted from the point of view of constitutional loyalty: to begin with, the innate speed of the Decree-Law does not fit in well with the reflection and the process of confluence of negotiations that the drafting of a regulation of legal rank requires in Parliament; and finally, although it is true that in the Spanish system it is usual for Decree-Laws to end up becoming laws ex art. 86.3 CE, we should not forget that the normative content of the Decree-Law is applied from its approval by the Government – or at least this is what is required by the very nature, urgency and extraordinary nature of this legal figure-, that once it enters the legal system it is difficult for its conversion into law to end up annulling the Decree-Law, and that it has finally dispensed with various controls (reports, opinions, etc…) that do surround the ordinary process of law-making and which are necessary for the coherent functioning of the constitutional order.

Thus, to return to the general approach to the subject, loyalty requires looking at each of the legal figures and dogmatic categories from a broad perspective, in order to give them a genuinely constitutional and non-fraudulent meaning. Loyalty is in fact the feeling of devotion, adherence and respect for the commitments, principles

[10] López Picó (2023).

and values that a Community decides to establish, but also for the people who nurture this common political project.[11] It is not enough to read each legal instrument from its literal regulation or from a simplistic and narrow interpretation, nor is it enough to approximate it to a superior value or a right. Loyalty requires a broader view, in order to connect each of the figures, institutions, rights, etc. with the system as a whole and its historical and contextual circumstances, responding to the why, what for and how.

Paradoxically, loyalty far from being identified with "fidelity" – which in the words of the Dictionary of the Royal Spanish Academy implies the mere observance of the faith that someone owes to another person[12]-, in our opinion is rather closer in its constitutional dimension to "compassion", understood according to the same Dictionary cited as the "feeling of pity, tenderness and identification in the face of someone's ills".[13] This is because loyalty is not inviting consideration of the effects our own actions have on others – on the system or the whole as a consequence – and thus the capacity to feel their fear, suffering, pain or needs, where it is only possible to arrive after understanding oneself.

Loyalty is, therefore, the opposite of a lenified, slow, weak, indolent, laissez-faire political system. It is the opposite of a "liquid" constitutional-democratic regime, *to* use Bauman's expression.[14] It is the search for a political system that adapts to changes and circumstances, but which does so without rigidities while at the same time without disregarding the constitutional pact and with attention to the harmonious functioning of the system, even more so when the constitutional system is subjected to tough challenges (pandemics, territorial issues, division of powers itself, the digital era, etc.[15]). This is why the subjective element becomes a core part of the principle of loyalty, because the "reading" of the political system by the legal-political operator takes on a special role.

3 The Objective Element of Loyalty

Beyond the element of subjectivity, in the determination of compliance with the principle of loyalty there is also, as we said, the objective element as a key factor. We refer to elucidating what actions embodied in the measure or norm and what

---

[11] In this sense, the Encyclopaedia Britannica, which offers the aforementioned reflections, is much richer and much closer to the principle of constitutional loyalty to which we allude (https://www.britannica.com). In contrast, our Dictionary of the Royal Spanish Academy is certainly sparse and imprecise, as it only identifies loyalty with legality, truth and reality. Vid. https://dle.rae.es/lealtad?m=form.

[12] Vid. https://dle.rae.es/fidelidad?m=form.

[13] Vid. https://dle.rae.es/compasión.

[14] Bauman and Bordoni (2016).

[15] In this regard, the collective work, VVAA (2022).

subsequent results determine whether or not an action is loyal to the constitutional-democratic system.

The answer is relatively simple, since loyalty is fulfilled when the legal-political operator uses the legal-democratic processes in their integrity and with coherence. When government action – understood in its broadest sense – is carried out in an "integral" manner, that is, both by seeking solutions to problems, addressing them from the different elements and circumstances that are actually at the root of specific problems – without partial or biased solutions – and by assessing to what extent the instruments used will offer the best results and, therefore, will be the most suitable in a decision-making process observed from the perspective of the protection of individuals, but also of the balance of powers. Because it is not a matter of simply appealing to the defence of fundamental rights, but of going further and reflecting beforehand on the best functioning of the different powers and on the risks of undesirable asymmetries; on the best balance of positions for the respect of the nature of all actors and, precisely, of the rights of individuals that form the basis of the constitutional pact.

The long episode of the Catalan sovereignty process offers us, precisely, some interesting reflections. Catalan nationalism's divergences with the state constitutional project in theory and in practice, and with various central governments that have succeeded one another, culminated – for the time being and after various convulsive episodes[16] – in a proposal for amnesty approved by the aforementioned Organic Law 1/2024, of 10 June, on amnesty for institutional, political and social normalisation in Catalonia, applicable to those who had committed some kind of illegal act or crime during the sovereignty process ("el procés"), to which was added the granting by the Council of Ministers in June 2021 of a pardon to nine people convicted in the aforementioned trial of the "procés".

Of course, there is no doubt about the need to adopt political-legal measures with an impact in order to resolve a very entrenched legal-political problem such as the one described above. Although this is not a peaceful issue and is beyond the scope of this study, it is even possible that this could be done by means of an amnesty, as there is no express prohibition in the Spanish constitutional order, and perhaps at a given moment extraordinary measures are required with the aim of wiping the slate clean.[17] However, it is the effects and consequences for the constitutional order – together with the intentions – which are transcendental from the point of view of the rule of loyalty, as this action can be carried out in accordance with the literalness of

[16] The intense process of approval of the Catalan Statute in 2006; the complex – and extensive – ruling of the Constitutional Court 31/2010, of 28 June, which resolved the challenge to the aforementioned Statute; the non-referendum referendum of 9 November 2014 and the referendum of 1 October 2017; the Supreme Court ruling handed down in October 2019, in which various political leaders were sentenced for their intervention in the referendum of October 2017, and a whole series of resolutions and proceedings affecting those who took part in the aforementioned referendum; and a whole battery of rulings by the Constitutional Court on "*el procés*", among other events. A summary in Alvarez Conde, Tur Ausina (2023), p. 195 ff.

[17] An interesting debate on this subject, in VVAA (2024a), pp. 15–111.

the legal framework of reference and the merely formal or material requirements, or we can ask ourselves whether constitutional democracy demands, as we think and defend, that this be done on the basis of the principle of constitutional loyalty with the objective requirements derived from it.

Indeed, the way to act in the latter case changes things significantly and has important repercussions on the proper development of the democratic-constitutional system. Thus, the rule of loyalty demands that the amnesty should take place using the legal instrument – and the political and legal processes that accompany it – that best guarantees the integrity and coherence of the political system. To begin with, because this measure, which indeed strictly requires an Organic Law, must be accompanied by a whole constitutional context that does not distort its application and generate undesired effects in the system: namely, a whole political process aimed at establishing a road map: a State pact, a broad political agreement, a protocol or "soft law" standard that sets out various political-legal commitments, good government action with adequate and firm leadership by the State Executive, a commitment that involves the Autonomous Communities – which are also a State and are also affected by the bilateral Catalonia-Central State movements – to one extent or another, a major political consensus to back it up – beyond the simple absolute majority needed to pass an Organic Law -, and governmental-parliamentary processes that provide the measure with the appropriate counter-powers (reports, opinions, etc….).. In relation to this last circumstance, the mere fact of having used a bill from a parliamentary group to launch the legal initiative of amnesty instead of a government bill already deprives the legal regulation of amnesty of a whole series of controls and accompanying measures (reports, opinions, etc.) which are of course required in an organic law on amnesty, which is something more than an "ordinary" organic law. Although it is "correct" to make an organic amnesty law on the basis of a bill, in our opinion it is not, however, loyal to the political system. Loyalty, which now helps to reinforce and anchor the dogmatic categories underpinning the political system, adds a further *plus*, as it takes into account in a particularly demanding way the constitutional purposes served by the measure adopted. Among all of them, in particular, updating and resolving the appropriate fit of the territorial model in our constitutional order. However, as we shall show, loyalty continues to remain in a legal limbo that is still diffuse or poorly elaborated in doctrine and jurisprudence, and perhaps also undervalued, despite the fact that it has solid doctrinal anchors such as the contribution of Jürgen Habermas on "constitutional patriotism",[18] to cite just a few points of reference.

[18] On Habermas' thought, with quotations from his work, see Gabriel de Mariscal (2010), Velasco (2023). On the claim for a principle of constitutional loyalty, Álvarez Álvarez (2008), and more recently, Freixes (2024).

4 Loyalty and the Separation of Powers: The Centrality of Checks and Balances

4.1 Crisis of the Spanish Political System. The Territorial Issue as a Constant Conflict

The exercise of power, both in its horizontal (territorial division) and vertical (traditional division of powers) dimensions, has faced complex situations on several occasions in the Spanish legal system.

Indeed, in the face of extreme or risk situations (pandemic, sovereignty crisis, failure to renew State bodies, etc.), the Spanish system has opted to accept, without further ado, certain measures of an extraordinary or exceptional nature, and in such cases it seems that this is justified because we are beyond the confines of the Constitution. The system itself is at risk, which is why states continue to make use of this type of instrument (amnesty, pardon, suspension of rights, the coercive mechanism of art. 155 CE on the Autonomous Communities, legislative reforms that confirm breaches of the constitutional order…), on the condition that their use is channelled through democratic instruments (a law) and with certain controls (parliamentary, judicial, constitutional). At present, it even seems that the spaces for constitutionality or unconstitutionality are becoming blurred, as we would simply be placing ourselves outside normality. And this is because it is simply a question of the Rule of Law surviving with this type of exceptional measures or safety valves in the system that make a merely formal and disloyal reading of our constitutional order.[19] Once the convulsive episode has passed, it is then back to everyday life as if nothing had happened. However, the grey area of loyalty-disloyalty that has accompanied these episodes seems to have been forgotten, and which makes it necessary to consider the adoption of different measures to "maintain" the system (*manutenzione costituzionale*), before, during or after these episodes occur. The possible (un)constitutionality that may come afterwards, when acts that do not fit with the constitutional order are challenged, are not enough. The political system cannot survive only at the cost of subsequent judicial sanctions and "daily" disloyalties.

In a certain way, the very concept of "sovereignty" beats in all this discourse, for we have to assume that it is no longer possible to take isolated, sovereign decisions outside the harmonious functioning of the system. There is no single sovereign, sovereignty is shared and must therefore be read in terms of loyalty. The fact that each one acts in the exercise of its competences, without feeling "obliged" to do so by what the other indicates, is a reduced, intellectually poor and problematic vision of the functioning of our current political systems, which is clearly seen in the territorial model, when the State or Autonomous Communities point out that they do

[19] Aguado Renedo (2024a), pp. 17–18.

not have to obey the guidelines that the other entity indicates to them. It is in these discourses and approaches that we observe that loyalty is conspicuous by its absence and that the system lacks corrective mechanisms and a full implementation of the democratic principle (and within it, the subprinciple of loyalty).

Appointments, amnesties, the use of legal instruments, in short, are sovereign acts that can only be carried out in a democracy in accordance with criteria of constitutional loyalty, without the mere resource of adopting measures "in accordance with the law" being valid, because then the formalist biases are evident. Their interpretation must be material in order to avoid abuses, arbitrariness… but this is not enough. Abuse, fraud or arbitrariness have a marked meaning in democracy and it is necessary to define these concepts in terms of loyalty. Certainly, Carmona Contreras points out that the EC is laconic in this sense. However, this does not imply that it is permissive, but rather that we need strong anchors that give coherence to the system, such as the principle of loyalty.[20]

And it is precisely this debate that lies at the heart of the discussions surrounding the aforementioned Amnesty Law of 2024. In fact, Alicia Gil tells us that both an amnesty and a pardon are correct mechanisms in a democratic-constitutional system, which can serve to avoid dysfunctions, even when these have been generated by a neglect of functions by the responsible political-legal operators themselves. And we also believe so, insofar as the principle of loyalty aims precisely at this: to correct the dysfunctions of the system, but to do so on a daily basis, preventing, correcting, detecting… and not only in extreme situations, in order to return to a certain extent to square one. Thus, Alicia Gil reaches this conclusion, without mentioning loyalty, when she warns about the conditions of these two measures, amnesty and pardon, which have to be agreed upon avoiding disorder, putting everything in its place, deciding in context or with other supporting measures that legitimise them.[21]

The law can be unjust because people are not perfect beings, nor do they pretend to be so at all costs; and loyalty is precisely a "maintenance" principle of the democratic system that attempts to iron out, redirect, shape or readjust… these injustices and even errors that have not been remedied. Precisely for this reason, because it is not a matter of punishing imperfect human beings, the principle of loyalty is aligned above all with a conception of constitutional law interpreted in preventive and restorative terms, and not so much in terms of punishment. Thus, returning to the previous theme, it could be concluded that amnesties and pardons are not *per se* incompatible with democracy, but they can be if they are adopted "under conditions of disloyalty".[22]

Moreover, the principle of loyalty also allows us to interpret constitutional "silences" in this way, since the fact that a measure is not prohibited in the

---

[20] Carmona Contreras (2024a), p. 20.

[21] Gil Gil (2024a), p. 21.

[22] Linde Paniagua, in the same survey, cites the conditions of loyalty – without mentioning the word – : very high consensus, commitment of those granted amnesty to the constitutional order, reintegration of those granted amnesty into society. Linde Paniagua (2024a), p. 24.

Constitution does not imply that it can be carried out without conditions and limits. These are precisely the ones that must be configured on the basis of the premises indicated by the very principle of constitutional loyalty. Another question, no less important, is to what extent the Constitutional Court will rule on this decision of the legislator based on the principle of constitutional loyalty. For it could be a good opportunity to seek the anchorage of a possible constitutionality/unconstitutionality through this approach.

In any case, perhaps one of the most obvious examples of disloyalty towards the political system is precisely the lack of a State Pact for territorial coexistence in more than 40 years of constitutional democracy, taking into account the high degree of decentralisation that characterises the Spanish territorial model and, consequently, the need for society to resolve the high level of potential and real conflict. The contributions of constitutionalist doctrine on the State of the Autonomies are many and very diverse, basically seeking constitutional reform and emphasising the lack of territorial cooperation and collaboration. Indeed, although it is true that the lack of centripetal or cooperative dynamics has been worked on and denounced in the legal-publicist doctrine, it is also true that perhaps because the principle of federal loyalty itself is not consubstantial to the model, it did not focus the attention of researchers as one of the pillars of the territorial model of the State. As Professor Biglino has pointed out, our State of autonomies is certainly not based on the very notion of the federal pact.[23] The deeper configuration and daily application of loyalty, therefore, is a pending element precisely because it is absent from the core of our territorial model of State.

Our territorial system, in theory and practice, is undoubtedly "centrifugal", focused on facilitating the process of decentralisation, on articulating the means for a generous and dynamic distribution of powers, on facilitating autonomous developments, but, at the same time, it is a system paradoxically conceived in the concern for nationalist excesses, showing a certain mistrust towards autonomous developments. The answer may lie, to a large extent, in the historical experience, certainly convulsive during the Second Republic,[24] unsatisfactory in the 19th century, as well as in the fears that the territorial question would block the constituent process in the 1970s, in the middle of the 20th century. Thus, the constituent response was not to tie up the model, but quite the opposite: to open the doors so that the democratic system itself could shape it with a certain amount of rationality, it is assumed, based on the contributions of the different legal-political operators. The result was a model in which the system of competences remains permanently open and dynamic, and articulated, moreover, on purposes and functions. Title VIII EC itself and its practical application are, in short, a good example of all this: precepts written in a negative key and with caution, with levers in favour of the central State and a certain suspicion towards the Autonomous Communities, mimetic developments without taking into account that not all the Autonomous Communities are equal, abuse of

[23] Biglino Campos (2004), p. 341.

[24] Varela Suanzes-Carpegna (2013).

the use of the Constitutional Court to resolve conflicts, lack of territorial State pacts, lack of development of the Senate as a true central State and a certain suspicion towards the Autonomous Communities, lack of development of the Senate as an authentic chamber of territorial representation (and cooperation) between the State and the Autonomous Communities, collaborations which, if they exist, have been forced by circumstances that go beyond the ordinary functioning of the territorial model itself (the case of the COVID-19 pandemic), etc.

In view of the above, one might wonder whether the constitutional text itself contains certain disloyalties. However, in our opinion, this is not exactly the case. It must be understood that the Constitution itself is a living document, partly a product of the historical moment in which it was conceived, and that it represents a channel for social conciliation. But at the same time, the constitutional text establishes those postulates that are essential for its citizens and introduces values and principles that must serve as a guide for the readjustment of its provisions. The fact that some particular contents of the constitutional text itself show disloyalty does not imply that loyalty itself is absent from the constitutional text, which is what matters to us. It is here, in the day-to-day development of the Constitution, that loyalty takes on its full meaning. It is the legal-political operators who have to shape it, with implementing legislation, public policies or even constitutional reforms, in order to seek loyalty: the coherent and harmonious functioning of the system.

However, loyalty, although absolutely necessary, as it has been designed so far in general terms – as a rule of good territorial government and linked more to the realm of politics than of law – is, for the time being, certainly inoperative.

4.2 The Control (Self-Monitoring) of Loyalty

In turbulent times, the need for the principle of separation of powers usually emerges in a marked way and requires rigorous reflection based on the principle of loyalty, which should be fully incorporated into the constitutional culture. Indeed, this implies starting from the basic idea of integral collaboration and the effective functioning of the internal and external checks and balances that inform the aforementioned principle of separation of powers. But it also implies assuming that all legal-political operators – both branches of government and counterparts – should be familiar with and implement the constitutional order, based on a panoramic vision of the political system.

This should be the case in the Spanish legal system, especially when, since 2010–2015, we have been living in a context of a certain systemic misgovernment, contaminated by a certain political and social fragmentation and, at the same time, by a marked polarisation that is, by definition, the staunch enemy of loyalty. A context and dynamics that can hardly be overcome – or will be overcome partially or insufficiently – without recourse to the principle of loyalty, which can thus show its full potential in the articulation of powers and counterpowers.

Even so, although we have pointed to the years 2010–2015 as a key moment in political fragmentation and polarisation because of the consequences this has had in recent years on the stability of the Spanish system, in reality it cannot be said that Spanish democracy in recent centuries has been characterised by a culture of pacts. Quite the contrary. Although there have been lucid moments (in the current Spanish democracy, the constituent moment itself, the functioning of the first stages of the Constitutional Court, the fight against terrorism, and a few others), the Spanish political system has generally lived in an atmosphere of "underground" or "emerging" conflict, depending on the stage, and where the leaderships have only mitigated the conflict on specific occasions. This means that the concepts of the coexistence pact and the constitutional pact are, to a certain extent, alien to Spanish society and that the tendency towards polarisation will emerge with a disturbing naturalness in any scenario.

Faced with this situation, we cannot help but ask ourselves directly about how to make the principle of loyalty operative and whether the jurisdictional bodies can make use of it and with what consequences, with the aim of generating a breeding ground for breaking down these intolerable asymmetries and disloyalties.

In this sense, it is currently difficult for actions that do not comply with the principle of loyalty to be controlled by the Constitutional Court. To begin with, because there is still a need for more doctrinal input and a more complete and better-armed configuration of the principle of loyalty, both in the Academy and in the courts. But it is precisely a question of going further and going beyond the use of the principle of loyalty understood merely as the identification of a desirable, albeit voluntary, action of "good governance" to which it seems to have been reduced.

Although the Constitutional Court is making progress in its development of the principle of loyalty, it must also be considered that the role of the Constitutional Court does not necessarily have to be omnipotent and exclusive in the implementation of the principle of loyalty. Perhaps it is not even advisable for this to be the case. Although this court is a privileged and especially authorised interpreter, it must also be deferential to other institutions and act in a collaborative manner, without intervening when the action can be exercised in a more effective, comprehensive and respectful manner with the legal system by other institutions. It must be remembered that the Constitutional Court is only one piece – albeit a very valuable one – of the constitutional machinery, and that it is also being affected by the drifts of democracy – including social and political pressure, which has increased in the digital era – and therefore by certain disloyalties. This is particularly true with regard to the appointments of the Court's own magistrates, since the risks of politicisation of these bodies are a reality and, in the case of the Spanish Court, it is excessively subject to political ups and downs (distribution of appointments by political quotas, delays in appointments, ineffective *hearings* in Parliament, etc.). Not to mention the fact that dialogue with other courts – supranational and infra-state – still needs to be strengthened.

On the other hand, the very day-to-day functioning of these higher bodies also requires a rethink based on the principle of loyalty. Indeed, there is a tendency to believe that when it comes to a technical institution – even one with political relevance – such as the Constitutional Court, the Supreme Court, or an advisory body such as the Council of State, its members detach themselves from their political ideology to become aseptic and neutral persons. However, the orientation in other political systems is precisely the opposite (United States, Germany…), since having been a member of a party or having been able to show one's own legal-political and social position on a certain matter of public relevance is a valuable element insofar as it allows one to know the commitment of that person to the constitutional order and to clearly observe his or her loyalty to the system, which leads to a more coherent and sincere subsequent development of his or her technical work. This avoids the use of disguised or hypocritical resolutions that mask an obvious political motivation. On the contrary, transparency and honesty make their work more loyal to the constitutional order. Talking politics in the hearings in Parliament, prior to their appointment as judges, will not in fact tarnish their technical work, but will make it more honest. It will demonstrate their commitment and loyalty to the constitutional system, so that the members of these bodies will have to match their doctrine with their ideology and do so in a transparent and technically impeccable manner. Otherwise, trying to show a superficial, aseptic, depersonalised image, etc., goes against the certain social commitment that is required when working in an institution of this magnitude.

On the other hand, to trust, once again, that a body such as the Constitutional Court or even the Supreme Court will assume the responsibility of demanding compliance with the principle of loyalty is to assume a merely partial vision of the political system and of Law. In other words, we should not rely solely on instruments of a coercive and repressive nature, since the preventive facet of the law, constitutional training and education, and self-control – which also form part of the legal world – must also contribute to making the principle of loyalty a reality. This is even more so in the field of public law and, in particular, constitutional law, which, unlike other legal disciplines, requires a social awareness of the meaning of constitutionalism in order for it to become a reality. In constitutional law, repressive law is of little use and, moreover, it is not very effective.

In the end, all this leads us to the classic debate about a political class that is "up to the task" of defending – and not boycotting – the constitutional order. We should not limit ourselves to recurrent political and social discourses that simply blame a mediocre political class and catastrophically warn of the emergence of an aristocratic democracy that will look after everyone. We forget, in fact, that we are also talking about working for an educated and informed society where citizens have some responsibility for the direction of their lives and their own political system, which also belongs to them.

It is about the recovery, in a certain way, of the space of politics as an innate part of the human being, which was lost precisely in the beginnings of contemporary constitutionalism, concerned as it was – which is logical – with conceiving the person as a subject immune to power and less with making him or her a true participant in politics as a patrimony of citizenship.

From this rather preventive and pedagogical approach, we should not underestimate, returning to the role of the high Courts, the work they carry out through *obiter dicta*, from where it is possible to launch authentic “soft law” messages to powers and counter-powers, thus contributing to generating a constitutional culture that is loyal to the system.

In any case, the co-responsibility/collaboration of all legal operators is required, a more comprehensive and balanced view of the work that different institutions and legal subjects can carry out. And this is so even though not all have the same capacity for action, since in contrast to some more technical bodies – justice at lower levels, the Courts of Audit – there are those who have greater legal-political action – such as the Constitutional Court, the Supreme Court or consultative bodies such as the Council of State and similar institutions in the sphere of the autonomous regions – , and others have a privileged capacity for action, such as the Parliaments or Governments themselves, or even the political parties, the latter being conceived in this respect as instruments of political socialisation.

5 Recovering the Principle of Loyalty. Towards the Search for a Constitutional Anchorage

The consideration of our democracy as “non-militant” has been to some extent an obstacle – but not the only one – to generating and consolidating a firm commitment to the constitutional order. We have consequently forgotten about militancy in the core of rights, principles and basic values of the constitutional order, and this in turn has led to the possibility of the education system itself dealing firmly and consensually with rights education being sidelined.

There were some attempts, such as Organic Law 2/2006 on Education, with the introduction of a subject on “Education for Citizenship”, and Organic Law 3/2020, with the subject “Education in civic and ethical values”, which could have marked a change of course. But instead, the so-called “school war” and the polarisation around the objectives of Education in the Constitution prevailed: those who think that constitutional education hides a form of state ideological indoctrination – the supporters of education as freedom – and those who believe that it is the mission of the state to educate in constitutional values – those who see education as a right.

In the end, this is a debate that requires committed efforts to configure an education system committed to its own Constitution and, therefore, to take risks and agree on the contents and scope of this education, since both prohibiting education in rights and imposing it from a single position are both disloyal, risky and polarised behaviours. This is because the Spanish political system must make freedom of expression compatible with a commitment to the constitutional spirit. However, as we already know, it is this commitment to pact and conciliation which, in short, has been lacking and has failed in the Spanish political system, installed in the aforementioned Democracy of adversaries, in the friends-enemies dialectic of which Adela Cortina spoke.[25]

From the above considerations, however, we find ourselves faced with a curious paradox. It is precisely in Art. 27 EC, which regulates the right to education, where, in our opinion, there is a solid normative basis for the duty to act loyally. We must remember that nowhere in the text of the Spanish Constitution is there any reference to the loyalty or loyal behaviour of institutions and citizens. Of course, one might think that this could be deduced from the articles devoted to the regulation of the Autonomous State and, in fact, it was the legislation developing the territorial model that came close to this issue. Specifically, art. 4.1 of Law 30/1992, of 26 November 1992, on the Legal Regime of Public Administrations and Common Administrative Procedure, in the wording given by Law 4/1999, configured the principle of "institutional loyalty" as a principle of relations between public administrations, which entailed: (1) respect for the legitimate exercise by other administrations of their competences; (2) the weighing of all public interests involved in the exercise of competences; (3) the provision of information between administrations; and (4) the provision of cooperation and active assistance between administrations.

In our opinion, however, and in accordance with previous considerations, the latter is a partial development of the principle of constitutional loyalty, due to the subjects affected, and due to the scope and configuration that we believe this principle should have.

In contrast to the above, the principle of constitutional loyalty has a more extensive scope which, as we have already announced, is effectively linked to art. 27.2 CE. This precept states that "The aim of education shall be the full development of the human personality with respect for the democratic principles of coexistence and fundamental rights and freedoms". It is therefore clear from its articles the political system is obliged to respect and commit itself to the constitutional foundations that sustain it, and it is understood that the reference to education in this reading that makes transcends the educational system itself to encompass the Spanish cultural-democratic system as a whole. In short, we refer to education understood as civic awareness and coexistence, civic responsibility and advanced social development (the "advanced democratic society" referred to in the Preamble of the Spanish Constitution).

We are clearly talking about an "education in the Constitution", in respect for the coherent and harmonious functioning of the constitutional system. A development of the political system which cannot betray its constitutional foundations and which requires proactive behaviour on the part of public authorities and citizens. It is, therefore, in our opinion, a precept that evokes the very constitutional loyalty to which we have been referring. In fact, it has been pointed out that it is in this precept

[25] Cortina (2010).

that we find the true "militant democracy" that the Spanish system must be,[26] since we do not believe that our democracy has any pretensions to commit suicide.[27]

But in addition to an "educational" approach, loyalty also has the effect of "forgiveness" for the mistakes made or the dysfunctions generated, in order to return to the correct channels of the constitutional system. For this reason, we cannot fail to connect loyalty with Art. 25.2 EC, when it states that "custodial sentences and security measures shall be aimed at re-education and social reintegration and may not consist of forced labour".

The precept refers particularly to the rights of convicted persons; a subject which, as is well known, incorporates a whole theory on the positioning of a State with regard to those who infringe the law, with criminal consequences. It should be noted that this precept is thus linked, from its basic approach, to Art. 27.2 by alluding to the need for the political system to "recover" and "reintegrate" those who have distanced themselves from the correct and harmonious functioning of the system, with the ultimate aim of making normal coexistence possible. Beyond expelling those who do not share the values and principles, those who are disloyal to the constitutional order, the Spanish Constitution evokes a spirit of conciliation between them and that order, as long as this takes place through the correct channels and with sufficient personal and material resources, without consequently falling into new disloyalties. In the end, the objective, as indicated in art. 25.2 CE, is security itself, which, far from constituting a fundamental right, is a legitimate constitutionally protected interest (STC 341/1993) which is only achieved precisely when the exercise of the system of rights and power is carried out in terms of loyalty.

6 Conclusion

The principle of constitutional loyalty deserves a place in the Spanish constitutional order. Not only because it strengthens the achievements of Spanish democracy itself, but also because it contributes to the solidification of European constitutionalism, whose axis, it should not be forgotten, continues to be each of the States that make it up.

Beyond the incorporation of the principle of constitutional loyalty through constitutional reform – a possibility that seems almost utopian, given the difficulties, above all political, that exist for reforming the constitutional text in Spain – there are other ways for this to happen. The privileged position occupied by the Constitutional Court makes it a perfect actor for this task, without prejudice to the fact that it could be accompanied in this task by other courts, both domestic and, above all, supranational, such as the Court of Justice of the European Union and the European Court of Human Rights.

---

[26] Monzón Julve (2009), Martín Guardado (2023).

[27] Torres del Moral (2006).

It is time to consider that, although constitutional texts and democratic processes are good, without loyalty there is a risk of falling into self-interested uses of the legal system, far removed from constitutional values and principles and, therefore, of a populist nature. Even if it is through the technique of *obiter dicta*, the Constitutional Court has sufficient authority to guide legal-political operators and citizens in a sense that is loyal to the system. Let us recall that it has done so on occasion, even if it did not mention the principle of loyalty itself. Pronouncements such as the following, and although it is only an occasional example in the history of Spanish democracy, regarding the so-called "tax amnesty" established by Decree-Law 12/2012, of 30 March, are illustrative. Thus, the Court pointed out the following in judgment 73/2017:

> In short, the adoption of measures which, instead of serving the fight against tax fraud, take advantage of it under the pretext of obtaining revenue that is considered essential in a scenario of serious economic crisis, entails the abdication of the State's obligation to make effective the duty of all to contribute to the support of public expenditure (art. 31.1 EC). It thus legitimises as a valid option the conduct of those who, in an unscrupulous manner, failed to comply with their duty to pay taxes in accordance with their economic capacity, ultimately placing them in a more favourable situation than those who voluntarily and on time fulfilled their obligation to contribute. The objective of achieving a collection that is considered essential cannot, on its own, be sufficient cause to legitimise a breach of the objective of justice that the tax system, in general, and the specific measures that comprise it, in particular, must aim to achieve in any case.

The Court's opinion is clear in this respect: using a legal figure (the tax amnesty), through an inappropriate source of law (the Decree-Law), and with a deviant and self-interested character, breaks the harmony of the constitutional system and breaks the objectives of justice. The Decree-Law was in fact declared unconstitutional, not because of disloyalty, but because it affected the essence of the duty to contribute to the support of public expenditure set out in art. 31.1 EC, which could not be done by means of the Decree-Law. However, in a pedagogical and exemplary manner, it leaves the previous warning, which is clear and evokes the principle of constitutional loyalty.

The constitutional doctrine, the Academy, has the obligation to follow in this wake, as it is also in a key position to measure the integrity of the legal system and to introduce the dimension of constitutional loyalty in a transversal manner in our work, beyond the particular, sectorial and specific analyses that we can make of the Spanish legal reality. Because we must not forget that the analysis of the dogmatic categories that we make and their continuous re-dimensioning is a task that serves to support the legal-political reality, and that our work is based on constitutional theory but also on auxiliary disciplines to constitutional law, such as the theory of the State, political science, history and sociology. All of these fields, together, allow for a better and more adequate configuration of the principle of constitutional loyalty.

References

Álvarez Álvarez L (2008) El principio de lealtad constitucional, Centro de Estudios Políticos y Constitucionales

Alvarez Conde E, Tur Ausina R (2023) Derecho constitucional, Tecnos

Bauman Z, Bordoni C (2016) Estado de crisis, Paidós

Biglino Campos P (2004) La lealtad constitucional en el Estado de las Autonomías. Revista Jurídica de Castilla y León, extraordinary issue: 51–74

Cortina A (2010) Las raíces éticas de la democracia. Publicaciones de la Universitat de, València

De Miguel Bárcena J (2024) Amnistía, una ley para olvidar, Athenaica

De Vega P (1985) La reforma constitucional y la problemática del poder constituyente, Tecnos

Freixes T (2024) Interview in Economistsjurist.es, 9 December

Gabriel de Mariscal J (2010) Habermas. El patriotismo constitucional. Academia Vasca de Derecho 20:87–113

Galvis Arenas G, Rodríguez Delgado M (2009) Fraude constitucional. Temas socio-jurídicos 27(57):135-152

Jiménez Campo J (2003) Lecture at the course held in October 2002 in Alicante. In: González Alonso A (2003) La lealtad constitucional. La Constitución como orden de valores o como procedimiento. Revista de Estudios Políticos 120:320–350

Laso Pérez J (2000) La lealtad federal en el sistema constitucional alemán. Cuadernos de Derecho Público 9:47–105

López Picó C (2023) ¿Una nueva era del procedimiento de conversión de los decretos-leyes en ley? De su fundamentación inicial a su auge actual bajo la fragmentación parlamentaria. CEFLegal, Revista Práctica de Derecho 270:83–112

Martín Guardado S (2023) La relevancia del deber (profesional) de lealtad constitucional en la enseñanza como medio para la defensa de la Constitución y el orden democrático-liberal. Revista de Trabajo y Seguridad Social, CEF 473:213–221

Monzón Julve M (2009) Orden constitucional y democracia militante: atención especial a la Educación para la Ciudadanía y los Derechos Humanos. Revista CEFLegal 107:53–98

Simões Nascimento R (2023) El argumento de la intención del legislador: usos y propuesta normativa. Doxa. Cuadernos de Filosofía del Derecho 47:105–133

Torres del Moral A (2006) Democracia militante. In: VVAA, Derecho Constitucional del siglo XXI, Aranzadi, Pamplona, pp 209–224

Varela Suanzes-Carpegna J (2013) La Constitución de 1931 y la organización territorial del Estado. Iura Vasconiae 10:323–354

Velasco JC (2023) Patriotismo constitucional. Nueva Revista, n. 186, Available at: https://digital.csic.es/bitstream/10261/335363/1/Patriotismo_constitucional.pdf, 44–53

VVAA (2022) Sujetos, derechos y lealtad constitucional, Aranzadi

VVAA (2024a) Encuesta sobre derecho de gracia, amnistía y Constitución. Teoría y Realidad Constitucional 54:15–111

VVAA (2024b) La ley de amnistía. Cuestiones constitucionales. Centro de Estudios Políticos y Constitucionales

Good Faith in Swiss Constitutional Law

Elif Askin

Abstract From a comparative perspective, the principle of good faith occupies a unique position in Swiss constitutional law. Article 9 of the Swiss Constitution elevates this principle to the status of a fundamental right, granting individuals a legally enforceable claim to be treated in good faith by the organs of the state. Furthermore, good faith is enshrined as a constitutional law principle under Article 5(3) of the Constitution, thus becoming a central normative standard that permeates the entire legal system. Unlike the fundamental right in Article 9, which can be invoked against the state, the principle in Article 5(3) serves as a guiding norm that explicitly binds both state authorities and private persons. However, the Swiss Constitution does not contain a precise definition of good faith and its requirements. The concept is historically rooted in private law and has been dynamically developed by the Swiss Federal Supreme Court, which continues to refine its contours in constitutional law jurisprudence. In practice, good faith plays a crucial role in the application of the law. A prominent legal manifestation of good faith is an individual's right to the protection of legitimate expectations, particularly when relying on incorrect advice or information provided by Swiss authorities.

E. Askin (✉)
Faculty of Law, University of Zurich, Zurich, Switzerland
e-mail: elif.askin@ius.uzh.ch

J. Podkowik et al. (eds.), *Gleams of Good Faith in Constitutional Law*, Ius Gentium: Comparative Perspectives on Law and Justice 132,
https://doi.org/10.1007/978-3-032-06486-8_12

1 Introduction

Trust, loyalty, and predictability – the foundations of good faith (*i.e., bona fide*)[1] – are essential to the very existence of the legal order of democratic states.[2] Good faith is not merely a maxim of human behaviour: it reflects a deeper attitude towards the law, the state, and the state's relationship vis-à-vis its citizens.[3] The principle of good faith fulfils diverse and important functions in legal contexts.[4] At its core, however, is the idea that a democratic legal order based on the rule of law depends on a basic consensus in which the members of the community act as autonomous subjects.[5] This becomes even more apparent in the context of democratic backsliding and growing political instability we currently face, given that authoritarian tendencies and attacks on the rule of law are increasingly prevalent worldwide. In these circumstances, the principle of good faith plays a decisive role. It provides an important counterbalance to arbitrary power ensuring that public authorities do not exploit legal formalism to the detriment of citizens and that individuals can rely on the law as a stable, predictable and just legal framework.[6] By requiring both the state and individuals to act in good faith, it reinforces the legitimacy and resilience of democratic institutions.[7]

In Switzerland, which is strongly shaped by its system of direct democracy, the principle of good faith occupies a prominent place in the constitutional law framework.[8] The Federal Supreme Court has established that good faith requires loyal and trustworthy conduct in legal relations and thus constitutes "a fundamental rule derived from ethical considerations which complements the rules governing individual legal relations and helps to determine their application".[9] The important role of good faith is particularly evident in the Federal Constitution of the Swiss Confederation of 18 April 1999 ("Swiss Constitution" or "Constitution").[10] Article 5(3) of the Constitution states that both the state and individuals must act in accordance with the rules of good faith. This provision enshrines good faith as a constitutional law principle that permeates the entire legal system as a normative

[1] For an etymology of good faith, see Kotzur (2009), para. 1.

[2] See Chiariello (2003), p. 7; Picot (1977), p. 119 et seq.

[3] Chiariello (2003), p. 7.

[4] See Sects. 4 and 5 below.

[5] Chiariello (2003), p. 7. See also Rohner (2014), para. 36.

[6] See Chiariello (2003), p. 7.

[7] See ibid.

[8] Kradolfer (2023), para. 59.

[9] DFC 83 II 345 E. 2 (own translation). *DFC* stands for Decision of the Swiss Federal Supreme Court (in German: Amtliche Sammlung der Entscheide des Schweizerischen Bundesgerichts (BGE); French: recueil officiel des arrêts du Tribunal fédéral suisse (ATF)).

[10] Federal Constitution of the Swiss Confederation of 18 April 1999, SR 101 (hereafter: Swiss Constitution); see for an English translation of the Constitution https://www.fedlex.admin.ch/eli/cc/1999/404/de.

standard.[11] Moreover, Article 9 of the Swiss Constitution guarantees that every person has the fundamental right not to be treated arbitrarily by state authorities, but in accordance with the rules of good faith.[12] Both provisions on good faith provide minimum guarantees of the rule of law and form part of Swiss *ordre public*.[13]

The codification of good faith as a *constitutional law principle* and *fundamental right* gives it a unique status in Swiss constitutional law as a guarantor of trust between the state and its citizens.[14] This dual function – guiding state action and protecting an individual right – illustrates how good faith serves as a foundational element of Swiss constitutionalism. However, as in many domestic legal systems and in international law,[15] the Swiss Constitution does not provide a precise definition of what constitutes good faith. As will be shown below, the high degree of abstraction inherent in the concept of good faith has led the Swiss Federal Supreme Court to develop a rich and dynamic jurisprudence that clarifies its various legal manifestations in Swiss constitutional law.[16]

In this chapter, I first examine the historical development of the principle of good faith and the process that led to its incorporation as a fundamental right in the Swiss Constitution (Sect. 2). The following section explores the contemporary functions of good faith in relation to democracy (Sect. 3). I then consider the legal sources of the principle of good faith in the Swiss Constitution (Sect. 4). Building on this, I provide a detailed analysis of the legal manifestations of good faith in the constitutional practice of the Swiss Federal Supreme Court (Sect. 5). Finally, the chapter ends with a conclusion (Sect. 6).

2 The Genesis of Good Faith in Swiss Constitutional Law

In Swiss law,[17] the principle of good faith has three primary legal sources, each with distinct manifestations:[18] Article 2 of the Swiss Civil Code of 10 December 1907 ("Civil Code"),[19] and Articles 5(3) and 9 of the Swiss Constitution. Article 2(1) of the Civil Code provides that "[e]very person must act in good faith in the exercise

[11] Schindler and Tschumi (2023), para. 63. See also Gächter (2005), pp. 125, 439.

[12] Article 9 of the Swiss Constitution stipulates two separate fundamental rights: the prohibition of arbitrariness (reasonableness) and the right to be treated in good faith.

[13] DFC 138 III 322, 4.1, 327; Tschentscher (2015), para. 1.

[14] See Rohner (2014), para. 36.

[15] See e.g., Futhazar and Peters (2020), pp. 189–228, 189.

[16] See Sect. 5 below.

[17] For an overview of Swiss law, see Thommen (2022), for constitutional law, see Oesch (2022), pp. 113–136; Egli (2020).

[18] Kradolfer (2023), para. 55. In addition to the provisions mentioned here, Swiss law also contains statutory provisions on good faith, such as those governing the revision of administrative decisions.

[19] Swiss Civil Code of of 10 December 1907, SR 210. An English translation is available at https://www.fedlex.admin.ch/eli/cc/24/233_245_233/en.

of his or her rights and in the performance of his or her obligations."[20] Historically, this private law provision served as the foundation for the Federal Supreme Court's case law on good faith and ultimately led to its recognition as a fundamental right in the Swiss Constitution.[21]

Although Article 2 of the Civil Code establishes the principle of good faith as a key concept of private law, its applicability in public law remained uncertain for a long time.[22] The Swiss Constitution at the time did not explicitly enshrine a constitutional law principle or a fundamental right to be treated in good faith.[23] However, the Federal Supreme Court addressed the concept in its jurisprudence.[24] Initially, the Court acknowledged the principle of good faith in public law but later rejected its applicability after the adoption of Article 2 of the Civil Code.[25]

It was only after the Second World War that the private law legacy of good faith began to evolve, gradually gaining acceptance in administrative and constitutional law, particularly in protecting legitimate expectations created, for example, by advice from state authorities.[26] From the 1960s onward, the Federal Supreme Court actively engaged with the principle of good faith in its case law.[27] In 1968, it recognized good faith as a manifestation of equality before the law (Article 4 of the Constitution of 1874) and, consequently, as a fundamental right.[28] In the following years, the Federal Supreme Court refined the contours of good faith and developed distinct categories for its application.[29]

In 1999, the Swiss Constitution underwent a total revision.[30] As part of this revision, the principle of good faith was formally codified in the Swiss Constitution.[31] As already mentioned, the application of good faith as a basic principle in legal relations between public authorities and private individuals had long been recognized in constitutional law practice and was also explicitly enshrined in private law even before the adoption of good faith in the revised Constitution.[32] Thus, the introduction of a fundamental right to treatment in good faith in particular was a

[20] Article 2(2) of the Swiss Civil Code reads: "The manifest abuse of a right is not protected by law."- The English translation of the Civil Code is available here: https://www.fedlex.admin.ch/eli/cc/24/233_245_233/en.

[21] Kiener et al. (2024), § 34, para. 1698.

[22] Kradolfer (2023), para. 56.

[23] See Swiss Constitution of 12 September 1984 and Swiss Constitution of 29 May 1874, an English translation is available at https://www.servat.unibe.ch/icl/sz01000_.html.

[24] Kradolfer (2023), para. 56.

[25] Ibid. See also e.g., DFC 48 II 182, 4. 187 et seq.; DFC 76 I 187.

[26] Kradolfer (2023), para. 56; see also Giacometti (1960), 290 et seq.

[27] Kradolfer (2023), para. 56. See also Chiariello (2003), 99 et seq.

[28] Chiariello (2003), p. 100.

[29] Kradolfer (2023), para. 56.

[30] The revised Swiss Constitution formally entered into force on 1 January 2000. For an overview of the historical developments of the Swiss Constitution, see Oesch (2022), p. 115 et seq.

[31] Kiener et al. (2024), § 34, para. 1698.

[32] Schindler and Tschumi (2023), para. 63.

significant yet undisputed innovation in the revised Constitution's catalogue of fundamental rights.[33] Today, good faith is firmly anchored in two constitutional provisions: Article 5(3) of the Swiss Constitution states that "State institutions and private persons shall act in good faith".[34] Article 9, in turn, stipulates that "[e]very person has the right to be treated by state authorities in good faith and in a non-arbitrary manner."[35]

The right to be treated in good faith (Article 9 of the Constitution) rapidly gained importance in Switzerland as the close nexus between public and private law became increasingly apparent, particularly in areas such as pension schemes.[36] Unlike fundamental rights, which offered only limited protection against these developments and in matters of state benefit, the flexible principle of good faith could be invoked against public authorities regardless of the scope of a specific right.[37] At that time, the Federal Supreme Court narrowly defined the right to be treated in good faith (Article 9) as the protection of legitimate expectations.[38] However, even before good faith was enshrined in the Constitution of 1999, it had legal manifestations that went beyond the protection of legitimate expectations, as will be shown below.[39] Article 9 therefore remains a highly flexible, overarching and multidimensional individual right that cannot be limited to specific issues.[40]

In the case of Switzerland, the codification of good faith as a fundamental right has also strengthened the position of the individual in a changing public law landscape, reflecting a shift towards a more human-centred legal system and rule of law-based administrative law.[41] This is crucial for the application of Article 9 of the Swiss Constitution and explains why the principle is mainly applied asymmetrically in constitutional law – in favour of the individual's right to be treated in good faith.[42] It is therefore not surprising that one of the most prominent examples of the state's duty to act in good faith towards individuals is explicitly enshrined in the Swiss Constitution.[43] Neither the European Convention on Human Rights (ECHR) nor the international human rights treaties (e.g., the International Covenant on Civil and Political Rights) contain a similar human right.[44]

---

[33] Botschaft über eine neue Bundesverfassung, 20 November 1996, 145. See also Kradolfer (2023), para. 58.

[34] Article 5(3) of the Swiss Constitution.

[35] Article 9 of the Swiss Constitution.

[36] Kradolfer (2023), para. 57.

[37] Ibid.

[38] Botschaft über eine neue Bundesverfassung, 20 November 1996, 134, 145.

[39] Kradolfer (2023), para. 58.

[40] Ibid.

[41] Ibid., para. 57.

[42] Ibid.

[43] Futhazar and Peters (2020), pp. 189–228, 222.

[44] Kradolfer (2023), para. 59. For the principle of good faith in international law, see Kolb (1998).

3 The Function of Good Faith in Swiss Democracy

In addition to the various legal manifestations that will be discussed in detail below,[45] good faith fulfils an important function in democratic states, including in Switzerland's democracy.[46] The principles of good faith, democracy, and the rule of law are closely interconnected.[47] It is therefore not surprising that Article 5(3) of the Swiss Constitution, which codifies the principle of good faith, is entitled "Rule of Law" and also encompasses other rule of law-based concepts such as the principles of legality and proportionality.[48]

The rule of law, which includes legal certainty, fosters individual confidence in the predictability of legal norms and the reliability of state actions.[49] At the same time, the state must be able to rely on a basic level of compliance by its citizens; the effectiveness and legitimacy of a legal order depend not only on enforceability but also on the willingness or "mindset" of its citizens to comply with applicable laws.[50] This mutual trust, deeply rooted in the principle of good faith, forms the foundation of any democratic society.[51] However, democracies also address the potential for mistrust in public institutions, limiting the exercise of state authority and subjecting it to checks and balances.[52]

The principle of good faith aims to counterbalance this tension between trust and mistrust, a role that is particularly important in times of crisis, such as political instability or a pandemic.[53] In situations where the law is vague or evolving, or where the state takes far-reaching measures that may interfere with people's rights, it is crucial that individuals can rely on the assurances and information provided by the authorities.[54] Similarly, the expectations of those affected by changes in the law or state measures on which they have legitimately relied on must be protected.[55] Moreover, good faith fosters trust between the government and the electorate, which is crucial in a direct democracy such as in Switzerland, where citizens actively participate in decision-making processes.

The principle of good faith requires that the specific behaviours it imposes be defined within the value system of a particular community.[56] Essentially, the

---

[45] See Sect. 5 below.

[46] Chiariello (2003), 7 et seq.

[47] Schindler and Tschumi (2023), para. 63.

[48] Article 5(3) of the Swiss Constitution.

[49] Ibid.

[50] Ibid.

[51] See Chiariello (2003), p. 8.

[52] Schindler and Tschumi (2023), para. 63.

[53] Ibid.

[54] Ibid.

[55] Ibid.

[56] Kradolfer (2023), para. 62.

principle reflects the socio-ethical perceptions of those to whom it applies.[57] Good faith in Swiss constitutional law and beyond thus serves as a mechanism for realizing the values enshrined in the legal system in which it operates.[58] This is crucial because a legal order cannot be maintained solely through legal instruments and procedures.[59] While good faith is a legal concept, it also transcends legal boundaries by appealing to the social, political, and moral responsibilities of the actors involved.[60] Due to its value-based nature, the application of the principle of good faith requires case-by-case assessments.[61] In a democratic state governed by the rule of law, these assessments must be conducted transparently, which is why the Swiss legal system – and the Federal Supreme Court in particular – operationalizes good faith through defined categories of application.[62] This unique role of good faith is also reflected in constitutional law norms, which will be discussed in the next section.

4 Constitutional Framework

4.1 The Fundamental Right to be Treated in Good Faith (Article 9 of the Swiss Constitution)

Article 9 of the Swiss Constitution explicitly provides a fundamental right to be treated in good faith. This provision acknowledges an "asymmetric" conception of good faith, which benefits individuals in their interactions with Swiss authorities.[63] Consequently, Article 9 is particularly significant in legal contexts where the state-individual relation is characterized by an unequal distribution of power.[64] As such, this provision is directed against the state and private persons who perform state functions.[65] In private law contexts, Article 2 of the Civil Code and its specific provisions (such as the prohibition of abusive dismissal in labour law) ensure the application of good faith.[66]

From a comparative perspective, one of the most notable examples of the duties of public authorities towards individuals can therefore be found in Article 9 of the Constitution. Additionally, as mentioned above, Article 5(3) requires state

[57] Ibid.

[58] Ibid.

[59] Futhazar and Peters (2020), pp. 189–228, 227.

[60] Ibid., pp. 227 et seq.

[61] Kradolfer (2023), para. 63.

[62] Ibid.

[63] See also ibid., para. 119.

[64] See also Futhazar and Peters (2020), pp. 189–228, 225.

[65] See Article 35(2) of the Swiss Constitution.

[66] Kradolfer (2023), para. 70.

authorities to act in good faith vis-à-vis individuals, which will be elaborated below. In this context, the constitutional law principle of good faith (Article 5(3)) reflects a duty of loyalty to individuals, characterized by state actions that are reliable and consistent.[67]

By allowing state authorities to rely on their past conduct, Article 9 protects the legitimate trust that individuals place in them.[68] For example, if a person has been given a promise by state authorities for which there is no sufficient legal basis, Article 9 of the Constitution requires that this promise must nevertheless be honoured by Swiss authorities.[69] The same applies where legitimate expectations of an individual have been created as a result of state measures that have a legal basis.[70] The Federal Supreme Court, for example, protected a construction project approved by state authorities under the principle of good faith, even though it violated the federal law on forests.[71] This case illustrates that the right to be treated in good faith may conflict with other legal norms.[72] In the case of the construction project just mentioned, the protection of legitimate expectations as a manifestation of Article 9 of the Swiss Constitution prevailed over the principle of legality.[73] Moreover, good faith may also sometimes conflict with the principle of equality before the law or even with the principle of democracy, particularly in cases involving legitimate expectations about changes in the law.[74] This requires a careful balance between the fundamental right to good faith and the relevant norms of constitutional law.[75]

In contrast to "traditional" fundamental rights, which typically protect against state actions related to specific issues (e.g., "life," "assembly," or "religion"), the right to good faith has a much broader scope of protection. It is not limited to a particular aspect of social reality but rather permeates all state actions across various areas of life, making it an overarching and comprehensive right.[76] Moreover, as discussed above, Article 9 may conflict with other norms, necessitating that it be considered alongside other constitutional law provisions. Importantly, the right to be treated in good faith is also reciprocal, meaning that individuals invoking Article 9 of the Swiss Constitution must themselves act in good faith when claiming a violation of this right.[77]

---

[67] Aubert and Mahon (2003), p. 46. See also Futhazar and Peters (2020), pp. 189–228, 222.

[68] Aubert and Mahon (2003), 96 et seq.

[69] Ibid.

[70] Ibid.

[71] DFC 108 Ib 377. See also Futhazar and Peters (2020), pp. 189-228, 222.

[72] Kradolfer (2023), para. 69.

[73] DFC 108 Ib 377. Article 5(1) of the Swiss Constitution enshrines the principle of legality: "All activities of the state are based on and limited by law."

[74] Kradolfer (2023), para. 69.

[75] Ibid.

[76] Ibid., para. 71.

[77] Ibid.

The right to good faith is enshrined in the Swiss Constitution in the same provision as the prohibition of arbitrariness (Article 9 of the Constitution). Both rights share some common features, such as similar historical roots and their overarching nature Uhlmann (2005), para. 104 et. seq. Nevertheless, the fundamental right to good faith and the prohibition of arbitrariness remain independent guarantees.[78]

The Federal Supreme Court has identified various categories of application as legal manifestations of the right to be treated in good faith, which are explored in detail below:[79] (1) protection of legitimate expectations; (2) protection of vested rights; (3) prohibition of abuse of rights; (4) prohibition of contradictory conduct; (5) protection of good faith in procedural law; and (6) interpretation of legal acts and relationships in good faith.[80] Article 9 of the Constitution can be invoked by both natural and legal persons, irrespective of their nationality or domicile.[81] Individuals holding state functions are also entitled to the right, providing they are not acting in a sovereign capacity and are affected in the same way as a private individual.[82]

4.2 *The Constitutional Law Principle of Good Faith (Article 5(3) of the Swiss Constitution)*

Apart from the right to be treated in good faith under Article 9 of the Swiss Constitution, Article 5(3) of the Constitution addresses good faith as a constitutional law principle that applies throughout the entire Swiss legal system.[83] While Article 9 focuses on the relationship between the state and the individual, Article 5(3) ensures that both state authorities and private persons demonstrate loyal and trustworthy behaviour.[84] The required standard of good faith aligns with commonly accepted norms of fairness and honesty in legal interactions.[85] Accordingly, Article 5(3) of the Constitution primarily serves to protect legitimate expectations in concrete legal relationships.[86]

Article 5(3) of the Constitution binds both public authorities and private persons. As noted above, the principle of good faith in Article 9 establishes a fundamental right vis-à-vis the state and can therefore be considered a *lex specialis*.[87] In legal

[78] Uhlmann (2005), 106.

[79] See Sect. 5 on constitutional practice below.

[80] Kradolfer (2023), para. 63; Tschentscher (2015), para. 15 et seq.

[81] Kiener et al. (2024), § 34, para. 1703.

[82] Ibid.

[83] Schindler and Tschumi (2023), para. 63.

[84] Ibid.

[85] Ibid.

[86] Ibid.

[87] Ibid., para. 64.

relations between private persons, the principle of good faith in Article 5(3) is directly applicable.[88] It applies both to private law (Article 2 of the Civil Code) and administrative law.[89] Furthermore, private persons are also obliged to act in good faith when interacting with Swiss authorities.[90] Due to the specific provisions of Article 9 of the Constitution (which governs claims by individuals vis-à-vis state authorities) and Article 2 of the Civil Code (which applies in private law), Article 5(3) of the Constitution is primarily relevant in two main areas: first, when state organs invoke the principle in their own interactions (e.g., between cantons and municipalities), and second, when the state accuses private persons of acting in bad faith.[91]

Consequently, Article 5(3) of the Constitution requires private persons to act loyally and reliably towards state authorities. The reason is that individuals' contradictory behaviour towards authorities is not legally protected.[92] Nevertheless, private persons are not bound by the principle of good faith to the same extent as the state; they retain the freedom to retract previous positions, and the state has greater resources to verify assurances made by individuals.[93] Generally, a significant legal relationship – such as administrative or judicial proceedings – is required for a person's actions to create legitimate expectations on the part of public authorities.[94] According to the Federal Supreme Court, contradictory behaviour occurs, for example, when an individual initially accepts a procedural action but later contests it.[95] Bad faith may also arise when individuals provide false information, for instance, during naturalization processes.[96]

5 Constitutional Practice

5.1 Overview

In Swiss constitutional law, the claims protected by the right to good faith (Article 9 of the Constitution) cannot be defined in general terms.[97] Rather, the case law of the Federal Supreme Court serves as the foundation for defining the concept of

---

[88] Ibid.
[89] Ibid.
[90] Ibid., para. 66.
[91] Ibid., para. 64.
[92] Ibid., para. 66.
[93] Häfelin et al. (2020), para. 717.
[94] Schindler and Tschumi (2023), para. 67.
[95] Ibid. See also DFC 143 V 66, 4.3.
[96] DFC 140 II 65.
[97] Kiener et al. (2024), § 34, para. 1704.

good faith and its various legal manifestations in Swiss constitutional law. This section examines the most significant practical manifestations of good faith.[98]

The protection of good faith plays a particularly significant role in the application of the law.[99] The most significant practical manifestation of Article 9 of the Swiss Constitution is the protection of individuals' legitimate expectations (Sect. 5.2). Under certain conditions, individuals may invoke the right to the protection of legitimate expectations even against the Swiss legislator (Sect. 5.3). Additionally, the prohibitions against abusive and contradictory behaviour by state authorities are enforceable aspects of Article 9 of the Constitution (Sect. 5.4). Finally, the principle of good faith may also extend to legal interpretation (Sect. 5.5).

5.2 *Protection of Legitimate Expectations*

The protection of legitimate expectations ("*Vertrauensschutz*") is a well-established doctrine of good faith under Article 9 of the Swiss Constitution.[100] Essentially, it protects individuals' trust in the predictability of legal norms and the actions of public authorities.[101] An individual must meet the requirements established by the Federal Supreme Court in order to successfully claim the protection of legitimate expectations.[102]

First, individuals' expectations must be legitimate to be protected.[103] If an individual knows that their expectation is based on incorrect information – for example, if a lawyer disregards incorrect government information that could easily be identified as incorrect by a legal professional – those expectations will not give rise to a claim under Article 9 of the Constitution.[104] Second, the protection of expectations applies only where arrangements have been made on the basis of them, with stronger protection being granted where significant steps have been taken, such as constructing a building based on an erroneous planning permission.[105] As such, the expectation must result in harm that is difficult to remedy; the mere disappointment of an individual's subjective expectation will not suffice in the absence of objective damage.[106] Third, there must be a causal link between the basis of the legitimate expectation and the arrangements made on that basis.[107] Fourth, a balancing test is

[98] For a good overview of the various categories of good faith, see Kradolfer (2023), para. 70 et seq.

[99] Kiener et al. (2024), § 34, para. 1705.

[100] DFC 146 I 105, 5.1.1., 126; Uhlmann (2022), pp. 163–181, 169.

[101] See also Futhazar and Peters (2020), pp. 189–228, 223.

[102] Tschentscher (2015), para. 15.

[103] Uhlmann (2022), pp. 163–181, 168.

[104] Ibid.

[105] Ibid.

[106] Kradolfer (2023), para. 89.

[107] Uhlmann (2022), pp. 163–181, 168.

required to weigh the proper application of the law against the protection of individual expectations.[108] Even where the expectations are legitimate and significant precautions have been taken, the public interest may outweigh an individual's financial interests.[109] For example, a person may be required to demolish a house built under a valid permit if it poses a high risk to an area.[110]

Administrative contracts typically establish legitimate expectations.[111] Rights conferred in such contracts may be regarded as "vested" rights.[112] Such rights can only be revoked with reasonable compensation.[113] Additionally, protection is afforded when a private person relies on an *administrative decision*.[114] Administrative decisions are addressed to individuals and resolve a specific legal situation.[115] A subsequent modification of an administrative decision is permissible only if the legal requirements for revocation are met and the public interest outweighs the protection of legitimate expectations.[116] However, according to the Swiss Federal Supreme Court, a decision may be irrevocable, particularly if it establishes a subjective right.[117]

Another important application of the doctrine of legitimate expectations concerns cases of *incorrect advice and misinformation* provided by Swiss authorities.[118] In both cases, advice or information must be provided on an individual basis, according to the Federal Supreme Court.[119] Additionally, the Court has established further criteria in this context.[120] The advice or information must be unconditional, issued by the competent authority, and based on factual and legal circumstances that have not changed since its provision.[121] For example, incorrect advice on legal remedies illustrates this principle. The protection of legitimate expectations applies in cases where an individual loses access to a legal remedy because they relied on incorrect advice from the public authorities despite exercising due diligence.[122]

---

[108] Ibid. See also e.g., DFC 137 I 69, 2.6.

[109] Federal Supreme Court, Judgment, 1C_567/2014 of 14 July 2015, 5.2. See also Uhlmann (2022), pp. 163–181, 168.

[110] Federal Supreme Court, Judgment, 1C_567/2014 of 14 July 2015, 5.2.

[111] Uhlmann (2022), pp. 163–181, 167.

[112] Ibid. Vested rights are similar to property rights.

[113] Ibid.

[114] Ibid.

[115] Ibid.

[116] DFC 137 I 69, 2.3; Kradolfer (2023), para. 95.

[117] Ibid.

[118] Uhlmann (2022), pp. 163–181, 167.

[119] Ibid.

[120] Ibid.

[121] Ibid.

[122] Kiener, Kälin and Wyttenbach (2024), § 34, para. 1709.

As far as legal effects are concerned, the protection of legitimate expectations aims to prevent harm to individuals who act in good faith.[123] If this protection is violated, Swiss law provides for various legal consequences. The state may be required to uphold the basis (e.g., an administrative decision) of legitimate expectations and apply the information or advice given, previous administrative practice, or former legal provisions.[124] If this is not possible – such as when it would conflict with public interests – alternative remedies may include financial compensation for losses incurred as a result of reliance on incorrect information.[125]

5.3 *Good Faith in Legislation*

Another area of constitutional law practice involving legitimate expectations relates to *legislative acts*. In Switzerland, the legislator is also required to act in accordance with the principle of good faith.[126] However, the criteria for applying the doctrine of legitimate expectations to legislative acts differ from those applicable to (individual) administrative decisions.[127] This is because legislation in democracies can be amended at any time.[128] Nonetheless, for a society to function effectively, a degree of stability is essential.[129] Consequently, the fundamental right to good faith under Article 9 of the Constitution does not prevent the legislator from amending or modifying laws.[130] However, good faith may impose certain limitations on such modifications.[131]

The Federal Supreme Court recognizes that individuals rely on Swiss laws in effect when a government action occurs, expecting not to face norms that retroactively evaluate their conduct.[132] Nevertheless, the *prohibition of retroactivity* applies only when the private conduct in question took place before the law changed.[133] In exceptional cases, retroactive application may be permissible if it is clearly stated in the law, limited in duration, does not create significant inequalities, and serves the public interest.[134]

---

[123] Ibid., para. 1727.
[124] Ibid.
[125] Ibid.
[126] DFC 128 II 112, 10b/aa; Kradolfer (2023), para. 111.
[127] Kradolfer (2023), para. 111.
[128] Ibid.
[129] Ibid.
[130] Kiener et al. (2024), § 34, para. 1719.
[131] Ibid.
[132] Ibid., para. 1720.
[133] Ibid.
[134] DFC 138 I 189, 3.4.

5.4 Prohibition of Abuse of Rights and Contradictory Behaviour

Article 9 of the Swiss Constitution protects individuals from *abuse of rights* by state authorities, while private individuals are protected by Article 2 of the Civil Code.[135] Whether the prohibition of abuse of rights is a justiciable element of the right to good faith is disputed.[136] Some legal scholars classify the prohibition of abuse of rights as part of the constitutional law principle of good faith under Article 5(3) of the Constitution, which is not enforceable in court.[137] Others, however, view it as part of the right under Article 9.[138] The Federal Supreme Court has established various categories of the prohibition of abuse of rights, typically including the abuse of a legal institution and the circumvention of the law.[139]

Article 9 of the Constitution also prohibits state authorities from acting in a contradictory manner (*venire contra factum proprium*).[140] This means that state authorities must act coherently and consistently in legal relationships.[141] A contradiction arises when public authorities depart from a previously binding position without objective justification, resulting in a disadvantage to an individual.[142]

5.5 Good Faith as a Source of Interpretation

Under certain conditions, the principle of good faith also applies to legal interpretation.[143] As such, the doctrine of legitimate expectations is an important source for interpretation: statements made in legal relationships between authorities and private persons should be understood in a manner that reflects good faith.[144] Statements should be interpreted based on their objective meaning.[145] As an interpretative source, the doctrine of legitimate expectations applies to administrative decisions as well as to contracts and concessions in public law.[146] Likewise, submissions from parties in legal proceedings should be interpreted according to this principle.[147]

---

[135] Kiener et al. (2024), § 34, para. 1712.

[136] Kradolfer (2023), para. 120.

[137] Ibid.

[138] Ibid.

[139] See Häfelin et al. (2020), para. 722 et seq.

[140] Uhlmann (2022), pp. 163–181, 169.

[141] Kiener et al. (2024), § 34, para. 1714.

[142] DFC 133 I 149, 3.3.

[143] Kradolfer (2023), para. 136.

[144] Ibid.

[145] Bickel (2014), § 9, para. 62 et seq.

[146] Kradolfer (2023), para. 137.

[147] Ibid., para. 138.

6 Conclusion

The principle of good faith is fundamental to democratic legal systems and fosters trust and predictability, which are essential for upholding the rule of law. In times of political instability, good faith is an important safeguard against the arbitrary use of power by public authorities. In Swiss constitutional law, the explicit protection of good faith is particularly robust compared to other domestic legal systems, highlighting its unique role within the Swiss legal system.

As stated in Articles 5(3) and 9 of the Swiss Constitution, good faith is more than just a constitutional law principle; it is a fundamental right that requires state authorities to act with loyalty and respect the legitimate expectations of their citizens. The case law of the Swiss Federal Supreme Court has played an important role in defining good faith by providing clear criteria for its application in different legal contexts, such as administrative decisions, legislative acts, and legal interpretation. Consequently, the principle of good faith helps maintain the stability of the Swiss legal system by enabling individuals to rely on the law and the obligations of Swiss authorities, thereby promoting a sense of justice and confidence in the rule of law.

References

Aubert J-F, Mahon P (2003) Petit Commentaire de la Constitution Fédérale de la Confédération Suisse du 18 Avril 1999. Schulthess, Zurich

Bickel J (2014) Auslegung von Verwaltungsrechtsakten. Stämpfli, Bern

Chiariello E (2003) Treu und Glauben als Grundrecht nach Art. 9 der schweizerischen Bundesverfassung. Stämpfli Verlag, Bern

Egli P (2020) Introduction to Swiss constitutional law, 2nd edn. Dike Verlag, Zurich

Futhazar G, Peters A (2020) Good Faith. In: Viñuales J (ed) The UN friendly relations declaration at 50. An assessment of the fundamental principles of international law. Cambridge University Press, Cambridge

Gächter T (2005) Rechtsmissbrauch im öffentlichen Recht. Schulthess Verlag, Zurich

Giacometti Z (1960) Allgemeine Lehren des rechtsstaatlichen Verwaltungsrechts. Polygraphischer Verlag, Zurich

Häfelin U, Müller G, Uhlmann F (2020) Allgemeines Verwaltungsrecht, 8th edn. Zurich/St.Gallen, Dike

Kiener R, Kälin W, Wyttenbach J (2024) Grundrechte, 4th edn. Stämpfli Verlag, Bern

Kolb R (1998) La Bonne Foi en droit international public. Revue Belge de Droit International 43(2):661–732

Kotzur M (2009) Good Faith (*Bona fide*). In: Peters A, Rüdiger W (eds) Max Planck Encyclopaedia of public international law. Oxford University Press, online

Kradolfer M (2023) Art. 9 [commentary]. In: Ehrenzeller B et al (eds) Die Schweizerische Bundesverfassung. St. Galler Kommentar, Band I, 4th edn. Dike/Schulthess Verlag, Zurich

Oesch M (2022) Constitutional law. In: Thommen M (ed) Introduction to Swiss law. Sui Generis, Zurich, pp 113–136

Picot F (1977) La bonne foi en droit public. Helbing & Lichtenhahn, Basel

Rohner C (2014) Art. 9 [commentary]. In: Ehrenzeller B et al (eds) St. Galler Kommentar zur neuen Bundesverfassung, 3rd edn. Dike/Schulthess Verlag, Zurich

Schindler B, Tschumi T (2023) Art. 5 [commentary]. In: Ehrenzeller B et al (eds) Die Schweizerische Bundesverfassung. St. Galler Kommentar, Band I, 4th edn. Dike/Schulthess Verlag, Zurich

Thommen M (ed) (2022) Introduction to Swiss law. Sui Generis, Zurich

Tschentscher A (2015) Art. 9. In: Waldmann B et al (eds) Basler Kommentar zur Bundesverfassung. Helbing Lichtenhahn Verlag, Basel

Uhlmann F (2005) Das Willkürverbot (Art. 9 BV). Stämpfli, Bern

Uhlmann F (2022) Administrative law. In: Thommen M (ed) Introduction to Swiss law. Sui Generis, Zurich, pp 161–182

Manifestations

Good Faith in Constitutional Interpretation

Krzysztof J. Kaleta

Abstract The purpose of this article is to clarify the concept of good faith in the context of constitutional interpretation. The need for good faith in constitutional interpretation stems not only from the specific political context of the crisis of liberal constitutionalism, but also from the very nature of constitution as a legal document, and above all from the irreducible sphere of discretion in constitutional interpretation. In my opinion, the concept of constitutional good faith should be understood as an instrument for limiting the discretionary power of interpreters and enhancing the legitimacy of the interpretative decisions they take. However, for the requirement of good faith to become an operative standard of constitutional culture it needs normative justification. In my view, such a credible justification for the concept of good faith in constitutional interpretation is provided by the philosophy of reflexivity. A reflexive account of good faith can be an instrument for limiting discretion in the process of constitutional interpretation, while at the same time contributing to deepening the social legitimacy of constitutional practice. In this way, such an approach can make constitutional practice more resilient to abuse.

This publication has been prepared within the framework of the research project "Reflexive constitutionalism as a response to the crisis of contemporary constitutionalism (PRACTIS: Power, Reflexivity And ConsTitutional crisIS)" financed by the National Science Centre (2021/43/B/HS5/00414).

K. J. Kaleta (✉)
Faculty of Law and Administration, University of Warsaw, Warsaw, Poland
e-mail: k.j.kaleta@wpia.uw.edu.pl

J. Podkowik et al. (eds.), *Gleams of Good Faith in Constitutional Law*, Ius Gentium: Comparative Perspectives on Law and Justice 132,
https://doi.org/10.1007/978-3-032-06486-8_13

1 Introduction

The concept of good and bad faith, which has been known to jurists for centuries, has relatively recently begun to be directly applied to constitutional interpretation. The notion of constitutional good faith expresses the well-known postulate of fidelity to the law (constitution) in jurisprudence. Its re-articulation in the context of the crisis of liberal constitutionalism demonstrates a search for a new constitutional language that better reflects the current challenges of constitutional interpretation. However, the transfer of the concept of good faith from the contractual relations of private law to constitutional law requires taking into account the specificities of constitutional interpretation.

The purpose of this article is to clarify the concept of good faith in the context of constitutional interpretation. This first requires identifying the context in which references to good faith are formulated in constitutional discourse. As I will try to show in Part I, the growth of interest in constitutional good faith represents a doctrinal response to the increasing instrumentalisation of the constitution by the ruling authorities. This trend led to a reinterpretation of the principles of liberal constitutionalism in an anti-democratic and illiberal spirit. The need for good faith in constitutional interpretation, however, stems not only from the specific political context of the crisis of liberal constitutionalism, but also from the very nature of constitution as a legal document, and above all from the irreducible sphere of discretion in constitutional interpretation. I will outline these conditions in Part II. In my opinion, the concept of constitutional good faith should be understood as an instrument for limiting the discretionary power of interpreters and enhancing the legitimacy of the interpretative decisions they take. However, for the requirement of good faith to become an operative standard of constitutional culture it needs normative justification. In my view, such a credible justification for the concept of good faith in constitutional interpretation is provided by the philosophy of reflexivity. This approach not only answers the problem of the legitimacy of power, but also provides objective criteria for operating in constitutional good faith. Therefore, in Part III, the claim of constitutional good faith will be interpreted as a kind of reflexive action. A reflexive account of good faith can be an instrument for limiting discretion in the process of constitutional interpretation, while at the same time contributing to deepening the social legitimacy of constitutional practice. In this way, such an approach can make constitutional practice more resilient to abuse.

2 Constitutional Good Faith and the Crisis of Liberal Democracy

Since the enactment of the first written constitution, disputes about constitutional interpretation have not been extinguished. They have resulted in the formulation of numerous theories that define the purpose and methods of constitutional interpretation in different ways. Against this background, the relatively recent adaptation of the concept of good faith for the purposes of constitutional interpretation should be interpreted as an expression of the search for new theoretical tools that allow for the adequate description and evaluation of constitutional practice in recent decades. The concept of constitutional good faith was incorporated into constitutional discourse to deal with a specific phenomenon within liberal constitutionalism, going beyond the hitherto known cases of incidental violations or instrumentalisation of the constitution.

This phenomenon is characterised in various ways. Most commonly, it refers to a series of political or legal actions taken by governments in many countries, which results in the hollowing out of constitutional institutions and principles, stripping them of their normative content while maintaining the guise of legalism. Practices referred to as *autocratic legalism*[1] or *abusive constitutionalism*[2] or *populist constitutionalism*[3] or *illiberalism*[4] are linked to the rise to power of illiberal movements, most often described as populist. The actions they undertake, which are presented to the general public as standard practices for interpreting the constitution, by way of negative synergy, result in the constitution losing its basic legal function. This blurs the distinction, fundamental to the liberal constitutionalism, between the current political game and the constitutionally guaranteed independent rules of the political game. Importantly, the essence of the phenomenon described is not a direct violation of the letter of the constitution, but an infringement of its spirit, in particular by challenging the specific (liberal) model of constitutionalism that the constitution represented at the time of its enactment. This is certainly the case when a constitution founded on the principles of liberal constitutionalism, instead of limiting power, begins to be used to consolidate it, leading to a breach of the fragile balance between democratic and liberal values in a constitutional democracy.[5]

It thus concerns the formation of a specific model of constitutional practice, which David Landau has called abusive constitutionalism. Within its framework, the constitution and constitutional institutions, originally designed in the spirit of liberal constitutionalism, cease to serve the protection of human rights and democratic values, becoming an instrument for their limitations.[6] The transformation towards an authoritarian regime can take place through both formal and informal constitutional amendments. The latter involve the reinterpretation of constitutional principles in an anti-liberal or anti-democratic spirit. Bad faith in constitutional interpretation most often manifests itself in a "highly superficial, selective and acontextual interpretation which inverts the democratic purpose of constitutional

[1] Scheppele (2018).

[2] Landau and Dixon (2019).

[3] Blokker (2019).

[4] Laruelle (2022).

[5] Scheppele (2018), pp. 557, 581–582.

[6] Landau (2013), pp. 195–200.

norms".[7] In practice, abuses of this kind may consist of absolutizing one of the constitutional principles that are useful to interpreters; interpreting the disputed provisions in isolation from the relevant axiological context (all relevant constitutional principles) or factual context (social conditions); and finally, misusing comparative law argumentation or ignoring historical interpretation in interpreting the concepts to which the constitution refers.

If constitutional court becomes subordinate to the ruling authorities play a key role in this process due to their strong position in the architecture of liberal constitutionalism. Their activity is described by David Landau and Rosalind Dixon as abusive judicial review. This phenomenon manifests itself in a variety of techniques of constitutional interpretation which, seemingly no different from the commonly accepted methods of interpretation, actually support antidemocratic and illiberal sub-constitutional legislation, deepening the process of consolidation of power in the hands of the ruling majority.[8] Abusive judicial review – whether weak, where courts uphold legislation or executive actions that significantly undermine the democratic minimum core, or strong, where courts actively remove or weaken democratic protections – is always executed through bad-faith interpretations, either of constitutional provisions or of the axiological or factual context addressed by the constitution.[9]

This phenomenon has also been recognised in analyses of the Polish constitutional crisis.[10] The practice of interpreting the constitution adopted by the government after 2015, with the significant participation of the Constitutional Tribunal, which was subordinated to the political majority, has been described explicitly as "hostile constitutional interpretation". As Jerzy Zajadło explains, acting in bad faith is a constitutive feature of this kind of practice:

> Hostile constitutional interpretation is a political strategy accompanied by specific perverse political rhetoric with quite a primitive, populist character. They serve the constitution, but at the same time they call the constitution "internally contradictory and conflictogeni" "postcommunist," "a constitution for elites, not for ordinary people," etc., etc., etc.. This strategy is not even overt but deeply concealed behind the screen of showy slogans. In the current situation, the often-repeated phrase "our legislature is compliant with the constitution, because it was confirmed by a verdict of the Constitutional Tribunal" is particularly perfidious, perverse, and even wicked. So in the final instance, the phenomenon of interpretation constitutionis hostilis is an example of extreme instrumentalization of recognizing the primacy of politics over the law, even at the level of the basic law.[11]

There is no doubt, therefore, that the rise of interest in the issue of good faith in constitutional law is linked to local unravellings in the broader process of the crisis of liberal constitutionalism. Constitutional interpretation, in the hands of its ideological opponents, is becoming the primary tool for the subversion of constitutional

---

[7] Dixon and Landau (2019), pp. 493–495.

[8] Landau and Dixon (2019), pp. 1318–1322.

[9] Landau and Dixon (2019), p. 1345.

[10] Garlicki and Derlatka (2024).

[11] Zajadło (2018), pp. 65–66.

axiology in an illiberal and undemocratic direction.[12] This has provoked a crisis of trust between participants in constitutional discourse. As a result, a reflection on the role of good faith in constitutional discourse is not only a reflection on the methods of constitutional interpretation itself, but also on the role of the constitution in liberal democracy.

3 Good Faith and the Specifics of Constitutional Interpretation

3.1 The Constitution as an Object of Interpretation

Justification for the requirement of good faith should be sought not only in current political circumstances, but first and foremost in the specifics of the constitution as an object of interpretation. As Sławomira Wronkowska, an eminent legal scholar and former judge of the Polish Constitutional Tribunal, aptly observes, the constitution is characterised by a "laconic linguistic dimension and a rich, extensive extra-linguistic dimension".[13] In these particular circumstances lies the paradox of constitutional interpretation: the laconic and general provisions of the constitution are expected to regulate extensive and complex matters of social life. This expectation poses specific challenges for constitutional interpreters.

The provisions of the constitution, apart from a narrow group of procedural rules, most often take the form of laconic and ambiguous principles and policy norms. They are used to set general objectives without specifying the manner or means of achieving them. Their instance and application is the fundamental aim of interpretation. The question of the scope of implementation of given constitutional principle is also never considered in isolation, and requires the consideration of legal (general constitutional principles) and factual (social determinants) circumstances. For these reasons, as we know, the directives of systemic and functional interpretation play a special role in the interpretation of the constitution.

However, the classical legal methods adopted within a given legal community do not always make it possible to arrive at unambiguous results. This is because the intrinsic open texture of the constitutional provisions is also considerably expanded by references to the so-called normative environment of the constitution. These are primarily the various doctrinal/philosophical concepts to which reference was made at the time when the constitution was drafted. These include such foundations of modern constitutions as the principle of the democratic state ruled by law, subsidiarity, social justice, the separation of power, or the natural (supra-positive) law in which most modern constitutions ground the concept of human dignity. Irrespective of this, the crucial concepts by which constitutional provisions are constructed, such

[12] Landau and Dixon (2019), p. 1326.

[13] Wronkowska (2016), p. 24.

as democracy, the rule of law and justice, are regarded as essentially contested concepts.[14] The interpretation of such provisions cannot be reduced to a matter of clarifying their linguistic meaning. They require contextualisation, recognition of both the tradition from which they originate and the contemporary, actual dimension of their functioning in specific domains of social life. Their intrinsically contested nature is expressed precisely in the fact that agreement between interpreters on their general, abstract meaning does not necessarily lead to agreement on the practical consequences of their application in a specific case.[15]

The need to recognise the normative environment of the constitution does not only refer to provisions with a strong axiological entanglement, such as those concerning human rights and freedoms or the principles of the socio-political system. Interpretation of the competence provisions, essentially of a procedural nature, also requires the recognition of the context of their application. This involves the need for a comprehensive and in-depth reconstruction of the circumstances in which the constitutional competences of public authorities are to be actualised, particularly in those cases where constitutional provisions refer to vague criteria. Sometimes the process of interpreting the constitution requires resorting to directives that make it possible to remove the legal loopholes that are revealed, at least *prima facie*, for example when the constitution provides for a specific conventional act (enacting or applying the law) but only partially defines the rules for its implementation, or does not define them at all.[16] Regardless of that, the competence provisions should always be interpreted in the light of the general principles, such as checks and balances, or the directive for public authorities to cooperate (as provided for in the preamble to the Constitution of the Republic of Poland).

Interpreting the constitution, especially within the framework of constitutional review, is not a mere technical comparison of two norms (constitutional and statutory). Rather, it involves determining whether, in light of all relevant constitutional principles and current knowledge of the regulated areas of social life, a given act of

---

[14] Waldron (2002), pp. 148–149; Pozen (2006), pp. 916–917.

[15] We should also not forget the anti-foundationalist background of modern liberal democratic constitutions. Such circumstances of constitutional interpretation were unanimously pointed out by philosophers as diverse in their views on constitutionalism as Hans Kelsen and Carl Schmitt. The latter criticised the dilatory character of constitutional provisions, which resulted from the postponement or even abandonment by the drafters of the constitution the final determination of the meaning of certain constitutional provisions (Schmitt (1985), pp. 62–63). What Schmitt regarded as a weakness of the liberal constitutionalism Hans Kelsen regarded as an immanent feature of the democratic regime. In his view, a democracy could only be founded on axiological relativism (Kelsen (1955), pp. 38–39). However, this influenced on his scepticism about making abstract provisions expressing human rights and freedoms the basis for constitutional review. As he noted in his work *The Essence and Development of Constitutional Justice*, such constitutional provisions only express a framework of interpretation, their final meaning should be determined in current legislation expressed a political compromise.

[16] During the Polish constitutional crisis, this problem came to light in the application of the prerogatives of the President, in particular the right of clemency, and also in the authority of parliament to enact a law setting out the rules for the appointment of members of the National Council of the Judiciary.

public authority (statute or judgement) represents a permissible concretisation of constitutional norms or exceeds constitutional limits. The concretisation of a constitutional norm is a kind of hermeneutical act of application, i.e. the reference of an abstract norm to the concrete conditions of social life. These specifics of constitutional interpretation are pointed out by S. A. Barber & J. B. Flaming when they write that this process involves two parallel tasks, i.e. establishing the true meaning or best interpretation of constitutional provisions and the truth or best account about the world to which constitutional provisions must apply if the Constitution is to be an effective instrument of its ends.[17]

This means that with the interpretation of the constitution, in addition to knowledge of the legal methods of its interpretation, a certain amount of information concerning the environment of the constitution is also necessary. This extra-linguistic dimension of the constitution cannot be fully grasped by means of strictly legal instruments. In the area of the normative environment of the constitution, the objects of interpretation are not only social ideas and concepts, but also historical facts (usually mentioned in the preambles), social phenomena, and statistical data, which are not the domain of law, but of philosophy, history, sociology or economics. Often each of these discourses uses different concepts and tools to analyse the same phenomena. As Marek Smolak notes, the ontological status of the "social market economy" is defined differently within demographic, social, economic or statistical sciences. Such conditions entail that:

> the judge's effort in interpreting the assumptions of the normative environment of the constitution is a truly herculean effort. He or she must possess knowledge, both as to the object of interpretation and the methods of its examination, which, by virtue of his or her profession, is not professional knowledge.[18]

3.2 Discretionary Power in Constitutional Interpretation

The starting point for considering constitutional good faith is therefore to recognise that constitutional interpreters have significant discretionary powers.[19] This discretion is both unavoidable (it results from the characteristics of the text itself) and desirable (it allows constitutional goals and values to be better fulfilled in a complex and changing social reality). However, it is also associated with specific risks, and may constitute an area of potential abuse. This is confirmed by the experience of abusive judicial review mentioned in the introduction.

Under the rule of law, discretion cannot, of course, provide an excuse for arbitrariness. Within an integrated legal culture, glaring examples of abuse are quite easy to identify as examples of misapplication of directives of legal methods. Hence,

[17] Barber and Fleming (2007), p. 191.

[18] Smolak (2016), 41.

[19] Wright (2018), pp. 47–48; Barnett and Bernick (2018), p. 29.

instances of inconsistent application of interpretive methodology are recognised by David Pozen as paradigmatic examples of subjective bad faith.[20] However, a conception of constitutional good faith based on a narrow legal discourse would not introduce new elements into constitutional culture. Such a narrow construction would enable the identification – *in media res* – of only simple cases of interpretation *contra and preater legem*. However, *ex ante*, in the context of the current constitutional dispute, it would not formulate any specific requirements for the participants in constitutional practice that would go beyond legal compliance. If, therefore, the concept of constitutional good faith is to genuinely protect the stability of the constitutional order, it must go beyond merely preserving formal correctness.

It is commonly argued that constitutional good faith serves to assess the process of applying and interpreting the constitution in a broad perspective that goes beyond the category of legalism.[21] The key to understanding the essence of good faith is a comprehensive view of constitutional interpretation. The constitution as a whole, being the product of the rational and deliberate action of the constituent power, has an identity and a function that is more than the sum of the purposes formulated in its individual provisions. Fidelity to the constitution is not only fidelity to its letter or even its spirit, but also to the broader political philosophy from which the constitution grows. Randy E. Barnett & Evan D. Bernick use the metaphor of a watch in this context:

> The Constitution can be thought of as describing a device or mechanism like a watch. Like the watch, the Constitution as a whole has functions or purposes (described in the Preamble). Like the flywheel, gears and springs of the watch, each of its clauses was designed to work harmoniously with the others to fulfil those functions. Like the watch, each of its constituent parts have their own secondary functions as means to the more general ends. Like a watch, the Constitution was consciously designed. Where the function or purpose of a provision is not obvious, we can attempt to 'reverse engineer' the design from close examination of its workings. But we can also seek out the explanations left behind by its designers. Whether these explanations were published or not, they would still help us to understand the functions of each constituent part as we attempt to use the device of the Constitution to perform its intended functions by seeking its spirit.[22]

No less important is the factual context in which the constitutional interpretation takes place. As Landau and Dixon emphasise, simply relying on the formal correctness of the court's reasoning is not sufficient to identify an abusive practice; an analysis of the context and the effects of the judicial decision is crucial in this case. As an example, they cite so-called abusive constitutional borrowing, which consists in transferring general ideas or specific institutional arrangements to a new context where certain social, political or economic conditions necessary for their proper

[20] Pozen (2006), p. 925.

[21] Pozen (2006), p. 894; Wright (2018), p. 49.

[22] Barnett and Bernick (2018), p. 53.

functioning do not exist. The same regulations in an unfavourable factual context can result in a weakening of democratic values.[23]

Controversies over constitutional interpretation need not arise solely from intentional actions, deliberate violations of canons of interpretation or ignoring factual circumstances. Indeed, fidelity to the constitution does not exclude the possibility of interpretive disputes between participants in constitutional discourse. Assent to the general meaning of key constitutional concepts and principles does not necessarily imply assent to their concretisation made in an individual act of constitutional application or interpretation. Participants in constitutional discourse may therefore be characterised by "rational disagreement" over the meaning of specific constitutional norms. As Balkin aptly points out fidelity to the constitution does not mean lack of disagreement:

> People with very different views will often see different things in the Constitution. They may understand the point or the effect of constitutional provisions quite differently. And when the Constitution features a tension between different values and principles-as it so often does-different people may resolve those tensions differently, all the while claiming to be faithful to the Constitution.[24]

Therefore, fidelity to a constitution founded on democratic values must also include a willingness to collaborate in seeking not just an one right interpretation, but the best possible interpretive settlement – one that enjoys the highest degree of both legal and social legitimacy. What is crucial, however, is the shared conviction among participants in constitutional discourse that they are engaging in the same practice,[25] based on the necessity of collaboration in a shared enterprise.[26] This means that the concept of constitutional good faith should have an inclusive function, serving to deepen trust between participants in constitutional discourse.

The integrative function of constitutional good faith can be considered from an internal perspective (within the legal discourse itself) as well as from an external perspective (between different discourses on the constitution in a democratic society). As far as the internal, legalistic perspective is concerned, it should be emphasised that the concept of constitutional good faith does not entail the need to adopt specific theories of constitutional interpretation, whether of a static or dynamic nature. The postulate of fidelity to the constitution, which is central to this concept, can therefore be interpreted either as fidelity to the original intention, to the spirit of the constitution or to the broader political philosophy out of which the constitution grows. The essence of good faith amounts precisely to a readiness to rethink and refine previously accepted methodological premises under the influence of new arguments or facts.[27] Constitutional good faith is thus a kind of meta-directive of interpretation that implicitly stems from the awareness of the existence of a sphere

---

[23] Landau and Dixon (2019), pp. 489–496.

[24] Balkin (2018), p. 160.

[25] Fallon (2017), p. 126.

[26] Wright (2018), pp. 46–47.

[27] Fallon (2017), p. 139.

of discretionary power in the process of constitutional interpretation, which traditional methods of interpretation are unable to eliminate. In other words, the concept of good faith does not relate directly to the methods of interpretation but to its purpose and participants.

The need for external integration, on the other hand, stems from the importance of the normative environment of the constitution in the process of its interpretation. Its full recognition requires the interpreter to be open to the extra-legal discourses in which the meaning of constitutional principles is discussed. I am firmly convinced that Wright's remark that "constitutional good faith exists at the intersection of culture and law"[28] should be interpreted in this way. In effect, only an interpreter who, in the process of interpreting the constitution, is able to access and appropriately use knowledge about the social dimension of constitutional functioning remains in good faith. The external integration of legal constitutional discourse is not an easy task, as it must not lead to a questioning of the autonomy of the law, which is the foundation of modern constitutionalism. This difficulty is recognised by David Pozen, who points out the disjunction in American legal practice between professional judicial discourse and social discourse on the constitution:

> Relative to other fields, constitutional law is distinguished not only by exceptionally low levels of bad faith talk inside the courts but also by exceptionally high levels of bad faith talk outside the courts.[29]

3.3 *The Purpose of the Concept of Constitutional Good Faith*

In summary, the purpose of the concept of constitutional good faith is to limit and subject to scrutiny the sphere of discretion that is involved in the interpretation of the constitution. It arises both from the characteristics of the constitutional text and the role that the normative environment of the constitution plays in its correct interpretation. In particular, this is the sphere in which legal discourse, based on traditional methods of interpretation, does not lead to unambiguous solutions, therefore it becomes necessary to refer to the general practical discourse. Importantly, decisions on constitutional interpretation need the broadest possible social legitimacy. The interpretation of the constitution, in particular undertaken by public authorities, is a social practice that demands legitimacy like any sphere of power in a democratic constitutionalism. Therefore, the postulate of constitutional good faith should be interpreted as a directive to deepen the social legitimacy of decisions based on the interpretation of the constitution.

---

[28] Wright (2018), p. 48.

[29] Pozen (2006), p. 918.

4 Towards Reflexive Good Faith in Constitutional Interpretation

4.1 The Objectivization of Constitutional Good Faith

For the concept of constitutional good faith to become an operative standard for constitutional culture, it requires objectivization. Interpreting good faith from the subjective side, i.e. the specific attitude of the interpreter, entangles us in a dangerous psychologism. The search for the unarticulated intentions of the interpreters is not only extremely difficult, but above all it is not conducive to building mutual trust between the participants in constitutional discourse. It runs the risk of reducing constitutional good faith to a rhetorical or moralistic category.

However, the objectivization of constitutional good faith is not an easy task. For the content of constitutional good faith is the specific attitude of the interpreters not only towards the constitution as an object of interpretation, but also towards the interpretation process itself and its other participants. This attitude is most often expressed in terms such as perfect commitment[30] or fidelity to the constitution. The latter is characterised by Balkin as follows:

> Fidelity is more than a set of techniques or methods-it means having the right attitude towards one's task. In constitutional interpretation, fidelity is not just a good thing. It is the whole point of the enterprise. But fidelity is not simply a property of an interpretation; nor is it merely a correspondence between one's interpretation and the thing one interprets. Rather, fidelity is also a feature of the self who interprets. Fidelity is an attitude that people have towards the object of interpretation and about the process of interpretation.[31]

Certainly, some of the expressions of good faith formulated in the literature constitute elementary principles of political culture. Their violations are indicated by David Pozen's unwillingness to compromise or negotiate across branch or party lines, unwarranted deviations from constitutional convention or evasion of the spirit of the bargain.[32] They play an important role in building trust between the participants in constitutional discourse but they relate little to the specifics of interpreting the constitutional matter itself. It is difficult to translate them into concrete obligations amenable to intersubjective verification. Striving to objectivise the notion of constitutional good faith, one should therefore seek standards of evaluation of interpretative actions undertaken by the interpreter. Following the classical formula of good faith, I propose to call these standards due diligence requirements.

Given the specificity of constitutional interpretation described above, it will be crucial to exercise due diligence while accurately, honestly and comprehensively reconstructing the normative environment of the constitution and the positions on constitutional interpretation formulated by the other participants in constitutional

---

[30] Pozen (2006), p. 926.

[31] Balkin (2018), p. 159.

[32] Pozen (2006), p. 292.

discourse. What remains in bad faith, therefore, is the interpreter who, by exercising due diligence, may have become aware of the key conditions of the normative environment or, knowing them, ignores the consequences for his or her argumentation arising from them. Similarly, an interpreter who ignores the opposing views formulated in public discourse on the subject of constitutional interpretation (whether of public authorities, in particular higher courts, legal doctrine, experts or civic movements) acts in bad faith.

By contrast, acting in good faith requires more than just reliability of the argumentation formulated, but also an attitude of philosophical scepticism, a willingness to acknowledge one's own fallibility in recognising the relevant contexts of interpretation, above all a willingness to face criticism of one's own findings.[33] From a hermeneutic perspective, it can be said that these activities serve to broaden the horizon of understanding of the constitutional norm and also to purify the interpreter's prima facie understanding of the constitutional norm from personal pre-judgements.

Understood in this way, the standard of due diligence can be seen as an ethical requirement, an imperative of self-restraint in the exercise of discretionary power. In this respect, however, it was rather an element of internal independence to protect the interpreter from what David Pozen calls bad faith in the Sartrean sense. For bad faith can also consist in the self-deception of the interpreter. This happens when there is a necessitarian assertion about what the law "must" mean or a minimisation of inconvenient facts about the constitution and the judicial role. Pozen here refers to the well-known observation that people may, through reflection or avoidance of reflection, distort or suppress information and beliefs of which they are prereflectively aware.[34] The problem is that, as he notes, the interpreter is not necessarily aware of being inauthentic, or untruthful towards herself.[35] Therefore, without questioning the ethical dimension of the good faith clause, one should look for measurable criteria that can be formulated in terms of concrete obligations incumbent on the interpreter. In those cases where the interpretation of the constitution is binding (e.g. within constitutional review), these criteria must also consider the legitimacy of authority. Only under such conditions can the concept of good faith function in constitutional discourse as an objective standard limiting the discretion of the interpreter.

[33] Barber and Fleming (2007), p. 192.

[34] Pozen (2006), pp. 934–939.

[35] Pozen (2006), p. 895.

4.2 The Philosophy of Reflexivity

Given the findings on the specificity of constitutional interpretation and the search for a broader philosophical justification for the concept of constitutional good faith, it is worth turning to the philosophy of reflexivity. Reflexivity is a fundamental concept of the social sciences,[36] including the legal sciences.[37] It can therefore also be successfully applied to constitutional practice as the practice of interpreting and applying the constitution. The notion of reflexivity grew out of the search for sources of legitimacy of the power exercised by modern social institutions, therefore it also perfectly responds to the signalled need to legitimise the discourse conducted around the interpretation of the constitution. It also provides concrete tools for limiting discretionary power in the process of constitutional interpretation.

The concept of reflexivity involves the self-reference of both action and cognition within social practice. Cognition and action are mutually interwoven, in the sense that reflexive practice is based on constant self-observation and modifications in the course of action. As A. Giddens argues, the basic principle underlying the social legitimacy of late-modern institutions is that they are capable of revising the foundations of their own action on the basis of incoming external information about these practices.[38] The reflexive operation of social institutions and practices involves using knowledge about the conditions of social life to organise and reshape the principles on which their ongoing functioning is based. It is therefore not so much a matter of adopting a critical attitude towards the correctness of one's own practice from the point of view of its internal assumptions (in the case of constitutional interpretation: focusing on legalism or the formal correctness of legal reasoning), as it is a readiness to transform one's own *modus operandi* under the influence of information arriving from outside, and therefore from other practices and social systems operating on the basis of quite different sources of legitimacy. It is therefore entails viewing one's own practice through the prism of other social practices with which one shares a particular field of action. Reflexive action, as it is oriented towards the constant verification of the legitimacy of one's own bases of action, should be characterised by a cognitive scepticism, leading participants in a given practice to prefer consensual forms of decision-making. As Levinson aptly notes, constitutional law requires not only formal entrenchment rules and appropriately designed institutional guarantees of compliance, but above all sociopolitical commitment.[39] Reflexive constitutionalism focuses attention on precisely this dimension of constitutional practice. As I will try to demonstrate later, linking the concept of good faith to the requirements of reflective thinking and action can solve the problem of legitimacy of constitutional practice, the risk of Sartrean bad faith and also provide better understanding of the demands of due diligence in constitutional interpretation.

---

[36] Beck et al. (1994); Luhmann (1998); Ricoeur (1974).

[37] Luhmann (2004); Habermas (1996); Teubner (1983); Nonet and Selznick (1978); Teubner (1993).

[38] Giddens (1990), p. 38.

[39] Levinson (2011), pp. 697–698.

In the domain of constitutional theory, the concept of reflexive constitutional interpretation refers primarily to societal constitutionalism,[40] with which it shares the view of the constitution not as an isolated legal act, but as a component of wider social practice. The actual sense of the constitution is negotiated between various social actors and social systems within this practice. The proposed concept also refers to the idea of reflexive constitutional identity.[41] Indeed, the interpretation of the constitution is the most important instrument of the reflexive self-understanding of the political community.[42] Reflection on constitutional identity should not be limited to a narrow legal discourse but remain open to other discourses in which the content of constitutional principles is deliberated. What is needed for this is an institutional condition that enables the pre-consciousness of legal thinking to be exposed through its social problematisation in the various discourses conducted around constitutional principles.

The essence of reflexive constitutionalism is thus the interweaving and interaction of different ways of thinking about the constitution. Constitutionalism is perceived as a type of reflection on the identity of the political community oriented towards the constitution understood as a text and as a practice of interpreting and applying that text.[43] This is done through the concretisation of the constitutional norm and thus the linking of the constitutional provisions to the concrete problems from which the need for interpretation arises. The interpretation of the constitution is always an attempt to solve a specific problem that has become apparent in the practice of the functioning of a given community. Resolving it appropriately requires examining the issue from different perspectives. It is through this kind of interaction that the concept of constitutional identity, which plays a special role in constitutional discourse, should take shape. This concept serves, especially in the forum of constitutional courts, to draw the line between constitutional interpretation and informal amendment.

4.3 The Need to Democratise Constitutional Interpretation

A reflexive approach to constitutional interpretation can also respond to the crisis of liberal constitutionalism, in particular the crisis of its social legitimacy, which has become a breeding ground for the development of various forms of abusive constitutionalism. Above all, it responds to the need to democratise constitutional interpretation. The sphere of discretion associated with the process of constitutional interpretation should not be an area reserved for exclusive legal reflection, but should become the subject of open, inclusive public debate. Reflexive

[40] Sciulli (1991); Teubner (2004); Thornhill(2018).

[41] Lindahl (2007).

[42] Nolte (2005), p. 4; Pichlak (2020), p. 59.

[43] Pichlak (2020), p. 60.

constitutionalism closely aligns with P. Häberle's concept of an "open society of constitutional interpreters", formulated years ago. It thus recognises the need to widen the circle of legitimate participants in the process of constitutional interpretation to include not only the public authorities (parliament, courts), but all political and social actors, both those directly shaping the content of constitutional norms and those affected by these norms in the practice of social life. According to Häberle's conception, anyone who is the subject of a particular state of affairs regulated by a constitutional norm (both when he applies the constitution and when the constitution is applied to him) becomes an indirect interpreter of that norm.[44] Whether his perspective has a chance to be publicly articulated depends on how the public sphere, in which authoritative judgements about the meaning of the constitution are made, is structured.

In the reflexive view, interpretation by professionals (lawyers, officials) should be a means of expressing "pluralistic public opinion", based on up-to-date knowledge of the actual conditions and possibilities for the implementation of constitutional norms. The idea, therefore, is to make constitutional interpretation an open and public process in which the actual state of compliance with constitutional standards is faithfully reflected. Such democratisation is only possible on the condition that constitutional interpretation is opened up to social normativity formed outside legal discourse. As K. Scheppelle suggests, "a successful constitution' is one whose ideas have spread beyond the boundaries of the text and into fields of social practice":

> Constitutions - or at least successful constitutions - manage to create their own social life. They do so by naturalising, channelling and/or legitimating power. Successful constitutions extend the idea of constitutionalism beyond any constitutional text and beyond the directly regulated political classes into a broader social world in which constitutional ideas shape social expectations and understandings, and come to be taken for granted. Constitutions, in short, rely for their maintenance on a general understanding of constitutionalism both in the political elite and in a broader public.[45]

This means that the official discourse around the interpretation of the constitution (e.g. in the forum of a constitutional court) should take into account the experience of its application, including what is sometimes called "the social life of constitutions",[46] "constitution in practice",[47] or "constitutional reality".[48] Those responsible for shaping the authoritative interpretation of the constitution should consider societal expectations about the understanding of constitutional principles, confronting them with their legal views in the process of applying and interpreting the constitution. As H. L. A. Hart demonstrated in *The Concept of Law*, the stability of the legal order ultimately depends on the consensual practice of officials and citizens recognising and accepting certain rules or practices. This means that there

---

[44] Häberle (1975), p. 297.

[45] Scheppele (2017), p. 35.

[46] Scheppele (2017), p. 55.

[47] Levinson (2011), p. 700.

[48] Häberle (1975).

must be convergence between understandings of constitutional principles within and outside the legal system.[49]

The realisation of this postulate requires the introduction into constitutional practice of instruments supporting professionals (judges, legal scholars) in the accurate recognition of social normativity. This means that the development of the concept of constitutional good faith and it influence on constitutional culture significantly depends on procedural solutions, e.g. the inclusion of instruments for articulating social normativity in the system of constitutional review. This is an important issue requiring further, separate elaboration. At this point, however, it should be signalled that this function is certainly fulfilled by a wide access of citizens to the institution of constitutional complaint, the real inclusion of social organisations as *amicus curiae* in the proceedings before the constitutional court, and the development of a professional analytical background that would provide essential information to the authorities in the recognition of the complex factual interdependencies (social, economic, technological) in the implementation of constitutional standards in various dimensions of the functioning of modern societies. These are the most important institutional conditions for making the constitutional good faith clause an effective standard for a reflexive constitutional culture.

4.4 Constitutional Interpretation Beyond Legal and Populist Constitutionalism

A reflexive interpretation of the constitution also breaks the duopoly that has dominated in constitutional discourse for some time – namely, that of legal and populist constitutionalism. The former is characterised by a narrow understanding of constitutional discourse as legal – and specifically as judicial – discourse. Under legal constitutionalism, the interpretation of the constitution is treated as an internal matter for lawyers.[50] It is often accompanied by legal formalism, which undermines the social legitimacy of the judiciary, thereby contributing to the weakening of the position of the judiciary towards the rule of law crisis.[51] Analyses of the state of constitutional practice formulated in the context of the Polish constitutional crisis confirm that one of the key weaknesses of liberal constitutionalism is the detachment of the practice of constitutional interpretation, above all in a judicial discourse, from social normativity. Skuczyński & Muszyński write in this context about the phenomenon of constitutional drift, which they consider to be one of the key determinants of the constitutional crisis in Poland:

> (…) after the adoption of the 1997 Constitution and until 2015, the constitutional provisions were subject to the process which we refer to as constitutional drift, which involved

[49] Levinson (2011), pp. 698–699.

[50] Blokker (2013), pp. 13–40.

[51] Matczak (2020), p. 421.

> marginalisation of the societal imaginary underpinned by the Constitution. During this period, more dominant liberal and communitarian imaginaries created grounds for a new paradigm of governance which strengthened the executive at the expense of the parliament, social partners, and other social actors in general.[52]

Paradoxically, the monopolisation of constitutional discourse by the courts, the recognition that judges have special insight into the meaning of constitutional principles and that judicial interpretation of the constitution is a professional practice immune from axiological and political disputes provides fertile ground for the development of the practice of abusive constitutionalism. Subordinated to the political majority, courts using an unreflective culture of adjudication based on argument from authority are a useful instrument in the process of dismantling the guarantees of the rule of law.[53]

Clearly, the practice of so-called populist constitutionalism, while providing a number of examples of constitutional bad faith in constitutional interpretation, is also unreflective. For it assumes the total primacy of politics over law, marginalising the role of legal discourse in the interpretation of the constitution. It should be emphasised that despite the specific rhetoric of populist groups, pitting the people against corrupt and isolated elites, populist governments do not at all take steps to encourage citizen participation in constitutional politics. In practice, it is the populist leaders who speak for the people as an imagined entity rather than a real political community. The practice of populist constitutionalism thus leaves no room for autonomous channels of articulating social normativity.

The dominant perspectives in contemporary constitutional discourse promote the inbred and monological view of constitutional interpretation, thus perceiving constitutional reflection as an "internal matter" of a particular social system (either legal or political) which, in the process of defining the constitutional identity, maintains full independence from the discourses of other social systems. This results in a static, one-dimensional perception of the constitutional identity, e.g. as a set of constitutional provisions that establish the objective boundary for constitutional politics (legal constitutionalism), or a completely extra-legal, homogeneous structure based on non-discursive ethnic, national or religious criteria (populist constitutionalism). Such approaches neglect the very nature of constitutional interpretation, which is located at the intersection of diverse social systems. Meanwhile, in the case of the reflexive interpretation of the constitution, it is not a matter of the arguments formulated in other discourses (moral, economic, political) replacing legal reflection. The point is that knowledge of them should be skilfully used within the framework of classical methods of interpretation (first and foremost, the directives of systemic and functional interpretation), so as to deepen the social legitimacy of the results achieved by this means. Conventional methods of interpretation are a kind of "filter" through which social normativity is incorporated into constitutional discourse.

---

[52] Muszyński and Skuczyński (2023), p. 2.

[53] Ginsburg and Moustafa (2008).

4.5 *Towards Reflexive Constitutionalism*

The concept of good faith emerged in constitutional discourse as a response to growing negative trends within the constitutional practice of liberal democracies. It was not part of a broader constitutional model or theory, but a consequence of an intuitive reach into the legal tradition in search of tools to understand and describe specific current problems of legal practice. Its significance in the discourse on constitutional interpretation, however, may be broader. The concept of constitutional good faith can play an important role in the transformation of constitutional culture. For this to happen, however, it requires objectification and further theoretical elaboration, which is possible provided that the concept of good faith is embedded in broader philosophical assumptions about the constitution as a legal act and a social phenomenon.

The aim of liberal democratic constitutionalism is to ensure the legitimacy of the legal order and to eliminate arbitrariness in the actions of public authority. Constitutional interpretation is a form of the exercise of power, one as expansive as the sphere of discretion available to the interpreter. Therefore, it requires both legitimacy and limitation. The monopolisation of the discourse on the interpretation of the constitution by any branch of government, be it the parliament or the constitutional court, in the long term leads to a consolidation of power that undermines the principle of checks and balances, which is the foundation of contemporary constitutionalism. On the other hand, the isolation of the process of constitutional interpretation from social normativity weakens the legitimacy of the constitution, which results in a weakening of its resilience to various manifestations of political instrumentalisation, thereby undermining the stability of the legal order.

The aspiration to eliminate arbitrariness and to deepen the legitimacy of the practice of interpreting the constitution lie at the heart of constitutional good faith. They also correspond to the fundamental goals of reflective thinking and action. Therefore, the concept of constitutional good faith should be interpreted as an imperative for reflexive action within the practice of interpreting the constitution. The philosophy of reflexivity provides a plausible justification for the concept of good faith in constitutional interpretation. This is because it brings to constitutional discourse a deeper understanding of the fidelity to the constitution. A reflexive constitutional good faith presupposes a holistic approach to constitutional interpretation, integrating the various dimensions of constitutional functioning. Meanwhile, as Barber & Fleming emphasise:

> fidelity in constitutional interpretation requires a fusion of philosophical and other approaches, properly understood. Within such a fusion, we would understand text, consensus, intentions, structures, and doctrines not as alternatives to but as sites of philosophical reflection and choice about the best understanding of our constitutional commitments.[54]

[54] Barber and Fleming (2007), p. 190.

Embedding the concept of constitutional good faith in the broader framework of the philosophy of reflexivity makes it possible to give it an objective and operative character. In this way, it not only contributes to counteracting acts of instrumentalisation of the constitution, but also makes it possible to build a culture of trust among participants in constitutional discourse. It protects against acts which, under the pretext of the "openness" of constitutional provisions, attempt to subordinate the law to particular political interests. It thus reinforces the autonomy of the constitution as a legal act. In that way it protects against practices that turn the law into a political weapon.[55] Opening up to a broad public discourse on the constitution, on the other hand, promotes a deepening of the legitimacy of constitutional practice. By making professional legal culture more responsive to public expectations, it prevents formalism in constitutional interpretation. As a result, reframing the concept of constitutional good faith helps to make the constitution a more democratic and at the same time more effective tool for constraining the exercise of power.

However, making constitutional good faith an operative standard of constitutional culture requires a properly shaped, reflexive public sphere – both within the professional (legal) domain and in relation to the functioning of civil society. At the level of professional legal culture, this requires first and foremost a reflexive culture of justifying interpretative decisions. The use of the sphere of discretion in the interpretation of the constitution cannot be masked by legal formalism but should be subject to transparent justification, which not only deepen the legitimacy of the judgment, but also protect the interpreter himself from the risk of falling into Sartrean bad faith. It should consist of confronting one's own views on the meaning of constitutional norms with the meaning adopted by other participants in constitutional discourse, including those formulated outside official legal discourse. This is only possible if there are institutions and procedures that mediate legal discourse with other discourses on the constitution. This implies the necessity of designing inclusive procedural solutions within the proceedings before public authorities, above all the courts, where binding interpretations of the constitution are formulated.

The successful incorporation of the good faith standard into constitutional culture in the reflexive manner also requires effort on the part of civil society. For Wright is right that constitutional good faith is first and foremost a "civic virtue that must be cultivated and inculcated".[56] There must be forums and channels of communication that articulate the civic perspective of understanding constitutional principles in a manner independent of government. There must therefore be autonomous bodies for generating knowledge about the constitution in action, knowledge that can be used to verify the arguments formulated in official constitutional discourse. These range from organisations protecting human rights, trade unions or self-governing professional bodies, to completely informal movements of contestation, bringing specific constitutional issues to the public. Most relevant, however, are the mixed, expert-citizen forums in which the professional (legal) discourse on the

[55] Scheppele (2018), pp. 573–574.

[56] Wright (2018), p. 49.

constitution is confronted with the experience of citizens. Therefore, a reflexive framing of constitutional good faith also requires support from the academy. The role of academic discourses is to provide knowledge about the actual conditions of constitutional application in different areas of social life.

5 Conclusion

The concept of constitutional good faith, understood as one of the instruments of reflexive constitutional interpretation, can contribute to strengthening the foundations of liberal constitutionalism, making it more resilient to the crises described at the beginning. This is because it strengthens the formal and informal guarantees for the implementation of the checks and balances principle, which is at the core of liberal constitutionalism's identity. It suffices to recall Article XVI of the Universal Declaration of the Rights of Man and of the Citizen of 26 August 1789, which stated that a society in which there is no guarantee of respect for rights or the establishment of the separation of powers has no constitution. In the optics of reflexivity, this demand, however, should be read more broadly than just in relation to the horizontal relationship between constituted authorities.[57] The separation of powers should also be respected in the vertical relationship between the constituent and constituted power. Fidelity to the constitution also presupposes fidelity to the citizens in whose name the constitution was established. Therefore, it will not only be a manifestation of constitutional bad faith to use the sphere of discretion to impose one's own extra-legal preferences through constitutional interpretation, but also to ignore the voice of citizens on constitutional matters. Importantly, the reflexive approach to constitutional interpretation revalues the pluralist approach to the identity of the people as constituent power, which underpins liberal constitutionalism but is challenged by populist movements.

The emergence of the question of good faith in constitutional interpretation was an intuitive response of legal doctrine to the visible manifestations of a crisis of constitutional practice within liberal democracies. It was an expression of the aspiration to take a broader view of constitutional interpretation, to go beyond the category of legalism, to link the process of constitutional interpretation more firmly to its social background. By turning towards the philosophy of reflexivity, the notion of good faith can be made an effective tool for the transformation of contemporary constitutionalism. A reflexive account of constitutional good faith can provide the impetus for discussing an original model of constitutional practice that would go beyond today's dichotomy of legal and populist constitutionalism. However, this requires further in-depth reflection on reconfiguring public sphere to foster citizen participation in constitutional interpretation, while enabling lawyers to use

[57] So: Wright (2018), p. 41.

knowledge of social normativity to deepen the legitimacy of judgements on constitutional interpretation.

References

Balkin JM (2018) Arguing about the constitution: the topics in constitutional interpretation. Const Comment 33(2):145–260

Barber SA, Fleming JE (2007) Constitutional interpretation. The basic questions. Oxford University Press

Barnett RE, Bernick ED (2018) The letter and the spirit: a unified theory of originalism. Georgetown Law J 107(1):1–63

Beck U, Giddens A, Lash S (1994) Reflexive modernization: politics, tradition and aesthetics in the modern social order. Stanford University Press, Stanford

Blokker P (2013) New democracies in crisis? A comparative constitutional study of the Czech Republic, Hungary, Poland, Romania, and Slovakia. Routledge, London

Blokker P (2019) Populism as a constitutional project. Int J Const Law 17(2):536–553

Chris Thornhill (2018) The citizen of many worlds: Societal constitutionalism and the antinomies of democracy. J Law Soc 45(S1) https://doi.org/10.1111/jols.v45. S1, https://doi.org/10.1111/jols.12104

Dixon R, Landau D (2019) 1989–2019: from democratic to abusive constitutional borrowing. Int J Const Law 17(2):489–496

Fallon RH Jr (2017) Arguing in good faith about the constitution: ideology, methodology, and reflective equilibrium. Univ Chicago Law Rev 84(1):122–145

Garlicki L, Derlatka M (2024) Constitutional review in abusive constitutionalism (continuation, corruption or disappearance?). In: Granat M (ed) Constitutionality of law without a constitutional court: a view from Europe. Routledge, New York

Giddens A (1990) The consequences of modernity. Polity Press

Ginsburg T, Moustafa T (2008) Rule by law: the politics of courts in authoritarian regimes. Cambridge University Press

Häberle P (1975) Die offene Gesellschaft der Verfassungsinterpreten. Juristische Zeitung, Vol. 10

Habermas J (1996) Between facts and norms: contributions to a discourse theory of law and democracy. MIT Press, Cambridge

Kelsen H (1955) Foundations of democracy. Ethics 66:38–39

Landau D (2013) Abusive constitutionalism. UC Davis Law Rev 47:189–260

Landau D, Dixon R (2019) Abusive judicial review: courts against democracy. UC Davis Law Rev

Laruelle M (2022) Illiberalism: a conceptual introduction. East Eur Polit 38(2):303–327. https://doi.org/10.1080/21599165.2022.2037079

Levinson DJ (2011) Parchment and politics: the positive puzzle of constitutional commitment. Harv Law Rev 124(3):657–746

Lindahl H K (2007) Constituent Power and Reflexive Identity: Towards an Ontology of Collective Selfhood. In: Loughlin M, Walker N (eds.) The Paradox of Constitutionalism. Constituent Power and Constitutional Form. Oxford University Press, pp 9–24

Luhmann N (1998) Observations on modernity. Stanford University Press, Stanford

Luhmann N (2004) Law as a social system. Oxford University Press, Oxford

Matczak M (2020) The clash of powers in Poland's rule of law crisis: tools of attack and self-defense. Hague J Rule Law 12:421–450. https://doi.org/10.1007/s40803-020-00144-0

Muszyński K, Skuczyński P (2023) Constitutional drift – exploring the deeper roots of polish constitutional crisis. iCourts Working Paper Series, No. 328

Nolte G (2005) European and US constitutionalism. Cambridge University Press

Nonet P, Selznick P (1978) Law and Society in Transition: Toward Responsive Law. New York

Pichlak M (2020) Constitutionalism as a reflection on political identity. In: Sulikowski A, Mańko R, Łakomy J (eds) Legal scholarship and the political: in search of a new paradigm. C.H. Beck, Warsaw, pp 57–74
Pozen DE (2006) Constitutional bad faith. Harv Law Rev 129(4):886–954
Ricoeur P (1974) The conflict of interpretations: essays in hermeneutics. Northwestern University Press, Evanston
Scheppele KL (2017) The social lives of constitutions. In: Blokker P, Thornhill C (eds) Sociological constitutionalism. Cambridge University Press, pp 35–66
Scheppele KL (2018) Autocratic legalism. Univ Chicago Law Rev 85(2):545–583
Schmitt C (1985) Political theology: four chapters on the concept of sovereignty. The MIT Press, Cambridge
Sciulli D (1991) Theory of Societal Constitutionalism: Foundations of a Non-Marxist Critical Theory. Cambridge University Press
Smolak M (2016) Wykładnia otoczenia normatywnego konstytucji. In: Smolak M (ed) Wykładnia konstytucji: Aktualne problemy i tendencje. Wolters Kluwer Polska, Warsaw
Teubner G (1983) Substantive and reflexive elements in modern law. Law Soc Rev 17(2):239–285
Teubner G (1993) Law as an autopoietic system. The European University Institute Press series. Blackwell, Oxford, Cambridge
Teubner G (2004) Societal constitutionalism: alternatives to state-centered constitutional theory? In: Joerges C, Sand IJ, Teubner G (eds) Transnational governance and constitutionalism. Portland, Hart Publishing, Oxford, pp 3–28
Waldron J (2002) Is the rule of law an essentially contested concept (in Florida)? Law Philosophy 21:137–164
Wright A (2018) Constitutional good faith. New York Univ Law Rev 93:41–49
Wronkowska S (2016) O niektórych osobliwościach konstytucji i jej interpretacji. In: Smolak M (ed) Wykładnia konstytucji: Aktualne problemy i tendencje. Wolters Kluwer Polska, Warsaw
Zajadło J (2018) Hostile constitutional interpretation. Gdańskie Studia Prawnicze 40:63–69

Good Faith in the State – Individual Relationships

Marcin Stębelski

Abstract The concept of good faith transferred to the field of constitutional law and considered from the perspective of various constitutional orders, expresses the obligation of state organs to undertake such actions that realise the fundamental constitutional principles. This approach relates directly to the essence of the constitution, whose normative layer, constituting the source of binding rules of conduct, rests on a foundation of values to be protected and realised in the process of its interpretation and application. Among the catalogue of values corresponding to the idea of a democratic state is respect for the rights of the individual. This entails ensuring that individuals have the conditions for a peaceful existence and, at the same time, granting legal guarantees through which they can develop as free subjects endowed with dignity. As a result, determining the status of the individual and their relationship to the state becomes one of the main axes of the constitutional system. It is therefore of particular research interest also in this aspect, which makes the principle of good faith one of the elements of modern constitutionalism.

The specificity of the state's action in relation to the individual is expressed in the obligation to shape the legal system and to direct governmental decisions in such a way as to ensure protection of the individual. The implementation of these basic principles requires acting in good faith, which is manifested, inter alia, by numerous principles relating to the rules of lawmaking. Acting in good faith by the state is also a basic assumption when public authorities introduce restrictions in the sphere of individual freedoms and rights. In this dimension, action aimed at constitutional goals is the initial condition for the admissibility of interference in the sphere of individual autonomy, as well as the criterion for assessing the legal effects of such interference.

Identifying the areas in which good faith relates to the relationship between the state and the individual ultimately leads to the conclusion that it is bilateral in nature. It imposes a specific obligation on the two parties to this relationship. This

M. Stębelski (✉)
Faculty of Law and Administration, University of Warsaw, Warsaw, Poland
e-mail: m.stebelski@wpia.uw.edu.pl

J. Podkowik et al. (eds.), *Gleams of Good Faith in Constitutional Law*, Ius Gentium: Comparative Perspectives on Law and Justice 132,
https://doi.org/10.1007/978-3-032-06486-8_14

is confirmed, in relation to the individual, by the obligation to obey the law, which is an expression of trust in the state, but also by the horizontally shaped obligation to respect the rights and freedoms of other subjects. This allows us to conclude that acting in good faith in fact permeates various spaces of constitutional regulation. To an equal extent, although in differentiated ways, it concerns the area of the state's authoritative actions, as well as the sphere of free, in principle, action of an individual. It thus indicates the universal character of the concept under discussion and its location at the very centre of constitutional solutions defining the relationship between the state and the individual.

1 Introduction

The search for manifestations of good faith in constitutional law should be carried out by referring to the basic features of the constitution. In this way, what constitutes the specificity of this normative act – i.e. first and foremost its particular content, legal force and form – becomes the point of reference for the consideration of good faith. Such a presentation of the topic stems from the conviction that good faith not only derives from the constitution, but also constitutes one of the essential instruments designed to secure its validity and thus also to enable the fulfilment of its fundamental functions.

At a more general level, one can say that the basic idea of a constitution, as it has developed over the past half-century, is to protect human rights. This corresponds, moreover, to the conviction expressed much earlier that there can be no constitution without respect for the rights of society.[1] This more general idea finds expression, for example, in the regulation of the status of the individual, i.e. the legal framing of their freedoms, rights and duties, constitutes one of the basic elements of the specific content of the constitution.[2] This shows at the same time that the constitution is more than just a detailed organisational act defining the mutual relations between the organs of the state counted among the various authorities. It not only makes the individual an essential subject covered by constitutional regulation, but also safeguards them against the sovereign actions taken by the state which are also addressed to them. This guarantee-protective function of the constitution allows, in a certain simplification, the conclusion that it expresses the idea of the state's duty of service to the individual.[3]

Even such a general observation regarding the position of the individual at the heart of constitutional regulation makes it possible to transfer the consideration of

[1] Article XVI of the 1789 Declaration of the Rights of Man and of the Citizen.

[2] This is the most extensive chapter of the Constitution of the Republic of Poland. See Bożyk (1999), pp. 21–37.

[3] See Piechowiak (2007), pp. 80, 90.

good faith to the level of the state-individual relationship.[4] The adoption of this perspective is based on the rather simple premise that if good faith is to be present in constitutional law, and thus to refer to the content of the constitution, it must surely be identifiable precisely in the sphere that shapes the legal situation of the individual in their vertical relation to the authority. For if it turned out that, acting on the basis of the constitution, the state is in no way bound by the principle of good faith in shaping the legal situation of the individual, it would be much more difficult to find an obligation or even a command to respect it in relations between organs of power. The purpose of this chapter is to show that what we call constitutional good faith is not only present in the state-individual relationship, but that it also very significantly affects the way the state exercises its powers. I present my findings in two parts. In the first, I briefly refer to the accepted understanding of good faith in constitutional law, deriving the obligation to respect this principle from the very essence of the constitution. In the second part, I analyse the manifestations of good faith in relation to the principle of the democratic state governed by law and the clause defining the conditions for limiting individual freedoms and rights. In doing so, I intend to show that good faith – by relating it to the sphere of the constitutional status of the individual – has its important place in constitutional matters and can then also be identified in other aspects of the functioning of state power under the constitution.

2 Good Faith in State-Individual Relations

Earlier studies have repeatedly referred to the basic characteristics of an action described as good faith, indicating that this category should also apply to constitutional law.[5] Characterising this concept is challenging because there is no legal definition of good faith. This is also the case in legal systems where good faith is explicitly mentioned in the constitutional text, such as in Switzerland or Romania. As a result, we mainly learn about the legal nature and elements of this principle from doctrine and case law.

The common denominator among many definitions of good faith is an action characterised by honesty, loyalty and fidelity to accepted obligations.[6] Certainly, each of these characteristics could be subject to more detailed analysis separately and it would probably be difficult to set very rigid boundaries for them. Good faith conduct, by its very nature, resists clear-cut classification, as it is not defined by a precise list of acceptable actions but rather by criteria that guide them. Good

[4] This is related to the general premise of liberal democracy, which is the requirement that citizens are treated by the state with respect for their equal dignity, thus giving rise to the formulation of a duty to act in good faith. See Gardbaum (2016), p. 160.

[5] See Blicharz (2025), Kałduński (2025).

[6] See Pozen (2016), pp. 888, 892.

faith presupposes such conduct which, within the framework of a specific relationship between two (more) entities, serves a common purpose. It thus envisages an interaction based on mutual trust.[7] It concerns an attitude that excludes actions aimed at taking advantage of one's position, misrepresenting or concealing the true motives of one's conduct. On the contrary, good faith requires transparency in action and consistency between the declared objectives and the methods intended to achieve them. Understood in this way, honesty means respecting the "rules of the game" established and binding on the parties, while at the same time refraining from actions that could raise doubts as to their admissibility and thus undermine the mutual trust of the parties to the legal relationship. It therefore involves not only respecting the "letter" of the provisions governing their relationship, but also taking into account the purpose of the obligations entered into when this "letter" does not give clear and unambiguous indications as to how one should act.[8]

The principle of good faith, which indicates the need to achieve the adopted objectives while requiring the use of honest methods to achieve them, is undoubtedly restrictive in nature. Although it does not unequivocally prohibit certain actions, it requires that they be considered in a broader context, taking into account the situation of the other party to the legal relationship, the main principles of the existing relationship, and the legal consequences of the decisions made. This is particularly important when such decisions are of a sovereign nature and may shape the legal situation of an individual. In such cases, the principle of good faith may be read as a directive for state action that builds trust on the part of its addressees and thus allows them to direct their conduct within the limits of the designated legal order. It may therefore apply not only to horizontal relations presupposing equality of the parties, but also play an important role in the vertical relations characteristic of constitutional law.[9] The principle of good faith will then give rise to the expectation that the authority (the state) will exercise its powers in such a way as to guarantee respect for the fundamental rights of the individual.[10]

---

[7] See Wright (2018), p. 46.

[8] This refers to the objective understanding of good faith, both in the passive and active sense. See Kałduński (2025), para 8.1.

[9] This extends the typical perspective that good faith is not necessarily compatible with the terms of constitutional law. See Gardbaum (2016), p. 159.

[10] This requires that the principle of *fiduciary government* underpinning the concept of *good faith constitutionalism* be preserved. See Bernick (2019), pp. 1–72.

3 Manifestations and Effects of Good Faith in State-Individual Relations

3.1 The Meaning of Good Faith

The definition of the meaning of good faith, as an action characterised, inter alia, by trust, certainty and predictability, relates directly to the basic features of the constitutional rule of law. Without undertaking a detailed analysis of this issue, it may nonetheless be stated that the introduction of the principle of the rule of law to the constitutional level is, on the one hand, a manifestation of a specific choice: namely, the recognition that the law – as a value in itself – is to constitute the basic instrument of state action. On the other hand, it sets the objectives of the state, whose raison d'être is to realise the principle of justice and respect for individual rights.[11] Thus, it imposes certain substantive requirements on the law, recognising that it must serve to realise principles that can be described as the axiological foundation of the constitution as a whole. The rule of law refers to a set of values that are either explicitly expressed in its text or derived from it in the jurisprudence of the constitutional court.[12] Their basic component, seen as the "hard core" of the principle,[13] is the recognition of the dignity of the individual which entails acknowledging their autonomy and framing the role of the state as one of safeguarding the individual and ensure the protection of their rights.[14] This also means that the state is obliged to use appropriate means to achieve these goals.

From this perspective, it follows that since the main determinant of the rule of law is the legal security of the individual, this goal can only be achieved under conditions of mutual trust. On the part of the state, it is a matter of acting loyally towards the individual, i.e. with the aim of safeguarding their situation and defining the legal space within which they can realise their intentions. On the part of the individual, it involves trust in the state, arising from the certainty and stability of the rules established and – as a result – acting in accordance with these rules.

It is worth adding that this general principle applies to the complex and diverse manifestations of the functioning of the state and its impact on the legal situation of the individual. Thus, it cannot be reduced to a closed catalogue of activities, but is intended to influence the manner in which sovereign powers are exercised in relation to the individual. It is not limited solely to the activities of the legislature, or to law-making activities in a broader sense, but also applies to the functioning of other authorities regardless of their systemic location. Thus, although the further analysis focuses on the state's lawmaking activities, this is because, in this context, it is easier to show the existence and necessity of acting in good faith. At the same time,

[11] Here, a distinction is made between the formal and substantive understanding of the principle.

[12] See Tuleja (2016), Article 2, para 19.

[13] See Zubik and Sokolewicz (2016), Art. 2, para 6.

[14] See Piotrowski (2018), p. 215. Grimm (2016).

this perspective makes it possible to identify the specificity of such conduct in the relationship between the individual and the state, without relating it exclusively to particular segments of public authority.

Placing good faith at the very centre of the state's relationship with the individual is not only due to a particular vision of the state and its role, but also to a more general perspective that takes into account the nature of the constitution itself as an intentional act. The idea here is to draw attention to this source of good faith in relation to the constitution, which is of a formal nature and linked to its fundamental features. In this respect, it is important to note that good faith action is not only embedded in the pursuit of specific objectives, such as those relating to the State in its relationship with the individual, but also refers more broadly to any action taken on the basis of constitutional norms. Every such action, although it must be based on specific constitutional norms, is at the same time directed towards the realisation of the values and principles underlying the adopted constitutional regulation. In other words, both in the process of interpreting and subsequently applying the constitution, all addressees of its norms are obliged not only to take these values into account, but also to realise, to the fullest extent possible, the principles that constitute the fundamental reason for establishing the constitution and giving it superior force in the legal order. The point here is to highlight this layer, which includes the axiological basis consisting of the values that define the identity of the constitutional regulation in question. These values require constant confirmation in constitutional practice, i.e. deliberate action aimed at achieving constitutional goals. As this directed action is precisely a bona fide action, this attitude seems to be necessary for the constitution to function as an act that produces concrete legal effects in the sphere of the functioning of the state and its organs.[15]

The link between good faith and acting on the basis of the constitution is of particular relevance with regard to the state, given that, firstly, state authorities may act only on the basis and within the limits of the law, and secondly, that in exercising the authority granted to them, they may use coercion and thus determine the scope of action of individuals permitted by law. Being bound by the principle of legalism, as a fundamental element of the rule of law, is intended to safeguard the individual against arbitrariness, while at the same time guaranteeing the stability and predictability of sovereign action. The problem often arises when the legal basis for action set out in the norms of competence does not provide an unequivocal answer to the question of what specific decisions (within the scope of legislative, executive or judicial power) may be taken. This situation involves granting a necessary degree of discretion to the legitimate authorities and, as such, does not raise any objections, as it is something obvious and, indeed, desirable. However, each time the state authority is granted a certain sphere of discretion on the basis of norms that are open to different interpretations, it may increase the risk of arbitrariness and thus lead to the exceeding of powers and violations of the law.

[15] By doing so, it minimises the risk of a so-called façade constitution. See Bożek (2023), pp. 3–24.

This problem appears even more frequently with regard to the legal bases determined by constitutional norms, which are characterised by a high degree of generality and thus require interpretation. If we add to this the aforementioned purposive nature of the constitution, which combines the level of norms expressed in the legal text with its axiological basis encompassing values, we can see that recourse to the principle of legalism alone will not always be sufficient to indicate precisely which actions are permissible and which are not. This issue may be the subject of dispute and, at times, of serious crises in which both parties claim to be acting on the basis of and within the limits of the law.[16] Against this background, the duty to act in good faith – i.e. to be oriented towards the objectives to be realised and to exercise powers honestly and loyally in pursuit of these objectives – seems to be a necessary component without which it is difficult to ensure the functioning of the state on the basis of constitutional norms.[17]

3.2 *The Effects of Good Faith*

What is noteworthy here is, firstly, the explicit placement of this obligation within the same constitutional provision that articulates the principle of legalism, proportionality and respect for obligations under international law.[18] This confirms the notion that good faith forms a coherent normative whole with other principles enshrined in the Constitution. At the same time, it complements the requirements arising from the rule of law by imposing additional, important, requirements on the organs of state power – loyalty, reliability and consistency. In this way, it links the rule to act on the basis and within the limits of the law to the constitutional objectives of the state. Referring to the Swiss example, it is equally important to grant everyone the right to be treated in good faith by the state authorities. In this context, it is significant that this right is linked to the concomitant prohibition of arbitrary treatment by public authorities. The doctrine of the protection of legitimate expectations, developed on this basis, confirms,[19] that the use of the principle of good faith has not only a protective dimension against unauthorised interference by the state

[16] Cf. the dispute over the manner in which the composition of the National Council of the Judiciary is to be statutorily framed and the divergent positions on the interpretation of Article 187 of the Constitution.

[17] It is still the text of the constitutional norms that is to be the starting point for an interpretation made with regard to their objectives. It is a matter of refocusing and seeking the appropriate context for the interpretation of constitutional norms. See Bernick (2019), pp. 1–72.

[18] In doing so, the principle of good faith itself is fundamental to the validity of international law. See Kałduński (2025). Thus, it can be said that also in this dimension it becomes an element of constitutional content. This is confirmed by the example of Romania, where the obligation to fulfil obligations under international agreements in good faith is explicitly enunciated in Article 11(1) of the Constitution there.

[19] See Askin (2025).

(passive aspect), but also serves to induce public authorities to take action implementing the constitutional guarantees of individual rights (active aspect).

The principle of the individual's trust in the state and the laws made by it, sometimes referred to as the principle of the state's loyalty to its citizens, is also a fundamental element of the clause of the democratic state of law adopted in the Polish Constitution.[20] It clearly emphasises the need for trust in relations between the state and the individual and – in this context – formulates the obligation of the state to act in a loyal and fair manner. At its core, this involves making decisions that provide a sense of stability and legal security. The well-established jurisprudence of the Polish Constitutional Tribunal has repeatedly and vividly pointed out that the law must not set "traps for citizens". Thus, it cannot contain vague and ambiguous provisions, as this makes it impossible for individuals to foresee the legal consequences of their actions.[21] The legislator must not take citizens by surprise and, at the same time, should guarantee them prospective recognition of those actions undertaken in accordance with the law in force.[22] In this way, the trust of citizens in the state is to be manifested concretely; on the part of the state this imposes certain limitations on the legislator, while obliging the state to shape the legal situation of the individual accordingly. This obligation can be very specific, as evidenced by a number of principles derived from the general principle of state loyalty. These include the requirement of legal determinacy, the prohibition of the creation of illusory powers, and the respect for justly acquired rights. Some of these requirements go so far as to oblige the legislator to secure the legal situation even of those individuals who have not yet acquired any rights, but who have embarked on certain undertakings on the basis of the hitherto binding norms, in the confidence that the state will fulfil its obligations and enable them to complete the actions undertaken.[23]

The invocation of the principle of citizens' trust in the state and the law it creates, in the context of manifestations of good faith in relations with the individual, could be justified if only for reasons of conceptual consistency. Since the essence of good faith is trust and mutual honesty of the parties in fulfilling their obligations, such an attitude should certainly characterise the state in its relations with the individual on the basis of this constitutional principle. The very perception of good faith in this context also has a deeper justification. It is related to the very nature of the principle in question, which, although so fundamental to the shaping of the mutual relationship between the state and the individual, remains at the same time so general and ambiguous that it requires clarification through the process of interpretation and application. It should be noted that neither the principle of trust in the state nor any of the specific principles derived from it specifies what a given public authority is

[20] Article 2 of the 1997 Constitution of the Republic of Poland. "The Republic of Poland is a democratic state governed by the rule of law, implementing the principles of social justice".

[21] See Florczak-Wątor (2025).

[22] See judgments of the Constitutional Tribunal: (2002), K 41/02, part V. A; (2008), P 16/08, part V, para 7.2; (2015) K 1/14, part III, para 9.4.

[23] Reference to the principle of protection of pending interests. See judgments of the Constitutional Tribunal: (2010) Kp 6/09; (2016) K 47/15.

supposed to do, but rather formulates certain expectations that also constitute the permissible limits of authoritative action. Whether the legislature will adequately realise these expectations, i.e. whether it will actually create a law ensuring security for the individual, depends, inter alia, on adopting an attitude known as good faith: orienting its one's actions towards the attainment of goals that are not explicitly included in the content of a given legal norm, but are an inherent part of it. This is well illustrated by reference to the rule of law, which has been framed in general constitutional norms that nonetheless impose specific obligations on the state. The necessity to act in good faith can be seen quite clearly in the case of the state introducing limitations in the sphere of constitutional freedoms and human rights. As with the rule of law clause, a more detailed discussion of the limitation clause is not necessary here. It is worth emphasising, however, that irrespective of how the individual elements of the proportionality test are formulated on constitutional grounds, i.e. how the legislator shapes the instrument for assessing the permissibility of the introduction of limitations , its basic condition is always the recognition of such a limitation as purposeful. This carries with it very important consequences. I would like to draw attention to two of them.

Firstly, this means that restrictions on the freedoms and rights of the individual may only take place for reasons that are justified at the level of the superior normative act – the constitution. Therefore, they cannot be a manifestation of arbitrary action by the state authorities, which would be the case when restrictions lack a constitutionally legitimate purpose.[24] Secondly, the purposefulness of the restrictions means that even the indication of the relevant purpose, must be further assessed with regard to the manner of its achievement. The issue here is to confirm that state interference does not consist of sham actions, i.e. actions which, despite official declarations, in fact aim at achieving hidden objectives.[25] The deliberate nature of the restrictions opens up space for good faith action, which, as emphasised above, is an attitude oriented towards the realisation of goals and constitutional objectives.[26] What is peculiar to good faith in this area is the fact that recognising an action as failing to fulfil the stated objectives, or as undertaken for purposes other than those declared, may result in a declaration of inadmissibility of the interference in question. In this way, the assessment of an aim-oriented action, i.e. an action in good faith, becomes an element in evaluating the admissibility of restrictions on individual freedoms and rights, which also testifies to its normative character.

The imposition of certain restrictions on the legislature when it intends to encroach on the sphere of individual autonomy is a consequence of granting legal subjectivity to the individual. It is intended to safeguard against possible arbitrariness on the part of the authorities and, at the same time, stems from assigning to the state the task of protecting the individual. The honest (loyal) fulfilment of this task

[24] See Podkowik (2025a in print).

[25] An action deemed to be undertaken in order to achieve ulterior motives (ulterior motive) may be deemed to violate the Convention. See Kochman (2025).

[26] See Podkowik (2025b).

consists, first of all, in respecting the criteria for restrictions provided for by law, i.e. the preservation of the statutory form and the demonstration of the constitutionally legitimate purpose of the planned interference. Next, it is crucial to link the objectives to the proposed instruments and to observe the appropriate proportion so as to make the restriction the least burdensome for the individual. Ultimately, even the fulfilment of all these criteria cannot justify a restriction that would override the essence of the individual right or freedom in question.[27]

The existing ambiguity of concepts relating to, for example, the objectives of limitations or the assessment of compliance with individual elements of the so-called proportionality test may in practice prevent the safeguarding of the legal situation of the individual, giving the formal criteria of limitations merely a façade-like character. There is therefore a need for these criteria, which have been enunciated at the constitutional level, to oblige the legislator, and subsequently the bodies applying the law, to direct their actions accordingly. That is, to ensure that, within the regulatory freedom granted to them, their actions will aim at realising the principle of the individual's trust in the state. The principle of good faith expressed in this way thus becomes an important element influencing the manner in which the state uses its sovereign powers. This is because it is closely linked to the need to remain faithful (loyal) to the individual as the addressee of the decisions taken. Numerous examples show that very often the legislator makes use of the possibility to limit the freedoms and rights of the individual, either despite the lack of a constitutionally legitimate aim or for purposes other than those declared.[28]

In the course of my deliberations, I have so far focused on that dimension of good faith which relates to the action of the state in relation to the individual. In this aspect, I have referred to the existence of limitations on the exercise of sovereign powers by the state and the necessity of orienting this action towards the protection of individual freedoms and rights. As is well known, the state is obliged to act loyally, and the source of this obligation is the concept of a democratic rule of law, which not only recognises the individual and their rights, but makes the individual the subject of its sovereign actions. This positioning of the individual in relation to the state stems from the recognition of human specificity, which is reflected the widespread emphasis on the principle of human dignity and – as a result – in the

[27] There is, in this respect, a far-reaching convergence of regulations involving constitutional limitation clauses in, for example, the Swiss constitution (cf. art. 36), Romania (art. 53), the Basic Law of the Federal Republic of Germany (art. 19) or the Constitution of the Republic of Poland (art. 31(3)).

[28] See Kochman (2025). Roznai (2021).

state's obligation to respect and protect it.[29] Acting in good faith is therefore, on the one hand, a consequence of the recognition of the individual as a subject, and, on the other hand, becomes indispensable so that the various manifestations of the State's sovereign influence over the individual can realise the protection of that individual's dignity as fully as possible. The outline presented in this way may be regarded as preliminary, but if we were to stop there, we would have to regard it as incomplete.

The reference to the principle of human dignity implies that one of the fundamental characteristics of the subject is to act freely and thus to make autonomous decisions relating to their own person. The law, including constitutional law, recognises this characteristic, which is manifested in the extension of human freedom to the protection exercised by public authority.[30] The sphere of autonomy of the individual thus delimited obviously creates the necessary space for self-determination, but at the same time imposes certain limitations on the individual. It obliges the individual to respect the law and thus establishes the requirement to respect the limits set by the law and subject to legal protection. In this interplay, it can therefore be seen that the state's duty to act loyally towards the individual is reflected and complemented in the duty imposed on the individual. This includes, firstly, an obligation on the individual to comply with the decisions addressed to them by the authorities and, secondly, a prohibition on acting in breach of the legal order. As a result, it requires the individual to direct their actions in a certain way so that, within the framework of the autonomy attributed to them, it is possible to comply with the rules whose guarantor is the state.

In doing so, it is worth noting that this constitutional shaping of the individual's space for autonomous action does not only relate to his or her relationship with the state, but also has an important horizontal dimension. It is expressed in the obligation of the individual to respect the freedoms and rights of others.[31] In this way, the constitution ensures the protection of the individual's freedom, thereby protecting the autonomy of the individual's action. However, it also expects the individual to – within the scope of their free conduct – take into account the obligation to protect the autonomy of others who are equal to them. There is therefore a kind of interaction here which provides for the complementarity of the action of the state and the individual. At the same time, it results in the inclusion of the individual, who is the subject of freedoms and rights, in the realisation of constitutional objectives.

---

[29] This formulation is explicitly provided in Article 1(1) of the German Basic Law; Article 30 of the Polish Constitution contains a parallel provision. Human dignity, as a fundamental constitutional principle, is protected in, for example, Article 7 of the Swiss Constitution and Article 1(3) of the Romanian Constitution, to confine myself here to the examples of countries already cited earlier in the text.

[30] Cf. Article 31(1) of the Constitution of the Republic of Poland: "Freedom of the person shall receive legal protection".

[31] This can be seen, inter alia, in the solutions contained in the Constitution of the Republic of Poland - Article 31(1), second sentence.

Both the obligation on the individual to obey the law and the injunction addressed to him to respect the freedoms and rights of others determine the space for acting in good faith. They define the scope of freedom in the exercise of the individual's freedoms and rights, indicating the necessity to realise the principles from which these freedoms and rights derive. At the same time, this shows that the observance of agreements and obligations characteristic of good faith and the pursuit of jointly defined objectives are also based here on the mutuality of the parties to such a relationship. In this case, i.e. with regard to the relationship between the state and the individual, this relationship obviously has features that are quite different from those between equal subjects.[32] On constitutional grounds, however, one can identify norms which seem to confirm that good faith as a specific directive of action also applies to the individual in their relationship with the state.

An example confirming the suggested bona fide bilateralism can be found in the provisions of the Romanian Constitution in its section on individual freedoms and rights. The general rule provided in this context is that the entitled subjects (Romanian citizens, foreign citizens and stateless persons) must exercise their constitutional rights and freedoms in good faith, without infringing the rights and freedoms of others.[33] What is noteworthy in this case is the juxtaposition of the injunction to act in good faith and the accompanying prohibition against infringing the rights and freedoms of others. Thus, while the prohibition of infringement refers primarily to actions contrary to the law, the exercise of rights and freedoms in good faith accentuates the dimension relating to the sphere of duty, which goes beyond mere legalism.[34] It relates to the honest and loyal exercise of one's powers, and thus to the determination of the conditions for action directed towards the exercise of the freedoms and rights granted to the individual in accordance with their purpose. The formula of good faith used here does not have a legal definition, but it indicates a course of action that is directional in nature and thus is intended to prevent arbitrariness and instrumentalisation of the rights enshrined in the constitution.

The juxtaposition of the injunction to act in good faith and the prohibition of violating the freedoms and rights of others is also significant in that it clearly broadens the scope of application of the first principle. It seems to indicate that the exercise of freedoms and rights in good faith applies to all situations in which an individual acts on the basis of constitutional norms. This is not limited to horizontal relations (e.g. with other individuals), but should also apply to actions taken in relation to the state (vertically). In effect, the imperative of honesty and loyalty fundamentally defines the attitude of the individual deriving certain rights from the constitution.

To complement the foregoing analysis, it is worth referring briefly to the norms contained in the Polish Constitution. This seems all the more interesting, as here too the subjects of constitutional freedoms and rights are obliged to use them in such a

[32] See Gardbaum (2023).

[33] Article 57 of the Romanian Constitution.

[34] See Stănescu (2025).

way as to "respect the freedoms and rights of others".[35] This obligation has – similarly to the Romanian injunction to act in good faith – the character of an obligation which is not limited to the prohibition of interference (negative dimension), but may also be read as requiring action to enable other subjects to exercise their freedoms and rights (positive aspect).[36] This appears to be the case especially when it concerns two parties to a specific legal relationship. In this context, the obligation to respect the rights of others should be linked to the pursuit of jointly accepted objectives. It therefore presupposes acting in good faith, the basis of which can be derived from the Constitution.

The attitude assuming honesty and loyalty of the individual towards the state is reflected in the catalogue of other constitutional duties. What I have in mind here is primarily the duty to obey the law, addressed to everyone[37] and the duty of loyalty to the Republic of Poland, which applies directly to citizens.[38] Referring to the first one, it was emphasised, inter alia, that apart from the legal duty, it is also of a moral nature, arising from a special relationship (bond) connecting an individual with the state, whose principles, system and basic tasks are defined by the Constitution.[39] The duty to obey the law, on the other hand, implies respect for the rules set by the state. This involves both an attitude of recognition of the legal boundaries and the taking of only such actions as fall within these boundaries. This understanding of the duty thus clearly complements the duty incumbent on the public authority with regard to the content of the law. This understanding of the duty to obey the law also corresponds explicitly with the understanding of the principle of good faith adopted in relation to the provisions of the Swiss Constitution. Indeed, it is worth recalling that the explicitly stated right of everyone to be treated in good faith (Article 9 of the Swiss Constitution) presupposes at the same time that the subject of this right behaves in an honest and loyal manner towards the state. The concrete manifestation of this mutual trust is respect for, and compliance with, the law. This bilateral relationship is not only firmly rooted in the principle of good faith, but also forms the basis of any democratic society defining its fundamental rights and obligations at the constitutional level.[40]

[35] Article 31(2) sentence 1 of the Constitution of the Republic of Poland.

[36] Particularly if we interpret this provision – Article 31(2) of the Constitution – in the context of the basic principles expressed in the introduction to the Polish Constitution, i.e. basing it, inter alia, on "respect for freedom". Garlicki and Wojtyczek (2016), Article 31, para. 5. Garlicki and Wojtyczek (2016), Article 31, para. 5.

[37] Article 83 of the Constitution of the Republic of Poland.

[38] Article 82 of the Constitution of the Republic of Poland.

[39] Działocha and Łukaszuk (2016), Article 82, para. 2.

[40] See Askin (2025), part 3 – The Function of Good Faith in Swiss Democracy.

4 Conclusion

The preceding analysis has made it possible to see that good faith action can also be identified in the relationship between the state and the individual. It stems from the very essence of a democratic state governed by law, together with its tasks, which – by definition – are intended to safeguard the individual by providing legal protection. The right granted to the state to shape the legal system sovereignly, and thus also to define the legal boundaries of the action of individuals, is closely linked to an influence that is intentional in nature. What can more generally be described as loyalty to the individual is a fairly broad field of action with a common denominator: the safeguarding of the legal situation of the individual, which manifests itself, inter alia, in the creation of stable and predictable norms and other authoritative decisions. Acting in good faith in relation to the various bodies exercising sovereign powers thus expresses an orientation without which it is not possible to realise constitutional principles, and thus it is not possible to confer a real meaning on constitutional goals concerning the individual in the practice of public authorities.[41] A concrete confirmation of the obligation to act in good faith with regard to the analysed relationship between the state and the individual can be found in the constitutions of Romania and Switzerland. However, this is not an exception revealing constitutional good faith only in these countries. Rather, it is an affirmation of a more general requirement, which stems from the endowment of the state with a specific constitutional model. Goal orientation and the need to take it into account and verify it in relation to the various manifestations of state action can also be observed when restrictions on individual freedoms and rights are introduced. The state's obligation to identify the constitutionally legitimate aim of restrictions and to show that the legal steps taken are likely to lead to it and are necessary to achieve it defines another specific sphere of sovereign influence on the individual – one in which action in good faith is essential.

References

Askin E (2025) Good faith in Swiss constitutional law. In: Podkowik et al. (eds) Gleams of good faith in constitutional law

Bernick ED (2019), Faithfull execution: where administrative law meets the constitution. Georgetown Law J 108(1)

Blicharz G (2025) Good faith in public law and the European legal tradition. In: Podkowik et al. (eds) Gleams of good faith in constitutional law

Bożek M (2023) The façade constitution – prolegomena. "Państwo i Prawo" 1

Bożyk S (1999), The constitution as the fundamental law of the state. In: Szyszkowska M (ed) Strong state. Białystok

Działocha K, Łukaszuk A (2016) Article 82. In: Garlicki et al. (eds) Commentary to the constitution of the Republic of Poland

[41] See above introductory chapter. Part III.

Florczak-Wątor M (2025) Good faith in polish constitutional law. In: Podkowik et al. (eds) Gleams of good faith in constitutional law
Gardbaum S (2016) Comparing constitutional bad faith. Harv Law Rev Forum, 129
Gardbaum S (2023) Online conversation with author
Garlicki L, Wojtyczek K (2016) Article 31. In: Garlicki et al. (eds) Commentary to the constitution of the Republic of Poland
Grimm D (2016) Constitutionalism. Oxford University Press
Kałduński M (2025) Good faith in international law. In: Podkowik et al. (eds) Gleams of good faith in constitutional law
Kochman A (2025) Good faith in the European convention of human rights. In: Podkowik et al. (eds) Gleams of good faith in constitutional law
Piechowiak M (2007) Servitude of the state towards man and his rights as the main idea of the Constitution of the Republic of Poland of 2 April 1997 - an achievement or a task? "Przegląd Sejmowy" nr 4
Piotrowski R (2018) Judges and the limits of democratic power in the light of the constitution of the Republic of Poland. Ruch Prawniczy, Ekonomiczny i Socjologiczny, No. 1
Podkowik J (2025a in print) Review of the constitutionality of the legislator's goals in the case law of the Constitutional Tribunal (in print)
Podkowik J (2025b) Good faith in the system of separation of powers. In: Podkowik et al. (eds) Gleams of good faith in constitutional law
Pozen DE (2016) Constitutional bad faith. Harv Law Rev 129(4)
Roznai Y (2021) Good faith in public law, conference statement, 23–24 September 2021 (online via Zoom), Oxford
Stănescu LS (2025) Good faith in Romanian constitutional law. In: Podkowik et al. (eds) Gleams of good faith in constitutional law
Tuleja P (2016) Article 2. In: Bosek L, Safjan M (eds) Commentary to the constitution of the Republic of Poland
Wright AM (2018) Constitutional good faith. N Y Univ Law Rev 93
Zubik M, Sokolewicz W (2016) Article 2. In: Garlicki et al. (eds) Commentary to the constitution of the Republic of Poland

Good Faith and the Separation of Powers

Jan Podkowik

Abstract This chapter focuses on the analysis of the principle of separation of powers in modern states and the role of good faith in the relationships between constitutional state bodies. The first part characterises the determinants of the separation of powers and examines the reasons why referring to the concept of good faith may be desirable in the context of interactions between various constitutional actors. This analysis excludes the relationships between central authorities and local governments, which are discussed in a separate chapter. Subsequently, building on the definition of good faith as an attitude oriented toward achieving constitutional goals and values, the chapter explores its fundamental characteristics and significance for the functioning of the state's institutional system. In the final section, an attempt is made to determine whether, and to what extent, constitutional good faith in the accepted sense can be enforced – both through judicial means and through extrajudicial mechanisms regulating inter-institutional relations.

1 Introduction

The aim of the chapter is to outline the theoretical framework for the concept of constitutional good faith in relation to the principle of separation of powers. The most frequent references to this concept in the discourse, and even accusations of lack of good faith,[1] appear against the backdrop of relations between state organs and their exercise of competences that affect the situation of other entities in the institutional structure of the state. Inter-institutional relations – as I will define them – by

[1] Pozen (2016).

J. Podkowik (✉)
Faculty of Law and Administration, University of Warsaw, Warsaw, Poland
e-mail: j.podkowik@wpia.uw.edu.pl

J. Podkowik et al. (eds.), *Gleams of Good Faith in Constitutional Law*, Ius Gentium: Comparative Perspectives on Law and Justice 132,
https://doi.org/10.1007/978-3-032-06486-8_15

their very nature give rise to disputes about the limits of jurisdiction and the catalogue of values promoted. In this context accusations of abuse or circumvention of the law are often made, including the use of the constitution to pursue current political goals or even personal gain, i.e. what can be described as the instrumentalisation of the constitution.

I argue that in systems based on the principle of constitutionalism,[2] the relationship between constitutional actors should be grounded in good faith, i.e. an attitude aimed at maintaining the supremacy of the constitution and preserving its fundamental role as an act that limits power and protects individuals. Constitutional good faith is intended to uphold the regulatory role of the constitution, regardless of whether one views the constitution as an emanation of an objective order of values or as a framework for regular politics.

While the proposed concept is not a safeguard of the state system against, what Jack Balkin terms "constitutional rot"[3] or constitutional crises,[4] it may make it easier to distinguish constitutionally acceptable practices from unacceptable ones, especially in ambiguous situations, regardless of whether we regard good faith as an enforceable legal norm, especially by courts.

The concept of good faith may at the same time offer methodological rigour for making choices in the application of constitutional provisions in situations where various alternatives are possible. In itself, it does not resolve the content of constitutional principles or their priority (hierarchy). Instead, it makes it possible – with reference to objectivised criteria – to justify why one course of action was taken rather than another in specific circumstances and, moreover, to relate it to the constitutional goals or objectives on which a given legal order is built. In this way, the concept creates the necessary space for constitutional actors, allowing, on the one hand, inherent disputes over the content of constitutional norms and the conditions for their realisation to arise, and, on the other hand, actions to be directed towards achiving the overarching goals that each constitution assigns to state organs. Paradoxically, recourse to the notion of constitutional good faith may not so much exacerbate disputes over the application of the constitution as serve to organise discussion on the application of the constitution in the formula of intersubjective construction.

The above assumptions form the framework for the following analysis. I will first characterise the conditions of the principle of separation of powers in modern states and, consequently, examine why recourse to the concept of good faith may be desirable in the relations between various constitutional actors. I leave outside the scope of consideration the relationship between central and local authorities, which is discussed in a separate chapter.[5] Then, starting from the book's definition of good faith as an attitude oriented towards the realisation of constitutional goals and objec-

---

[2] Barber (2018), pp. 1–20.

[3] Balkin (2018).

[4] Whittington (2002), Balkin and Levinson (2009), Balkin (2018), Mojski (2023).

[5] Sułkowski (2025).

tives, I will set out the basic predicates and their relevance for the functioning of the relations between the organs of separated power or, more broadly, between the entities constituting the institutional system of the state. In the last part, I will try to clarify whether, and to what extent, constitutional good faith can be enforced, both judicially and extrajudicially, in relation to inter-institutional relations.

2 Determinants of the Separation of Powers in Modern States and Their Consequences

In classical political thought, the theory of the separation of powers originated in opposition to the dominant, absolutist monarchy, wherein all power was concentrated in the hands of a single entity. In Montesquieu's terms, this theory presupposed the division of state functions among the three basic branches – the legislature, the executive and the judiciary – a principle known since antiquity. More importantly, it also required their relative separation in personell and competence separation, as well as the creation of a system of checks and balances. This was primarily to safeguard human freedom and thus prevent the tyranny of the reigning monarch. Although the separation of powers and its objectives have been characterised differently over the years, the focus has most often been on the separation of these three essential branches of state activity and common set of values that the separation of powers was intended to serve, such as freedom, the rule of law, the efficiency of government, and the accountability of power.

This simplified outline of the separation of powers and the values underlying this idea has many advantages. Undoubtedly, it allows for a fairly easy definition of the state system and the interrelationships between its branches. However, it does not reflect the entire complexity of inter-institutional relations found in the vast majority of democratic states, if not all of them. When examining the conditions of contemporary democratic systems, we can conclude that their picture is far more complex and multidimensional than the isolated three monolithic blocks designed to secure individual rights.[6] As Aziz Z. Huq and Jon D. Michels argue, any consideration of the separation of power system should take into account the existence of "normative pluralism" and "institutional heterogeneity",[7] which co-shape this system.

When it comes to the former, the state system is permeated not by just a handul of values such as individual freedom, governing efficiency or accountability, but by many competing values, which, in addition, cannot be realised to their full extent at the same time. The separation of powers, as Huq and Michels observe, has an instrumental justification. It allows for the realisation of a pluralism of values in which diverse values are harmonised and promoted,[8] while at the same time preventing the

[6] Carolan (2009).

[7] Huq and Michels (2016), p. 351.

[8] Huq and Michels (2016), p. 382.

imposition of one value as dominant. It thus prevents not only physical but also normative tyranny. Take, as an example, the disputes over the relationship between freedom and security or the efficiency of the administration (implying the reduction of formalism and the acceleration of decision-making processes), as well as the rule of law and social participation, which in turn require the existence of formal rules of conduct and the involvement of various actors, sometimes delaying given actions and their expected effects.

It can be hypothesised that the separation of powers not only serves to negotiate and harmonise diverse values, as the abovementioned authors point out, but also to negotiate and thus shape the normative content of constitutional provisions, especially those referring to vague doctrinal and philosophical concepts or socio-economic ideas. Concepts such as the common good, the rule of law or individual freedom – despite the fact that they have (and must have) a minimal semantic core embedded in the text of constitutional provisions and commonly shared by all participants in public life[9] – ultimately evolve through the practice of their interpretation by constitutional actors, not only the courts, but also by other actors. A prime example is the concept of the rule of law, once understood strictly formally (acting on the basis and within the limits of the law) and now supplemented by further substantive requirements, about the existence and scope of which there is currently a lively dispute. The separation of powers of the state creates the conditions for discourse, disputes and compromises as to the meaning of individual values encoded in the content of constitutional regulation, or more broadly – the provisions regulating the operation of individual institutions. In a sense, it prevents interpretative tyranny.

The second predicate, institutional heterogeneity, means that the distribution of power should not be reduced to treating the three basic branches of government as standing in isolation, like monoliths, with functions and objectives separate from each other. The system of power should be seen through the prism of a "dense political environment", consisting of a diverse group of actors operating inside and outside each authority.[10] These include the institutions within each authority, which are an integral component of it (e.g. the chambers of parliament in a bicameral system; the government and the president sometimes assisted by additional independent agencies and offices forming the executive branch; the various organs of the judiciary separated from each other in terms of competence and organisation, responsible for civil, public affairs or constitutional review). There are also other actors within the institutional system, such as the already mentioned independent bodies (the ombudsman, independent audit offices, government agencies) that do not fit into the classical model of separation of powers, as well as local authorities or

[9] Rejecting the view that there is a certain agreed minimum content of constitutional norms, we would have to conclude that con-stitutional interpretation becomes a relative act – dependent each time on the ability of those currently in the majority to impose their own reading of the provisions. Under such an assumption, the decisive argument for the validity and application of the constitution would be the argument of force.

[10] Huq and Michels (2016), p. 392.

political parties, civil society, the media, and foreign actors. Each of these actors – in different ways and on different terms – participates in shaping the values of the constitutional system. Take political parties, for instance. They are not always mentioned in constitutional provisions and singled out in discourse in the context of the separation of powers, yet they play a key role in decision-making processes in the state. This is because their activities not only influence the functioning of parliament and thus the direction and nature of the disputes or decisions made there, but in parliamentary-cabinet systems, they also have a leading role in shaping the government and authorising its activities. Furthermore, they influence the relationship between the different branches of government, particularly when parliament composed of party representatives is empowered to elect certain state organs (e.g. judges, ombudsmen and overseers). By reflecting the views of the electorate and their expectations of a particular vision of social order, political parties thus have an important influence in promoting constitutional values and setting priorities. Conservative parties will generally promote strong state structures, the centralisation of power, and a commitment to traditional values, while liberal parties will priorities on limiting state interference as well as protecting freedom or equality.

This necessarily brief overview of the determinants of the functioning of the contemporary state system does not exhaust all the complexities. It does, however, illustrate the background accompanying the practice of applying the constitution under conditions of separation of powers, which – on the one hand – involves various actors with differing expectations and interests (and sometimes individual ambitions and constraints) and, on the other hand, normative pluralism, which requires the constant negotiation of the content of values and the degree to which they are realised. Added to this is the subtle intertwining of the competences of the different actors operating in the constitutional system, which may either require them to cooperate or make them mutually dependant.

Given that the division of power is, at its core, based on mechanisms of mutual inhibition and balancing and, as Madison maintained, the idea of "ambition counteracts ambition",[11] the presence of multiple actors with different values that require agreement and negotiation naturally creates the risk of conflict. This is especially true if the aim of political actors is to strengthen one's own position, remain in power, gain the electorate's approval and promote a specific socio-political agenda, or return to power to realise a different vision of the state to that promoted by the present government. Such disputes occur not only between the main branches of divided power (legislative and executive or between the courts and the other authorities), but also between individual components (e.g. between the chambers of parliament on an issue requiring joint action, between the president and the government or between the various organs of the judiciary), and even with the participation of other actors (e.g. political parties), if, for example, a cross-party consensus in parliament is required for a decision. Disputes between the courts and the legislative and executive branches over the admissibility of restrictions on fundamental rights and

[11] Federalist No 51.

judicial interference in the sphere of legislative and executive activity, or between parliament and the government over the limits of parliamentary scrutiny of government representatives, have been well known for years.

The constitutional doctrine has described various disputes between constitutional actors, their course and characteristics.[12] I do not wish to refer to these findings here. I will, however, draw attention to two fundamental points that will help – in my view – to illuminate more clearly the need to introduce the concept of constitutional good faith into the scholarly discourse in the context of the separation of powers.

Firstly, a characteristic feature of the constitution is the semantic and axiological openness of its provisions, and the use of the language of balancing principles and, to a lesser extent, the language of specific rules. Moreover, many provisions, even those having the status of an unambiguous rule (e.g. competence provisions) remain structurally open, in the sense that they do not specify the circumstances in which the provision may be applied and they leave a certain sphere of discretionary action to the addressee. Finally, a characteristic feature of the constitutional text is its silences.[13] In situations of ambiguity regarding the scope of competence, an authority may take action (consciously or unconsciously as a result of misinterpretation or incomplete knowledge of the circumstances) that will be challenged by other actors. Take, for example, the existing provisions in various constitutions establishing the President's right to veto a law, which usually do not specify the prerequisites for the exercise of this power (e.g. Article 122(5) of the Polish Constitution, Article 10 of the French Constitution, Article I, Section 7 of the US Constitution) or the provisions requiring the consent of one authority to appointments or other decisions made by the other authority (e.g. Article 179 of the Polish Constitution provides for the appointment of judges by the President at the request of the National Council of the Judiciary, without deciding whether it is permissible to refuse to appoint the person named in the request,[14] or Article II, Section 2, Clause 2 of the US Constitution requiring the consent of the Senate to the President's appointment of judges and other officials, which does not specify the conditions for granting consent or the time within which the President's request should be considered[15]). Other examples are provisions allowing a special procedure for the enactment of laws, permitting the adoption of a government bill without a vote in parliament, such as the solution found in the French system (Article 49(3) of the French Constitution) and the Romanian system (Article 114 of the Romanian Constitution), linking the enactment of a law to a vote of confidence or a vote of no confidence, or the conditions allowing the executive to issue decrees with the force of a law (Article 86 of the

[12] Vermeule and Posner (2008); Tushnet (2004); Fishkin and Pozen (2018).

[13] Loughlin (2018).

[14] Which at one time triggered a competence dispute between the National Council of the Judiciary and the President of the Republic of Poland, eventually ending with the discontinuation of proceedings by the Polish Constitutional Tribunal in the decision of 23 June 2008, ref. no Kpt 1/08.

[15] Which has historically triggered many disputes between the President and the Senate, not only at the level of the Supreme Court, but also in the federal courts: Chafetz (2005), Arkush (2014).

Spanish Constitution). They do not resolve when and under what conditions the government may exercise this power.

Such regulations are found in every constitution. Deciding on the content of individual provisions, the circumstances of their application and the limits of competence is a routine part of constitutional practice.

Secondly, there is a strong interpenetration of law and politics in the sphere of inter-institutional relations. Public authorities may seek to overstep the limits of constitutional competence and encroach on the jurisdiction of another body or block the action of another body, hoping for a one-off or permanent strengthening of their own position vis-à-vis other actors, or for a particularistic advantage connected with promoting a specific vision of the state and social order, etc.[16]

Moreover, legal mechanisms can, on the one hand, be used by particular actors to promote constitutional values such as administrative efficiency, the rule of law or individual freedom. On the other hand, the same mechanisms can be (and usually are) used to promote a particular actor's current political goals and vision of values in the institutional system of the state. These two funtions are not always opposed. During the COVID-19 pandemic, legislation was passed in many countries around the world granting new powers to the executive to combat the spread of the pandemic and protect health, even if these regulations strengthened government institutions in relation to other bodies and weakened the protection of individual rights. Similarly, the presidential veto can be used when the president deems a law passed by parliament to be contrary to the public interest, but at the same time allows the president to block key legislative initiatives of the opposing party, thereby weakening the opposing political camp and strengthening his or her own camp. A presidential veto may pursue one or both of these objectives at the same time. The appointment to official or judicial posts of persons who share and defend the values of those who have the power to appoint them (the appointment of constitutional judges, whose job it is to resolve disputes over competence or to examine the constitutionality of laws) may facilitate the pursuit of political goals by the president or the parliamentary majority,[17] although it may also be regarded as promoting normative pluralism. The same is true for the application of other constitutional regulations with ambiguous content, such as the aforementioned Article 49(3) of the French Constitution or Article 114 of the Romanian Constitution. As demonstrated by constitutional practice,[18] such solutions enable the executive to push through the introduction of important social projects that would be impossible or difficult to pass under the ordinary legislative procedure, especially under time pressure, when at the same time there is no risk of building a majority to dismiss the government using this mode of lawmaking.

---

[16] More than two decades ago, this phenomenon was described by Mark Tushnet, referring to it as "constitutional hardball". Tushnet (2004).

[17] Levinson and Sachs (2010); Landau and Dixon (2019).

[18] Safta (2013).

It is sometimes a characteristic feature of the actions of state organs that certain practices are accompanied by a formally unobjectionable legal and axiological justification, but the factual circumstances surrounding a particular situation may indicate that the real aim is to achieve some political objective, sometimes falling outside the constitutional framework or leading to the weakening of other constitutional principles, or even serving a purely private objective. In the most general terms, this refers to situations in which real intentions – with constitutionally dubious justifications – are masked by a neutral veil to lend credence to the constitutionality of the action taken.[19] An emblematic example from constitutional practice is the decision to prorogue (suspend) the UK Parliament in 2019, ultimately overturned by the UK Supreme Court, in the circumstances of the ongoing dispute between parliament and the government over the terms of Brexit.[20] Boris Johnson, who became Prime Minister in July 2019, wanted to achieve an exit from the EU by 31 October 2019, even without a deal ("no-deal Brexit"), which was opposed by a majority of parliamentarians, who proposed to pass regulations blocking the Prime Minister's implementation of such a solution. In August 2019, Johnson asked Elizabeth II to suspend parliament for 5 weeks. He argued that the prorogation was needed to prepare the Queen's Speech, which is traditionally delivered at the start of a new session of parliament and contains the government's legislative plan. The Prime Minister's critics, however, argued that the real purpose of prorogation was to prevent parliament from effectively opposing Brexit without a deal, as this left parliament with no legislative process. Ultimately, the Supreme Court, in a precedent-setting judgment,[21] overturned this decision, indicating that prorogation had "extreme consequences" for the functioning of parliament and the performance of its constitutional functions, such as the scrutiny of government. At the same time, the Supreme Court indicated that unless there is a legitimate purpose – which was lacking in this case – the decision is unlawful.

Similarly, in Poland, following the Law and Justice party's victory in the autumn of 2015, a number of measures were adopted to bring the Constitutional Tribunal under political control.[22] These included the enactment of a law regulating the procedure before the Constitutional Tribunal,[23] which, inter alia, increased the size of the full bench from nine to thirteen judges, and established the obligation to consider all cases initiated by parliamentarians or other state bodies exclusively in full bench, and in the order of their receipt, without the possibility of derogations from these rules. In addition, the law was to enter into force on the day of its announcement, and thus without the required *vacatio legis.* As the representatives of the parliamentary majority argued during the legislative work, the aim of the regula-

---

[19] Sajó (2021), pp. 284–300; Sadurski (2023), p. 209–241.

[20] Elliott (2020).

[21] UK Supreme Court (2019). *R (Miller) v The Prime Minister* [2019] UKSC 41.

[22] Radziewicz and Tuleja (2017); Sadurski (2019), pp. 58–95.

[23] Act of 22 December 2015 amending the Constitutional Tribunal Act (Official Gazette 2015, item 2217).

tion was to ensure that constitutional cases could be thoroughly heard as soon as possible. In a precedent-setting ruling, the Constitutional Tribunal held that although the Polish Constitution empowers parliament to regulate in a statute the procedure before the Tribunal, the real aim of the legislator was to block the review of the constitutionality of the statute, which in itself violates the Constitution.[24]

The occurrence of disputes over the scope of particular constitutional norms defining the relations between organs and other entities constituting the institutional system of the state may be beneficial for the legal system. They make it possible, as indicated, to negotiate the normative content of the provisions and the values underlying constitutional regulation, or to clarify the limits of the competences of individual bodies. Such disputes are a characteristic feature of constitutional democracies and are even inscribed in the nature of such a system. They undoubtedly foster the development of constitutional law[25] and the transformation of the state system.[26] At the same time, they also entail costs. When especially intense, these disputes can lead to institutional paralysis (as experienced, for example, by Spain in connection with the political dispute that blocked a compromise on the election of members of the judicial council,[27] or by Poland in the dispute over the functioning of the Constitutional Tribunal and the statutory regulation of the rules on the election of members of the judicial council[28]). They can also deepen polarisation and, in the worst case scenario, degrade the regulatory role of the constitution, which then ceases to be perceived by citizens as setting the rules of the game and is reduced to another tool of day-to-day politics.[29]

This raises the question of whether it is possible to resolve doubts as to which practices are constitutionally acceptable and which practices are beyond the scope of the constitution under ambiguous provisions coupled with the political context accompanying their application by constitutional actors. What is the limit of opportunism and the pursuit of partisan advantage?

Despite the scepticism emerging from some of the chapters in this book regarding the possibility of effectively resolving disputes at the interface between law and politics, and of preventing constitutional abuses,[30] one should not abandon attempts to search for adequate concepts or doctrines that-even if they do not solve all the problems of instrumentalising the constitution-can assist decision-making or analytical processes. The concept of constitutional good faith, discussed in the book, may be an answer to these dilemmas.

[24] Constitutional Tribunal of Poland, 2016 *Judgment of 9 March 2016, Ref. No. K 47/15*; See also: Radziewicz (2017).

[25] Vermeule and Posner (2008), p. 925.

[26] Tushnet (2004), p. 532.

[27] Torres Pérez (2018).

[28] Sadurski (2019), pp. 58–131; Szwed (2023).

[29] Whittington (2023a, b).

[30] Vidal-Naquet and Magnon (2025).

3 Predicates of Constitutional Good Faith in a System of the Separation of Powers

We make the initial assumption in this book that constitutional good faith means the attitude of all constitutional actors directed towards the realisation of constitutional aims and objectives. The essence of this attitude is, in particular, to recognise the restrictive and purposive character of the constitutional provisions in the exercise of one's own tasks and competences and, moreover, to strive to interpret those provisions in a consistent and predictable manner. Acting in good faith serves to ensure that the values of fundamental importance to the political community, which underlie the basic aims and objectives of the constitution's establishment, also shape the context in which the constitution operates. The actual realisation of the constitution can only take place if all actors, in their actions, respect its provisions and are guided by the principles underlying its adoption. The proposed concept is inscribed in the essence and basic functions of the constitution as the fundamental law of the state, the validity of which binds the political community together and secures the basic values of the functioning of this community.

Although it is difficult to formulate an exhaustive definition of the concept of good faith, the common denominator in discussions across the various branches of legal science is conduct characterised by honesty, loyalty and fidelity to accepted commitments. It usually involves conduct within a bilateral or multilateral relationship, based on mutual trust and the pursuit of common goals, and characterised by transparency of action and consistency between the declared objectives and the methods intended to achieve them. These essential characteristics can also be applied to constitutional good faith,[31] and in particular to the inter-institutional relations described here.

Relating good faith to the principle of separation of powers and to the conditions for its implementation outlined earlier, it should be noted that constitutional good faith obliges all constitutional actors to view the state, the constitution itself and the institutions of the state system as part of a "shared enterprise".[32] The upholding of this duty is entrusted to all actors operating in the state system, regardless of their legal position, tasks and competences. This means that the interests of individual functionaries or the institution they represent (institutional loyalty) let alone self-interest, although immanently embedded in the process of applying the constitution, cannot be the determining factors in the way the constitution is interpreted and applied. Constitutional good faith opposes excessive opportunism.[33] It excludes arbitrary actions, i.e. those motivated solely by partisan goals.[34] The above assumption refers directly to the observation that, in the sphere of constitutional law, acting

[31] Podkowik and Stębelski (2025).

[32] McCanse Wright (2018), p. 47.

[33] Leib and Galoob (2019).

[34] Fallon Jr. (2009), p. 984.

in good faith is closely related to the realisation of the public interest.[35] This requires each actor to adopt a perspective in which all those who make up and influence the institutional system of the state accept the common goals and objectives set by the constitution and wish to remain within constitutional boundaries, even despite possible disagreement on the content of particular provisions or the underlying values. Figuratively speaking, they all agree that they are playing the same game and under the same rules.

In a sense, good faith corresponds to the concept of treating public offices as fiduciary, as developed in American constitutional law[36] or the principle of "fidelity to the constitution", sometimes *expressis verbis* enshrined in the constitution in relation to the head of state (cf. Article 130 of the Polish Constitution, Article II clause 3 of the US Constitution, Article 61 of the Spanish Constitution) or other officials (Article 54(2) of the Romanian Constitution).

Good faith requires constitutional actors to do more than just formally follow the rules. It requires demonstrating a commitment to the constitutional project. As is pointed out in the discussion of the Spanish concept of constitutional loyalty,[37] it is more than mere compliance with the rule and observance of the law. Namely, it implies an attitude of respect for the constitutional order, openness to cooperation, and rejecting opportunism. It thus serves the proper functioning of the democratic system, as well as its effective and coherent development. This corresponds, in a sense, to the understanding of constitutional loyalty developed in the jurisprudence of the Romanian Constitutional Court,[38] which includes loyalty to other constitutional actors and loyalty to the Constitution itself.

Constitutional good faith in the proposed sense goes beyond individual conduct and practices, although recourse to it may prove particularly useful in contentious situations. It is an enduring attitude on the part of actors involved in the application of the constitution, consisting in showing of a willingness and taking action directed towards remaining within the constitutional framework and a commitment to the implementation of the constitution. Adopting such an attitude is not an emanation of the subject's will for self-restraint (forbearance) or adherence to the standards of political culture. It should be – as we pointed out in the introductory chapter – seen as a normative obligation, deriving from the essence of the constitution itself, entwined with the entire constitutional system and embedded in its foundations.

Although the constitutional provisions of the vast majority of states do not contain an explicit provision obliging constitutional actors to act in good faith, the existence of such an obligation should not be questioned even if the constitution is silent on the subject. After all, the basis for the reconstruction of a constitutional norm obliging actors to act in good faith in a particular system may be provided by various constitutional provisions and constitutional principles, which, read together,

[35] Sadurski (2023).

[36] Leib and Galoob (2019), Leib and Kent (2021).

[37] Tur Ausina (2025).

[38] Stănescu (2025)

make it possible to reconstruct such an obligation. With regard to entities operating in a system of the separation of powers, these bases may be found in the provisions defining their oath, taken upon taking office, which requires loyalty and fidelity to the constitutional system from public officials as well as in the basic principles of the political system: legalism, cooperation of powers and the common good.

The good faith attitude in inter-institutional relations is characterised by at least two key features: formal and material legalism, and institutional cooperation.

Firstly, formal legalism implies a commitment to the law, which requires the observance of unambiguous and concrete rules of conduct, but also of existing and well-established conventions and unwritten norms, widely recognized as valid in a particular sphere of relations, as well as respect for established judicial decisions setting standards of conduct and past practice in the application of particular rules. It is a matter of both respecting the existing procedures and the substantive scope of competences in accordance with their prevailing understanding, and finally respecting court rulings and other decisions determining in a binding manner, in accordance with the rules of a given system, the rights and obligations of a given entity. After all, the condition for maintaining good faith is to remain within the legal framework in force,[39] no matter how demanding.[40] Such an approach makes it possible to maintain a coherent and uniform understanding of concepts and institutions, which can be seen as one of the conditions protecting the process of constitutional interpretation from instrumentalisation.

Formal legality alone, in the above sense, is not, however, sufficient to declare a given action constitutional, especially if the provisions on which a given action or legislative act is based are ambiguous and thus there are potentially alternative ways of behaving in certain situations or there is a lack of practice that would enable the reconstruction of a normative pattern of conduct. Since authoritarianism can hide under formal legality,[41] and doubts most often concern not the violation of explicit provisions, but "the essence and spirit of the constitution",[42] it should be additionally required that the application of ambiguous provisions, leaving the addressees a margin of discretion, be accompanied by the obligation to carefully demonstrate that the act or practice in question is justified by some constitutional value. In other words, every action of a state organ should not only have a formal basis, but additionally a substantive justification in constitutional aims and objectives. Credible justification of the material premises and basis of the actions of state organs, not only when challenged by other actors, minimises arbitrariness in the application of

---

[39] Although in some jurisdictions it is explicitly written into constitutional provisions that acting in good faith may exclude liability for wrongful acts (Articles 50 and 98 of the Zimbabwean Constitution) or such concepts have emerged in judicial jurisprudence (Leon doctrine in the US).

[40] Venice Commission, *Opinion No. 1203/202 on the Draft Constitutional Amendments Concerning the Constitutional Tribunal and Two Laws on the Constitutional Tribunal*, 141st Plenary Session, Venice, 6–7 Dec. 2024, § 67.

[41] Scheppele (2018); ECHR *Ukraine v Russia*, 25 June 2024, nos. 20958/14 and 38334/18, § 1334.

[42] Whittington (2002).

the law[43] and fosters a culture of mutual trust in which the concept of good faith is embedded.

The appeal to constitutional good faith therefore dictates that the question of the purpose of certain actions taken by constitutional actors, and their justification, must be posed in each case. Is the only explanation the fact that the law grants such a possibility, or is there also an axiological justification behind the practice in question, confirmed by constitutional norms and values as well as by the purpose of the competence provisions or by more general constitutional assumptions?

The assessment of the good faith of constitutional actors will be the subject of a separate study.[44] Here, it suffices to point out that a particular practice should be objectively regarded as useful for the realisation of the value that constitutes its material basis and, at the same time, that this value must be pursued in a way that does not undermine other, more important constitutional principles. In particular, it must not lead to the undermining of the fundamental role of the constitution as an act limiting power and protecting the rights of individuals. Therefore, actions that may find some constitutional justification but undermine the elementary assumptions of the constitutional system are constitutionally impermissible. For instance, parliamentary obstruction which has been recognised for centuries as a mean of defending the rights of minorities.[45] Its use may lead to significant impediments to the functioning of the collegial body, but it can hardly be considered *prima facie* constitutionally impermissible, even if it results in the blocking of individual decisions (such as the election of a person to a position, the passing of a law or a vote of confidence). The assessment of the admissibility of the use of obstruction would probably be different if its effect were to permanently block the work of a given body and render it incapable of exercising its constitutional powers. In the same way, a presidential veto – used occasionally, even for the opportunistic purpose – cannot be deemed to violate the constitution, unless its effect is to actually block the work of parliament.

When identifying and assessing the material purpose of an action, it is by no means a question of examining the subjective intentions or motivations driving individual actors. In fact, it is rightly noted that they are difficult to ascertain,[46] and are often, as I have pointed out, mixed with constitutionally impermissible motivations and objectively acceptable goals that remain within the constitutional framework. To declare a particular practice unconstitutional, political intention or personal motivation should generally be irrelevant. Instead, it is necessary to determine whether the effects,[47] of a given act or practice undermine constitutional aims and objectives or fail to remain consistent with the constitutional axiology.

---

[43] Kochman (2025), Leib (2025).

[44] Podkowik and Stębelski (2025).

[45] Jellinek (1904).

[46] Pozen (2016); Vidal-Naquet and Magnon (2025).

[47] Petrov (2024), pp. 192–194.

Relevant to the assessment of a specific situation and to whether it has a substantive constitutional basis without the same time undermining the assumptions of the constitutional system is the context in which the action is taken. Context is everything. This can be seen in the examples of the prorogation of parliament in the UK, where the assessment of the constitutionality of Boris Johnson's decision would probably have been different in the absence of the ongoing work in parliament to determine the terms of Brexit. A similar point can be made about judicial reform in Poland: if a cross-party consensus had been guaranteed in electing the members of the National Council of the Judiciary, and no other changes had been introduced affecting the functioning of the courts – changes that raised the possibility of political influence over judicial decisions – the evaluation would also have been different. Similarly, if an appropriate *vacatio legis* had been ensured, allowing for a review of the constitutionality of the measures relating to the operation of the Constitutional Tribunal, the Tribunal's assessment in case ref. K 47/15[48] might have been different as regards the unconstitutionality of the legislator's actual aim. A specific context may support recognising the admissibility of a certain action or, on the contrary, show that the assessed action does not serve the realisation of constitutional aims and objectives, but has an instrumentalising character. In any case, it must be assumed that the context of the action cannot be the leading factor determining the way in which the constitution is interpreted. In other words, constitutional interpretation should not be conducted to justify a political decision already taken or planned, but to answer the question of the permissibility of such a decision in the light of the constitutional standard.

The above assumption – that an essential requirement of interpreting and applying of the constitution is respect for the existing understanding of the law and the limits of competence – does not, of course, imply that changing the interpretation or practice is impermissible. The law is not, and cannot be, static. It remains open to negotiation and compromise, which are necessary in conditions under normative pluralism and a dynamically changing reality. Changes in practice may result from shifting social and cultural circumstances (e.g. the evolution of the idea of equal treatment or the notion of privacy in the digital age), from identifying errors in earlier understandings of the law, or even from a political will to emphasise constitutional norms differently or to resolve value conflicts in new ways. Good faith, therefore, does not enclose the constitution in a hermetic wrapping of once-established standards. It does not oppose the hard constitutional game or the constitutional showdowns between actors as to the content of the norms and their mutual relations, which remain the driving force behind the development of constitutional law and are characteristic of the relations between authorities. It does, however, require that deviations from hitherto accepted interpretation or historically shaped practice must be duly and honestly motivated by constitutional values and genuinely serve their realisation, while ensuring that the new practice and its effects

[48] Constitutional Tribunal of Poland, 2016 *Judgment of 9 March 2016, Ref. No. K 47/15.*

remain consistent with other constitutional principles or its basic assumptions.[49] Some aspects of interpreting the constitution in good faith have been highlighted in a separate chapter of the book.[50] In this sense, constitutional good faith sets the conditions for negotiating constitutional values and norms, so as not to undermine of the constitution's role as an act limiting power, nor to reduce it to a mere instrument of political struggle.

Secondly, good faith should not be reduced to a requirement of formal and substantive legality. In particular, in inter-institutional relations, where a particular act requires the involvement of more than one actor, good faith implies an obligation of loyal and honest interaction and thus a perception by the individual actors of their systemic role not as isolated atoms, but as part of a broader whole with common goals. As Barber notes, in the most abstract terms, inter-institutional relations should be characterised by benevolence (comity), manifested both in the pursuit of a common goal for all authorities, namely the well-being of citizens, and in the use of their distinct competences to promote such goals.[51] The need for all authorities to work together to protect fundamental rights has recently been highlighted by Aileen Kavanagh. In her view, protecting rights in a democratic system is not the sole responsibility of the courts or parliament, but a shared responsibility of all three branches of government: the executive, the legislature and the judiciary. Each branch plays a distinct yet complementary role, working together in a spirit of mutual respect and cooperation. Rather than competing for constitutional supremacy, all institutions should cooperate to accomplish this task.[52] Such collaboration is equally necessary in other areas of state functioning, including those not directly affecting fundamental rights.

The relationship between constitutional good faith and the duty to cooperate is highlighted in various national legal orders, such as in Poland, Romania, Germany or Spain, as well as in international law.[53]

How, then, can this cooperation manifest itself? Two basic manifestations can be identified, which, it should be added, are not exhaustive. The first is an attitude reflecting the will to exercise one's own powers or competences within the framework of complex activities requiring the involvement of more than one entity. Constitutional good faith thus opposes the unjustified withholding of the cooperation required to take a decision. For instance, the dispute surrounding the appointment of a US Supreme Court judge in 2016, when the representative of the Senate majority declared that the Senate would not deal with any proposal coming from an end-of-term president from the opposite political camp;[54] or the dispute concerning the Spanish judicial council, where representatives of two opposing political camps

---

[49] Kochman (2025).

[50] Kaleta (2025).

[51] Barber (2018), pp. 71–72.

[52] Kavanagh (2023).

[53] Klamert (2025), Kałduński (2025), Kochman (2025), Stanescu (2025), Tur Ausina (2025).

[54] Fishkin and Pozen (2018), p. 917.

were unable to agree on the renewal of the council's composition, which in practice paralysed its functioning for many years. A further example is the lack of willingness to work together to solve the crisis around the Polish Constitutional Tribunal and the judiciary. Good faith therefore requires a willingness to consult, openness to arguments, and a readiness to change one's own position in order to reach a compromise – an attitude that must be adopted by all actors involved.

The duty to cooperate also has a positive dimension, especially if the constitutional norms establish a complex procedure requiring the involvement of more than one entity, but do not specify time limits for the implementation of individual steps. In such cases, the duty to act promptly, appropriate to the circumstances, should then be assumed. For example, the Polish regulations on judicial appointments did not specify a deadline for the President to consider the motion from the National Council of the Judiciary. Leaving aside whether, and in what situations, the President may refuse to appoint the person indicated in the motion – an issue that was itself disputed – the motion should be considered without undue delay. A situation where the President does not take any decision for several months should be considered unacceptable, as it may not only violate the rights of those seeking appointment but also impair the functioning of the courts.

4 Enforcement of Constitutional Good Faith in Constitutional Practice: Key Challenges

A significant challenge for the concept under discussion is enforceability. As Pozen notes, judicial enforcement of constitutional good faith is problematic and – at least in American practice – rather limited. This stems from epistemic and evidentiary difficulties and, finally, from judges' fear of jeopardising their own legitimacy by enforcing rules that appear vague or subjective, particularly in matters with strong political ramifications. The risk is compounded by the possibility that judges could be accused of bad faith when applying discretionary standards.[55]

If, in the jurisprudential practice of various states or international bodies, there are few cases of enforcing good faith in the sphere of relations governed by constitutional law, this is – as the considerations in this book show – most often observed in matters of fundamental rights, and thus of state-individual relations, with the assessment focusing in particular on whether a certain action can be considered as pursuing constitutionally permissible or non-arbitrary objectives. Such a procedural mechanism can be found in the case law of the ECtHR[56] and in the case law of other constitutional courts, applying in particular the principles of proportionality and equality.[57] The enforcement of standards of good faith – linked above all to the

[55] Levinson (2016), p. 170.

[56] Kochman (2025).

[57] Leib (2025); Podkowik and Stębelski (2025).

absence of ulterior motives and illegitimate aims of interference – in the review of individual acts of law application (e.g. decisions of the administration concerning individuals) and the review of the constitutionality of norms restricting fundamental rights, despite some criticism, is in principle part of the constitutional task of the courts to resolve disputes between individuals and the state. This seems, after all, a safer matter for the judiciary than being an arbiter of inter-institutional disputes, of which they themselves may be a part, especially if the other authorities take measures aimed at limiting the jursdiction of the courts or regulating the methods of selecting judges. It is therefore rare to enforce good faith in constitutional relations.[58] Above all, this is the case when supreme or constitutional courts are endowed with the power to settle competence disputes, but also when reviewing the constitutionality of provisions regulating the status of other authorities. This leads some authors to formulate the thesis that constitutional good faith is either an unenforceable norm of constitutional law,[59] or it serves as a rule of conduct but not nearly as often as a rule of decision.[60] In this sense, the norm of good faith obliges one to behave in a certain way, which cannot be effectively enforced before the courts.

The issue of enforceability is undeniably complex and multidimensional, conditioned by the assumptions made in a particular regime as to the role of the courts and the limits of judicial review of the activities of other constitutional actors. Accordingly, it is not possible to make comprehensive and universal proposals for ensuring the effectiveness of constitutional good faith. Some aspects are addressed in other chapters of this volume. However, one may be tempted to identify provisional lines of discussion in the sphere of inter-institutional relations, which could be deeloped in further analyses.

Firstly, the possibility of judicial enforceability arises in spheres in which an action or practice relating to institutional relations takes the form of an act of law-making and, at the same time, a system of control of the constitutionality of the law exists in the state. Judicial enforcement of good faith will amount to an assessment of the constitutionality of the act in question against the perspective of constitutional norms, without necessarily requiring that the action of the legislature be labelled lacking in good faith. An example is the assessment of the constitutionality of the provisions regulating the organisation and proceedings before the Constitutional Tribunal, one of the key stages of the constitutional crisis in Poland, where it was found that the solutions introduced by the legislator defining the manner and principles of adjudication of cases, in conjunction with the entry into force of the law on the day of its promulgation, were in fact aimed at blocking the operation of the constitutional court, violating the principles of efficiency of public

[58] Reference to this concept is characteristic of the Israeli Supreme Court, e.g. in the case on the permissibility of refusing to countersign presidential acts of pardons – Minister of Justice v. Zohar, HCJ 219/09, Israeli Supreme Court, 29 November 2010, or in the recent high-profile judicial reform case – Movement for Quality Government in Israel v. The Knesset, HCJ 5658/23, Israeli Supreme Court, 1 January 2024. See also Roznai (2023).

[59] Pozen (2016), p. 987.

[60] Leib (2025).

institutions and the principles of appropriate *vacatio legis*.[61] Another example is the assessment of the admissibility of prorogation of the parliament in the Miller v. Prime Minister case mentioned above. Finally, the courts are capable of dealing with various manifestations of abuse or circumvention of the law in the course of the legislative process.[62] Judicial enforceability may furthermore come into play in the review of acts of law application, including those affecting directly or indirectly the status of the individual, or in the procedure of settling constitutional disputes between constitutional bodies, as evidenced by the Polish or Romanian experience.[63]

Secondly, enforcement may occur in the system of constitutional accountability, e.g. within the framework of the impeachment procedure for the president or the accountability of other functionaries for constitutional torts in the framework of which the manner in which constitutional powers are exercised is the subject of assessment, as well as through instruments of political accountability (e.g. a vote of no confidence in members of the government).[64]

In the first and second cases, the question remains open as to the consequences of ascertaining (suspecting) a lack of good faith and the significance of this for the pending proceedings, in particular whether it must result in to a declaration of the unconstitutionality (invalidity) of the assessed act or whether other sanctions may apply in connection with a violation of the constitution. Adopting the thesis that the lack of good faith means, in essence, a failure to realise constitutional aims and objectives, it may be argued that the lack of good faith is tantamount to a violation of the constitution and thus produces effects such as a violation of other constitutional provisions. On the other hand, solutions that embed the assessment of good faith in the procedural rules on the burden and standard of proof appear to be possible. For example, a substantiated allegation of lack of good faith may alter the general rule of the burden or standard of proof in constitutional proceedings (shifting the burden of proof to the party alleged to lack good faith) or affect the level of assessment within the existing standards of assessment in a given jurisdiction.

Thirdly and finally, the whole sphere of extra-judicial (non-constitutional) ways of promoting of good faith and stigmatising manifestations of its absence in the practice of constitutional actors is not insignificant.[65] As Pozen notes, "bad faith talk", can on the one hand, harm constitutional culture, but on the other, also enhance and regulate it. Although often toxic and destructive, it can also be an important tool for enforcing accountability in conditions of weak formal control over bad faith actions. Calling out a lack of good faith in public debate can function as a soft social sanction (pressure, shame, reputational damage), help exclude extreme or dishonest

[61] Constitutional Tribunal of Poland, 2016 *Judgment of 9 March 2016, Ref. No. K 47/15.*

[62] Brzozowski (2014); Denning and Kent (2014).

[63] Florczak-Wątor (2025); Stănescu (2025).

[64] See, e.g., the position of the U.S. House of Representatives, Committee on the Judiciary (2019) in the course of the attempted first impeachment of President Donald Trump over allegations of abuse of power in withholding military aid to Ukraine motivated by personal interest and failure to cooperate with Congress in providing materials and testimony.

[65] Pozen (2016), pp. 951–954.

arguments from serious constitutional discussion, or pave the way for the application of more "hard" institutional measures.

5 Conclusion

The principle of separation of powers, enhanced by constitutional good faith, requires state institutions to cooperate constantly in order to achieve constitutionally defined goals and conduct constitutional disputes in accordance with the rules of the constitutional framework. The system of government can be compared to a symphony orchestra, where each instrument and musician plays a specific part according to the score – the constitution. Only by playing in accordance with these requirements, while respecting the roles of the other musicians, and pursuing a common goal can a harmonious and meaningful result be achieved. Disharmony resulting from arbitrariness, opportunism, or disregard for the principles of cooperation leads to chaos and the disruption of the system as a whole. Good faith in relations between state bodies is therefore not only desirable, but also necessary for the political community as a whole to be able to "hear" the coherent, transparent tone of the constitutional project. While the proposed concept raises further questions regarding its implementation, it can serve as a useful tool for analysing and evaluating institutional practices in the context of observed global democratic crises and in the day-to-day functioning of the state.

Legal Documents

The UK Supreme Court, R (Miller) v The Prime Minister [2019] UKSC 41.

Venice Commission (2024) Opinion No. 1203/202 on the Draft Constitutional Amendments Concerning the Constitutional Tribunal and Two Laws on the Constitutional Tribunal, 141st Plenary Session, Venice, 6–7 December, para. 67.

European Court of Human Rights (ECHR) (2024) Ukraine v Russia, 25 June, nos. 20958/14 and 38334/18, para. 1334.

Israel, Supreme Court (2010) Minister of Justice v. Zohar, HCJ 219/09, 29 November 2010.

Israel, Supreme Court (2024) Movement for Quality Government in Israel v. The Knesset, HCJ 5658/23, 1 January 2024.

Poland, Constitutional Tribunal (2016) Judgment of the Constitutional Tribunal of 9 March 2016, ref. K 47/15.

Poland, Constitutional Tribunal (2009) Decision of the Constitutional Tribunal of 20 May 2009, ref. Kpt 2/08.

United States Supreme Court (2014) National Labor Relations Board v Noel Canning, 573 U.S. 513.

U.S. House of Representatives, Committee on the Judiciary, 2019. Impeachment of Donald J. Trump, President of the United States. H. Rept. 116–346. Washington, D.C.: Government Publishing Office. Available at: https://www.congress.gov/congressional-report/116th-congress/house-report/346/1

References

Literature

Arkush DJ (2014) The senate and the recess appointments. Harv Law Rev Forum 127:1–10

Balkin JM (2018) Constitutional crisis and constitutional rot. In: Graber MA, Levinson S, Tushnet M (eds) Constitutional democracy in crisis? Oxford University Press, Oxford, pp 11–26

Balkin JM, Levinson S (2009) Constitutional Crises. Univ Pa Law Rev 157(3) [dokładne strony nieznane, wymagają uzupełnienia]. [Dodano brakujący numer tomu i poprawiono formatowanie]

Barber N (2018) The principles of constitutionalism. Oxford University Press, Oxford

Brzozowski W (2014) Obejście konstytucji. Państwo i Prawo 9:3–18

Carolan E (2009) The new separation of powers: a theory for the modern state. Oxford University Press, Oxford

Chafetz J (2005) Unprecedented? Judicial confirmation battles and the search for a usable past. Yale Law J 114(7):1262–1320

Elliott M (2020) Constitutional adjudication and constitutional politics in the United Kingdom: the miller II case in legal and political context. Eur Const Law Rev 16(4):625–646. https://doi.org/10.1017/S1574019620000401

Fishkin J, Pozen DE (2018) Asymmetric constitutional hardball. Columbia Law Rev 118:915–982

Florczak-Wątor M (2025) Good Faith in Polish constitutional law. In: Podkowik J, Chmielarz-Grochal A, Stębelski M, Sułkowski J (eds) Gleams of good faith in constitutional law. Springer, Cham

Huq AZ, Michels JD (2016) The cycles of separation-of-powers jurisprudence. Yale Law J 126(2):346–437

Jellinek G (1904) Parliamentary obstruction. Polit Sci Quart 19(4):579–588

Kałduński M (2025) Good faith in international law. In: Podkowik J, Chmielarz-Grochal A, Stębelski M, Sułkowski J (eds) Gleams of good faith in constitutional law. Springer, Cham

Kaleta KJ (2025) Good faith in constitutional interpretation. In: Podkowik J, Chmielarz-Grochal A, Stębelski M, Sułkowski J (eds) Gleams of good faith in constitutional law. Springer, Cham

Kavanagh A (2023) The collaborative constitution. Cambridge University Press, Cambridge

Klamert M (2025) Good faith in European Union law. In: Podkowik J, Chmielarz-Grochal A, Stębelski M, Sułkowski J (eds) Gleams of good faith in constitutional law. Springer, Cham

Kochman A (2025) Good faith in the European convention on human rights. In: Podkowik J, Chmielarz-Grochal A, Stębelski M, Sułkowski J (eds) Gleams of good faith in constitutional law. Springer, Cham

Landau D, Dixon R (2019) Abusive judicial review: courts against democracy. UC Davis Law Rev 53(3):1313–1387

Leib EJ (2025) Good faith in U.S. constitutional law. In: Podkowik J, Chmielarz-Grochal A, Stębelski M, Sułkowski J (eds) Gleams of good faith in constitutional law. Springer, Cham

Leib EJ, Galoob S (2019) Fiduciary principles and public office. In: Criddle E, Miller P, Sitkoff R (eds) Oxford handbook of fiduciary law. Oxford University Press, Oxford, pp 303–322

Leib EJ, Kent A (2021) Fiduciary law and the law of public office. William Mary Law Rev 62:1297–1348

Levinson D, Sachs BI (2010) Political entrenchment and public law. Yale Law J 119(4):402–482
Levinson, S (2016) Trash talk at the supreme court: reflections on david pozen's constitutional good faith. Harv Law Rev Forum 129:166–175.
Loughlin M (2018) The silences of constitutions. Int J Const Law 16(3):922–935. https://doi.org/10.1093/icon/moy064
McCanse Wright A (2018) Constitutional good faith. N Y Univ Law Rev 93:41–49
Mojski W (2023) Kryzys konstytucyjny. Zagadnienia teorii konstytucji. Wydawnictwo Uniwersytetu Marii Curie Skłodowskiej, Lublin
Petrov J (2024) How to detect abusive constitutional practices. Eur Const Law Rev 20(2):191–221. https://doi.org/10.1017/S1574019624000142
Podkowik J, Stępelski M (2025) Dobra wiara w prawie konstytucyjnym - prolegomena. Przegląd Sejmowy, 2:9–33
Pozen DE (2016) Constitutional bad faith. Harv Law Rev 129(4):885–955
Radziewicz P (2017) Refusal of the polish constitutional tribunal to apply the act stipulating the constitutional review procedure. Rev Eur Comp Law 28(1):23–40. Available at:. https://doi.org/10.31743/recl.4309
Radziewicz P, Tuleja P (eds) (2017) Konstytucyjny spór o granice zmian organizacji i zasad działania Trybunału Konstytucyjnego: czerwiec 2015 – marzec 2016. Wolters Kluwer Polska, Warszawa
Roznai Y (2023) Clownstitutionalism: making a joke of the constitution by abuse of constituent power. Jurídica Anuario del Departamento de Derecho de la Universidad Iberoamericana 15:51–98. https://doi.org/10.48102/ji.15.220
Sadurski W (2019) Poland's constitutional breakdown. Oxford University Press, Oxford
Sadurski W (2023) Constitutional public reason. Oxford University Press, Oxford
Safta M (2013) Separation of powers and constitutional loyalty. Jurid Trib 3(1):182–193
Sajó A (2021) Ruling by cheating: governance in illiberal democracies. Oxford University Press, Oxford
Scheppele KL (2018) Autocratic legalism. Univ Chicago Law Rev 85(2):545–583
Stănescu L-S (2025) Good faith in Romanian constitutional law. In: Podkowik J, Chmielarz-Grochal A, Stępelski M, Sułkowski J (eds) Gleams of good faith in constitutional law. Springer, Cham
Sułkowski J (2025) Good faith and the vertical division of power. In: Podkowik J, Chmielarz-Grochal A, Stępelski M, Sułkowski J (eds) Gleams of good faith in constitutional law. Springer, Cham
Szwed M (2023) Fixing the problem of unlawfully appointed judges in Poland in the light of the ECHR. Hague J Rule Law 15:353–384. https://doi.org/10.1007/s40803-023-00191-3
Torres Pérez A (2018) Judicial self-government and judicial Independence: the political capture of the general Council of the Judiciary in Spain. Germ Law J 19(7):1769–1800
Tur Ausina R (2025) Good faith in Spanish constitutional law. In: Podkowik J, Chmielarz-Grochal A, Stępelski M, Sułkowski J (eds) Gleams of good faith in constitutional law. Springer, Cham
Tushnet M (2004) Constitutional Hardball. John Marshall Law Rev 37:523–553
Vermeule A, Posner EA (2008) Constitutional showdowns. Univ Pa Law Rev 156:991–1048
Vidal-Naquet A, Magnon X (2025) Good faith in French constitutional law. In: Podkowik J, Chmielarz-Grochal A, Stępelski M, Sułkowski J (eds) Gleams of good faith in constitutional law. Springer, Cham
Whittington KE (2002) Yet another constitutional crisis? William Mary Law Rev 43(5):2093–2149
Whittington KE (2023a) Bad Faith Constitutionalism. Available at: https://balkin.blogspot.com/2023/05/bad-faith-constitutionalism.html
Whittington KE (2023b) A typology of constitutional crises. Hoover Institution Working Paper

Good Faith and Judicial Power

Anna Chmielarz-Grochal

Abstract The purpose of this chapter is to identify and analyse the basis and manifestations of constitutional good faith in the activities of the judiciary. The analysis proceeds from the presumption of good faith arising from the essence of the constitution as the supreme legal act. The main thrust of the analysis concerns the judicial application of the law, where good faith is manifested in the duty of loyalty and respect for the constitution, as well as honest conduct. Good faith is linked to the role of the courts in a democratic state and to the conception of the judicial office, the assumption of which is preceded by the taking of an oath. Judges have not only a legal but also a moral obligation to respect the constitution and apply its provisions in good faith. Due to the specificity and openness of the text of the constitution, its judicial application has certain distinctive features. Two of them are of fundamental importance. First, the interpretation of the constitution cannot be undertaken in isolation from the purpose of the regulation and its underlying axiological assumptions. Second, the established goals and objectives of constitutional provisions must be treated as a mandatory point of reference in the application of laws (i.e. pro-constitutional interpretation). This serves to realise the normative function of the constitution. Judges, being subject to the constitution, have the legitimacy to ensure that these values are respected and to guard the constitutionally defined limits of the operation of political power. The chapter concludes with an examination of judicial review and the implementation by courts of the role of "guardians" of the constitution.

A. Chmielarz-Grochal (✉)
Faculty of Law and Administration, University of Lodz, Lodz, Poland
e-mail: achmielarz@wpia.uni.lodz.pl

J. Podkowik et al. (eds.), *Gleams of Good Faith in Constitutional Law*, Ius Gentium: Comparative Perspectives on Law and Justice 132,
https://doi.org/10.1007/978-3-032-06486-8_16

1 Introduction

The judicial power is an inherent element of the democratic system, which is based on the principle of the separation and balance of powers. It is an authority endowed with special powers, as it performs the function of administration of justice, and is therefore associated with the protection of fundamental rights, as well as a supervisory function in relation to other authorities (e.g. review of the constitutionality of the law).[1] According to the theory of separation, it is independent of other authorities. The separation of judicial and political (legislative and executive) powers promotes the stability of the democratic system, which is related to the basic functions of the judiciary. The independence of the judiciary is also a defining element of the legal status of judges, including their rights and duties.[2] It can be argued that the very purpose of courts in a liberal-constitutional democracy stems precisely from their ability to administer justice independently.

In constitutional law scholarship there have been attempts to define constitutional good and bad faith.[3] Constitutional good faith is treated as a key component of the political system and an essential element of the rule of law. It is assumed to be both cultural and legal in nature, applying to the activities of all constitutional actors, including the judiciary. Acting in good faith requires not only formal compliance with the law, but also respect for values and the pursuit of constitutional goals. Constitutional good faith is connected to the exercise of discretionary power, which is particularly evident in the activities of the courts.

There is no doubt that the actions of the judiciary, like any other authority, must comply with the law, including the constitution. The text of the constitution, which is a set of rules, principles, values and "silences", defines the framework for delegating powers and imposing limitations to any political and judicial authority. If we posit the thesis that constitutional good faith is embedded in the essence of the constitution, it follows that the activities of public authorities, including the judiciary, rest on a presumption of constitutional good faith. As a result, the conduct of judges acting in good faith should be equated with honesty, sincerity, loyalty to the constitution, and fair dealing.[4] Constitutional good faith in this sense can be an essential means of protecting the rule of law and fundamental rights.[5] This is consistent with the basic functions of the judiciary, which should act to defend the liberal-democratic constitutional order.[6]

The purpose of the chapter is to consider how constitutional good faith can be manifested in the activities of the judicial power. This applies both to the judicial administration of justice and the settlement of disputes about the law, as well as to

---

[1] See e.g. Smilov (2012).

[2] Cf. Gisbert (2022).

[3] Pozen (2016); Wright (2018).

[4] Pozen (2016), pp. 892–893, 929; Wright (2018), p. 46.

[5] Cf. Wright (2018), pp. 44, 45.

[6] Cf. Landau and Dixon (2020), pp. 1315, 1321–1322.

judicial review of the activities of other authorities or the effects of such activities in light of their compliance with the constitution. The identification of constitutional good faith is based on the assumption that the judicial power should ensure constitutional stability in the state, and therefore its loyalty or integrity to the constitution and the values expressed therein must be all the stronger. The judicial power should also act loyally, respecting the functions and competences of the other powers – the legislative and the executive – in accordance with the principle of the separation and balance of powers. It is an open question whether good faith can be a criterion for judicial review of the actions of the legislative and executive branches. At the same time, even in the most stable constitutional system, the risk of abuse of power or control exercised by the judiciary, as a manifestation of abusive constitutionalism, cannot be excluded.[7]

2 Justification for the Judiciary to Act in Constitutional Good Faith

In the activities of the courts, which are aimed at upholding the rule of law and protecting individual freedoms and rights, what must be present is "a sense of loyalty to and respect for law", "the absence of dissimulation, deceit and fraud", and "a sincere belief that one is acting in accordance with the law".[8] The doctrine has attempted to develop a comprehensive theory of good faith adjudication focused on the ethics of adjudication.[9] The presumption of judicial good faith of judges should serve to safeguard the possibility of making lawful judicial decisions even when judges exercise broad discretion. Judicial discretion is permissible by definition: discretion and the indeterminacy of law do not undermine the legitimacy of adjudication in a constitutional democracy. The application and interpretation of the law are activities that in a democratic state of law must meet standards of fairness, equity and due process in resolving disputes.

By virtue of the democratic legitimacy of the judiciary, judges may be regarded as representatives of the people and depositaries of the sovereign power to judge.[10] Before taking office, judges (including constitutional court judges) take an oath – a promise, among other things, to obey the law, be faithful and loyal, and support the constitution.[11] It may be debated whether this promise to obey and be faithful to the constitution can be viewed as a contract: in exchange for receiving power and taking

[7] Cf. Landau (2013); Petrov (2024), p. 6.

[8] Basdevant (1960), pp. 91–92.

[9] Burton (1992).

[10] Cf. Piotrowski (2018), pp. 222–224.

[11] See e.g.: 28 U.S. Code § 453: Oaths of justices and judges, https://www.govregs.com/uscode/expand/title28_partI_chapter21_section453; Section 38: The judicial oath of the German Judiciary Act, Federal Law Gazette I, p. 713 as amended, https://www.gesetze-im-internet.de/englisch_drig/englisch_drig.html.

office, a judge accepts limits on his or her freedom.[12] However, judges are trustees rather than parties to a contract – the voluntary assumption of office, coupled with the judicial oath, creates an actual fiduciary relationship.[13] As a result, judges have a legal and moral obligation – to citizens – to uphold the constitution in good faith.[14] This seems reasonable: on the basis of the constitution, judges are entrusted with the power to adjudicate, which they must exercise within defined legal framework, in accordance with the constitution.[15]

The role of judges in a democratic state under the rule of law is to make decisions in accordance with existing standards (sometimes creating a binding standard themselves, as in a *common law* system). The primary binding standard for judges is the law (with the constitution at the forefront), but the wording of the judges' oath of office indicates that judges are also obliged to take into account extra-legal principles or values when adjudicating. A judge should demonstrate loyalty to the law and to values such as the "truth" and "justice", as expressed in the text of the oath of German judges. The power of adjudication rests on the obligation to obey the law while maintaining a moral attitude towards the law and values such as justice, fairness and honesty[16]. Therefore, it can be assumed that judges have a duty to observe and apply the constitution in good faith. Acting in good faith – interpreting the law and justifying decisions in accordance with the constitution, its literal content, and the principles and values underlying it – fosters citizens' trust in the judiciary.

The justification for judges to act in good faith can be derived from the law. In Romanian law, for example, good faith functions as a principle governing the exercise of judicial power. The current Law on the Status of Judges and Prosecutors states that "judges (...) shall conduct their work in good faith and impartially, including the appearance of impartiality" (Article 4 para. 3).[17] The obligation to act in good faith arising from this provision has been linked to the principle of impartiality, which is crucial in the adjudication process and closely connected with the principle of judicial independence from political power. Today, good faith is not merely a standard of conduct for judges in their relationships at work and in society, as it was in the previous law on judges, where it appeared alongside respect.[18] Good faith has acquired the status of a principle of law: no longer merely an ethical or deontological criterion, it applies generally to the exercise of judicial office and the operation of judicial power. Therefore, the sources of good faith as a principle of judicial

---

[12] Easterbrook (1998), p. 1122.

[13] See e.g. Leib et al. (2013).

[14] Barnett and Bernick (2017), p. 20.

[15] Cf. Wright (2018), p. 44.

[16] Cf. Leiter (2020).

[17] Law no. 303/2022 of 15 November 2022 on the status of judges and prosecutors, Official Gazette of Romania, No. 1102 of 16 November 2022, https://www.iccj.ro/wp-content/uploads/2023/11/Legea-303-2022-eng.pdf.

[18] Article 90 para. 2 of Law no. 303/2004 of 28 June 2004 on the rules governing judges and prosecutors, Official Gazette of Romania, Part I, No. 576 of 29 June 2004, https://legislationline.org/sites/default/files/documents/2b/Romania_law_on_statute_judges_prosecutors_2004_am2009_en.pdf.

power should be sought in values such as judicial integrity, impartiality, and equality before the law.[19] Furthermore, the normative nature of the duty of judges to act in good faith is confirmed by Article 52(3) of the Romanian Constitution,[20] which establishes the material liability of the state for damages caused by judicial errors. According to this provision, the state's liability is determined by law and does not preclude the liability of judicial officers who acted in bad faith or with criminal negligence.

3 Good Faith and the Application and Interpretation of the Law in the *Common Law* System

Issues concerning constitutional good faith and the judicial application and interpretation of the constitution in good faith are analysed in American jurisprudence. Various theories of constitutional interpretation are presented, such as originalism, with its commitment to the original meaning of a constitutional provision, and living constitutionalism, which is associated with judicial activism.[21] The theory of constitutional interpretation depends largely on the conception of the constitution itself.[22] Judges do not have to agree on the best theory of constitutional interpretation, or on a single interpretive methodology. However, they must act within the constitutional framework – in accordance with the constitution. They are also subject to certain limitations that arise from the social, cultural, political and institutional features of the constitutional system. A limitation on the discretionary power of judges as interpreters may lie in the duty to act in good faith.

Contemporary constitutional originalism points to the usefulness of "good faith" in the process of judicial application and interpretation of the constitution. Randy E. Barnett and Evan D. Bernick present a theory of constitutional construction, which they base on the concept of *common law* long used in contract and trust law – the duty of good faith performance.[23] The originalist theory of interpretation is based on attachment to the "letter" or original meaning of the constitution (not excluding the intent of its drafters), while construction consists of translating the semantic content of the provision, established through interpretation, into rules (norms) of constitutional law. Good-faith constitutional construction presupposes "faithful" implementation of the constitution by judges who establish and adhere to the original functions, purposes or objectives of the constitution, i.e. its "spirit".

[19] Stănescu (2025).

[20] See https://www.presidency.ro/en/president/constitution-of-romania.

[21] Solum (2019); Barber and Fleming (2007), *passim*; cf. Balkin (2011), *passim*.

[22] Balkin (2016).

[23] Barnett and Bernick (2018); cf. Barnett and Bernick (2017).

The concept of good-faith constitutional construction is based on the idea that judges are trustees of the people (*public fiduciaries*).[24] A fiduciary relationship is created when a judge voluntarily takes office and an oath: "to support the Constitution", according to Article VI, Clause 3 of the Constitution of the United States.[25] The discretion entrusted to judges, especially when it is as broad as in the US constitutional system, is the basis for corresponding fiduciary duties, such as the duty to uphold the constitution and the duty to act in good faith. The judicial oath "functions as a bridge between the document and the duty to obey it".[26] Having voluntarily taken the oath, judges – as fiduciaries – are morally and legally obligated to "faithfully" obey the instructions contained in the constitution, which authorize and set the limits of their authority (as Article III of the Constitution of the United States). Fidelity to the constitution means that judges should exercise their discretionary authority in accordance with the "letter" and "spirit" of the constitution.[27] Moreover, once a judge takes an oath to uphold the constitution, he or she gives up the ability to amend the constitution through adjudication.[28] Judges are required to be loyal, diligent and honest in the exercise of their office.[29]

The fiduciary duty of constitutional good faith justifies the originalist concept of construction. The authors of this concept believe that judges need a methodology to exercise discretionary power: such discretion must be exercised in good faith. Good faith is to guide and constrain judicial activity in the sphere of construction. Judges are obliged to employ good-faith construction when the interpretation of the original meaning of a constitutional provision is not sufficient to resolve a case or doubts that have arisen, e.g., when a provision is unclear. Good-faith construction involves, first, accurately determining the "spirit" (or original function) of a constitutional provision at the time of its enactment, and second, formulating rules to give effect to both the "letter" and "spirit" of the text in a given case and in future cases. It can be argued that good faith is a directive of judicial interpretation of the constitution, which sets the limits of judicial discretionary power. The opposite is bad-faith construction, which involves the judge's opportunistic use of discretion to disregard or undermine the original "letter" or "spirit" of the constitution in pursuit of personal extra-constitutional preferences. However, no theory of constitutional interpretation will guarantee that judges will not abuse

---

[24] A more traditional model sees judges as agents or servants of the law; it can be considered as more consistent with the judicial oath, the rule of law, and the role of courts in the democratic system – see: Harris (2020).

[25] Constitution of the United States, https://constitution.congress.gov/constitution/.

[26] Re (2016), p. 308.

[27] Barnett and Bernick (2018), pp. 21–26.

[28] Barnett and Bernick (2018), p. 36.

[29] See e.g. Code of Conduct for United States Judges. Guide to Judiciary Policy, Vol. 2A, Ch. 2, canons 1 and 3, https://www.uscourts.gov/administration-policies/judiciary-policies/ethics-policies/code-conduct-united-states-judges#d.

the trust of the people if they are determined to do so, guided by personal preferences and indifferent to their oath.[30]

4 Good Faith and the Application and Interpretation of the Law in the *Civil Law* System

The application and interpretation of the law by the courts depends on assumptions about the role of the courts in the legal system, but also on how the role of the courts is viewed by the judges themselves. Some will carry out the will of the legislator and apply the provisions of law regardless of their extra-legal evaluation. For other judges, the provisions of the law will be only a starting point in the adjudication process, and the main goal will be to administer justice and issue a ruling that corresponds to the principles of equity, social needs or other criteria depending on the axiological assumptions adopted.[31]

In the *civil law* system, as a general rule, a judge is not authorized to make a ruling if there is no validating basis (a norm of state law), even if considerations of justice (or another value considered moral) require it. This is a consequence of the clear distinction between the powers of the legislature and the judiciary. Therefore, in continental legal culture, in the process of judicial application of the law, interpretation is of crucial importance. In the process of interpretation, the decisive criterion need not be only the literal meaning of the law and the intentions of the legislator, but also the requirements of justice or current social needs and conditions. This is confirmed, for example, by the jurisprudence of the Polish courts.[32]

The judge is most often seen as a faithful (honest) "servant" of the law,[33] which is consistent with his or her oath, the rule of law and the role of judges in a democratic state. He or she is obliged to comply with the applicable law. The court's task is to determine the linguistic meaning of a provision of the law and to interpret and implement the intention or will of the legislator (intentionalism). Interpretation may also be based on recognition of the public meaning of the text of the law at the time of its enactment or application (textualism).[34] It seems that as an honest "servant", a judge is obliged to act in good faith in order to most faithfully implement the intention of the legislator expressed in the legal text. Such actions by judges serve to realise the principle of the rule of law, which is essential to society as the foundation of legal security. Departure from the model of the judge as a faithful, honest "servant" of the law may result in arbitrariness in the application of the law and a corresponding loss of legal certainty.

---

30 Barnett and Bernick (2018), pp. 26–37.

31 See more Solan (2010).

32 Pietrzyk (2023).

33 Cf. Pietrzyk (2023), pp. 4–12.

34 Cf. Manning (2005); Waldron (2006).

On the other hand, courts act as organs of justice. Accordingly, judicial decisions must meet the requirements of justice, righteousness, equity, fairness or any other criteria that the judge deems important. This approach was advocated by Ronald Dworkin, according to whom a judge is able to interpret the law in a way that best harmonises with the moral values of fairness, impartiality and due process, and ensures the coherence of the entire legal system.[35] Courts are a kind of counterweight to the legislature and part of the checks and balances mechanism.[36] Judges have democratic legitimacy to review the work of the legislature and assess the meaning of legal provisions through the prism of values. This includes both legal values (especially those expressed in the constitution) and commonly accepted non-legal values (such as justice, social needs or morality).[37] Justice is a universal value, and it is sometimes expressed explicitly in the constitution as its axiological basis.[38] In addition, in the *civil law* system, courts also have the ability to interpret lawmaking or modify the provisions of laws so that they are in line with constitutional values or correspond to current social conditions. These are actions that go beyond searching for the meaning of a legal provision, which – referring to the findings in the American doctrine – are the equivalent of "construction".[39] It seems that such actions by judges to make a just ruling can be viewed as a manifestation of constitutional good faith.

Good faith action by courts in the *civil law* system can take the form of pro-constitutional interpretation. The use of pro-constitutional interpretation is supported by the presumption of the constitutionality of laws, which is a consequence of the principle of constitutional supremacy. From this presumption comes the principle that, in case of doubt, a constitutionally compatible interpretation of a law should be adopted. The judge strives to achieve an interpretive result that allows for the fullest realisation of the values protected by the constitution. It can be assumed that the judge acts in good faith, as he seeks to ensure that only those norms that meet constitutional standards are included in the legal system.[40] In this case, the judge acts as a harmoniser of the legal system.[41] Pro-constitutional interpretation of laws, which is a manifestation of judicial activism, has a *sui generis* law-making character. Giving the provisions of a law a meaning supplemented by the axiology of the constitution is acceptable in the civil law system, as long as the pro-constitutional interpretation does not lead to an arbitrary modification of the linguistic meaning of the legal provision and its application *contra legem*.[42]

[35] Cf. Dworkin (1986); Dworkin (2011).

[36] Gonzalez (1996).

[37] Pietrzyk (2023), pp. 17–21.

[38] See e.g. the Preamble of the Constitution of the Republic of Poland of 2nd April 1997 (Official Journal No. 78, item 483), https://www.sejm.gov.pl/prawo/konst/angielski/kon1.htm.

[39] Cf. Schauer (2021).

[40] Cf. Zajadło (2018), p. 69.

[41] Cf. Pietrzyk (2023), pp. 14–17.

[42] Kaczmarczyk (2021).

5 Good Faith as a Directive of Judicial Application of the Law

Applying and interpreting the law (including the constitution) in good faith – whether *in the common law* or *civil law* system – involves the obligation of the courts to act within the limits of the powers conferred on them, which is a consequence of the principle of the separation and balance of powers. There is no doubt that the power entrusted to the courts must be exercised with regard to the functions, objectives and purposes of the constitution; the power to adjudicate is not unlimited.[43] In democratic states, the main task of courts, including constitutional courts (tribunals), is to safeguard the dignity and fundamental rights of the individual, which are guaranteed in principle by the constitution.[44] A judge, who pledges to uphold the law and be faithful (respectful, supportive, and so forth) to the constitution, thus has a dual obligation: to uphold the rule of law and protect individual rights. The performance of the courts' adjudicatory function requires them to act within the limits of the constitution, and judicial decisions should be made, where possible, with reference to the overriding goal of justice.

Constitutional good faith directs the process of judicial application and interpretation of the law to achieve the goals and values that the constitution protects. This requires a certain attitude on the part of the judge – first of all, fidelity to the object and process of interpretation.[45] It should be borne in mind that the constitution is a legal act characterized by the generality of its provisions and openness to the underlying value system, which does not always take the form of written legal principles. Interpretation of the constitution at the level of the language of norms may therefore be insufficient to determine the meaning of a provision, while constitutional principles or values may be ambiguously interpreted. Indeed, the judge has a fairly broad discretionary power. Therefore, the judge's adoption of a reflective but also contextual approach to determining the meaning of constitutional provisions can be considered a sign of good faith and can contribute to eliminating arbitrariness in the interpretation process. It would seem that it is in this way that a judge loyal to his or her oath of office should interpret the constitution in good faith. At the same time, in the process of interpretation, the judge should exercise due diligence, which can be linked to the ethical requirement of self-restraint in the exercise of discretionary power.[46]

In addition, legal reasoning and argumentation in constitutional and statutory cases depend on the values recognized by judges as interpreters of the law and the interpretive methodology they choose. In the *common law* system, what matters is the theory of constitutional interpretation adopted by the judge (originalism, textualism, intentionalism, living constitution), and in the *civil law* system it is the

[43] Cf. Fallon (2009), p. 984.

[44] See e.g. Velaers (2016).

[45] Balkin (2018), p. 159.

[46] See Kaleta (2025); cf. Kaleta (2014); Pichlak (2020).

method of interpretation (linguistic, purposive, functional, axiological).[47] In the case of constitutional interpretation, it is not enough to simply "follow the law" without the reflection necessary for the initial determination of its meaning. Constitutional argumentation in good faith should be based on a reflective balance between the methodological assumptions made by the judge and intuitive legal judgments about the appropriate (morally and practically desirable) results of interpretation in individual cases. This requires taking into account not only the peculiar nature of constitutional provisions, previous findings and their application in practice, but also the axiological and factual (social) context of constitutional validity. Judges guided by good faith will not use interpretation to arrive at solutions that merely satisfy their own preferences. However, they should be ready to develop or rethink accepted methodological assumptions under the influence of new arguments or facts.[48] While remaining within the judge's discretion, acting in good faith is largely a matter of discerning between potentially conflicting imperatives.[49] Furthermore, a judge may disagree with the assessment of fellow judges adjudicating the case (*votum separatum*). A difference of opinion among judges adjudicating a given case is possible as long as they remain within the limits of the constitution.[50]

The application and interpretation of the law by judges in good faith must be aimed at achieving the goals and objectives of the constitutional legal order. Judges may not act on the basis of mere will, beliefs or preferences that are not grounded in law, even if these extra-legal beliefs or preferences are professed by the legislature, the executive branch, or the judges themselves.[51] The duty of judges is to respect the law, which should be linked to the requirement of moral and ethical behaviour.[52] Good faith manifests itself in the judge's loyalty to his or her oath and fidelity to the law, as well as faithful action. The faithful action of judges is a basic rule of conduct that can be linked to the fiduciary conception of office, even if it is not directly enforced in the same way as the rule of decision-making.[53] In the case of the judiciary, public expectations of such faithful action are higher than for the legislature or the executive branch, and this is related to the constitutional role of the courts, regarded as the last line of defence of the liberal-democratic constitutional order.[54]

Complementing the interpretation of the law in good faith is the courts' adherence to the constitutional standards of due process and procedural fairness, which

[47] Pietrzyk (2023), *passim*.

[48] Cf. Fallon (2017).

[49] Cf. Wright (2018), p. 48.

[50] Cf. Levinson (2016).

[51] Barnett and Bernick (2018), p. 6.

[52] Wright (2018), p. 48.

[53] Leib (2025), p. 11.

[54] Landau and Dixon (2020), p. 1313.

guarantee the protection of individual rights in judicial proceedings.[55] The principle of good faith can be (as in Romania) a principle of judicial procedure, according to which a judge is obliged to act in accordance with the general principles of law and the requirements of fairness and good faith.[56]

Judges should be guided by the principle of good faith in order to ensure fairness and justice in the process and in the judgements they deliver. In all proceedings – civil, criminal, or administrative – it is necessary to respect procedural rules and values, in particular justice, equality and human dignity. The procedure must be based on such elements as the impartiality and independence of the judge, the predictability of the court's action, the openness of the proceedings, the stability of judgments, as well as the fair treatment of the participants in the proceedings, the principle of equality of arms, the right to be heard, the right to participate personally in the proceedings, and the right to a justification of the decision.[57] A judicial process that is fair, justice-oriented, humane and respectful of human dignity can be regarded as a manifestation of the court acting in constitutional good faith. If an independent and impartial judge acts in good faith and adheres to the principles and values that define the procedure in question, it is possible to achieve fair and just outcomes.[58] Erroneous decisions or misconduct, such as unnecessary delays in hearing cases, are not excluded, although they do not necessarily reflect ill will on the part of judges. Judicial errors of jurisdiction or procedure, in the assessment or application of the law or in the evaluation of evidence, may be dealt with by judicial review on appeal. Conversely, other judicial failings that cannot be remedied in this way (e.g. protraction) may give rise to claims by litigants against the state. Demonstrating that unfair judicial conduct is a point of contention in a case opens up the possibility of applying the principle of good faith. Judicial proceedings will be a manifestation of constitutional good faith if the procedure is used by the judge as an instrument to realise constitutional values such as the rule of law, human dignity and justice. These values correspond to the objectives of the judiciary. Therefore, it follows that judges should not be subject to personal civil liability for claims directly relating to their good faith exercise of judicial functions.[59]

---

[55] Cf. Resnik (1977).

[56] Stănescu (2025).

[57] Cf. Chauvin (2019).

[58] Cf. Summers (1974); Tyler (1994).

[59] Consultative Council of European Judges (CCJE), Opinion no. 3 of the Consultative Council of European Judges (CCJE) to the attention of the Committee of Ministers of the Council of Europe on the principles and rules governing judges' professional conduct, in particular ethics, incompatible behaviour and impartiality. Strasbourg, 19 November 2002, point 55.

6 Good Faith and *Judicial Review*

In democratic states, the organs of judicial power, in addition to resolving disputes over the law, exercise supervisory powers over the legislative and executive branches, as well as public administration in the broadest sense. The supervisory function of the judicial power vis-à-vis the other authorities is justified by the principle of supremacy of the constitution in the national legal order. Judicial control is one of the *checks and balances*. The procedure and scope of this review vary across jurisdiction. Courts (tribunals) have the power to rule on the constitutional responsibility of those occupying the highest state offices, review the legality of decisions made by such entities, verify the validity of elections, check finances, and review the constitutionality of the goals or activities of political parties. One of the most important aspects of judicial review is ruling on the constitutionality of laws – by ordinary courts in *common law* countries (and supreme courts such as the US Supreme Court) or special constitutional courts (tribunals) in *civil law* countries.[60]

The courts competent to review the constitutionality of laws in both legal systems have a special systemic role as "guardians" of the constitution. On taking office, constitutional judges take an oath in which they undertake, in particular, to support and uphold the constitution.[61] Such a judge thus has not only a legal but also a moral duty of fidelity, honesty and loyalty to the constitution in carrying out the tasks and competences of the constitutional courts. The primary purpose of the constitutional courts (tribunals) empowered to review constitutionality is to protect constitutional rights (especially minority rights) and to ensure the constitutional balance between the organs of public power in a system operating with the separation of powers.[62] Their task is to protect constitutional values by assessing laws on the basis of general principles of law, such as, inter alia, the principle of justice, equality, or human freedom.[63] They are also considered one of the main defence mechanisms against unfair constitutional amendments or even attempts to replace the existing constitution.[64] For this purpose, the courts use tools such as the doctrine

[60] Cf. Sinani (2024); Rosenfeld (2004); Kelsen (1942); Strzępek (2023).

[61] See e.g.: Article 134(4) of the Constitution of the Slovak Republic, Act no. 460/1992 Coll. as amended, https://legislationline.org/sites/default/files/2024-06/Constitution%20of%20the%20Slovak%20Republic%202023.pdf; § 8(1) of the Constitutional Court Act 1953 – Verfassungsgerichtshofgesetz, GBl. Nr. 85/1953 (WV) as amended, https://www.ris.bka.gv.at/Dokumente/Erv/ERV_1953_85/ERV_1953_85.pdf, http://www.ris.bka.gv.at/Dokumente/BgblPdf/1953_85_0/1953_85_0.pdf; Article 4(1) of the Act of 30 November 2016 on the Status of the Judges of the Constitutional Tribunal, Journal of Laws of the Republic of Poland on 19 December 2016, item 2073, https://trybunal.gov.pl/fileadmin/content/dokumenty/Akty_normatywne/The_Act_on_the_Status_of_the_Judges_of_the_Constitutional_Tribunal__as_amended_in_2017__en.pdf.

[62] Issacharoff (2011), p. 1002; see more Issacharoff (2015); cf. Tommasini (2024).

[63] Cf. Comella (2004).

[64] Dixon and Landau (2021), p. 81; Landau and Dixon (2015).

of unconstitutional constitutional amendment.[65] In European countries, there is an emphasis on the need for constitutional courts to protect "constitutional identity", which is an expression of the fundamental values of the state, especially the values that form the identity of the nation.[66] The canon of such principles includes, in particular, sovereignty, the principles of democracy, the rule of law, and the protection of fundamental rights and freedoms.[67]

Therefore, the presumption of constitutional good faith in the process of applying and interpreting the constitution by the constitutional court is justified. This court not only interprets the constitution, but also shapes the content and meaning of constitutional provisions, taking into account its axiology and political or social context. For example, the German Federal Constitutional Court (*Bundesverfassungsgericht*), based on the concept of the constitution as an "objective order of values", has repeatedly concretised, developed and adapted – through interpretation – constitutional norms with regard to the current needs of social life.[68] This confirms that the constitutional court is the real and ultimate interpreter of the Basic Law, which influences the understanding and application of constitutional law. Moreover, only the constitutional court's interpretation of the constitution is legally binding.

The good faith conduct of the constitutional judge – who is the democratically legitimised ultimate interpreter of the constitution – should be based on an interpretive methodology that takes into account the constitution as a coherent, logical-teleological whole. Good faith interpretation of the constitution should be based on a "faithful" decoding of the content of the constitution and its goals (objectives) and values, which either justify or complement the content of the constitutional provisions. Applying and interpreting the constitution requires the right attitude of a constitutional judge – loyalty to the constitution, and not to the political power that most often participates in his or her appointment. In this sense, good faith can be considered an objective standard that limits the freedom of the constitutional interpreter. Complementing the constitutional judge's action in good faith should be his or her adherence to the rules of professional ethics. In the process of interpreting the constitution, there must be an implied consistency of good faith and honest conduct. In practice, acting in constitutional good faith also depends on how constitutional judges view their role in a democratic legal state and whether they are resistant to the influence of political power oriented toward the monopolisation of power.

The judicial power, despite its independence, may not be able to defend itself against the actions of political actors seeking to consolidate power.[69] Political power may use various techniques to subjugate the judiciary, especially the constitutional

[65] See Roznai (2017).

[66] See e.g. Drinóczi (2020).

[67] Cf. Nagy (2024).

[68] Cf. Stremler (2017).

[69] Ginsburg (2008).

court, in order to legitimise political decisions.[70] As a result, courts may engage in judicial review that undermines rather than protects or promotes democracy and the rule of law. This phenomenon is referred to as *abusive judicial review*. It is the subject of a broader doctrinal analysis, which is based on examples from the practice of various countries (e.g. Poland, Venezuela, Hungary).[71] Abusive judicial review might be pursued as a political strategy, when a power with authoritarian tendencies subjugates the courts and uses them to carry out anti-democratic constitutional amendments. There are two forms of abusive judicial review: in the first case, the courts uphold legislation or executive actions that significantly undermine the minimal core of democracy ("weak" abusive judicial review); in the second, the courts themselves remove or undermine democratic safeguards ("strong" abusive judicial review).[72] In the constitutional discourse on abusive judicial review, there are also references to the concepts of good and bad faith. If the judge's intentions and his or her decisions are aimed at undermining the foundations of liberal-constitutional democracy, then one can speak of acting in bad faith. By issuing decisions with anti-democratic overtones, judges may deliberately distort the meaning of the constitution and rely on concepts and doctrines designed to protect liberal democracy in a truly offensive manner that undermines their basic meaning and transforms them into tools for attacking liberal democracy.[73] The question is whether it is possible for judges to act in constitutional good faith in a situation where political power has taken control of the courts.

Above all, independent judges must be faithful to the constitution, its fundamental principles and democratic values at all times, especially in moments of crisis for constitutional democracy. They can do so through the strength of the constitution-based reasoning contained in the legal justification of their decisions, using a methodology that takes into account the established judicial understanding of the concepts or institutions of constitutional law in case law. Such an attitude on the part of the judge would be an expression not of good faith, but of genuine faith in the constitutional importance of the judiciary for the defence of the liberal-democratic constitutional order. On the other hand, it cannot be ruled out that judges coerced into a political strategy may choose to uphold anti-democratic actions for prudential reasons, so as not to provoke political power to undermine the independence and jurisdiction of the courts. Judges may in good faith assume that, in the long term, issuing a constitutionally questionable or even anti-democratic decision may preserve their capacity to resist more serious threats to democracy. It would seem more reasonable – and consistent with constitutional good faith aimed at protecting the rule of law and the long-term independence of the judiciary – for judges to exercise restraint. This could include, for example, deferring the issuance of decisions that

[70] Poland's experience shows that the techniques used by political power to neutralize and absorb judicial power can lead to the erosion of constitutional democracy – see e.g. Garlicki (2019); Sadurski (2019).

[71] For more extensive discussion, see Landau and Dixon (2020); Dixon and Landau (2021).

[72] Landau and Dixon (2020), pp. 1345–1353; Dixon and Landau (2021), pp. 94–98.

[73] Landau and Dixon (2020), pp. 1334–1345; Dixon and Landau (2021), pp. 83–93.

are important to the functioning of the constitutional order.[74] However, it is questionable, to say the least, whether this kind of judicial strategy is appropriate in a situation of serious threat to the essential core of the constitutional democratic order, which is precisely what the courts are supposed to protect.

It should also be remembered that, in a democratic state under the rule of law, it is up to the judicial power to make the final determination of what is constitutional. Because good faith arises from the essence of the constitution, the judicial assessment of the actions of the legislative or executive authorities should take into account the presumption of constitutional good faith of the authorities' bodies. Good faith may appear in judicial proceedings as an exception that protects public officials in situations of wrongful action.[75] Compliance by the reviewed entities with standards such as respect for the law, loyalty, honesty, and integrity in cases of error, e.g. regarding the consequences of an act or decision, may determine the recognition of such action taken in good faith. On the other hand, actions disregarding these standards or even harming fundamental constitutional values should lead to such conduct being classified as legally void or even criminal, due to the bad faith on which it was based.[76] Judicial enforceability of good faith is not excluded, but may prove difficult or even impossible.[77] Courts may be reluctant to decide cases requiring an assessment of whether public officials acted in constitutional good faith.[78] It would then be necessary to examine the intentions or motives of a public official, and courts do not have the tools to do so. When deciding political cases, the courts themselves may be suspected of improper motives, which would negatively affect their authority and public confidence in the judiciary. It is understandable that the courts maintain a certain distance from engaging in the evaluation of political disputes. American constitutional law scholarship points to reasons why good faith and bad faith are not judicially enforceable.[79] In practice, courts apply the concept of the *political question doctrine* developed by the US Supreme Court, according to which courts should not decide questions that fall within the exclusive competence of the legislative and executive branches. Courts apply this doctrine to assess their own institutional capacity to resolve politically sensitive disputes; however, it does not absolutely preclude judicial review.[80]

[74] Landau and Dixon (2020), p. 1328; Dixon, Issacharoff (2016), p. 699; cf. Gardbaum (2015).

[75] Pozen (2016), pp. 898–900.

[76] Cf. Criste (2019), pp. 90–91.

[77] Podkowik (2025).

[78] Fallon (1997), p. 72.

[79] Pozen (2016), pp. 909–917.

[80] Bradley and Posner (2023).

7 Conclusion

The foregoing analysis suggests that the activities of the judiciary in a constitutional democracy can be based on the presumption of good faith. Constitutional good faith, as a substrate of sincerity, honesty, loyalty to the constitution or honest action, is linked in some natural way to the concept of an independent judiciary and the role of judges in a democratic state under the rule of law. Such a presumption of good faith could strengthen the legitimacy of the judiciary, which, in the classical separation of powers, has competencies oriented toward protecting the rule of law and human rights and controlling the other authorities. The following arguments may be advanced in its support.

Firstly, constitutional good faith can be regarded as the standard of judicial conduct required by the constitution as the basis of the state's legal order. The constitutions of democratic states entrust precisely the courts with the protection of the fundamental values on which the constitutional order is founded (such as dignity, democracy, the rule of law, justice, equality). The legitimacy of recognizing good faith as a standard for the operation of judicial power is reinforced by the adoption of the fiduciary conception of the office of judge, which finds a basis in the text of the judicial oath. The pledge of judges to obey the law and to be faithful, respectful, loyal, and supportive of the constitution justifies the view that the activity of the courts should rest on the obligation of constitutional good faith. Judges are bound by the constitution as the supreme law of the state, which implies an obligation to observe and respect not only the "letter", but also the principles and values on which the framers founded the constitution. Related to this duty is not so much the legal as the moral responsibility of judges to society.

Secondly, constitutional good faith can be considered a directive of judicial application and interpretation of the law, in the first instance the constitution itself. For a judge to act in good faith in these spheres is not only to follow the law in its semantic layer, but also to take into account its axiology, especially values of a universal and constitutional nature. Theories of constitutional interpretation in the *common law* system or rules of interpretation applied by judges in the *civil law* system are helpful in determining the actual meaning of the content of constitutional provisions, taking into account their object and purpose. A specific example of good faith interpretation is pro-constitutional interpretation, which in Poland is a product of direct judicial application of the constitution. At the same time, constitutional good faith sets limits on the discretionary power of judges. Judges are always bound by the constitution, so the normative judgments they make should be consistent with the goals and objectives of the constitutional legal order.

Thirdly, constitutional good faith can be understood as a kind of decision-making rule. A judicial decision made in good faith should reflect the seriousness of purpose in seeking to understand the constitution and its underlying axiology as a basis for determining the meaning of a legal provision, as well as the personal and institutional impartiality of the court. Confirmation of a good-faith decision can be provided by judicial reasoning, especially when the court adheres to established standards of legal reasoning, thereby fostering a sense of legal certainty. Equally important is the courts' adherence to the principles of procedural fairness. Possible judicial errors, such as incorrect assessment of the probable effects of a decision on the legal order, do not necessarily imply a lack of good faith if the justification of the goal is an expression of the judge's genuine conviction about the meaning of the law. On the other hand, a judge's going beyond the "letter" of the law in accordance with constitutional values and objectives such as justice or fairness is permissible under the rule of law, but it must not result in the judicial power encroaching upon the sphere of powers reserved to the legislature in a system of separated powers. In this sense, the judiciary is obliged to maintain loyalty and fairness towards the legislature, which may itself be regarded as an expression of constitutional good faith.

Fourthly, constitutional good faith is inherent in the activities of constitutional courts. Being the "guardians" of the constitution, they are obliged to observe the "letter" and "spirit" of the constitutional provisions, since it is for them to have the final say on the validity of the law independently of political considerations. Therefore, a constitutional judge should be expected to maintain an attitude of special fidelity and loyalty towards the constitution, and to employ adjudication in multifaceted, reflective and contextual constitutional argumentation. Rulings of constitutional courts typically draw on textual arguments, as well as historical arguments (referring to the assumptions and intentions of the framers), doctrinal arguments, and arguments based on axiology and teleology. In practice, constitutional courts shape the content and meaning of constitutional provisions through interpretation, taking into account their axiology, goals, objectives and functions, as well as their political or social context. This enables them to prevent unconstitutional constitutional amendments. Unfortunately, as the experience of many countries in recent years has shown, courts – especially constitutional courts – can, through various techniques used by political actors with authoritarian tendencies, be instrumentalised to facilitate anti-democratic constitutional amendments. In such circumstances, it is doubtful that the constitutional good faith of a constitutional judge can serve as a convincing argument that no abuse of judicial review has occured.

Fifthly, the use of good faith by the judiciary as an additional criterion for reviewing the constitutionality or legality of an action (omission), normative act, or decision of public authorities cannot be ruled out. The issue of judicial enforceability of good faith has been discussed in more detail in the previous chapter.[81] The question remains open as to whether entrusting such a power to the judiciary, whose potential for acting in bad faith cannot be absolutely ruled out, would involve an excessive risk of instrumentalising the constitution.

[81] Podkowik (2025).

References

Balkin JM (2011) Living originalism. Harvard University Press, Cambridge

Balkin JM (2016) The framework model and constitutional interpretation. In: Dyzenhaus D, Thorburn M (eds) Philosophical foundations of constitutional law. Oxford University Press, pp 241–264

Balkin JM (2018) Arguing about the constitution: the topics in constitutional interpretation. Const Comment 33(2):145–260

Barber SA, Fleming JE (2007) Constitutional interpretation. The basic questions. Oxford University Press, New York

Barnett RE, Bernick E (2017) The letter and the spirit: the judicial duty of good-faith constitutional construction. Georgetown University Law Center (working paper), http://perma.cc/TXH4-MEKR

Barnett RE, Bernick ED (2018) The letter and the spirit: a unified theory of originalism. Georgetown Law J 107(1):7–18. Available at SSRN: https://ssrn.com/abstract=3049056 or https://doi.org/10.2139/ssrn.3049056

Basdevant J (1960) Dictionnaire de la terminologie du droit international, Paris

Bradley CA, Posner EA (2023) The real political question doctrine. Stanford Law Rev 75:1033–1090

Burton SJ (1992) Judging in good faith. Cambridge University Press, New York

Chauvin T (2019) Procedural justice as a rule of law and expression of respect for human dignity. Studia Iuridica 79:48–67. https://doi.org/10.5604/01.3001.0013.1881

Comella VF (2004) The European model of constitutional review of legislation: toward decentralization? Int J Const Law 2(3):461–491. https://doi.org/10.1093/icon/2.3.461

Criste M (2019) Le rôle des principes généraux dans la globalisation du droit constitutionnel. Fiat Iustitia 1:88–104

Dixon R, Issacharoff S (2016) Living to fight another day: judicial deferral in defense of democracy. Wis Law Rev:683–731. Available at SSRN: https://ssrn.com/abstract=2726045 or. https://doi.org/10.2139/ssrn.2726045

Dixon R, Landau D (2021) Abusive judicial review: abusive borrowing by and of constitutional courts. In: Abusive constitutional borrowing: legal globalization and the subversion of liberal democracy. Oxford University Press, pp 81–115

Drinóczi T (2020) Constitutional identity in Europe: the identity of the constitution. A regional approach. German Law J 21(2):105–130. https://doi.org/10.1017/glj.2020.1

Dworkin R (1986) Law's empire. Harvard University Press, Cambridge

Dworkin R (2011) Justice for hedgehogs. Harvard University Press, Cambridge

Easterbrook FH (1998) Textualism and the dead hand. George Wash Law Rev 6:1119–1126

Fallon Jr RH (1997) Foreword: implementing the constitution. Harv Law Rev, Vol. 111(1), pp. 54–152. https://doi.org/10.2307/1342131

Fallon RH Jr (2009) Constitutional constraints. Calif Law Rev 97(4):975–1037

Fallon RH Jr (2017) Arguing in good faith about the constitution: ideology, methodology, and reflective equilibrium. Univ Chicago Law Rev 84(1):123–145. Available at: https://chicagounbound.uchicago.edu/uclrev/vol84/iss1/7

Gardbaum S (2015) Are strong constitutional courts always a good thing for new democracies? Columbia J Transnatl Law 52:285–320. Available at SSRN: https://ssrn.com/abstract=2552816

Garlicki L (2019) Constitutional court and politics. The Polish crisis. In: Landfried C (ed) Judicial power. How constitutional court affect political transformation. Cambridge University Press, pp 141–162

Ginsburg T (2008) The global spread of constitutional review. In: Caldeira GA, Kelemen RD, Whittington KE (eds) The Oxford handbook of law and politics. Oxford University Press, pp 81–98

Gisbert RB (2022) Judicial Independence in European constitutional law. Eur Const Law Rev 18(4):591–620. https://doi.org/10.1017/S1574019622000347

Gonzalez CE (1996) Reinterpreting statutory interpretation. North Carolina Law Rev 74:585–730. Available at: https://scholarship.law.unc.edu/nclr/vol74/iss3/2
Harris D (2020) Judges as agents of the law. Mitchell Hamline Law J Public Policy Pract 41(2), Article 1. Available at: https://open.mitchellhamline.edu/policypractice/vol41/iss2/1
Issacharoff S (2011) Constitutional courts and democratic hedging. Georgetown Law J 99:961–1012, 1002. Available at SSRN: https://ssrn.com/abstract=1580211
Issacharoff S (2015) Fragile democracies: contested power in the era of constitutional courts. Cambridge University Press
Kaczmarczyk H (2021) Pro-constitutional interpretation of statutes. A few remarks related to the dispute about judicial activism. Rev Eur Comp Law 46(3):93–107. Available at:. https://doi.org/10.31743/recl.12330
Kaleta KJ (2014) Between reflexivity and effectiveness: dilemmas of the democratic legitimacy of constitutional justice. In: Cserne P, Konczol M, Soniewicka M (eds) The rule of law and the challenges to jurisprudence. Central and Eastern European Forum for Legal, Political, and Social Theory Yearbook Vol. 3, pp 113–123
Kaleta KJ (2025) Good faith in constitutional interpretation. In: Podkowik J, Chmielarz-Grochal A, Stębelski M, Sułkowski J (eds) Gleams of good faith in constitutional law, Springer Nature, Cham
Kelsen H (1942) Judicial review of legislation: a comparative study of the Austrian and the American constitution. J Polit 4:183–200. https://doi.org/10.2307/2125770. Accessed 15 Jan 2025
Landau D (2013) Abusive constitutionalism. UC Davis Law Rev 47:189–260
Landau D, Dixon R (2015) Constraining constitutional change. Wake Forest Law Rev 50:859–890. Available at SSRN: https://ssrn.com/abstract=2624842
Landau D, Dixon R (2020) Abusive judicial review: courts against democracy. Univ Calif Davis Law Rev 53:1313–1387
Leib EJ (2025) Good faith in U.S. Constitutional law (January 08, 2025). Fordham Law Legal Studies Research Paper No. 5088420. Available at SSRN: https://ssrn.com/abstract=5088420 or https://doi.org/10.2139/ssrn.5088420
Leib EJ, Ponet DL, Serota ME (2013) A fiduciary theory of judging. Calif Law Rev 101:699–753. Available at SSRN: https://ssrn.com/abstract=2029001
Leiter B (2020) The roles of judges in democracies: a realistic view. Revista Estudos Institucionais 6(2):346–375. https://doi.org/10.21783/rei.v6i2.508
Levinson S (2016) Trash talk at the supreme court: reflections on David Pozen's constitutional bad faith. Harv Law Rev 129(4):166–175
Manning JF (2005) Textualism and legislative intent. Va Law Rev 91:419–450. Available at SSRN: https://ssrn.com/abstract=2853690 or. https://doi.org/10.2139/ssrn.2853690
Nagy G (2024) The protection of constitutional identity in some east-central European countries. Opolskie Studia Administracyjno-Prawne 20(2):123–140
Petrov J (2024) How to detect abusive constitutional practices. Eur Const Law Rev 20(2):191–221. https://doi.org/10.1017/S1574019624000142
Pichlak M (2020) Constitutionalism as a reflection on political identity. In: Sulikowski A, Mańko R, Łakomy J (eds) Legal scholarship and the political: in search of a new paradigm. C.H. Beck, Warsaw, pp 57–74
Pietrzyk M (2023) Role of courts & interpretation in civil law culture (November 2, 2023). Available at SSRN: https://ssrn.com/abstract=4672007 or https://doi.org/10.2139/ssrn.4672007
Piotrowski R (2018) Judges and the limits of democratic power in the light of the constitution of the Republic of Poland. Ruch Prawniczy, Ekonomiczny i Socjologiczny 1:215–229
Podkowik J (2025) Good faith and the separation of powers. In: Podkowik J, Chmielarz-Grochal A, Stębelski M, Sułkowski J (eds) Gleams of good faith in constitutional law, Springer Nature, Cham
Pozen DE (2016) Constitutional bad faith. Harv Law Rev 129(4):885–955

Re RM (2016) Promising the constitution. Northwest Univ Law Rev 110(2):299–356. https://scholarlycommons.law.northwestern.edu/nulr/vol110/iss2/1
Resnik D (1977) Due process and procedural justice. Nomos 18:206–228. Available at JSTOR: http://www.jstor.org/stable/24219206
Rosenfeld M (2004) Constitutional adjudication in Europe and the United States: paradoxes and contrasts. Int J Const Law 2(4):633–668. https://doi.org/10.1093/icon/2.4.633
Roznai Y (2017) Unconstitutional constitutional amendments: the limits of amendment powers. Oxford University Press
Sadurski W (2019) Poland's constitutional breakdown. Oxford University Press
Schauer F (2021) Constructing interpretation. Boston Univ Law Rev 101:103–132
Sinani B (2024) Global patterns of constitutional judicial review systems: two major models of constitutional judicial review in the world. Juridical Tribune—Rev Comp Int Law 14(1):156–173. https://tribunajuridica.eu/arhiva/y14v1/10.%20Blerton%20Sinani.pdf
Smilov D (2012) The judiciary: the least dangerous branch. In: Rosenfeld M, Sajó A (eds) The Oxford handbook of comparative constitutional law. Oxford University Press, pp 859–873
Solan LM (2010) The language of statutes: laws and their interpretation. The University of Chicago Press, Chicago
Solum LB (2019) Originalism versus living constitutionalism: the conceptual structure of the great debate (January 11, 2019). Northwest Univ Law Rev 113(6):1243–1296. Available at SSRN: https://ssrn.com/abstract=3324264
Stănescu L-S (2025) Good faith in Romanian constitutional law. In: Podkowik J, Chmielarz-Grochal A, Stębelski M, Sułkowski J (eds) Gleams of good faith in constitutional law, Springer Nature, Cham
Stremler M (2017) The constitution as an objective order of values. Kutafin Law Rev 4(2):498–526. https://doi.org/10.17803/2313-5395.2017.2.8.498-526
Strzępek K (2023) Constitutional review in Poland. On the 220th anniversary of Marbury v. Madison. Przegląd Prawa Konstytucyjnego 6:355–366. https://doi.org/10.15804/ppk.2023.06.25. Accessed 15 Jan 2025
Summers RS (1974) Evaluating and improving legal processes—a plea for "process values". Cornell Law Rev 60:1–52
Tommasini N (2024) Judicial self-empowerment and unconstitutional constitutional amendments. Int J Const Law 22(1):161–190. https://doi.org/10.1093/icon/moae009
Tyler TR (1994) Governing amid diversity: the effect of fair decisionmaking procedures on the legitimacy of government. Law Soc Rev 28:809–831. https://doi.org/10.2307/3053998
Velaers J (2016) Constitutional versus international protection of human rights: added value or redundancy? The Belgian case, in the light of the advisory practice of the Venice commission. Revue interdisciplinaire d'études juridiques 77:265–295
Waldron J (2006) The core of the case against judicial review Yale Law J 115(6):1346–1406. Available at: https://doi.org/10.2307/20455656 or https://www.jstor.org/stable/20455656
Wright AM (2018) Constitutional good faith. N Y Univ Law Rev 93:41–49
Zajadło J (2018) Hostile constitutional interpretation. Gdańskie Studia Prawnicze XL:63–69

Good Faith and the Vertical Division of Power

Jarosław Sułkowski

Abstract The division of power in the state is not limited to maintaining the separation of powers in a horizontal sense. In every country, regardless of its form, there is a need to protect the autonomy of local authorities against interference from the central government (the vertical aspect of the division of powers). The scope of this autonomy is derived from the form of the state and is wider in a federal state than in a unitary state. Good faith is therefore applicable both where power is decentralised and in a state where federal entities partially exercise sovereign power (federal states, unitary states). It is also important in relations between units of decentralised power.

Good faith in the abovementioned vertical relationships is a mutual obligation which has its source in the provisions of the state constitution. This obligation is understood in terms of cooperation and loyalty. Its function is to facilitate effective and legitimate authority by prohibiting the arbitrary exercise of power at the central level and the arbitrary threat to, and undermining of, confidence in legitimate central authority by local (regional) authorities. Therefore, the question arises whether the public law vertical dimension of the idea of good faith is gaining recognition in national legal systems and what its manifestations are. The examples of Spain and Germany show that the principle of loyalty is applied in constitutional law, and examples from practice confirm its importance for the stability of power in the state. In contrast, US law does not recognise such a principle, probably because the structures of state and federal governments are much more distinct.

The mere expectation of mutual loyalty between the authorities from a vertical perspective may turn out to be insufficient. Therefore, the constitution provides for mechanisms for the judicial resolution of competence disputes, including those concerning the scope of autonomy of local (regional) authorities. The assessment of these mechanisms depends on many factors, in particular the legitimacy of the enti-

J. Sułkowski (✉)
Faculty of Law and Administration, University of Lodz, Lodz, Poland
e-mail: sulkowski@wpia.uni.lodz.pl

J. Podkowik et al. (eds.), *Gleams of Good Faith in Constitutional Law*, Ius Gentium: Comparative Perspectives on Law and Justice 132,
https://doi.org/10.1007/978-3-032-06486-8_17

ties initiating these proceedings, the level and manner of shaping procedural guarantees, and the effectiveness of court decisions and their legal and financial consequences. The thesis that cooperation and loyalty may determine the direction in resolving manner of resolving competence disputes that arise in practice seems justified.

1 Introduction

For a long time, public law scholarship has drawn attention to the ongoing crisis of state institutions of the constitution itself.[1] Among the many causes of this state of affairs is, the primacy of procedural democracy over deliberative democracy,[2] which has led to the primitivisation of the decision-making process, stripping it of debate, factual assessment and analysis, and a thereby reducing it to a caricature of representative democracy. The phenomenon of the erosion of democratic mechanisms is accompanied by the rise of populism, which for many years has been[3] regarded as an anti-democratic "virus" of our times,[4] a force that enables those in power to depart from democratic principles and contributes to *democratic backsliding*.[5] The view that the polarisation of political rhetoric is the cause of the crisis is also legitimate.[6]

Threats to the democratic system can be at least partly neutralised if both central and local authorities act in good faith.

The aim of this article is to assess the usefulness of constitutional good faith in the relationship between central and local government, seen through the prism of the specific nature of this relationship. *Bona fides* is characterised by relationality: the actions of political actors in good faith must be based on their mutual attitude. It will be interesting to see whether good faith, by definition applied to equal actors, can be useful in vertical relations and whether the specificity of state-local authority relations justifies the need for at least a partial redefinition of *bona fides*. The discussion on good faith will be carried out independently of the model adopted for the state's territorial system and cooperation mechanisms.

[1] Skąpska (2018), pp. 276–301; Landau (2013).

[2] Tully (2008), p. 102.

[3] However, it must be stressed that in many countries where populist forces have gained ground in recent years, they have not led to a significant set back of democracy. Western and Northern Europe have experienced the rise of populism in the last ten years, but in countries such as Denmark, France, Germany, Italy, the Netherlands, Sweden and the UK, it has not resulted in a significant deterioration in democratic standards.

[4] Galston (2018), pp. 5–19.

[5] Bellamy et al. (2023), pp. 563–583.

[6] Svolik (2019), pp. 20–32; McCoy and Somer (2019), pp. 234–271.

2 Vertical Power-Sharing as a Platform for Good Faith Action

The state is the essential and primary subject of public law, but "alongside" the state, the legal order allows for the creation of other subjects of public law, including subjects of local self-government.[7] It has become a constituent element of the modern democratic state. Local self-government is not only an institution of public administration, but also an institution of democracy; the democratic idea and the idea of self-government have complementary functions, and local self-government and local democracy balance the omnipotence of the state.[8]

In order to consider the importance of good faith in the relationship between central and local government, there is no need to go into any more depth regarding the understanding of the vertical division of power. The requirement of a vertical division of power referring to its decentralisation was long sinced emphasised by Benjamin Constant.[9] In his view, local authorities are in a vertical position vis-à-vis the central executive and are protected by the principle of subsidiarity and autonomy, thus becoming a counterweight to the central authority.[10] The vertical division of power does not consist of singling out an additional area of substantive government activity (in addition to the legislature, the executive and the judiciary), but refers to the distribution of power between decision-making centres at different levels of the organisational structure of the state (between the unions, the Länder, and local government). In horizontal terms, therefore, all authorities pursue different objectives but at the same level, whereas in vertical division of power, units at different levels act to achieve the same objective. Vertical division is just as important in a state as horizontal division, but it is more conducive to deepening and maintaining democracy. This is because it is, by definition, "closer" to local communities. It should also be emphasised that local authorities do not have state sovereignty and are not competitors to the central authority. In turn, the state should not take over the affairs of local communities. In this view, the principle is mainly about self-governance. In every country, regardless of its form, there is a need to protect the autonomy of local authorities from interference by the central government. The extent of this autonomy is derived from the form of the state. It exists both in states where power is decentralised and in those where federal entities partially exercise sovereign authority (e.g. unions, provinces, states). It is also relevant in the relations between units of decentralised power.

The functioning of local self-government is based on a dichotomy, in that there are both central field authorities and self-governing entities at the regional or local level. The distribution of tasks between them depends on whether the sovereign perceives the scope of public affairs as suitable for relatively autonomous

---

[7] Kasznica (1946), p. 63.

[8] Doliwa and Doliwa (2015).

[9] Constant (1836), p. 126.

[10] Cf. Vargam (2021), p. 123.

administration by legally empowered communities.[11] The distribution of public tasks between central and local government is decided by the former, guided by constitutional criteria, among which the principle of subsidiarity is fundamental.[12] The principle of subsidiarity does not make it possible to identify authoritative premises for determining the catalogue of tasks that can be effectively performed by local self-government units. Therefore, the state (mainly the legislature and the judiciary) has a wide discretion in interpreting what public tasks should be performed by the local government and to what extent.[13]

The constitutional vertical relationship is based on the legally-designated autonomy of the local government vis-à-vis the state and its organs. Hence, local government entities have a public subjective right to administer and manage public affairs, and the state and its bodies have the right to supervise whether this administration and management is carried in accordance with the law. Local government entities generally have a high degree of autonomy in the performance of public tasks. This ability to self-regulate systemic and organisational matters ensures – at least in theory – that the performance of public tasks is optimised by adapting the conditions for their implementation to the requirements of reality. The scope of action and *the ratione materiae* of a given local authority depends on the model adopted by the constitution, the interpretation of its provisions by the central authority, the scope of protection of local self-government provided for by law and the manner of its implementation by the judiciary. Expressions of the position of the local authority include legal autonomy, task autonomy, and organisational autonomy determining the way in which public tasks are performed. On the legal level, local self-governments have constitutionally guaranteed financial and revenue independence, but in this respect scholarship, practice and reality indicate the relative ineffectiveness of adopted legal solutions and their weakening in time.[14]

Constitutional good faith may be an important *novelty* for the interaction between local and central government. It is based on a constitutionally derived mutual obligation of cooperation and loyalty. The question arises-whether the public-law vertical dimension of good faith exists in national legal systems and how it is implemented. The examples of Spain, Germany and Switzerland show that the principle of loyalty is applicable in constitutional law, and examples from practice confirm its importance for the stability of power in the state. At the same time, a caveat must be made that the expectation of mutual loyalty between authorities may not be sufficient. Therefore, the law provides for mechanisms for the judicial resolution of disputes of competence, including over the extent of local authority autonomy. The effectiveness of these mechanisms is crucial for constitutional practice, including the good faith action of authorities. For this reason, the modalities of judicial protection of local authorities must be evaluated, which depends on the legitimacy of the actors

[11] Niżnik-Dobosz (2020), p. 24.

[12] Springer (1996), p. 111.

[13] Chmielnicki (2005), pp. 67–68.

[14] Cámara Villar (2004), pp. 197–240; Scharpf (2008), pp. 509–521.

initiating these proceedings, the level and design of procedural guarantees, the effectiveness of judicial decisions and their legal and financial consequences. The thesis that constitutional good faith may determine the direction of the resolution of competence disputes arising in practice therefore appears justified.

3 Justification for the Application of Good Faith in the Local Authority: Central Authority Relationship

Good faith in constitutional law by its very nature covers all spheres to which its material scope applies. It is difficult to identify, at the constitutional level, any constitutional relations that could be excluded from the fair and honest conduct of political actors, both vis-à-vis the constitution and vis-à-vis each other. This general statement, although sufficient to support the expectation of the application of good faith in relations between local and central government, should be extended to include other weighty rationales justifying the absolute obligation to be guided by good faith in these relations.

Firstly, local self-government derives from the concept of state sovereignty, which exercises power directly and through its own organs, but may delegate some of its power to local communities. The functioning of self-government is based on the decentralisation of administration – the scope of its activity does not differ from that of state administration, but it constitutes a distinct organisational form. Thus, self-government is a legal institution established to handle part of the affairs of state administration. It is a separate legal entity from the state, entering into legal relations with it and possessing its own rights and obligations, which give it an equivalent position to the central authorities. This equivalence means, among other things, that the local authority, like any authority, bases all forms of its action on the law, including in particular the constitution. The duty to act in good faith implies an obligation to act in a manner oriented towards achieving constitutional objectives and goals.

Secondly, in a modern parliamentary democracy, all parts of the state are constructed through democratic mechanisms. Thus, the sovereign exercises power at both central and local levels. Smaller communities interact with larger ones, so the views of smaller communities must be protected. The mechanisms for this protection are multifaceted and generally apply when a dispute arises. Meanwhile, at the stage before a dispute arises, it is appropriate to pursue constitutional objectives in such a way that it this pursuit has a preventive dimension – aimed at preventing potential divergence and conflict. The good-faith conduct of political actors at all levels of government can contribute to raising the standard of cooperation between authorities, including in the vertical dimension of power.

Thirdly, constitutional law *in genere* regulates the position of the state in its external and internal relations, the locus of supreme power in the state, the forms in which the sovereign exercises that power, the status of the individual in the state, with particular regard to the rights and freedoms to which he or she is entitled and the duties imposed on him or her, as well as the principles of organisation and functioning of state organs and the relations between them. All these elements relate to local authority, which enters into relations with the state primarily in its internal dimension. The essence of self-government is public trust, understood as the satisfaction of citizens' interests by local authorities.[15] The importance of local self-government is expressed above in the aspect of power sharing, which should not become an antagonising factor. The relationship is also reciprocal: the central authority has a duty to act loyally towards the local authority. Such respect requires the creation of an efficient public administration, capable of serving the broad public interest. This, in turn, requires a clear definition of the scope of matters relevant to the local structure as a whole, together with the objectives for whose realisation it is responsible; a specification of the scope of autonomy necessary to achieve these objectives, including the means of legal protection; the establishment of a system of instruments that prioritises the objectives of the lower levels in relation to higher ones and provides incentives directing the work carried out by lower levels towards the objectives they are responsible for realising; and defining rules for the supervision of local authorities, with the proviso that such supervision may be exercised only on the basis of law, and that state interference in local affairs may occur solely in specific, legally defined cases.[16] It should also be noted that local communities naturally seek an appropriate degree of freedom and autonomy in managing and resolving their own affairs. However, the empowered higher-level body is entitled to intervene and assume the tasks of a lower-level entity if that entity has failed to fulfil its assigned tasks. Therefore, in some cases it will be necessary to transfer certain tasks that are unsolvable at a lower level to the higher level.

Fourthly, the relationship between central and local government is extremely dynamic and, by definition, can result in tensions of various kinds. On the one hand, the principle of subsidiarity makes it a natural requirement to seek local solutions at the local government level. The European Charter of Local Self-Government affirms that public tasks must be carried out primarily by the administrative body closest to the citizen, while the delegation of tasks to another body must depend on the nature and scale of the task, as well as on considerations of efficiency and economy.[17] The allocation of tasks in practice depends on the state's prudent approach to delegation. Unwarranted interference by higher levels of government in the sphere of competence of lower levels is therefore undesirable. More importantly, the higher level may only intervene in the affairs of the lower level in order to assist it.

On the other hand, loyal cooperation between the state and local government must be based on respect for the autonomy of local authority. This autonomy – following F. Fleurke and R. Willemse – has at least three dimensions. The first is the

[15] Zaleśny (2015), p. 26.

[16] Madurowicz (1977), p. 60.

[17] European Charter of Local Self-Government, drawn up in Strasbourg on 15 October 1985, OJ 1994, No. 124, item 607, as amended; See https://rm.coe.int/european-charter-of-local-self-government-eng/1680a87cc3 (Accessed: 10.02.2025).

extent to which the local authority defines its own agenda, which is related to the freedom to choose the solutions most beneficial to its territory. The second dimension of autonomy refers to political independence and indicates the extent to which the local authority is free to shape its policies, including the organisation of local elections. The third dimension of autonomy refers to decision-making independence and indicates the extent to which a local authority is independent of other bodies for its decision-making.[18] Autonomy is a right of a community other than the state, and while it should be broad, it does not protect actions that fall outside the framework set by law. As an autonomous body is part of a larger political system, the principle of autonomy must be reconciled with the principle of unity of the state. In this broad field of cooperation the threat of disputes is high and the ability to properly interpret constitutional norms is crucial.

Good faith is an essential criterion for the functioning of local government. A balanced and sensible central government policy, grounded in a sound understanding of constitutional assumptions and preceded by a proper identification of constitutional objectives, is essential for the interaction between the two centres of power. Importantly, a self restraining central authority, delegates to local authorities powers that it cannot later arbitrarily claim back to the central level. In order not to undermine trust, the central authority not infrequently gives up its right to decide on an issue, making the power in question permanently local. Local communities are expected to perform intrinsically local tasks, and to carry them out themselves, with an emphasis on the principle of subsidiarity reinforced by good faith conduct.

Last but not least, good faith in the relationship between central and local government is applicable in the context of changing functions of the state and local government. As pointed out in the 2008 report "Decentralisation and local democracy in the world. First Global Report by United Cities and Local Governments"[19] the powers, responsibilities and degree of decision-making autonomy of local authorities have increased significantly in most countries. Moreover, national policies depend on their implementation by local authorities, the more so as these authorities are thereby able to de facto influence national policies. They can also create distortions at the local level, compelling the central government to partially accommodate the demands of local government.[20] This phenomenon is accompanied by an increasing interpenetration of private law and public law. A free-market economy – together with a society in which individuals are able to make free choices, cooperate and associate – favours the application of principles and institutions characteristic of private law to the field of public law. It is therefore possible to use the concept of good faith. It is important to recognise that the traditional centralised state model has reached its limits, and that its current development is based on the expansion of the legitimacy of power and the increasing diversity of

[18] Fleurke and Willemse (2006), pp. 71–87.

[19] Decentralisation and local democracy in the world First Global Report by United Cities and Local Governments, United Cities and Local Government & World Bank, 2008.

[20] Ibid, 159.

state functions, some of which are transferred to local authorities. In addition, the liberalisation of trade and the globalisation of the economy are contributing to the blurring of state boundaries, the growing importance of local authorities, the acceleration of decentralisation processes and, consequently, a change in the perspective on the perception of cooperation between the centres of central and local power. The view that acting in constitutional good faith with a view to realising constitutional objectives acquires particular significance in light of the increasing role of local self-government, which is becoming an important public-law entity and a participant in important systemic processes, appears well-founded.

4 The Importance of Constitutional Good Faith in the Relationship Between Central and Local Government

Good faith in the process of applying the constitution in the relations between the central and local authorities should be understood in the same manner as in the relations between the legislature, the executive and the judiciary. Every political actor, irrespective of his or her affiliation to a particular branch of power, is obliged to treat the addressees of his or her actions loyally, based on respect, on the one hand, and – obviously – on the constitution, on the other. Thus, M. Safta aptly stated that the assumption of the duty of constitutional loyalty constitutes a significant "enrichment" of the principle of separation of powers. This point is all the more important, since respect for the rule of law cannot be limited to the implementation of explicit and formal provisions of the law and the constitution. Respect for the rule of law also encompasses constitutional conduct and practices that promote compliance with formal rules by all constitutional bodies and mutual respect between them. In the absence of such conduct, the principle of the separation of powers would be stripped of its content, which would mean that conduct contrary to the idea of the rule of law could be permitted under the protection of the constitution.[21]

Although the requirement to act in good faith applies to all public authorities, at least four features can be identified in the central authority-local authority relationship which can be qualified as the *differentia specifica* of this relationship: (a) the unequal position of the parties; (b) the permanent and ongoing nature of the interaction between central and local government; (c) the existence of numerous dialogue and cooperation mechanisms, which *mutatis mutandis* can be considered as the "soft law" of constitutional law; and (d) the possibility of judicial resolution of disputes, including disputes of competence, between the state and local government.

[21] Safta (2013), p. 3.

The unequal position of the parties in the vertical relationship is due to the stronger position of the central authority, as it is within its constitutional and legal framework that the local authority functions. Regardless of the structure of the state (federal or unitary), the extent of the autonomy of its constituent parts and the effectiveness of the existing mechanisms for cooperation and dispute prevention it is the state that ultimately determines the systemic position of the local authority. State legislation, implementing the provisions of the constitution, regulates the division of powers between central and local government. The financing of local government activities, which determines the possibility of implementing the activities assigned to local (regional) authorities, also depends on the final shape of the state budget or budget-related legislation which is also the responsibility of the central government. Depending on the form of the state and the extent of the autonomy of local authorities, there are various means by which the central authority can influence local (regional) authorities. The extent of state interference varies, but the most far-reaching measure is always the subordination of local authority to central authority (which, moreover, takes a variety of forms). Ultimately, the state, as a structure, is the entity within which the local authority operates. The unequal legal position of the two parties in the vertical relationship is of direct relevance to good faith. *Bona fides* is, after all, intrinsically based on the equality of the parties (in both civil law relations and in international law). Since a distinctive feature of vertical relations is the non-equivalence of the parties, the weaker position of the local authority should be corrected by a mechanism favouring the "weaker" party to the relationship, i.e. the local authority. A presumption of good faith on the part of the local authority could therefore be considered, which could be rebutted by legal steps taken by the central authority, with the onus placed on it to demonstrate circumstances indicating bad faith on the part of the local authority. However, this issue would require further study.

The second feature of vertical relations is their continuity and ongoing nature. Leaving aside whether the local authority is a constitutionally distinct, separate authority within the framework of the vertical relationship, or merely a form of the distribution of power (its decentralisation), it is indisputable that the local authority has legislative, executive, and, in some countries, even judicial competences. Subjectively, therefore, the interaction between the two sides of the vertical relationship is based on a certain degree of symmetry. The local legislature will continually encroach on the area of statewide legislation, which at the regional level is subject to specification, implementation or further development, and the area of possible inconsistencies (and sometimes collisions) is extensive. Similarly, the exercise of law at the local level "overlaps" in substance with that of the central executive. Of course, within the framework of the division of competences, the two spheres of action of the authorities must be distinguished, but even in this respect the probability of collision between the central and the local authority is high. The risk of conflict within the judiciary generally applies to structurally complex states, but even in this branch of power such disputes are not an uncommon phenomenon.

Thus, taking into account the uninterrupted, constant and dynamic process through which central and local authorities operate in overlapping areas of activity (legislative, executive and judicial), good faith should be regarded as a particularly useful concept. This additional criterion provides an opportunity for central and local authorities to continuously analyse the effects of their actions. Constitutional good faith thus imposes an obligation on the state and local authorities not only to respect the competences of the other party in the vertical relationship, but also to remain within their own legally permissible scope of action. Loyalty and cooperation between authorities must also be seen as an obligation to perform tasks in a certain manner, i.e. they must not be carried out in a spirit of confrontation with the other party in the vertical relationship, and, in addition, the local authority must also take into account the interests of the local community.

Thirdly, vertical relations are also characterised by a multitude of preventive mechanisms designed to foster cooperation and prevent disputes. One of these is – based on the German concept of the *Bundestreue*[22] – federal loyalty,[23] which, in its most general sense, means mutual respect between central and local authorities.[24] As J.R. Nato points out, the ways in which this respect manifests itself in legal systems vary considerably.[25] The requirement of loyalty to act may be a principle of conduct without binding legal force. In a state, there may be procedural requirements imposed on government bodies to consider the impact of their actions on local authorities. The law may explicitly prohibit harm to a local partner in the exercise of powers. It may even, although rarely, impose substantive requirements for the fair treatment of federal partners. Differences can also be observed with regard to the consequences of breach of loyalty in vertical relations. Courts may order negotiation measures, while a less frequent consequence may be the invalidation of acts violating the principle of loyalty.[26] Interestingly, federal loyalty can be seen as an element that has contributed to the universalisation of the requirement of

[22] The principle of "federal fidelity" ("Bundestreue") or benevolent relationship to the Federation obliges such interaction within the framework of the constitutional division of tasks that takes into account the legitimate interests of the Federation and the Länder. This principle applies both in the relations of the Federation with the countries as well as between the Länder. As the Bundestreue principle is a general unwritten "good manners" clause, it only applies in a subsidiary manner and cannot serve to alter constitutional competence. Neither is it able to establish legal relations between the Federation's partners; it merely justifies and limits the rights and obligations that exist within the framework of the legal relations linking the Federation and the countries. The principle is primarily a prohibition on the abuse of law – Arban (2017), p. 259.

[23] In French-speaking Belgium, the term is similar to the English "loyauté fédérale". In Italian, "leale collaborazione" means "loyal cooperation". An interesting connotation can be observed in the German term "Bundestreue", which is specific to the highly developed German federal loyalty – see Nato (2019), p. 9.

[24] Da Silva (2023), p. 221.

[25] Nato, *Passim*.

[26] *Passim*.

loyalty in vertical relations.[27] In the view of the German *Bundesverfassungsgericht*, it has even been considered as an exportable model, useful for other states.[28]

The Bundestreue concept is important, but it does not exhaust the rich catalogue of mechanisms for vertical cooperation. According to the Council of Europe report "The relationship between central and local authorities. Report of the European Committee on Local and Regional Democracy" (CDLR), communication between the different levels of government is the most frequently mentioned form of cooperation indicated by Member States. Mutual consultation, guidance or exchange of information between local authorities and central government are cited as examples of good practice in the countries analysed in the report. This cooperation extends to policy formulation and consultation on legislation, contacts during the implementation of policies for advice, monitoring the implementation of state policies, and the resolution of disputes.[29] There is no need to analyse the various forms of cooperation in greater detail, but – from the point of view of the specific application of the concept of good faith to vertical relations – it is worth highlighting some of them.

In almost all Council of Europe Member States, consultation is regarded as the most common form of cooperation. Mandatory consultation on local issues legal, budgetary, or fiscal is carried out with associations of local authorities. Dialogue generally takes place between associations of municipalities and representatives of central government offices. In addition, many countries have formal consultation structures (such as conferences or working groups) that meet periodically – annually or quarterly. In decentralised states, these structures are often regional, although there may be issues that must also be dealt with at the federal level.[30]

The report also notes that central authorities play an important role in advisory activities towards local authorities. Typically, relationships in this respect are more informal, with officials and individual municipalities as participants. They less frequently take the form of institutionalised contacts at the political level. In some

[27] As Marieta Safta notes, the Constitutional Court of Romania established this duty of constitutional loyalty by interpreting the norms of the Basic Law. The Court's jurisprudence has evolved from simply defining the concepts of "loyalty" and "loyal behaviour" to defining certain "principles of constitutional loyalty" derived from a principle explicitly enshrined in the Constitution – the principle of separation and balance of powers. The Federal Constitutional Court of Germany has also included a similar principle in its case law. The principle of faithful cooperation between authorities and the principle of good behaviour towards the Federation oblige the Federation and the Länder to respect each other, and the Court has stated that, by analogy, the principle of loyal cooperation between authorities applies to relations between the constitutional organs of the Federation. The Federal Constitutional Court initially left open the question of whether such a constitutional principle existed and, if so, whether it could be invoked by an applicant in a constitutional complaint procedure. However, the Court explicitly recognised this principle in later decisions – Safta (2013), p. 2.

[28] Schneider (2009), p. 99.

[29] Council of Europe Report *The relationship between central and local authorities. Report of the European Committee on Local and Regional Democracy (CDLR)*, prepared in collaboration with Prof. Alba Nogueira López of the University of Santiago de Compostela, Spain, 2007, https://rm.coe.int/1680747fbc, p. 57.

[30] Ibidem, 33–34.

cases, guidance or information is accompanied by the training of local staff. Several initiatives in Member States seek to expand ways to reach out to local authorities to explain how to identify local tasks.[31]

Also of interest are the numerous examples presented in the report of cooperation in defining policy objectives, managing public affairs and providing financial support between local and central authorities.[32] It is worth highlighting the importance of good practices in the field of finance, particularly those concerning the bilateral estimation of the revenues needed by local authorities to fulfil their responsibilities and to provide an adequate level of services to citizens.

The diversity of levels and forms of cooperation – which is constantly deepening – undeniably influences the way in which the concept of good faith is framed in the relationship between central and local government in three ways. First and foremost, the cooperation common in the states, though diverse in form, is conducive to the mitigation of conflicts and shifts the burden of good faith from the traditional formalised methods of interaction between authorities to less formal means. Their importance, however, should not be underestimated. Moreover, with the multiplicity of forms of cooperation between the two centres of power, assessing their actions in the context of good faith and trust in the provisions of the constitution requires reference to the effectiveness of the cooperation mechanisms, their frequency, commitment to the implementation of the agreements reached. In other words, these factual actions are not indifferent to the assessment of the implementation of constitutional goals and objectives. Finally, the priority of the use of "soft" methods of cooperation, as preventive measures to prevent the emergence of disputes, should, it would seem, be accepted. Thus, in this sense, the perception of good faith in vertical relations should be complemented by the obligation to use such cooperation mechanisms.

A final distinguishing element of the *bona fides* of the relationship between central and local government is the existence of formalised procedural means

---

[31] Ibidem, 33–34.

[32] France has developed structures for cooperation between state and territorial authorities Firstly, Contrats de Villes (CDVs) between state and territorial authorities aim to prevent social exclusion. CDVs target action in urban neighbourhoods at risk of social exclusion due to unemployment, housing problems or violence. Secondly, Contrats locaux de sécurité (CLS) are concluded between those authorities that can work together to improve security conditions. to improve security conditions.

A cooperation agreement setting out the framework for relations between the State and local authorities was concluded in Iceland in February 2006. Its main focus is to establish a formal structure for the relationship between the State and the municipalities and to harmonise public management policies. Committees of experts from both levels meet periodically to discuss common issues. In Italy, the provision of cooperation is a regional function. Each region has a unit responsible for cooperation and administrative support. Administrative. In the main policy areas, there are usually bodies providing cooperation. In addition, a specific cooperation mechanism has been established in Italy: in order to implement extraordinary programmes to strengthen law enforcement and security services, the Minister of the Interior and the prefects (prefetti) can sign agreements with the regional government and local authorities, providing for logistical, instrumental and financial contributions from the region and local authorities – see ibid., 39.

(including at the constitutional level) which, in judicial proceedings, can be used to settle political, legal, competence and financial disputes in a binding manner. The final form of these legal instruments depends on many factors. The attempt to universalise procedural remedies would, by its very nature, face the accusation of a simplistic and even superficial treatment of the issue. Despite the danger of oversimplifying the problem and thereby diminishing an understanding of the meaning of good faith in vertical relations, it is necessary to make certain assumptions on which the usefulness of dispute resolution mechanisms in vertical relations will depend.

It must be stressed that such disputes may concern any of the spheres of government. On the political level, as the Spanish experience shows, the insubordination of local power pursuing separatist aims could lead to the desintegration of the state structure. Regardless of the political assessment of the action taken by Madrid, it must be noted that the changes introduced into the legal order in 2015,[33] including the legal effects of the judgments of the Constitutional Court together with the existing competences of the Court of Auditors and the Supreme Court, helped to overcome one of the most serious crises of statehood in Spain. The actions of Catalonia and previeously those of the Basque Country flagrantly contradicted the principle of constitutional loyalty and were challenged by the relevant central judicial authorities.[34]

Disputes in the relations between central and local authorities may also concern the legislative sphere. Therefore, it is necessary to ensure, at the constitutional level, a basis for the review of local law in terms of its compliance with the state-wide law, including the constitution, combined with the possibility of derogating local law inconsistent with the constitutional order. The sphere of law enforcement must also be subject to the possibility of judicial settlement of disputes arising within it. It is therefore reasonable to expect the creation of mechanisms for the settlement of competence disputes between central and local government bodies.

The issue of the financial (and, to some extent, fiscal) autonomy of local authorities cannot be excluded from judicial dispute resolution mechanisms. Disputes over the adequacy of financial support for local authorities for their assigned tasks are not isolated. It should also be noted that the limit on the indebtedness of local budgets

[33] Law 12/2015, of 22 September, amending Organic Law 2/1979, of 3 October 1979 on the Constitutional Court to establish preventive control of draft organic laws concerning the statutes of the Autonomous Communities or their amendment, and Organic Law 15/2015, of 16 October, on the reform of Organic Law LO 2/1979, of 3 October 1979 on the Constitutional Court, to implement the resolutions of the Constitutional Court.

[34] Judgment of the Special Chamber of the Supreme Court of Spain of 27 March 2003 dissolving the political parties Herri Batasuna, Euskal Herritarrok and Batasuna, ordering the deletion of their registration in the register of political parties and the immediate dissolution of these parties and the immediate cessation of their activities; order of the same court dated 24 April 2003 ordering the dissolution of the Batasuna parliamentary group in the Basque Parliament – see Bilbao Ubillos (2003), p. 249 et seq.

the amount of which may disrupt the budgetary stability of the state may prove to be a problem.[35]

The key areas within the scope of local government activity must be subject to judicial review, given the wide field of potential conflicts between central and local government. It is important to shape procedures for recognising and adjudicating disputes arising in vertical relations between central and local government. Competence in this regard must be conferred on the judicial authority, – primarily on the constitutional courts (and possibly, to some extent, on supervisory bodies). The capacity to commence proceedings before the competent authority must be granted to both the parties to the vertical relationship, as well as to the actors acting as guardians of the rule of law (such as prosecutors and ombudsmen).The procedural remedies available to both parties must be based on the principle of equality of arms (shifting the burden of proof to the central authority is not excluded). The time taken to adjudicate a dispute must not nullify the efficiency of the dispute resolution procedure and, if the competence to resolve disputes is not vested in the highest judicial instances, it is necessary to introduce the possibility of appealing against the decision of the court of first instance (or the decision of a non-judicial review body). It is also reasonable to assume that the enforceability of the contested act may be suspended until the judicial conciliation procedure has been completed and, obviously, the effects of the judicial authority's decision should, of course, be indisputable, final and enforceable (non-compliance should trigger restrictive measures).

In the sphere of vertical relations, the creation of procedural guarantees linked by legal science directly to federal loyalty – may, by analogy, serve to promote good faith action. Elements associated with federal loyalty, such as the separation of powers between central and local government, cooperation in the performance of public tasks, observance of the principle of solidarity, protection of the legal and financial autonomy of local government, and judicial dispute resolution procedures-function simultaneously as mechanisms for safeguarding constitutional *bona fides*. The boundary between federal loyalty in vertical relations and constitutional bona fides is blurring. Indeed, the constitutional position of local self-government is by definition a constitutional matter.

In conclusion, it is reasonable to it may be asserted that good faith constitutes an essential element of vertical relations. Both the central and local authorities are bound to conduct their activities in every sphere in a manner consistent with the preservation of the state's territorial, functional and institutional integrity. It is the duty of the authorities to cooperate in mutual trust by fostering bilateral relations, offering mutual assistance and support, consulting on matters of common interest, coordinating activities and legislation, adhering to agreed procedures, and

[35] It is for this reason that Article 135 of the Spanish Constitution was amended providing, inter alia, for the prohibition of excessive indebtedness by the Autonomous Communities – "Reforma del artículo 135 de la Constitución Española, de 27 de septiembre de 2011". *Boletín Oficial del Estado* (núm. 233, de 27 de septiembre de 2011).

refraining from initiating legal proceedings against one another. The existence of judicial dispute resolution mechanisms serves as a guarantee of respect for constitutional provisions, and as an indirect, formal safeguard for acting in good faith.

5 Conclusion

Respect for the constitution cannot be limited to the literal implementation of its provisions. Its essence lies in the fact that, in addition to guaranteeing human rights, it provides a framework for state and local authorities and defines their powers and duties. The purpose of these provisions is to enable the smooth functioning of institutions based on their loyal cooperation. Parliament, the executive, the judiciary and local government all serve the common purpose of promoting the interests of the state as a whole, rather than the narrow interests of a particular institution, political party or a specific community.

The importance of *bona fides* in vertical relations cannot be overestimated, especially as the systemic dependencies between centres of power create the temptation for the central authority to impose its position. The day-to-day nature of the interaction between central and local authorities entails the risk of conflict. The existence of numerous dialogue and cooperation mechanisms should be seen as instruments for the implementation of constitutional good faith, and in the event that they prove insufficient, vertical relations must be safeguarded by the possibility of activating judicial mechanisms for the settlement of disputes, including disputes over competence. The central and local authorities must be required to use instruments that guarantee harmonious cooperation in the processes of political and administrative decentralisation. They are united by an obligation to assist, cooperate and loyally exchange information and raise reservations relevant to vertical relations.

Regardless of the form of state, every local authority and every central authority should act in good faith, as this obligation derives from the binding of all public authorities to the constitution as the act standing hierarchically at the top of the legal order. This thought was emphatically expressed by the Spanish Constitutional Court, which, in its judgment on the Statute of Catalonia, stated that the normative articulation of the regime governing local government must correspond to the structural requirements of the constitutional order, which, like the principle of cooperation of each autonomous community with the State and all of them with each other, can only be clearly deduced from the Constitution itself.[36] The supremacy of the Basic Law and the willingness to honestly decode the objectives contained therein are the essence of good faith. *Bona fides* thus becomes an indispensable element of the modern understanding of the principle of constitutionalism.

[36] Judgment of the CT of 28 June 2010, delivered in the case STC 31/2010.

References

Arban E (2017) Exploring the principle of (federal) solidarity. Rev Const Stud 22(2):259

Bellamy R, Kröger S, Lorimer M (2023) Party views on democratic backsliding and differentiated integration. East Eur Polit Soc Cult 37(2):563–583

Bilbao Ubillos JM (2003) Guión para el debate sobre la disolución de los grupos parlamentarios vinculados a partidos que han sido ilegalizados judicialmente. Revista Española de Derecho Constitucional 68:249 et seq

Chmielnicki P (2005) "An essential part of public tasks" and the principle of subsidiarity as constitutional directives defining the scope of action of local self-government and their implementation in legislation and jurisprudence. In: Sarnecki P (ed) Samorząd terytorialny. Systemic principles and practice. Sejm Publishing House, Warsaw, pp 6768.

Constant B (1836) Cours de politique constitutionnelle. ed.by Jean-Pierre Pagès. Didier, p 126

Council of Europe Report The relationship between central and local authorities. Report of the European committee on local and regional democracy (CDLR), prepared in collaboration with prof. Alba Nogueira López of the University of Santiago de Compostela, Spain, 2007., https://rm.coe.int/1680747fbc, p 57

Da Silva M (2023) Federal Loyalty and the 'nature' of federalism. Rev Const Stud 11:221

Decentralization and local democracy in the world First Global Report by United Cities and Local Governments, United Cities and Local Government & World Bank, 2008, p 159

Doliwa K, Doliwa A (2015) Local democracy and decentralization - in institutional, legal and philosophical terms

Fleurke F, Willemse R (2006) Measuring local autonomy: a decision-making approach. Local Gov Stud 32:71–87

Galston WA (2018) The populist challenge to liberal democracy. J Democr 29(2):5–19

Kasznica S (1946) Polish administrative law. Poznań, p 63

Landau D (2013) Abusive constitutionalism. UC Davis Law Rev 47:189–260

Madurowicz W (1977) Z zagadnień decentralizacji w terytorialnym przekroju gospodarki narodowej, Problemy Radów Narodowych 38:60

McCoy J, Somer M (2019) Toward a theory of pernicious polarization and how it harms democracies: comparative evidence and possible remedies. ANNALS Am Acad Polit Soc Sci 681(1):234–271

Nato J R (2019) "Development of duties of Federal Loyalty: lessons learned, conversations to be had" (Winner of Baxter family competition on federalism), online (pdf): McGill www.mcgill.ca/law/files/law/2019-baxter_federal-loyalty-lessons-discussions_jan-nato.pdf, p 9

Niżnik-Dobosz I (2020) Local government Vis-à-Vis the principle of separation of powers. Ruch Prawniczy, Ekonomiczny i Socjologiczny 4:24

Safta M (2013) Separation of powers and constitutional loyalty. Juridical Tribune 3(1):3

Scharpf FW (2008) Community, diversity and autonomy: the challenges of reforming German federalism, pp 509–521

Schneider H P (2009) Loyalty-solidarity-subsidiarity. Three principles of a judge made federalism in Germany. In: idem/Jutta Kramer/Beniamino Caravita di Toritto (eds), Judge Made Federalism? (Nomos, Baden-Baden)

Skąpska G (2018) Insulting constitutionalism and constitutionalism insulted. A sociological reflection on the crisis of liberal-democratic constitutionalism in post-communist Europe. Public Philos Democr Edu 7:276–301

Springer W (1996) Subsidiarity as a systemic principle in a federal state - a member of the European Union (on the example of Germany). In: Milczarek D (ed) Subsidiarity. European Center of Warsaw University, Warsaw, p 111

Svolik M (2019) Polarization versus democracy. J Democr 30(3):20–32

Tully J (2008) Public philosophy in a New Kaey. Cambridge, p 102

Vargam A (2021) Local self-governments and the vertical division of power. Public Gov Adm and Financ Law Rev 6(2):122

Zaleśny J (2015) Financial independence of the municipality - assumptions and results. Const Law Rev 5:26

Correction to: Good Faith in the European Convention on Human Rights

Aleksandra Kochman

Correction to:
Chapter 5 in: J. Podkowik et al. (eds.), *Gleams of Good Faith in Constitutional Law*, Ius Gentium: Comparative Perspectives on Law and Justice 132, https://doi.org/10.1007/978-3-032-06486-8_5

The institutional author's name "European Commission" was mistakenly listed as a co-author of the chapter instead of being added to the author's affiliation. The text "European Commission" has now been taken out from both the PDF and the online version of Chapter 5. Furthermore, we have incorporated "European Commission" text into the author's affiliation section.

The updated version of this chapter can be found at
https://doi.org/10.1007/978-3-032-06486-8_5

J. Podkowik et al. (eds.), *Gleams of Good Faith in Constitutional Law*, Ius Gentium: Comparative Perspectives on Law and Justice 132,
https://doi.org/10.1007/978-3-032-06486-8_18

MIX
Papier aus verantwortungsvollen Quellen
Paper from responsible sources
FSC® C105338

If you have any concerns about our products,
you can contact us on
ProductSafety@springernature.com

In case Publisher is established outside the EU,
the EU authorized representative is:
Springer Nature Customer Service Center GmbH
Europaplatz 3, 69115 Heidelberg, Germany

Printed by Libri Plureos GmbH
in Hamburg, Germany